D1287416

GOVERNMENT AND SOCIETY
IN CENTRAL AMERICA,
1680–1840

A MAP OF
THE KINGDOM OF
GUATEMALA

Government
and Society
in Central America,
1680–1840

MILES L. WORTMAN

Columbia University Press   New York, 1982

Library of Congress Cataloging in Publication Data

Wortman, Miles L., 1944–
   Government and society in Central America,
1680–1840.

   Bibliography: p.
   Includes index.
   1. Central America—Politics and government.
2. Central America—History—To 1821.
3. Central America—Economic conditions.
4. Social classes—Central America—History.
I. Title.
JL1408.W67   306'.2'09728   81-12286
ISBN 0-231-05212-X   AACR2

Columbia University Press
New York   Guildford, Surrey

Clothbound editions of Columbia University Press books are Smyth-
sewn and printed on permanent and durable acid-free paper.

To my parents, Ruth Nacht Wortman
and
Joseph R. Wortman

Contents

Preface   ix

Part One: El Reino de Guatemala
1. The Conquest and the Settlement   3
2. The Kingdom Under the Hapsburgs   17
3. Cross and Crown   41
4. Colonial Society   64
5. Crisis and Continuity, 1680–1730   91

Part Two: The New Order
6. The Transformation of the Colony   111
7. The Bourbon Reforms in Central America   129
8. At the Mercy of the World Market   157
9. The Indian Under the Later Bourbons   172
10. The Economy Collapses   184
11. José de Bustamante and the Crisis   195
     in Colonial Government

Part Three: The Center Gives Out
12. The Widening Gyre   215
13. The Republican Experiment: In Search of Order   229
14. States Into Nations   247
15. Caudillos, Castes, and Conclusions   268

Appendix A: Annual Income from the Church Tithe   279
Appendix B: Annual Remissions to the Royal Coffers,
     by Administration, 1781–1819   284
Appendix C: Sales of and Profits from Tobacco,
     Diverse Years, 1766–1828   286

x   *Contents*

Appendix D: Population Statistics   288

Abbreviations   291

Notes   293

Glossary   339

Bibliography   341

Index   359

Preface

VOLCANOES DOMINATE Central America. Rising dramatically from broad bases to pointed cones, one after another, they form a zigzagging line from Chiapas south to Costa Rica. Volcanoes hover majestically over the old colonial capital, Antigua, over Guatemala City, San Salvador, and San José, all richly verdant and serene against the dark blue Central America sky. Two stand over the placid water of Lake Nicaragua like stark pre-Columbian pyramids.

The volcanic cordillera divides the isthmus, creating the highlands where Central American civilization centers. Here, amongst these mountains, volcanic ash became fertile tablelands that attracted Amerindian groups and, later, Spanish settlers. The rich soil fed the Amerindians' *milpas*—the organized production of corn—and, after the conquest, the Europeans' wheat fields and cattle herds. The wealth of the soil nourished the highland civilizations; Mayan and then Spanish cities thrived.

The volcano is evidence of the fractures in the earth crust, of the presence of fissures that divide vast earth plates and allow gases and molten rock to escape and form the young, rich land that yielded civilization. But the action of the plates, the platonic movement, destroyed civilizations as well. Earthquakes changed the courses of rivers, destroyed cities, and overthrew civil order. Volcanic ash covered land, trees, and buildings, gas fried all living matter within its reach, while molten rock transformed the landscape. When volcanoes erupted or the earth quaked, society was overcome by turmoil and washed by waves of religious fervor. Men were diverted from farming, compelled to repair or rebuild damaged or razed structures. Food supplies diminished. Elites fought among themselves for profit from the dearth of food, labor, and building materials.

Outside the volcanic cordillera, the hotlands bordering the Caribbean and the Pacific yielded wealth for the highland civilizations, paying tribute to them and trading in cacao, cotton, dyes, and salt. To the east, in the humid hotlands that border the Caribbean, population was sparse. When Christopher Columbus sailed along its shores in 1502, he saw rich tropical vegetation and called it "Costa Rica," rich coast, an ironic appelation for lands where malaria, yellow fever, and typhoid would discourage European settlement. Rather than colonists, these open lands were haven to herds of wild cattle and to Afro-Amerindian communities of escaped slaves. These foreign buccaneers, loggers, and contrabandists plied their trades with impunity, a constant symbol of the fragility of Spanish rule throughout the colonial period.

To the west of the highlands, the dry hotlands bordering the Pacific yielded wealth. Pre-Columbian Indians produced cacao and traded it north to Mexico, an enterprise later usurped by the conquistadores. Spaniards introduced wheat, expanded cotton production, and discovered the dyeing properties of indigo, the plant that was to give Central America an important place in the world economy.

The Spanish invasion of Central America was but one in a long history of economic and military incursions. The Cakchiquels and the Quiché who occupied the Guatemalan highlands were there but five hundred years when Pedro Alvarado conquered the region.[1] Trade along the Caribbean and Pacific coasts and on this land bridge between Meso- and South America had introduced cultural changes for well over a millennium.[2]

If the Hispanic invasion was not unique, it was significant, certainly as important as the Quiché and Cakchiquel migrations. It transformed the landscape, the political structure, and ultimately the racial and social composition of the region. It caused an immediate demographic catastrophe. It expanded what had been coastal trade to world commerce. And it opened the American world to wave upon wave of cultural and intellectual innovation.

The sixteenth-century Spain of the Catholic monarchs, Ferdinand and Isabella, the devout Charles, and then the Counter-Reformation embued colonist and Amerindian alike with an orthodox Catholicism, remnants of which are still present today throughout all of Latin America. Traditional Iberia transmitted pre-industrial institutions—*encomienda* for labor, *cabildos* for municipal rights and patrimonial privilege, and the church for local cohesion. The loose union of realms under one monarch that was the Spanish monarchy insured local autonomy in the Americas. The sixteenth-century Vitoria school in Salamanca revived renaissance humanism and accepted Bodin's "voluntarist" notion of sovereignty as "power not bound by laws." The "divine" Hapsburg king accepted the authority given from the community, the power to make law but not to alienate the "land" (the *patria*).[3]

Orthodox Catholic and voluntarist Hapsburg Spain was transmitted to America, the one seemingly a unity, the other, an amalgam. In America it merged with local institutions, the *mita* of Inca Peru, the tributary system of Aztec Mexico. It suffered the excesses of conquistadores. It adapted to the landscapes of the altiplano of Peru, the lowlands around the Caribbean and the volcanic cordillera. It sought natural resources, population for land, fertile soil, and, above all, minerals for instant wealth.

The common cultural institutions produced a seemingly united Spanish America. But the local conditions and autonomy produced variations. We twentieth-century historians, especially we from outside the region, tend to forget these differences. Even within the geographical unity called Central America a broad variety of cultures and civilizations existed. By the seventeenth century Spanish and Indians lived side by side in the Valley of Guatemala, but there were few Spanish in Verapaz and few Indians remaining in Honduras. The mulatto of the hotland cacao plantation, the mestizo of the *hato*, the small plot, the Amerindian of the pueblos and common lands of highland Quezaltenango, the traditional Creole oligarch of Santiago de Guatemala, and the poor Creole farmer of Salvador were as different as the topography of the volcanic cordillera and the moist and the dry lowlands.

Central America was at the same time similar and dissimilar to the rest of Spanish America. As traditionally Catholic and patrimonial as Lima, it lay outside the silver belt extending from the mines of Potosí to Europe. Its institutions replicated those of Mexico, but its civilization resembled more closely that of Quito. It was a backwater in comparison with Mexico City or Lima, but no more so than most of the regions within the jurisdiction of the viceroyalties of New Spain and Lima.

The land tenure pattern of the *grande domaine*, as Chevalier has called it, may have prevailed in central Mexico, with large numbers of Indians living in debt peonage on large haciendas, defended by Creoles from the demands of Spanish officials.[4] But this was not the case in Central America, at least through the first half of the eighteenth century. The *repartimiento* was still the chief manner of gaining labor from the large stock of persons living in Indian towns in highland Guatemala, Chiapas, and Verapaz, as well as from smaller settlements elsewhere in Central America. Large haciendas existed, but few of their owners were sufficiently prosperous or powerful to support debt peonage systems. Ironically, some haciendas were owned by Indians themselves, through *cofradías* and communal holdings, while many Spanish landholdings were small and poor.

This is not to suggest that Amerindians lived "better" in Central America. That judgment cannot be made. Both Mexico and Central America were colonies inherently: outsiders ruled subjugated peoples and survived on the fruits of their labors. But each colonial system was qualitatively different.

Among the disparate peoples and landscapes of Central America there was one unifying factor, the patrimonial government. The Hapsburgs called it "El Reino de Guatemala," the Kingdom ruled from Santiago, whose *vecinos* represented the *patria*, the traditional rights over land and labor derived from the conquest. Here, in Santiago and its highland areas, the preponderance of the colony's Amerindian population lived, providing labor for the city. Here Alvarado established his authority and here the crown created its offices.

Santiago, in fact as well as in law, was the center of Hapsburg power. Because of a dearth of settlers and an abundance of colonized Amerindians, government assumed the essential shaping force to maintain the conquest. From the end of the conquest period through the mid-eighteenth century, bureaucrats gathered goods from Indians in tribute payments or by the legal compulsion of repartimiento of goods and sent the commodities to Spanish cities to provide food for colonial survival and articles for colonial trade. Officials administered Indian labor forces and provided them for use on Creole farms. The government granted and distributed pensions to colonists that derived from Indian produce. And it guarded and continued the conquest through the church, the ecclesiastical bureaucracy that was an essential part of the colonial government.

Colonists from the highlands came to the capital to convert goods paid in tribute by Indians into currency, prelates sent tithed crops to the diocesan seat. Merchants from Lima, Mexico, and interior Central America came through and bartered their wares. Privileged, landed encomenderos lived here from the fruits of Indian labor like hidalgo noblemen in the Spanish tradition. In Santiago de Guatemala they socialized with those of their class and protected their power through seats on the municipal council, the cabildo, or through marriages of heirs to bureaucrats or other Creoles.

Of course other towns and cities developed in Central America:

San Salvador and San Miguel where indigo production centered, Comayagua for mining, and, later on, Granada and León in Nicaragua through which trade passed to New Granada or Lima. But these were small towns in comparison with the capital, with relatively small indigenous populations. In Santiago de Guatemala was the bureaucratic seat, the large labor force, and the trade to Mexico.

The Spanish towns, the Indian pueblos, the rural hatos, cattle ranches, and milpa common land provided for subsistence. The trade of the pueblo and of poor Spaniards and castes was local, scarcely affected by the outside world. Through the mid-eighteenth century economic dependency relationships were weak, if they existed at all. Government had to force production through taxation and most trade through tributary articles. An international and intercolonial commerce did exist, but it scarcely affected the semi-sufficient economies of Central America—the Indians of Verapaz, Chiapas, or Quezaltenango, the oligarchy of Santiago, who prospered from Indian tributary pensions, from traditional privileges, and from some colonial trade. Unlike the late eighteenth century, survival in this baroque society was affected more by nature than by commercial fluctuations.

Thus, in this colony, with a dearth of settlers, an abundance of colonized and dispersed, semi-subsistent economies, government was the essential shaping force. It channeled to the New World the medieval Spanish traditions upon which Hapsburg law was based; it maintained that vague outline of common jurisdictions, institutions, rights, and ultimately culture; it provided sustenance, and, perhaps most important, it was the mediator to which the different sectors turned to resolve crises.

Through the colonial epoch the manner in which government administered and mediated colonial affairs changed, most dramatically during the period of this study. In 1680 an exhausted Castile, "ominously pessimistic," in Vicens Vives' term,[5] reverted to a hardened, traditional respect for regional privileges, and by 1700 Hapsburg rule ended, replaced by a Bourbon monarchy whose absolutist philosophy contrasted dramatically with that of its weakened predecessor. Centralizing reforms were introduced. The bureaucracy was transformed. Nevertheless, Hapsburg institutions, local rights, the church, the legal structure continued to function under assault from new ideas in government. And, within a century, Bourbon authority itself came under attack from enlightened, liberal republican doctrines that supplanted it in the early nineteenth century. Finally, a traditional, nativist reaction in 1838 tried to restore many institutions that resembled, if they did not copy, those of the Hapsburg monarchy of 140 years before.

But this is not only a study of government in Central America.

Rather, it is an inquiry into the relation between society and government, how the changes in rule and ruling philosophy were introduced, accepted, and resisted. The Hapsburg system of the late seventeenth century may have been decayed, but its institutions and values had been the basis and foundation for colonial rule for 150 years. They remained in Central American society to be attacked by absolutism, a world economy, and the enlightened intellectual movement. Semisubsistence, local economies were overwhelmed by the forces of the world economy and an integrated colonial economy developed with government assistance. New colonials arrived with new ideas and allies, overcoming the traditional elite, and eventually rivaling Bourbon absolutism. The eighteenth century was more than a Bourbon epoch, it was a social revolution here as elsewhere, and these forces of change encountered resistance. How they interacted upon the patrimonial society, the Hapsburg creation, and upon the diverse societies throughout the colony, is critical to this history.

As an overview this study examines tradition and change: the tradition of Amerindia as it was transformed by Hapsburg institutions and evolved into a tradition of Central America which came under attack in the enlightened age and, in turn, fell to the attack of a nineteenth-century nativist movement. It is the constant theme of Central American history: defensive insularity versus invading forces, resistance, adaptation, or submission. The Creole elite that led the independence movement was not a traditional force, for it overcame and submerged traditional rights and families. Rather, it was an invading force that attacked Bourbon absolutism when it attacked merchant prerogatives and the force of the western economy. The nativist revolts of the 1830s were a response to that invasion.

Finally, this study is concerned with the fragmentation of that modicum of unity of Hispanic, Catholic, and Hapsburg society, the fragmentation that culminated under the Central American Federation. Why did a colony that, like a dormant volcano, was at peace for 250 years and that peacefully achieved its independence erupt, collapsing in disunity and violence, first between regions and oligarchs and then between races and classes, transforming the landscape?

What social and political factors led to the anarchy that pervaded the nineteenth century and that still remains, like the omnipresent volcanos, the social and political inheritance of Central America?

Much of the research for this study was done in the Archivo General de Guatemala and the Archivo General de Indias in Seville, Spain. My infinite gratitude to the *porteros* in those institutions, those men who climb up and down the stacks and stairways to retrieve documents so that a history like this may be written, and to the officials of those institutions who provide a service that benefits not only their nation, but the world.

My thanks also to the Archivo General de la Nacion (Mexico), the Archivo Eclesiástico de Guatemala, the Bibliothèque Nationale, the British Museum and the Public Record Office, the Archivo Segreto Vaticano, the Archivum Romanum Societatis Iesus, and the New York Public Library.

Numerous friends and colleagues have supported me and provided advice and useful criticism of this volume. In France, the faculty of the Ecole Pratique des Hautes Etudes, VIième Section, provided the training and criticism for my doctoral dissertation upon which this work is based in part. Ruggiero Romano directed my studies and research and provided invaluable advice and guidance. My deep gratitude to him for his patience and understanding. Julian Pitt-Rivers gave the initial impetus for which I will always be grateful. Frédéric Mauro and Pierre Vilar were particularly helpful in analyzing the manuscript.

In the United States, Ken Andrien, Jacques Barbier, Herbert Klein, Murdo Macleod, and John TePaske read, criticized, and improved the work. My thanks to each of them. To Myrna Chase Wortman, my love, not for her advice and support which so much improved this work, but for herself.

Research for this work was supported by the Tinker Foundation and the State University of New York Foundation to whom I express my gratitude. My thanks also to the Geneseo Foundation that provided assistance for the preparation of the manuscript.

GOVERNMENT AND SOCIETY
IN CENTRAL AMERICA,
1680–1840

PART ONE

El Reino de Guatemala

CHAPTER ONE

The Conquest
and the Settlement

TWO ALIEN WORLDS met, the European and the Amerindian, with a violence surpassed only by the clash of the region's substrata plates and the resultant earthquakes and volcanic explosions. Thousands of Indians were slaughtered in battle. Hundreds of thousands died of disease. Of those who survived, many were enslaved. Most were resettled. Their leadership was removed, their religions suppressed. The land was altered. Virgin forests were felled and European animals introduced. The soil eroded.

Out of this violence, out of this joining of Europe and America, emerged a new American social order, a settled and relatively peaceful colony comprised of Amerindians, castes, and Creoles under a Hapsburg monarchy and a Spanish, Christian god. In the early, violent days, conquerors sought wealth greedily. After the initial shock, a more rational economic and political life emerged. Law was established, boundaries created, and elites formed.

It is this process of normalization, the establishment of the colonial social structure, that concerns us. The rules and traditions, the hierarchies and beliefs, and the bases and suppositions for social order formed in the first century of the colony continued through the colonial period and exist, to some degree, today.

Christopher Columbus came first. He sailed along the Caribbean coastline and named the cape at Gracias a Dios and the land of Costa Rica. His explorations and those of other Spaniards for the next ten years were tentative, seemingly unimportant. They may have given rise to stories and fables among Mesoamerican peoples. More important, they probably transmitted a destructive and unseen invader, European disease, for we now know that before Hernán Cortés and

Pedro Alvarado conquered the region, an epidemic occurred that, by one estimate, killed a fourth of the dense population of the Guatemalan highlands.[1]

The epidemic was a portent. Hernán Cortés conquered Aztec Mexico in 1519 and deputized his lieutenant, Pedro Alvarado, to lead an expedition of Spanish and Tlaxacalan and Cholutecan Mexican Indians south into the Guatemalan highlands. Unlike the great Aztec empire at Tenochtitlán, Guatemala was not unified and so was conquered piecemeal. At first, Alvarado made alliance with the Cakchiquels. He crushed the Quichés and Tzutuhils. Labor obligations led the Cakchiquels to revolt. Alvarado suppressed the revolt with equal violence.

In twenty years a few thousands of European men subjected most of Mesoamerica. The victories of Hernán Cortés and Pedro Alvarado showed the great disparity in military technology between Amerindia and Europe. The arrows and spears of a multitude of Amerindians attacked the few, armored Spanish without effect. The conquerors' horses, their fighting dogs, and the frightening sound of their guns were all new to America, shocking the defending peoples into submission. Spanish alliances with Amerindian nations divided and conquered. And the invisible ally, European germs, wrecked havoc among indigenous peoples who lacked natural immunities.

This Spanish domination was repeated elsewhere. In southern Central America, in Nicaragua and Costa Rica, slavers came from Panama in search of laborers for the mines of Santo Domingo and later for use as bearers in the conquest of Peru. From Cuba, Martín Estete invaded Honduras in search of gold.

The conquests were rapid. Indian resistance dissipated quickly. Rivalries among conquistadores soon became more prevalent than indigenous rebellions. The Contreras family took control of Nicaragua and extended their slave raids into Honduras and Salvador. They were repulsed by Alvarado's faction. Cortés invaded, attracted by rumors of mineral wealth in Estete's Honduras. He marched through the Yucatan and the hotlands of Verapaz, passing the island of Petén. Here he was feted by the Itzá nation, a people that would not be conquered until the end of the seventeenth century. Most of his army perished from illness in the hotlands, as had Estete and most of his troops. The rumors of minerals unfounded, Cortés abandoned Honduras and returned to Mexico. Soon after, Francisco de Montejo came south from the colony he founded in the Yucatan and took control of the province.

The search for immediate wealth was the prime concern of these conquerors, the first generation of colonists. Between 1521 and 1550 they fought among themselves for territorial control, and they used Indian labor brutally. Indigenous populations declined precipitously. Government power scarcely existed, marked only by the existence of three independent factions, the Alvarados and later Maldonados of Guatemala, Francisco de Montejo in Honduras, and the Contreras family in Nicaragua.

By far the most destructive search for wealth occurred in Nicaragua and southern Honduras. The slavers sought bodies for export. They raided and depopulated areas that were said to have had "more people than hairs on all the deer." The commerce continued until mid-century, when depopulation, royal legislation, and the lure of Incan wealth to the south put an end to it, leaving a vacuum for other populations and for cattle to fill.

In Guatemala settlement and the exploitation of Indians took different forms. Spanish wealth was not derived from the export of humans, rather it came from the fruits of Indians' work. The first conquistadores were awarded *encomiendas* of Indians, licenses to collect tribute for the crown that were, in reality, permissions to compel Amerindian labor in personal service. Columbus had instituted the medieval custom in Hispaniola to try to create stable populations under royal control. It was repeated throughout the Spanish Americas. The greatest number of Indians went to the most powerful in the conquest, Pedro Alvarado received the most, followed by his brother, Jorge. In 1548, six captains of the conquest still held pueblos with more than five hundred Indians each; two had over a thousand. Lesser conquerors, however, who had been given smaller pueblos, became impoverished when disease killed their Indians.[2]

Those Indians who did not fall under encomiendas were enslaved. If this slaving did not result in massive depopulation as had occurred in Nicaragua, it was nonetheless violent and destructive. Most conquerors enslaved without regard to the formal Spanish laws of conquest that prescribed slave status only for those taken in battle. New slaves were branded on the face; slaves who were sold were rebranded; and freed slaves were counter-branded to cross out the original mark.

In the early years of the conquest the two labor systems existed side by side. Encomenderos and slave owners—the two were frequently the same—sent their workers to Honduras for mineral production, ordered them to gather cacao, or rented them as bearers or *tamemes*. These alien and hard labors upset the pre-Columbian work pattern, forcing Indians to travel through climates to which they were not adapted. With no road system and no carts, with few and expensive beasts of burden, tamemes were compelled to carry wood and stone for construction and minerals and foodstuffs for commerce. Heavy burdens, long hours, and variations in climate led to death. Of four thousand Indians that set out on one expedition only six survived.[3]

The conquerors in Nicaragua gained their profit from slaving, those in the north sought minerals. Their Indians panned the rivers of Central America and they discovered fairly quickly the value of Honduras. Alvarado invaded Montejo's domain and established a settlement at Gracias a Dios. Gold was also found at San Pedro and Trujillo, both in the same province. At least 24,000 pesos were found throughout Honduras in 1540 and 45,000 two years later in San Pedro and Trujillo alone.[4]

With gold production, the crown attempted to assert its authority over the conquistadores. It established in 1541 the first ruling tribunal or *audiencia* in Central America at Gracias a Dios—with jurisdiction extending from Tabasco and the Yucatan south to Costa Rica—to collect the traditional *quinto* tax, a fifth of all mineral production. But within a decade gold yields declined precipitously at Gracias a Dios, and complaints from the northern provinces about the long distance to the audiencia seat led to a transfer of the body to the more central location at Guatemala.

Still other areas were developed for quick mineral exploitation. In Olancho in Honduras and Segovia in Nicaragua, Indians rebelled against servitude and African slaves were imported. These too were difficult to control. Nevertheless, silver and gold production surpassed all other areas in the 1540s, reaching its peak around mid-century. Twenty-six thousand pesos in taxes were sent to Spain in 1553. But, as in the other areas, production declined within a decade. Streams were panned out and manpower was short. For the rest of the colonial period, Honduras was the area where minerals could be found. But most mining, be it in gold panning or silver production, did not yield large amounts, certainly never the sums that were obtained from Mexico or Peru. Indian laborers were scarce. New veins were found, mined, and quickly abandoned. For most of these three hundred years mineral production and the miners themselves were poor.

Thus, Central America fell outside the "silver belt," the regions of the Americas where coinage was prevalent and where the crown, merchants, and farmers were most attracted. Instead, Central America had to gain its wealth from agriculture. The colony's survival, its marketing structure, and its labor systems developed for the production of food, cotton, and cattle for subsistence and cacao, indigo, and other commodities for trade with the outside world.

The first conquerors quickly appreciated the wealth that could be earned from agriculture. In the Chiapas region of Soconusco they usurped what had been the traditional Amerindian production and trade in cacao to Mexico. The colonists did not take over direct control. Rather, Spanish encomenderos collected a tribute tax on every cacao tree while compelling Indians to trade or barter goods with them at unfair prices, selling food expensively and buying cacao cheaply.

But, as with mining, the initial spurt of cacao wealth quickly subsided. Epidemics killed many of the hotland Indian farmers. The burdensome levies and the unfair trade in commodities led to a decline in production. Encomenderos reacted by compelling the survivors to increase plantings and production, but Indians resisted and allowed trees to die. Royal officials, allied with the colonists, created the office of *juez de milpas*, a judge to supervise and order greater plantings, but to little avail. The epidemic of 1545 killed many of the remaining Indians. Guatemalan highland Indians were transferred to the Soconusco hotlands, but the change in the climate and the harsh labor killed them as well. With the establishment of effective royal government and the opposition of highland colonists to population transfers, Soconusco cacao encomenderos were deprived of replacements and the industry lost its importance.[5]

Most of the first generation of conquistadores and encomenderos lost power and wealth within twenty years of their arrival. Some sold their encomiendas to *nouveaux-arrivés*. Some became impoverished as their Indians died. Still others left to seek their fortunes in South America. Pedro Alvarado himself left in 1530 with a large group of Spaniards and Indian retainers to conquer Quito.

With few sources for immediate wealth and the surviving Indian population already distributed, Central America became a transit point on the way south from Mexico to Peru. A shipbuilding industry developed in Realejo (Nicaragua), where the readily available pitch and hardwoods were converted into vessels for the Pacific traffic. By 1542 Bishop Marroquín could say about Guatemala that "this city has always been inn and hospital for everyone. It is now and will be since it is on the way to everywhere."[6]

The first two decades of the conquest were violent and anarchic. Royal control was limited at best. Then the fury of the collision of the two worlds ebbed. Thanks in part to Bishop Las Casas' observations of the destruction of Central American Indians and to his criticisms of Spanish labor policy, the crown promulgated the "New Laws" of 1542 to eliminate slavery and encomiendas. It dispatched officials throughout America to enforce the radical provisions. The effectiveness of the laws and their enforcers varied from colony to colony. In Mexico resistance led to the restoration of the old encomiendas, although no new ones were granted thereafter. In Peru the laws led to revolt and the death of the royal enforcer.

Alonso López de Cerrato was sent to Central America. He traveled throughout the colony, enforcing the laws. His accomplishments were clear: he freed slaves, eliminated encomiendas, reduced tribute, and inspected and ruled upon the administration of Indians. On the other hand, he did not suspend all encomiendas. The wealthiest colonists were confirmed in their holdings, and, indeed, new ones were rewarded to Cerrato's family. But this inconsistency was not unusual; the combination of effectiveness in government against weaker sectors of the colonial elite, ineffectiveness against the most powerful, and personal or family reward was a characteristic of the next century and a half of Hapsburg government, as we shall see.[7]

The Cerrato reforms marked the beginning of effective royal government in Central America and the end to the anarchy of the initial collision of the two worlds. Life became more ordered. The original conquistadores, a military class, held Amerindians in low esteem as defeated enemies. The second generation of colonizers, some holding encomiendas, others as merchants and farmers, looked upon the Indian as a necessary source of labor. Rather than private control, the government took control of the administration of labor in the repartimiento of Indians.

To be sure, the Cerrato reforms were only a first sign of stability in government. A decade later the audiencia of Guatemala was dissolved because of corruption linked to the cacao trade, its jurisdictions divided between Panama and Mexico. Seven years later it was restored. Official corruption never ended. Neither did abuse of Indians. In areas where cash crops and minerals were exploited, laborers were overworked to the point of death, others were exploited by colonial officials. Corruption and the harsh use of Indians existed through the colonial and into the national period. But in the center of royal administration, in Guatemala and the surrounding highlands, the rhythm of work became more regular, the pueblo protected (even if the protection was ineffective at times), and the colonial population more settled.

Nor did the decline in Amerindian population cease with the Cerrato reforms. The change in work patterns from pre-conquest times, the movement of peoples from cool highlands to hot lowlands for production of money crops, and the failure of Amerindia to develop resistence to European disease, all contributed to the reduction in population that lasted, perhaps, until the last decade of the sixteenth century. Severe pandemics spread throughout the colony in 1519–20, 1545–48, and 1576–78. After each, the demand for labor rose and with it greater abuse of the surviving populations.[8]

By the end of the century the population curve turned. Still, this did not mean that Indians ceased to suffer from disease. In the varied and undulating topography of Central America, with its dry and hot Pacific lowlands, its moist and hot Atlantic lowlands, and its cool tablelands, regional epidemics occurred that sometimes were limited to the altitude and climate of a single pueblo. More widespread epidemics, in the Valley of Guatemala at the turn into the eighteenth century, and in Chiapas eighty years later, provide vivid proof of the continued vulnerability to disease. But in gross terms the total population of Amerindia stabilized around 1600, particularly in the Guatemalan highlands, and from that point on grew, not steadily but zigzaggedly. Just as the Cerrato reforms were a first sign of stable administration, though certainly not indicative of strong and honest government, so the turn of the century marked the beginning of demographic stability that was periodically interrupted thereafter.[9]

The demand for labor affected the survival of the Indian populations. And the demand for labor rose with the ability of the colonial elite to find a suitable cash crop for a market abroad. In the thirty years following the Cerrato reforms, cacao was such a commodity. As had occurred in Soconusco, a small group of encomenderos in the Salvadoran hotlands of Izalcos gathered great and rapid wealth through the collection of tribute on cacao trees and the commodity's trade north to Mexico. The prosperity of the encomenderos attracted merchants and other colonists who gained their livelihood from the peripheral trade in food crops and clothing in the town of Sonsonate. The commerce earned one encomendero at least 140,000 pesos in the thirty-year period. But, as in Soconusco, the boom ended because the pandemic of 1578 reduced the Indian population by as much as 90 percent. Encomenderos tried to exact more tribute from the survivors, causing even greater loss of life. Some laborers were imported from the Guatemalan highlands, but with opposition from Spanish officials and colonists in that region it ceased. By 1590 cacao production was a fraction of that of the boom era. It continued here as well as elsewhere in the colony, but never reached the great quantity and profit of the early years. In the seventeenth century cacao from Guayaquil and Caracas sold on the Mexican market in greater quantities and at cheaper prices, eliminating the demand for the Guatemalan variety.[10]

In both the Soconusco and Izalco industries, encomenderos sought help from the government to compel Indians to plant cacao trees. The jueces de milpas were empowered to force Indians to maintain sufficient cacao trees to satisfy tribute requirements and government needs, and, at first, they seemed to succeed in increasing the production. But as a consequence of the pressure, Indians lacked sufficient time and labor to plant foodcrops and were themselves weakened and succumbed to the epidemic.

The juez de milpas did not end, however, but was used whenever Indians failed to supply sufficient commodities in tribute to the colonial population. It was a major source of corruption. Officials who gave their services to those merchants who offered a sufficient bribe were tempted to create the office until the long appeal process to Spain extinguished it. Periodically, throughout the seventeenth century, the audiencia resurrected the juez office and then the crown banned it.

More important, the juez de milpas was the only minor position that had legal approbation to violate the pueblo. Spanish alcaldes and their aides could order labor drafts, head counts, and tribute collections, but they could do so only through the Indian cabildo and the Indian alcalde. Whenever a demand for labor was not met, the Indian alcalde was jailed and beaten. However, the juez de milpas had the right to regularly visit pueblo common lands and demand that the Indians work them. Clerics fought this invasion and the crown usually concurred. Still, the institution did not die until the second half of the seventeenth century.

With minerals drained and cacao profits limited to a few powerful encomenderos, the search for exportable commodities continued. Sarsaparilla was recognized in Europe for its medicinal qualities, but demand was not sufficiently great to stimulate trade. There was some success in Realejo with the construction of boats for the Pacific trade as well as with the extraction of Nicaraguan pitch for use in fabricating boats and casks for Peruvian wines. The dye cochineal required too much labor, was too vulnerable to Central American weather and locusts, and was better exploited in Mexico. This attempt to find a money crop—a *produit moteur* as Murdo MacLeod labelled it, following the Chaunus—to attract capital, shipping, and the interest of Seville merchants and to trade for Spanish cloth and wine as well as other articles of conspicuous consumption was constant throughout the colonial period. And for most of the epoch, from 1580 until independence and after, they looked to the blue dye, indigo, as the commodity to fill this function.[11]

Indigo was grown in the Pacific lowland areas, particularly in the regions around and between Sonsonate, Santa Ana, San Miguel, and San Salvador, or in most of what is today the Republic of El Salvador. Produced from xiquilite (*indigofera tinctoria*) since before the conquest, the Spanish crown became interested in its properties in 1558 when it asked the colonial government in Guatemala for samples and a description of how to cultivate the plant, produce, and use the dye. From 1585 til 1608, indigo amounted to over 23 percent of all commodities shipped from the Bay of Honduras to Spain. With the drop in cacao production at the end of the sixteenth century it became the primary export commodity until 1640, when demand in Europe, Spanish naval power, and the entire Atlantic trade declined.[12]

Indigo demand and production rose at the time of greatest royal concern for the Indians' well-being in what had been the cacao-producing area of Salvador. Workers were scarce. Like sugar farming, indigo required little labor except for three months a year when the bushes were cut, brought to the workhouses or *obrajes*, loaded into vats, emptied out, cut up, and packaged. Though the work lasted only three months, it took its toll. The residue that indigo left in the vats yielded sickening fumes. Large swarms of flies, which were attracted to it, plagued the workers with bites that transmitted disease. Concerned for the dwindling labor supply, the crown repeatedly issued orders in the last half of the sixteenth century against the use of Indians in the obrajes. The orders went unheeded; the prosperity of the dye was more important than the crown's ire. Toward the end of the century an inspection system was established to insure that the workhouses functioned without Indians. But the interdict only made the indigo more expensive.

A royal order declared in 1636 that "experience has shown the great damages that the Indians of [Salvador] have received and receive in the indigo obrajes . . . so that what are today obrajes were once pueblos now extinct and abandoned." Inspectors visited obrajes, were bribed, and then levied a small fine. Farmers preferred to pay this "tax" rather than give up their labor force. When the bishop of Guatemala inspected Salvador in 1671—the first such *visita* in thirty years for some towns and eighty for most—the indigo farmers "asked me that the alcalde mayor should not make annual inspections for the harm that results." But, the cleric opined, not to perform such inspections would result in increased contraband trade and abuses of indigenous labor. Indeed, the inspection by alcaldes was needed to maintain royal authority and to enable the official to gain some profit from the production. Rather than eliminate the labor, the system reinforced it, as officials' support depended upon bribes from its practice.[13]

On the other hand, the royal action did limit the supply of laborers, providing legal power to Creoles and officials in other areas who wished to protect their labor forces. Repartimientos of Indians, that is Indians administered by royal officials, could not be used legally in indigo areas. Of course, here too, bribed royal officials violated the law, diverting labor forces to indigo lands. And Indians were in repartimiento but three months a year; nothing prevented their hire to farms during the remainder of the year, especially if they fell in debt. Still, large transfers of labor forces from afar were hampered as clerics and other farmers used the law to keep Indians near their pueblos. The law also raised the cost of production with bribes at a time when commerce to Europe became more expensive and dangerous, thus making indigo an unprofitable commodity. The indigo farmers worked against the legislation throughout the seventeenth century. In 1630 they offered the crown contribution of 40,000 pesos, eight times the annual tax paid by all Creoles in the colony, in exchange for repeal. But the law remained until the early eighteenth century.[14]

The farmers looked to purchase African slaves to provide adequate labor and some haciendas did employ them. But the supply was limited and the price, therefore, high. The Indian labor, supported by the bribe system, was more economical than the purchase of slaves. Authorities and colonials alike feared the growing population of *cimarrones*, escaped slaves, in remote areas; most segments of the colony supported interdictions of the import of slaves.

Indigo production continued through the century, even after trade with Spain was cut after 1640. If commerce was not as concentrated or as large as it had been before the break, the dye was to serve as a continuing agent of exchange, a connection with the outside world, with Mexico, Peru, Cartagena, and, illegally, with Holland and England. It would expand again with the eighteenth-century industrial revolution.

The export of commodities, be they cacao or indigo, and the consequent abuse of Indian labor and the corruption of royal officials attracted the attention of rival merchants, of clerics, and of government officials, who reported to the crown, in countless complaints and reports, the tax evasions and abuses perpetrated by their enemies. But this well-documented drama overshadowed a far more important, less controversial, and therefore less documented development in Central American society: the growth of a regularized, internal economy that produced for the subsistence of the entire colony.

The early conquistadores sought immediate wealth; the later colonists created a more stable society and economy. Wheat farms and sugar plantations emerged in the valley of Guatemala and around León, Nicaragua. Cotton was cultivated in the Pacific hotlands of Escuintla and Chiapas. Sheep for wool were introduced into the highlands. Spanish friars and wealthy Creoles developed farms not for quick riches, as with cacao and gold production, but to provide the colonial population with necessary goods.

Labor was regularized. The encomienda that had been a crucial element of the cacao trade ceased to play an important role with the reduction in Indian populations and the refusal of royal officials to award other Indians as replacements to the hotlands. Rather, the encomienda was transformed into a pension system with tributes from Indians-in-encomienda given as rewards and for the upkeep of loyal Creoles and peninsulares.

In the encomienda's place, the division or repartimiento of Indians by *corregidores*, *alcaldes mayores*, and *ordinarios* and their aides became the major supplier of labor for the colony until the end of the eighteenth century. Each week every Indian alcalde was legally compelled to furnish a labor force equal to one-fourth of the pueblo's male population. Theoretically that labor force was to work from eight in the morning until five in the afternoon from Monday to Friday with a two-hour rest at noon and were paid a *real* for each day's work. The Spanish officials, the *repartidores*, then distributed the laborers to farms, haciendas, and public works for which they received one-half of one real for each laborer.[15]

Towns close to urban centers were liable to drafts for urban projects, construction and maintenance of public buildings, roads, and streets by Creole alcaldes ordinarios. "When public works are approved, a diabolical work of the devil," a Franciscan redundantly decried, "six, eight, or ten Indians must travel to cut wood, bring their own carts and their own instruments, axes, machetes and the rest." When calamities struck, like earthquakes, the subsequent pressure for work increased the demand for labor, and thus forced up the price of the free labor work force (of mestizos, mulattoes, and blacks).[16]

Labor abuses and Indian mortality depended frequently upon the geographical location of pueblos and historical and natural accidents. The town of Aquajapa provides a specific example of an individual settlement's misfortune. Situated on the royal road, near four major wheat-producing haciendas, the pueblo had to contribute labor to transport people and goods upon the road as well as provide work forces to the farms. When, in the first half of the seventeenth century, the next town along the royal road, Salpaltagua, was destroyed by an epidemic, the burden upon Aquajapa to transport goods and people on the road was increased by twice the old distance. The populace was now forced to bear the burden of communication and transportation over some seventeen leagues. Overwork on the road and in the wheat fields caused illness, a decline in population and still greater pressure for labor.[17]

Over the years repartimientos developed into custom, with each piece of cultivated land enjoying the traditional, if not legal, right to an Indian work force. Indeed, the number of Indians determined the value of certain farms, and sometimes land was purchased for the labor force which was then transferred to another enterprise. Thus, a lumberer purchased a cattle farm in 1663, transferring the Indians to cut wood and abandoning the cattle. The same year a sugar farmer bought small ranches to move their workers to his *trapiches*.[18]

There were, of course, great opportunities for corruption and abuses. Lesser officials, lieutenants of the alcaldes, who depended upon the half-real per worker for their profit ignored population loss and insisted upon the continued supply of the same number of Indians. Indians were frequently not paid for the travel needed to reach distant farms. Sometimes they were transferred, illegally, to hotland areas.

However, because the value of land was determined at least in part by the number of Indians it possessed, producers had a vested interest in the well-being of their laborers. Any official who excessively abused Indians earned the wrath of Creoles and clerics alike. Indians could not be transferred from highland to hotland areas without facing the ire of some sector that understood the fatal results of such a practice as well as the consequences of the depopulation of regions. As a result, the repartimiento of labor, in the sense of the assignment of a certain number of laborers to a farm as determined by tradition, became a well-entrenched system, with farmer, official, and Indian working to support its regular administration. In contrast to the six-teenth century, when greed and ignorance led to death and destruc-tion, by the seventeenth century a stable labor practice led to a status quo which all sectors supported.[19]

The labor of Indians became regularized. The harsh work of ta-memes was reduced as mules and horses became more prevalent and cheaper. Roads were constructed that enabled the use of carts. Colonials, officials, and clerics in the highlands guarded against the export of Amerindians to the fatal labor of cacao and indigo fields. Indians were now needed to work in the wheat fields and on public projects, to build roads, government offices, and churches, to supply the growing population of the highlands with fish from Lake Atitlán, lumber from the mountains, and clothing from their home work.

This tension between production for the external market, whether in minerals, cacao, or indigo, and that for internal subsistence was and is a constant in Central American history. The tension was particularly great with the demographic decline. Without much silver, those colonists and officials who sought goods for export to Spain did so because they saw their future in the Iberian Peninsula and needed exportable wealth to transfer to the old world or they coveted Spanish luxuries, cloth and ornaments, and needed goods for trade. Only two necessities came from Europe at the end of the century: hardware, not yet a critical item, and wine for sacrament, but that was now produced in cheaper and larger quantities in Peru.

And thus, if some export industries such as cacao or indigo suffered from "depression," the internal economy did not. Unlike urban Mexico, where throughout the colonial period there were chronic food shortages and labor for wheat fields was in short supply, highland Guatemala and the rest of Central America rarely suffered from a dearth of food. "Depression" in the internal economy was caused by drought and locusts, not by the obstacles of war, the unavailability of ocean vessels, or the demand in Europe.

True, some officials, merchants, and encomenderos suffered. The three encomenderos who gained their fortunes from cacao exploitation in Izalcos left. But Central American life at the end of the century became regularized, especially in the highlands—William Sherman calls it "a more stable social mileau"—so that when the Franciscan friar Miguel Aguía visited Guatemala at the turn of the seventeenth century he saw better conditions there than in Peru, where the rich silver mines of Potosí were creating an affluent colonial society.[20]

This was not Peru. Neither was it the central valley of Mexico, where the shortage of labor created abuses that drove Amerindians to the protection of the hacienda and into debt peonage. Central America was, by and large, outside the "silver belt," the mining regions and affiliated farms and cities that sent minerals to Spain.

Despite pandemics, highland Guatemala had sufficient labor to avoid the debt peonage of its northern neighbor. It lacked the great public works like the drainage system that absorbed so many Indian laborers in Mexico.[21] And it lacked the mines that tempted the crown as well as the Creoles to take Indians away from agricultural production.

By 1600 Central America was settled and its citizens were concerned with the provision of sufficient food, cloth, and trade. The violence of the conquest had ended.

CHAPTER TWO

The Kingdom Under the Hapsburgs

THE CREATION OF a government structure in the sixteenth century marked the establishment of a stable social network that linked all sectors of the colony. Cabildos (municipalities) governed Creole towns and cities, gaining control over labor administration. In Indian pueblos colonial authorities replaced the traditional leadership and imposed Indian cabildos. At the national level, the king's secular and spiritual appointees mediated among the requirements of empire, colony, region, and the Indian.

Similarly a Hapsburg philosophy evolved throughout the empire, a philosophy that balanced the needs of each region with those of the empire in order to maintain control over its vast domains. The structure of the system was flexible, bowing to local conditions and political realities, and recognizing local traditions as having force in law. It rewarded loyalty, granting offices and pensions to those who served the crown well. The system accepted regional and individual self-interest, licensing the collection of taxes to private individuals or municipal corporations, selling offices, and overlooking minor corruption on the part of royal officials.

The Hapsburg system functioned well while Peruvian mines sent ample silver to Spain and rival European states were still weak. The loyalty and *hispanidad* (Spanishness) of seventeenth-century Mexico and Central America testify to this. But Spanish power could not be maintained under what was a fundamentally weak, decentralized state unable to amass sufficient resources to repulse the incessant attacks of European states and Caribbean pirates. Deprived of fiscal resources, offices were sold, and the bureaucracy became increasingly inept; the empire lost territory. When, in 1700, Louis XIV's grandson, the Duke of Anjou, succeeded to the throne of Spain as Philip V, he and his Bourbon ministers challenged the loose, if well-entrenched, Hapsburg system. Much of the Bourbon epoch in Spain was a struggle to replace the sixteenth- and seventeenth-century melange of laws and customs with institutions that stressed direct compliance with written law and the annihilation of autonomous Hapsburg bodies. The history of eighteenth-century Central America that is described in this book is one of conflict between Hapsburg society, attitudes, and institutions and the Bourbon reformers.

Looking back from the epoch of independence, we can appreciate the strengths of the Hapsburg system that, unlike its successor, developed a system of rewards through the tax structure and pension system that tied colonials to the empire even during times of greatest state weakness. The church functioned under the direct control of the crown, uniting the needs of localities with the Catholic hispanidad of the metropolis. Despite the vast distances and the lack of communication at the end of the seventeenth century, all groups in Central America recognized the supremacy of the crown. Attempting to reform colonial government, the Bourbons destroyed not only principles of local autonomy but also this sense of national integration. They undermined the church. At the end of the seventeenth century the Americas remained loyal to a feeble Hapsburg Spain; at the beginning of the nineteenth, alienated, they revolted from a weak Bourbon empire.

Though it ruled the largest and wealthiest empire in the world, Hapsburg power was not sufficient to enforce its will, and thus the balancing of interest groups and the power of the colony itself kept a check on the will of the emperor. This system had developed during the conquest of Iberia when Spanish sovereigns joined together their kingdoms or *reinos* to dispel the infidel and then to unite, first under the Christian monarchs Ferdinand and Isabella, later under the Hapsburg monarchy. The Hapsburg Charles created the basis for an empire by allowing local princes to retain their authority and traditions. With the conquest and settlement of the Americas, new kingdoms were formed: "viceroyalties" were established in New Spain and in Lima, and "kingdoms" in Guatemala and other smaller areas.

Distance from the metropolis enabled both conquistadores and settlers to maintain power sufficient to compel the crown to balance local with imperial interests and to recognize the autonomy of its independent units and officials. Groups rivaled each other within and between the American colonies: Spanish merchants and local businessmen were in conflict over trading rights and prices, large and small farmers quarreled about the allocation of a scarce supply of laborers, and regular and secular clerics disputed questions of ecclesiastical privilege. The crown's bureaucracy joined in factions with colonial sectors: peninsulares governors, corregidores, and alcaldes mayores were appointed by and allied with president and *oidores* of the audiencia; they worked closely with Spanish and Creole merchants and producers; and their decisions were frequently influenced by the interests they represented rather than by law. As Creole and mestizo populations developed and African slaves were introduced, there was conflict with Spaniards and Indians over the rights and duties of each group in the economic and social life of the colony. The crown mediated between the several interests—all groups were still further divided into classes and occupations—first, through its appointed officials, and ultimately, through the Council of the Indies. As the crown mediated, it also weighed colonial interests with those of the dominant Iberian provinces, the needs of the crown, and those of the empire as a whole.

Colonial government was administered under a system of written laws and unwritten customs through the sixteenth and seventeenth centuries. With the metropolis involved in a series of disastrous wars, direct, centralized administration was impossible. The frontier nature of the region and the fragility of the empire militated against control. Royal orders from the Council of the Indies were sometimes unenforceable; violations were rarely prosecuted. Creole producers and merchants, Spanish bureaucrats, clerics, Indian and caste populations, all recognized and proclaimed the supremacy of the crown. However, whenever new legislation met with united opposition, the crown was too weak to act. A system of government thus developed that was based upon a melange of established traditions, royal legislation, and local factors, all contributing to the structure of colonial administration and law.

The crown was not without weapons to enforce its will. As economic and political interests disputed their rights, the crown and the Council of the Indies received comprehensive reports and complaints from each of the factions, the various hierarchies within the church, the Indian communities, and the Creole population. The divisions within the colony could insure that the council's decision was enforced. Overcorrupt officials could be detained in unhealthy prisons for long periods; they could be returned to Spain in chains. Loyal and honest officials were granted sizable pensions and were promoted to valued offices.

For the two centuries of their rule, then, Hapsburg decrees could only reflect or channel the diverse political forces of their empire. In essence, law was a broad general framework that defined loyalty and disloyalty. In marked contrast, their Bourbon successors enforced orders in the colonies that were diametrically opposed to the interests of some of the most powerful forces in colonial society. Hapsburg tools to enforce the royal will—the royal bureaucracy, the control of intra-empire trade, and the spiritual aegis of the church—were insufficient weapons; the strength of the colonies and kingdoms relative to the metropolis was much greater in the sixteenth and seventeenth centuries than it was to be in the eighteenth. Hapsburg law recognized that royal decrees might not be "justly" suited to all areas at all times. The duty of the highest colonial officer, the president, was not ultimately to enforce the royal will, as it would later be under the Bourbons, but to preserve order and the loyalty of the kingdoms to the emperor.[1]

The best example of the functioning and philosophy of the Hapsburg system in the seventeenth century is the history of the battle over trade in Peruvian wine and oil, a history involving Salvadoran indigo farmers, Peruvian shippers, Andalusian lords and, ultimately, the crown itself. In devout Central America wine and oil were vital necessities. Without them the sacrament could not be performed and souls faced damnation. Merchants had always profited from the traffic in these religious commodities. The Dominicans held the legal wine monopoly in Central America, but all sectors of the society were interested and smuggling was prevalent. Spanish wine derived from Andalusia and its producers, such as the Dukes of Medina Celi and Osuna, held vast vineyards around Seville and were among the most powerful men in the empire. The wine traders of Seville sat in the cabildo and the merchant guild (*consulado*) and provided loans to the crown to finance its war efforts throughout the Hapsburg epoch. Both the lords and the merchants were staunch supporters of the monarchy and, in turn, expected it to defend their prerogatives.

Spanish olives and wine grapes were introduced into Peru in the sixteenth century and within a century challenged the peninsula trade. By the mid-seventeenth-century trade between Guatemala and Spain was stifled by European wars and Caribbean piracy. Commerce with Vera Cruz and Mexico was irregular and the cost of land transportation, taxes, and the great number of middlemen between Guatemala, Mexico, and Vera Cruz made Spanish wine and oil much more expensive in Guatemala than the Peruvian products.[2]

The wine traffic became a critical part of the Peruvian-Central

American commerce, involving the needs of the crown as well as the Creoles. Peru produced only two items needed in Central America— silver and wine. Boats sailing north in search of produce could make the voyage profitable if they could fill their empty holds with wine casks; any restrictions on the wine trade limited the incentives for the commerce. Similarly, restricted trade routes chagrined Central American merchants who could not export their goods to Europe except through the long, expensive, and ultimately unprofitable channel of Vera Cruz. Central American products had good markets to the south, however; indigo for Quito obrajes, wheat to Lima, and pitch to the wine fields for the making of casks. Even boats built in Realejo could be exchanged for Peruvian wine and oil. Wine was linked not only to spiritual salvation but to the material well-being of Central American farmers and merchants.

The crown's interests were no less vitally concerned. The imposition of a complete ban on traffic between Peru and Guatemala would reduce tribute income. Silver was the lifeline of the empire, and Central America depended upon Peru for its piece of the lifeline. Constantly short of coinage because the economy was basically one of agriculture and barter, Guatemalan royal officials found it difficult to convert Indian tribute goods (corn and wheat) to money to send to Spain. Without silver, the king and his pensioners who had been granted tribute from Indian encomiendas would be deprived of income. Royal officials and clerics sent for a few years to positions in the colony could not take their wealth when they returned to the Peninsula. Faced with the interests of powerful Peninsula wine growers and traders, and those of Peruvians, Guatemalans, and royal agents in the colonies, the monarchy had to balance all sides and serve its own interest in Guatemala's steady supply of Peruvian silver.

The consulado of Seville, with many grape and olive interests, was much more influential than the new world merchants by virtue of its contribution to the finances of the crown. Therefore, in 1620, the Council of the Indies banned the trade of Peruvian wine to Guatemala, allowing only two *naos* a year to trade between the areas if the boats carried at least 200,000 pesos in coinage. The interdict was ineffectual. In Guatemala the President removed it periodically when minor revolts along the Pacific coast threatened the colony. Boats with legal products brought Peruvian "vinegar"—the taste of wine and vinegar was difficult to differentiate in the seventeenth century. In fact, the trade rarely, if ever, ceased, though there were fines, bribes, and occasional seizures by zealous officials enforcing the interdict. The ban inflated the price of wine as contraband traffic flourished. In 1643, in Sonsonate, one official permitted the importation of Peruvian wine to fill a shortage in the colony and was deluged with 6,000 barrels or three times the annual average import of Spanish wine between 1647 and 1677. Despite its inability to enforce the interdict the monarchy had to maintain it to satisfy the Peninsulares.[3]

All sectors of Central America, including the church, argued vociferously for the legalization of the wine trade to support religious ceremonies and to stimulate trade. The Council of the Indies received proposals from various Central American groups steadily throughout the seventeenth century. In 1670, for example, a deputation of Guatemalan merchants suggested that the crown permit 5,000 barrels (*botijas*) of wine to enter from Peru and 10,000 from Spain with the Spanish product to be paid for with indigo. The proposition would have brought Spanish vessels to the Bay of Honduras and stimulated the depressed indigo market. It was a challenge to the Seville consulado to provide regular commerce to the Bay of Honduras. The merchants of Seville rejected the project, repeating their arguments that indigo could not be sold in Europe and that "no one will make a trip to the Port of Honduras because there is no force to oppose the pirates that infest those coasts."[4]

Estimates of the amount of wine required annually by Central America varied. The Council of the Indies recommended 40,000 barrels, the merchants of Guatemala 50,000, and the dean and cabildo of the Guatemalan diocese, "at least" 100,000. Whatever the need, there is no doubt that Spain failed to provide sufficient quantities. In the thirty-one years during which there are complete, extant figures of Spanish wine imports (see table 2.1) and during which Peruvian wine was illegal, the annual average received in Central America was 1,900 barrels. Between 1673 and 1679 three boats arrived from Spain with some 4,600 barrels while 18,000 barrels from Peru arrived and paid taxes during the same period.[5]

A shift in the attitude of the Spanish crown towards the Peruvian wine trade came about in 1680. The loss of tax revenues and the inability to the Seville consulado to supply either Central America or New Spain led to a reassessment. Partial legalization would not affect the price of Spanish wine, the Council of the Indies claimed, over the objections of the merchant guild, because the Spanish product was rarely imported into Central America. After five years of appeals, a royal *cédula* was issued that legalized commerce in Peruvian wine for the first time in the century.[6]

Despite a series of natural disasters in the late 1680s, commerce flourished as Central America became an entrepôt for Peru and Mex-

*Table 2.1: Spanish Wine Entering Central
America, 1647–1677*

Year	Barrels	Year	Barrels
1647	5,569	1660	108
1648	7,252	1661	734
1650	2,375	1662	116
1651	2,208	1663	2,629
1653	134	1665	108
1655	2,571	1668	4,120
1656	3,970	1667–77	24,691
1659	2,242		

SOURCES: *1647–66:* A. G. I., Guatemala 279, the
cabildo of Guatemala, 4/11/1668; *1667–77:* the cabildo
of Guatemala, 11/28/1677.

Note: The wine indicated entered via the Bay of
Honduras and from Mexico. In those years not listed,
no wine entered through official channels.

ico, underlining the importance of the wine trade in stimulating Pacific
commerce in other goods. Abuses increased as well in the temporary
commercial boom that resulted from the Council's permission to carry
on the wine trade. Cacao from Guayaquil was smuggled illegally into
Sonsonate for transport to Mexico, much to the horror of Central
American cacao producers who had fought successfully to ban such
traffic. Mercury, a government monopoly, was imported illegally by
private individuals for sale in Honduran and Mexican mines. Spanish
and Asian clothing was exported illegally from Mexico through Sonsonate and Realejo to Peru. The final abuse stood revealed when a
Peruvian vessel was caught trying to smuggle more than 300,000 pesos
worth of silver to Europe through Nicaragua. Costa Rican and Nicaraguan officials and merchants were implicated along with the
Peruvians.[7]

The wine trade prospered for a few years. With the entry of English
pirates to the Southern Sea around the 1680s and the War of Spanish
Succession, the enemy began to harass the Pacific traffic as effectively
as it had the Caribbean. Pressured by war and dependent upon Seville's
merchants for loans, the newly installed Bourbon monarchy withdrew
permission for the Peruvian wine trade in 1713. Combined with the
war's effect—ending virtually all commerce in the Atlantic and Pacific—and several natural disasters, the crown's decision caused the
greatest unrest in Central America since the early days of the conquest.
City and town leaders expressed great indignation, pointing to the

inadequate markets in Spain for their goods and the fact that no boats had come from the metropolis since 1695—nor would one arrive until 1725. They complained that goods brought overland from Mexico were too expensive for the scarce resources of Central America. In Nicaragua, they said, "one no longer buys or sells with money and only the fruits of the land are exchanged."[8]

Tension grew as Central American merchants fought for commercial survival. During the fifteen previous years farmers and merchants were bankrupted because warfare prevented contacts. Now, with the ban on Peruvian wine closing yet another exit for colonial goods, the very survival of the export trade was at stake. When, in 1714, a vessel arrived in Sonsonate bearing Peruvian wine, the Guatemalan president was forced to act: the local population was determined to unload the ship despite the Bourbon prohibition. There were vestiges of the Hapsburg flexibility left among the authorities, and the president claimed to the crown that the boat left before the 1713 interdict arrived in Sonsonate. He added that his ultimate responsibility was to "conserve the peace in the kingdom" and he therefore allowed the wine to enter. Two more boats arrived in 1716 and they were again allowed to unload because of the "general clamor." In all cases, the crown agreed with the president's decision in the interests of order.[9]

In conclusion, the century-long battle reflected both the strengths and weaknesses of the Hapsburg system. Royal decrees placated the powerful Seville merchants and wine producers who were opposed to commerce in Peruvian wine. Government officials in Guatemala periodically allowed the trade to keep the peace; unofficially, they recognized that without legal sanction the trade would continue, irregularly and at a higher cost because of bribes. Any determined effort to halt it would end in revolt. All recognized that the crown and an important elite in the Peninsula could not receive their tribute and pensions unless there was sufficient silver to convert Indian commodities and Peruvian silver came north with the wine.

Under the Hapsburgs, then, the monarchy and the bureaucracy preserved the support of the Seville elite and the peace of Central America with a minimum of force, maintaining control over this fraction of the large empire. Given the realities of power, interests, and geography, Hapsburg "flexibility" continued to be practiced by the incoming Bourbons.

The peninsulares who governed were responsible for overseeing Indian labor, remitting taxes to Spain, and insuring the defense and loyalty of the colony. The president was the chief official, his power tempered by the *real audiencia*, the judicial body which he served as president, and by the appeal process which provided recourse to the Council of Indies and to the crown.

The colony was divided into provinces under the jurisdiction of governors, alcaldes mayores and corregidores until the Bourbon *intendant* reforms of 1786. The four *gobiernos* that existed in the sixteenth and seventeenth centuries at Comayagua, León, Soconusco, and Costa Rica were established to control mining, shipping, cacao and indigo production, and to complete the conquest of Costa Rica. The less important regions of San Salvador, Ciudad Real (Chiapas), Tegucigalpa (Comayagua), Sonsonate, Verapaz, Suchitepéquez, Nicoya, Amatitique, and the mines of San Andrés de Zaragoza were established as alcaldes mayores with eighteen other less-settled and colonized areas under corregidores. Later, in the Hapsburg period, the distinction between alcaldias and corregidores blurred as the two offices differed in name only.[10]

The functions of the governor, the alcalde, and corregidor were similar, though the governor's position was considered far more important than the others and merited greater salary and ceremony. All three officials administered the collection of tribute and the distribution of Indian labor (repartimiento) to agricultural holdings.

The central fact, acknowledged by Hapsburg bureaucrats and colonists alike, was that the colony would be impossible to maintain without Indian tribute. Without the tribute, taxes would not be sufficient, no food would be grown, the basic elements of commerce would go uncollected. In Mexico and Peru mineral production thrived, coinage existed, and a prosperous trade was carried on with primary materials produced under the direct control of the Spaniard. But in Central America most commodities were grown or manufactured by the Indian and collected from him in taxes or forced trading by government officials or *encomenderos*. In this structure the Indian remained in the tribe, and the primary producing group was preserved. When tribute as the economic base was destroyed, as it was in indigo production, tribes were weakened or destroyed.

Every healthy, male Indian between the ages of eighteen and fifty was obliged to pay commodities worth two pesos in annual tribute to the king. The levy supported defense, government, and church expenses as well as remissions to Spain—80 to 90 percent of all income to the royal coffers.[11] Unlike Peru or New Spain, where merchants and mineral and agricultural producers contributed sizable revenues to the crown, the non-Indian populations in Central America administered and profited from the fruits of the Indian tribute to the extent that they barely paid taxes.

The dependence of the governmental structure and the economy upon Indian tribute exerted enormous pressure on the Indian population. Officials and natives alike had to maintain tribute levels and the royal income despite fluctuations in population from epidemics and natural disasters. The president, and more locally, the corregidor and alcalde mayor, maintained receipts or faced the wrath of the crown. Officials failed or refused to take new head counts, demanding that Indian alcaldes furnish the same tribute payments they had in the past. The ill, the young, and the aged were pressed for labor, which further increased mortality. Natural calamities thus led to greater disasters; populations with small declines suffered for their losses.

In addition to its function as a tax measure, tribute provided the commodities to support Creole trade. Corn, wheat, cotton, wool, cacao, and thread collected by corregidores and alcaldes mayores were auctioned in towns and cities at *almonedas*, a storage area that also served as an auction house. Theoretically legal, the auctions were open to corruption—agreements by merchants to offer lower prices, or arrangements between officials and favored businessmen. This process enabled the state through its fiscal system to maintain an internal trade in subsistence goods, compelling the Indian to produce.[12]

The lack of minerals in the colony affected the conversion of tributary articles into coinage. Remissions to the crown, funds taken to Spain by officials and clerics, encomiendas and pensions sent to the peninsula, all drained the colony of specie. The slight commerce and the relative unimportance of Guatemalan products in Mexico and Spain caused a crisis in specie. Merchants and government competed for silver. In the last half of the seventeenth century officials complained that merchants hoarded or exported Guatemala's limited supply of precious metal rendering the conversion of tribute impossible. The crown was, in fact, compelled in 1685 to permit a restricted wine trade with Peru as long as specie accompanied the wine.

This depression in the Creole economy may have benefited many Indians, however. With few outlets for goods, the pressure on labor in the Guatemalan highlands was reduced. The lack of silver lowered the price and the demand for Indian food and goods with the government periodically compelled to distribute food free of charge in order to rid itself of unwanted commodities.

Prosperous Indian communities thus paid tribute, but, ironically, the crown was unable to convert the wealth of corn and beans into silver. Royal officials tried to coerce merchants to accept goods for specie. The government issued receipts (*libranzas*) in payment for goods sold to it which were exchangeable in tributary goods. When, in 1676, the president learned that Mexican merchants were in Suchitepéquez purchasing cacao, he forced them to buy government goods. Thus, some of the weight of the tributary system was shifted to the commercial sector.[13]

Alcaldes mayores and corregidores were officially responsible for overseeing Indian tribute and making repartimientos of labor forces. Their unofficial functions were as important, if not more so, than their official duties. In Central America the colonial population was too small, too urban, to employ the labor resources of the rural indigenous population. Areas like Verapaz or Quezaltenango had between them less than a hundred colonists, many of whom were too poor to practice any sizable production. In such areas, the royal official was the dominant commercial agent together, perhaps, with the clergy. Alcaldes mayores and corregidores insured the civil control of the province as they integrated the interior indigenous areas into colonial society by forcing labor obligations upon them.

This integration was accomplished through the repartimiento of goods, an institution that was repeatedly banned but nevertheless integral to colonial life in Central America and southern Mexico. Officials and their assistants traveled throughout their jurisdictions, purchasing Indian commodities and wares and selling other goods. As with labor repartimiento, the repartimiento of goods became traditional with both official and Indian working within the trade system. Abuses were prevalent. The official who came to Central America for a limited number of years was not usually a wealthy man. His salary did not cover expenses and the cost of his office as well as the expenses of his family and retainers, especially after 1630 with the imposition of the *media anata* salary tax. The official had to borrow to finance his voyage and upkeep until he could establish his position. Then, he had to support either the president of the audiencia who appointed him or an ally in Spain who worked for his appointment. In the former case, a lesser official had to channel a steady amount of commerce to the president or an ally in Guatemala. He formed alliances with Creole businessmen. In periods of economic depression, or slack trade, or decline of indigenous population that led to reduced production, the indebted alcalde or corregidor faced enormous pressure to maintain his economic position. He then compelled Indians to produce more, sell commodities at unreasonably low prices, and purchase goods at abnormally high prices. Such practices fostered Indian or clerical resistance, heightening the conflict and contributing to further abuses. Nevertheless, by the eighteenth century, in most instances, these illegal practices were much less harsh than those of the sixteenth century that caused so many fatalities.

Royal officials ordered all classes of goods to be produced. Generally, Indians sold corn, beans, chile, and vanilla to officials who, in turn, sold these goods in the cities or in other towns. Indians produced commercial goods according to local conditions. In the Guatemalan highland regions of Tecpatitlán, Totonicapán, and Quezaltenango, male Indians were compelled to gather cotton in the coastal hotlands and sell it to officials. The cotton was distributed, *repartido*, to Indian women to be spun. Women were beaten if they failed to spin the thread sufficiently fine. Alcaldes mayores forced Indians in Chiapas to leave their pueblos to collect wild cochineal or to gather salt and cotton. In the Chiapan city of Ciudad Real Indians were forced to sell corn to the alcalde mayor, who then distributed it to other Indians to grind, make tortillas, and sell for his profit. In Nicaragua, repartimientos of honey and tar required Indians of Nueva Segovia, Granada, and Realejo to search for these goods in wild areas.[14]

Generally, the use of repartimientos of goods or the repartimientos of labor was determined by the particular condition of each pueblo. Repartimientos of goods were practiced in those areas where colonists and colonial commodities were scarce and repartimientos of labor existed where colonials lived and earned their livelihood. In fact, the alcalde mayor or corregidor served as the agent of Spanish society, maintaining the conquest in semi-frontier areas by directing the production of Indian articles and their introduction to the Creole and, sometimes, the export economies. The official sent the commodities to the cities where they were sold either to an allied official, a merchant, or the local populace, using Indians as door-to-door salesmen. In this way, the sizable indigenous population which was distant from Creole centers was forced to participate in the economy of colony and empire.

In those areas where the interests of different sectors overlapped with repartimiento there was opposition. In their need for labor Creoles resisted repartimientos of labor to other areas. They attacked repartimiento of goods because it compelled Indians to produce for officials rather than colonists. This resistance was particularly strong in the wealthy, indigo-producing region of Salvador. The Creole alcaldes ordinarios of Salvador controlled labor within the city, exporting Indians to indigo haciendas in the countryside, while Spanish alcaldes mayores distributed labor from pueblos outside the city's limits. The two sectors frequently clashed. The Creoles claimed the Spaniards violated jurisdictions by forcing Indians from the city to bring them cacao, balsam, cotton, achiote, and vanilla, "although these miserable native people do not possess these fruits [and] must travel to far off lands to purchase or gather them." Local farmers complained that the officials forced them to purchase merchandise at exorbitant prices using their power as suppliers of Indian labor for compulsion. The officials retorted that the Creoles used Indians in repartimiento in obrajes, illegally, rather than for the public works for which the repartimiento was meant.[15]

Generally, complaints concerning unfair repartimientos of goods and labor concerned the unfairly low price paid by officials for goods or the excessively high one paid by Indians. Most typically, officials purchased Indian goods at a third of their market value and sold goods to Indians at double the normal price. Clerics complained that officials paid for goods with clothing obtained from other Indians, unnecessary clothing that was priced too high. Indigenous populations were forced to travel away from their milpas during harvest time, paid five reales for a week's work that began Monday morning at six and ended Saturday evening at six, allowing them no time to go to and from their homes. Indians who arrived late or left early lost a day's pay. Many times Indians received only a half real for a week's work after they paid the high prices for food and other goods. Indians were made to purchase their tools or allowed only two or three weeks a year to rest and farm their own fields in violation of the law that stipulated only three months of labor. When a man could not report to work because of illness, or if he had fled the town, his wife, son, or daughter had to take his place.[16]

Prelates served as the guardians of Indians, living among them—some in the same pueblo for as many as fifty years—and reporting to higher authorities. In the tradition of Las Casas, regular clergy detailed specific abuses, pointing to the society's moral contradictions. Thomas Gage told of a situation in 1642 that was typical for the next hundred and fifty years. The alcalde mayor of Nicoya (Costa Rica) employed Indians "like slaves," without pay, to make a thread called *pita* from agave that, when dyed with indigo, brought high prices in Spain. The local friar opposed him and charged the Indians from his pulpit not to obey "any such unlawful commands from their alcalde mayor." The official, a military veteran who had served in Milan, "came one day resolutely to the friar's house with his sword drawn," and he attacked the priest, slicing off two fingers before the intercession of Indians ended the confrontation. The official was excommunicated, but "as

he was a man of high authority, he soon got off his excommunication."
Subsequently, he complained to Guatemala and forced the cleric's
removal from the region.[17]

Stories of official abuses were sent to the Council periodically
throughout the seventeenth and early eighteenth centuries, emotions
frequently reaching such peaks that even the crown was attacked for
the actions of its agents. "The officials your Majesty appoints," one
friar exclaimed curtly, "are damned to hell because of the practices
that continue." Priests would not accept the charge that Indians were
lazy and required supervision: "no other people work and farm all
classes of produce except them." Indeed, it was the Spaniard, mestizo,
and mulatto, who were lazy and depended upon the Indian for his
every need. Apart from labor in the fields, the Spaniard used Indians
for personal service at home, to wash, to cook, to construct houses,
and to run errands.

In the seventeenth and eighteenth centuries the Franciscans
were, among all the regular orders, the most outspoken defenders of
the Indian. One fiscal of the audiencia—the king's lawyer and "protector of the Indians" by title and by function if not corrupted—
claimed that only the Franciscans reported the truth. "The other religious orders are interested [in maintaining the repartimientos] because they have large sugar works where many Indians in repartimiento labor."[18]

But while one arm of the Hapsburg state, the church, criticized
Indian labor policy, the other, the civil authorities, with the sole exception of the fiscal, by and large, defended it. Appeals to the president
of Guatemala either brought no action or else recriminations because
most alcaldes and corregidores were related to or allied with the chief
official. Presidents of the audiencia could not support moves that
attacked the system from which they took a share through trade with
lesser officers.

Fundamentally, the entire Central American colonial society depended on the repartimiento for the production of foodstuffs and
commodities for commerce and for the construction and maintenance
of roads, churches, and other public works. The response to royal
interdicts of repartimiento was the same throughout the colonial period: "the universal good of the colony is at stake . . . Those that
solicit the absolute liberty of the Indian place this kingdom in the
greatest danger." Central America was not Peru or Mexico, it was
asserted, where mines and mints paid for slaves or laborers. Here,
Indians were needed to build churches and farm wheat, "bread being
the only subsistence of man." Elsewhere, clerics had slaves to support

them or their hospitals, but here, they had "no one else to serve them, to provide for them and clean their houses." Finally, how would the indigenous population pay the king his due tribute without the repartimiento?[19]

The labor disputes illustrate the nature of the Hapsburg system where local political and economic motives superseded legal considerations. Although the Spanish official was prohibited from trading, from business agreements, and from marrying Creoles, he had to make private alliances to survive. If he suspended the repartimientos of goods, his superiors in Guatemala would find their share of the commerce limited and seek his dismissal. Creoles would agitate against him for failing to deliver goods to the city. The trade of goods from repartimientos required connections with merchant groups. In controversies over taxation, labor policy, or land or mine ownership, alcaldes and oidores made decisions based upon these private agreements. The tactic of the reforming President Cerrato, who allied with leading encomenderos while persecuting others, was repeated through the eighteenth century.

Unlike the Bourbons who understood the need to maintain fiscal capital within the colony and to build a powerful internal administration and who, indeed, sent revenue to Central America from other sections of the Empire, the Hapsburgs were content to draw their annual tribute, continuing governmental practices that were at least a century old. Their weakness was their inability to adapt the state to the changing world.

The responsibility for tax administration fell to the president of the audiencia, with the senior oidor functioning as the treasurer, and the fiscal in his role as the crown's attorney overseeing the entire process. Under the law, the treasury inspection board, *tribunal de cuentas*, located in Mexico City, supervised Guatemalan tax collection, but during the entire colonial period that body never received a report from Guatemala.

A number of levies were charged to the non-Indian population as their tribute, the annual revenue the crown expected from the colony. The sales tax (*alcabala*), ordered for Guatemala in 1576 but not charged until 1602, was levied, theoretically, at a rate of 2 percent each time an item was sold, but, in practice, only the first sale was taxed. It was accompanied by a *barlovento* tax of 1 percent. Introduced in 1638 during the Union of Arms of the Spanish provinces, it was meant to support the Caribbean coastal fleet (*flota de barlovento*). The sales tax was the most important levy for non-Creoles in terms of amounts collected. A royal fifth, or *quinto*, taxed mineral production but, despite its name, it was rarely charged at that rate. The common rate was 10.5 percent because of the poverty of the region's mines. The lack of government administrators in Honduras meant that most mineral output went untaxed in the dispersed panning and small mining areas. It was illegal to sell or trade silver without the government seal, but untaxed silver was prevalent in the informal economy; it was, for example, regularly reported among the remains of deceased merchants, bureaucrats, and clerics.[20]

Royal officials and clerics had to pay a one-time tax worth one-half a year's salary on their positions (*media anata* for secular bureaucrats and *mesada eclesiástica* for the clergy). Spread out over the term of office, the levy was, in reality, a bookkeeping maneuver to reduce salaries, as it was deducted from the salary before it was paid. All encomiendas and pensions had to pay a similar amount. Towards the end of the seventeenth century the crown increased taxes on salaries and encomiendas in an effort to preserve the state's resources in the face of military expenses. They were charged an additional media anata three separate times between 1680 and 1715. These forced contributions reduced further the low salaries most officials received, pushing them to maintain their upkeep from extra-official sources.

The state received other income from the sale of official paper (*papel sellado*), from fees to confirm land titles, and from tribute from some free mulattoes and blacks. The tribute became less important as the century progressed and these populations received exemption for militia service. Then, the terror wrought by the Sambos and Mosquitos led the government in León to exempt mulattoes and blacks in an effort to appease the local population.

In addition, the state received one-ninth of the church tithe from Chiapas, Guatemala, and Nicaragua, and the entire tithe from Comayagua where the central treasury supported all ecclesiastical expenses because the district was so poor. In almost all instances the royal ninth reverted to the church for the construction of temples, for pensions, or for sacramental wine.

The major controversies over taxation during the Hapsburg epoch concerned the alcabala (sales tax), which affected Creole commerce. The alcabala and barlovento were not always collected by the government. In Mexico, Lima, and Guatemala, the collection was contracted or farmed out to either the city's merchant guild or a "committee of the city's commerce" (*diputación del comercio*). Each year one of these groups of private individuals paid the government a set sum (established by auction, theoretically), which gave the private organization the right to collect the tax in the central city and, in turn, to farm the privileges in the interior of the colony to other local groups. The practice linked the fortunes of tax-farming merchants throughout the colony with those of the colonial government and provided the state with a guaranteed annual income. The licensed tax collectors had a competitive advantage over other merchants whom it taxed. The existence of tax farming was an indication of government weakness, the inability to gather resources through its own bureaucracy.[21]

For the first half of the seventeenth century the cabildo of Guatemala was assigned the right to collect the levies. When the audiencia assumed direct control over sales tax collection in 1656, it continued to farm out the alcabala in interior regions, not trusting the alcaldes mayores and corregidores to administer the levy and lacking the resources to establish an independent fiscal administration. The crown received only token sums from most towns: San Antonio Suchitepéquez gave between 200 and 250 pesos annually, the cacao-producing area of Soconusco, 70 pesos, and the rich agricultural town of Chiquimula de la Sierra, 25. Only Salvador and its adjoining regions paid a substantial amount—roughly 1,000 pesos a year—which varied, depending upon the quality and quantity of the indigo crop. The largest amount of money collected thus came from Guatemala City and the commerce that passed through it. Goods retailed in Guatemala from 1667 to 1672 paid 23 percent, and commodities passing through to other areas paid 63 percent of total net income. The city was the seat of colonial rule and thus had to support the tax burden.[22]

Hapsburg rule assumed the personal self-interest and "corruption" of its officials and colonists. Officials gained a thorough training in contemporary concepts of justice in the seventeenth century, as Góngora asserts,[23] but the crown assumed that these bureaucrats would work for their own self-interest once they reached the New World. The kingdom lacked the resources to pay large salaries or to maintain an adequate inspection system, thus encouraging corruption. But officials feared punishment and worked for the rewards the crown preferred. Heavy fines brought destitution and imprisonment in the dark, damp quarters of the crown's jails that meant illness. Officials whose greed was excessive, however, usually had friends in Spain who could work on their behalf. Although they might be fined or jailed at the court of first instance, the Council of the Indies did not uphold the decisions. Still, the superior tribunal reassigned offending officials to other, less favorable areas, or, if they caused too much trouble, removed them from public service.[24]

The Hapsburg system had incentives as well. An official who performed well, adjudicated fairly, maintained the loyalty to the crown, and did not excessively abuse the power of his office received annually encomiendas or pensiones from the tribute money for himself and his descendants. The encomienda-as-reward was a basic foundation of Hapsburg rule. It guaranteed the rule and obedience of major colonial officials, particularly in less important areas where supervision was difficult. The encomienda was worth much more than an official might earn from gross illegal practices in Central America. A president, oidor, or corregidor, could never earn large amounts of specie that could be smuggled back to Spain. True, he might gain land or Indian labor, but these were temporary possessions subject to seizure when he lost power. A pension of 1,000 or 2,000 pesos provided support for the official and at least one descendant.[25]

The regime of Martín de Mencos illustrates the Hapsburg's use of encomienda for their functionaries. President of Guatemala from 1659 to 1668, a particularly turbulent period in the colony's history, Mencos was the first of many military presidents to govern as a consequence of the rise of English and French power in the Caribbean. As pirates extended their activity, with the annual fleets between Honduras and Spain merely a memory, the merchants had shifted their attention to Peru and were engaged in illegal commerce in the southern area. Cacao production and mining had virtually ceased. Fiscal income was stagnant. During half of Mencos' tenure a locust plague disrupted food and indigo production and an earthquake had destroyed part of Guatemala City. In his ten years Mencos was involved in the illegal trade in indigo and silver with Holland. He admitted his guilt, but was nonetheless awarded a sizable pension for his earlier service as general of the armada and for his firm rule in Guatemala—encomiendas of Indian tribute which guaranteed 8,000 pesos a year. His pension continued to support the Mencos family until it was suspended ninety years later as part of the general Bourbon attack on Hapsburg encomiendas in the colonies. Mencos understood in the Hapsburg manner the local residents' need to engage in illegal trade. He sanctioned minor violations of the laws in order to maintain the commercial activity of the region. Further, he converted the illegal activity into revenue for the crown by imposing new taxes on Pacific Ocean traffic that financed some Caribbean fortifications against pirates.[26]

Mencos resolved the long-standing controversy over the regulation of Indian labor, a fight that pitted the Amerindians and the crown's edicts against the audiencia and Creole population. Since the early days of the colony, judges were employed by alcaldes, corregidores, and governors to supervise the planting of food or cacao crops. These jueces de milpas were established to ensure that sufficient cacao trees were maintained so they might be taxed, but the decline of population and of the cacao trade eliminated the need for the judges, who nonetheless continued to exist, urging Indians to produce commodities that judges or alcaldes purchased. Throughout the first half of the seventeenth century repeated royal cédulas banned the positions only to have the audiencia reinstate them. The audiencia argued that the Indians lacked corn and were eating poisonous herbs and roots, and tribute was not being paid, nor cacao planted. "In Soconusco which used to yield 30,000 *cargas* (loads) of cacao, now only 100 are produced." The jueces de milpas caused "the land to be abundant and fertile," it was claimed. When, in 1645, the crown banned the jueces again, criticizing the audiencia, the president of Guatemala waited a year and then reinstated the office. The provinces, he claimed, were in a "miserable state" because the Indians failed to plant crops. Some towns had to send as many as twenty leagues to get sufficient food for the Indians, with corn costing five times its usual amount. Only the jueces could ameliorate the situation.[27]

The Franciscans led the opposition to the judges, as well as to the repartimientos of labor and goods. To the colonial officials, the Franciscans "for their particular ends [were] working against the well-being of these provinces." The clerics detailed the abuses: days before the judge arrived the town had to clear the road and prepare food for his visit. As he and his entourage of ten to twenty assistants arrived the populace had to greet them with trumpets (failure to do so led to the imprisonment and eventual death of an Indian alcalde in Samsaquez). The judges brought goods with them, either to be purchased by the town at high prices or exchanged for local produce at an inequitable rate. The officials and their assistants had to be cared for during their stay, carried on to the next destination, and provided with provisions for the trip. The Franciscans, in a series of letters throughout the period, agreed that the Indian was better off without any official; the Indian alcalde sufficed to maintain the well-being of the town.[28]

The jueces de milpas served to enrich colonial officials as well as to provide substance for intra-colonial trade. The resistance by many strong colonial sectors to the interdict of the office perpetrated its existence for two-thirds of the seventeenth century. When Mencos arrived in Guatemala he saw the damaging effects of the juez and recommended that the judges be banned. The Council of the Indies once again banned the office and astonished all in Central America by going one step further, eliminating all repartimientos of labor and

goods. This measure attacked the existence of the colony, which depended on such repartimientos for most food, labor, and commerce.
Realizing that the colonials and many officials would not tolerate the
repartimiento ban, Mencos disallowed it, eliminating only the jueces.
The crown reiterated its law. Mencos appealed again. Eventually, the
repartimiento ban was vacated.[29]

Mencos also reformed the antiquated fiscal system. A review of
the old system indicated that the city of Guatemala paid 5,000 pesos
annually for the alcabala, an amount he viewed as insufficient. Salvador's indigo regions annually produced 800,000 pounds worth four
reales per pound. The most powerful citizens of Guatemala controlled
much of the indigo commerce with Mexico so that city paid only the
taxes they wished. In addition, the illegal wine shipments from Peru
were entering Sonsonate without tax, as were exports of indigo to
Peru.[30]

The Council of the Indies agreed with Mencos and ordered him
to assume control of the collection of taxes. The reform produced
immediate results (table 2.2). Alcabala and barlovento revenue increased one-and-a-half times in the first year of its collection by the
audiencia. Over a long term, the results were dramatic, income increased two-and-a-half times during the economic period which, at
best, remained stable. The system was not completely effective. The
government collected taxes only within Guatemala City and continued
to farm out its collection in interior regions. It did not trust the alcaldes
mayores and corregidores to administer the levy fairly or honestly and
it lacked the resources to establish an independent fiscal administration.

Mencos was not incorruptible. In 1663 he was accused of trading
with Holland, an activity he admitted, pleading personal poverty. More
accusations were made, but the Council of the Indies refused to pass
judgment and sent the affair to the crown. The crown also refused to
prosecute, despite Mencos' admitted guilt. After his tenure in Guatemala Mencos returned to Spain and was called into sessions of the
Council of the Indies whenever Central America was discussed. It is
clear that he was greatly respected, had contacts at the highest levels,
and had been an able and loyal servant. For this he received his
valuable pension.[31]

Within the colony encomiendas and pensions were granted to
powerful Creoles as well, which tied the most powerful families to the
fortunes of the colonial government. Like the Spanish officials, a colonist's encomienda or pension was granted for two generations, though
his was worth much less than that of a peninsular—usually less than
half—a difference Creoles resented.[32]

Table 2.2: Alcabala and Barlovento Tax Income, After Expenses, Diverse Years 1656–1723

	1656–67	(Ann. Av.)	1667–78	(Ann. Av.)	1688–89	(Ann. Av.)	1694–1702	(Ann. Av.)	1711–25	(Ann. Av.)
Alcabala	57,500	(5,000)	150,213	(13,656)			70,972	(7,886)	270,997	(18,066)
Barlovento	8,000	(1,455)	19,505	(1,773)						
Total	65,500	(6,455)	169,719	(15,429)	38,851	(19,425)				

SOURCES: *1656–78*: A. G. I. Guatemala 983B, Contador de Alcabala, 5/15/1679; *1694–98*: Guatemala 679, "Relacion de todos los tributos, rentas. . . "; *1697–1700*: Guatemala 216, Contador de Alcabala, 6/30/ 1702; *1688–89*: Guatemala 639, Report of Contador de Cuentas; *1700–03*: Guatemala 682, Contador de Alcabala, 3/16/1725; *1711–25*: Guatemala 342.

Note: The city of Guatemala collected colonial taxes prior to 1667, the audiencia, thereafter. The expenses deducted were those incurred in the collection of the taxes, and not those used to finance other functions (i.e., defense) which are frequently included under "expenses" in colonial documents.

Table 2.3: Encomiendas Granted in Spain and Guatemala, 1600–1680

Years	No. in Spain	Total Amount (pesos)	Average Amount (pesos)	Years	No. in Guatemala	Total Amount (pesos)	Average Amount (pesos)	No. of Other Encomiendas Without Listed Value
1600–20	33	21,375	648	1610–20	24	8,253	344	26
1620–40	28	33,871	1,210	1620–40	68	34,789	512	3
1640–60	18	28,721	1,596	1640–60	51	26,520	520	0
1660–80	50	64,435	1,289	1660–80	64	35,847	560	16
Total Annual Average	1.6		1,150		3		509	

SOURCES: A. G. I. Guatemala 212 Relación de las mercedes que S. M. ha hecho en encomiendas de Indios del distrito de la Audiencia de Guatemala. . . desde el año 1600 hasta fin de 1681.

There were two ways in which encomenderos collected tribute, either through government officials, with the corregidor or alcalde mayor controlling the labor of the Indian as in repartimiento, or through a personal administrator or agent. The latter was preferred, because it kept the control of the money in private hands. Personal administrators collected well over half of all Central American encomiendas until 1720 when encomienda was abolished. These agents did not control Indians as they had been under the sixteenth-century system. Usually merchants arranged for the collection of tribute and transferred it to Spain, perhaps profiting from the various barter exchanges involved in the process.[33]

The Hapsburgs enhanced their authority by renewing these pensions every two generations. The crown could not ban encomiendas—the threat of general rebellion was too great—but it could reward those who were loyal and ignore less desirable political forces. Naturally, it alienated those without encomiendas. In the first eighty years of the seventeenth century, the monarchy granted almost 150,000 pesos worth of annual tributes to encomenderos for an average of one and a half generations (see table 2.3), while officials in Central America granted 105,000 pesos, always for two generations. Manipulating Indian tribute grants thus united the Hapsburg empire at its weakest point.

The state suffered from this manipulation of the private sector by Indian tribute and labor. Some 50 percent of all tribute at mid-seventeenth century went to pensions rather than to state expenses. Only toward the end of the century did the crown begin to enact measures—too late—to regain these vital funds.

While the loyalty of the empire was maintained through the pension-reward system and the balancing of the interests of each colonial sector, the crown lacked sufficient funds to finance an adequate defense and force to compel tax contributions and military service. The Dutch defeat of the Caribbean armada in 1650 and the English seizure of Jamaica in 1655 were dramatic symbols of a fundamental weakness. Buccaneer raids had already cut Caribbean commerce. They seized and razed the Honduran, Nicaraguan, and Costa Rican regions from 1630 onward. Englishmen appeared with slaves at the Walis or Belize River to exploit logwood for dyes. The coastal islands were lost. Renegade slaves mixed with Indians and some whites, forming the Sambos and Mosquitos peoples. They gained control of most of the Caribbean coast of Honduras and Nicaragua and allied with the British in raids on the colony. England went so far as to propose to the Spanish court in 1665 that it grant a monopoly to the English on indigo exploitation in Guatemala.[34]

Creoles living in a fairly peaceful, subsistence economy in Guatemala and Salvador resisted attempts to provide for an effective defense of the colony. They fought increased barlovento taxes; the crown met most military needs from vacant pensions, Indian tribute that no longer was assigned to crown or pensions. Creoles opposed Mencos' efforts to organize an expedition against Granada buccaneers. Mencos' successor, Rosica de Caldas, earned Creole enmity by compelling an expedition south.[35]

If Spanish territorial and military hegemony was reduced, so too was its ability to control and profit from Central America's resources. Contacts with Dutch tradesmen in Curaçao and with British merchants along the coast led to increased contraband trade as the century progressed; President Mencos' commercial dealings with the Dutch provides some evidence of it. There were many such cases involving officials and Creole merchants. The Council of the Indies examined the problem of the vecinos of Trujillo, Comayagua, and Costa Rica, who traded freely in hides, cacao, sarsaparilla, dyes, and other items along the coast.[36]

Illegal trade within the empire was also rampant. We have seen the extent of the illegal wine trade in the Pacific. This was complicated by traffic in Guayaquil cacao and goods from the Manila galleon. Untaxed Peruvian silver was smuggled through Central America to Holland. Some Central Americans used the aegis of the church to trade without taxation to Mexico and Spain.

How much of this illegal trade occurred? This we do not know, and guesses are perilous. President Mencos declared in 1655 that all trade was at a standstill, but ten years later he claimed that the colony annually exported 800,000 pounds of indigo or three times the amount sent to Spain legally during earlier boom years. Neither estimate can be considered accurate. Clearly, production did not approach the boom years of the the last half of the eighteenth century, but it continued as labor reports and smuggling accusations indicate. Much of the illegal trade was barter for European cloth, wine, and hardware, which makes measurement even more difficult. We, like the crown, are unable to ascertain the extent of smuggling.

The very beauty of the Hapsburg system—its loose, permissive structure which tied, through bonds of loyalty, sectors of the colony to the crown—was its fatal weakness. Its stable social and bureaucratic structure, so unlike the anarchy of the sixteenth century, the growing Indian population, the Catholic-hispanidadismo, and the tax structure, pension and judicial system that united the vast, diverse empire were remarkable accomplishments over the century, but were too weak, too decentralized, to supply the resources needed to repel invaders, to control commerce, and to maintain an honest bureaucracy. The Hapsburgs looked too much to silver mines, and too little to agricultural production, too much to remissions of tribute in silver to Spain and too little to the construction of a colonial defense. These were the weaknesses that the Bourbons faced upon accession to power in 1700.

CHAPTER THREE

Cross and Crown

THE CHURCH WAS the bedrock of Hapsburg rule. While the crown mediated, the church bridged the empire's diverse interests, linking them into one cultural unity, maintaining a common catholic-hispanic identity and ideology. The diverse ecclesiastical institutions were able to serve and defend the interests of the crown, Creole colonial society, and the Indian pueblo. It was a Spanish institution that became fully American, so well entrenched in the Latin American social fabric that it outlasted its Hapsburg partner, its Bourbon rivals, and its liberal, republican enemies.

The Spanish church was fundamentally a Hapsburg institution, an integral part of the system of rule. Under the *Patronato Real*, the agreement between the crown and the papacy, the monarchy had direct control over the colonial church in all non-doctrinal matters. The king was responsible for all appointments and the king's Council of the Indies received all ecclesiastical reports.

Taken together, however, the church was far more powerful than the Hapsburg civilian administration. It collected alternative taxes, ruled more at the local than national level, and kept most of its wealth within the Americas rather than remit its revenue to Spain as secular authorities did.

But it was the strength of the church in defending local community values and economies and in spreading the word of Christ that was important. Ecclesiastics protected Amerindians from labor abuse, guarding their pueblos from cultural and economic invasion, and providing sustenance in times of scarcity. Clerics and friars saw to the supply of vital food to Spanish cities, defended the urban elites, gave shelter to widows and unmarried women, and provided social services—hospitals, orphanages, and schools. While the secular authorities created the framework, the church integrated and unified the colony through religion and its vast fiscal power. It insured the loyalty of the colony to the empire through proselytizing hispanic-catholicism. Where the state lacked soldiers to stem uprisings, the church was present.

Although we speak of "the church," the institution was scarcely monolithic. In Central America it was comprised of secular clerics in urban parishes and a dozen regular orders in Indian pueblos, Spanish cities, on haciendas, and in nunneries. High clergy and low, peninsulares and Creoles, each defended his flock in different ways. The cross symbolized ecclesiastical unity, a common if vague loyalty to Rome. But the plethora of saints, some resembling pre-Columbian gods more than Christian figures, the centrality of Mary, and the variations in ritual belied religious unity except that of Christ and the Cross.

Ecclesiastical authority was divided into the dioceses of Guatemala, Comayagua, León, and Ciudad Real until 1744 when Guatemala was elevated to an archdiocese and given authority over the other regions. As the leading ecclesiastical official in Central America, the Guatemalan bishop was the second most important figure in colonial government, reporting to Spain all ecclesiastical disputes and those secular conflicts involving the church. Along with the president, the audiencia, the cabildos, and a few private individuals, his words were influential with the Council of the Indies. Working closely with the dean and cabildo eclesiástico, the Creole governing board of the diocese, the bishop usually represented colonial society more than the views and values of secular authorities.

The early sixteenth-century church established the pattern for Central America: some clerics served the Creole colony and others, Amerindian pueblos. Francisco Marroquín, the first bishop of Guatemala, was a close friend of Pedro Alvarado and a leader of the encomenderos-colonists. He used but little influence to alleviate the plight of the Indians. In contrast, Bishop Pedraza decried the abuse of indigenous groups from his pulpit in Honduras. Bishop Valdeviera's attack on the leadership of the governor of Nicaragua led to his murder. The most famous of all Latin American colonial clerics, Bartolomé de Las Casas, brought a group of Dominican priests to Chiapas to contest the rule of local encomenderos. While the friars conquered Amerindia spiritually, Las Casas reported the labor conditions to the crown, exposés that led to the New Laws of 1542 and the Cerrato Reforms.

The church bridged Amerindia and colony. In this Hapsburg empire, far too weak to control its vast domains with secular officials, but still concerned that Amerindians remain loyal, pay tribute, furnish labor and material, and yet were not abused, the ecclesiastical institutions were a critical component of the monarchy. While Hapsburg officials and colonists used Indians in repartimiento, connecting them with the colonial economy, clerics defended the pueblo and served as its religious leader.

In many areas Franciscans and Dominicans attempted to establish an alternative existence for colonial society, Kingdoms of God that arose around monasteries, supported by and employing large numbers of Indians. Elsewhere, individual friars spent their lives living isolated in the pueblos. Wherever, the orders saw their mission as holy and their subjects as wards to be protected against incursions by colonists or officials. The division between religious and secular activity was sometimes hard to distinguish, to be sure, with clerics running large wheat, sugar, and indigo plantations using Indian labor that government officials and colonists desired.

Most prelates lived among the numerous, populous highland communities where the sustenance of the pueblo and the small church was their chief concern. For his support the prelate received emoluments from the town. Each pueblo was responsible for the upkeep of the cleric through payments of goods, services, and, sometimes, coinage. In Chiapas in 1695 every town in the province had to pay each cleric at least five reales daily, twelve eggs, a *fanega* of corn and fish on Fridays. Workers were provided daily to farm and serve as porters, horsemen, woodcutters, cooks, "an assistant to go for water," grinders of corn for tortillas, and guardians of livestock. Every church ritual had to be paid for by the Indians: marriages and interments cost as much as two pesos each, special masses, three or four pesos; baptisms were free, however. Pueblo fiestas cost the town about three pesos each, depending upon their importance (there were usually a minimum of five fiestas a year, although there could be as many as twelve).[1]

In most towns, sodalities (*cofradías*) played an important role in the upkeep of the clergy and the maintenance of capital within the community. Theoretically, the sodality was established to finance the celebration of the town's saint, the Virgin, Jesus, and the sacrament. Large images of these figures were maintained and brought out on the saints' days, Christmas, Easter, and other days of fiesta when masses were celebrated. Supported by contributions from the pueblo and by a portion of the common land, well-administered sodalities in wealthy areas could accumulate sizable amounts of money. In many areas, Indians gave in goods or labor more to sodalities than they paid in tribute. The fund became an economic defense against the demands of Spanish society. It paid for tribute, and bribes, and debts. It financed masses and the upkeep of the cleric. A 1637 complaint that echoed through the eighteenth century was that there were too many sodalities and they were multiplying every day. Many were begun without diocesan license; a testimony to the cultural independence these brotherhoods manifested. Indians contributed to them to support fiestas and had nothing left to pay tribute to the encomenderos, the complainants claimed. The drunkenness and dances of the ten to twelve fiestas celebrated each year "renewed more the memory of old idolatry than the devotion toward Christian images." A visita in Nicaragua in 1667 revealed that there were "so many cofradías that the Indians are occupied with them all the time with no time for their milpas."[2]

Rich Indian cofradías were frequently involved in commercial dealings with colonial society though it is difficult to ascertain either the degree of independence that the Indians had in these dealings or the amount of pressure that colonial society exerted upon them. In Nicaragua, Honduras, and Salvador the cofradias became involved chiefly in cattle raising. Creoles complained constantly of expanding cofradías that competed with them for lands, markets, and labor. By 1756 cofradías supplied almost a third of the cattle to Guatemala for consumption and a decade later a major bureaucratic battle erupted over whether to tax cofradía receipts. The rich cofradías in San Juan Amatitlán received from three to seven pesos annually from its members and were so wealthy that prominent Creoles had loans outstanding to the brotherhoods. Some large cofradía holdings may have fell under prelate or Creole control. The 23 cofradias in Mita that held over 4,600 pesos, over 3,000 head of beef cattle (each worth 5 pesos), plus numerous horses, burros, and land, and the 24 cofradías in Jutiapa that held over 3,000 head of cattle and large areas of land attracted usurpers. The wealthy Indian cofradías of the Valley of Guatemala had to contribute a portion of their receipts annually to support the maintenance of the Cathedral of Guatemala. Others gave their commercial power to Guatemalan creoles. The major Indian town of Chiapas authorized such an arrangement in 1666. Who profited from it we cannot tell. The same year, the convent of San Agustín in the valley of Petapa purchased a wheat farm from the Indian cofradía of Nuestra Señora del Rosario of Petapa and then sold it immediately to a Creole, Joseph Agustín de Estrada in a suspicious dealing. Still, the large number of Creole complaints against cofradías in both the seventeenth and eighteenth centuries testify to the relative independence of most Indian brotherhoods from the dominant society.[3]

The cofradía was more than an economic defense. In settled areas, traditional Mayan practices were absorbed into the liturgy of Christianity; cofradía rituals often were closer to pagan than Christian beliefs. Legislation banned Quiché dances, the *Tum Teleche* and *Trompetas Tun*, and Tzutuhil ritual, the *Lox Tun*, but with little success. In the eighteenth century, they were still practiced by cofradías in Guatemala and Chiapas. Clerics attempted to control pagan rituals but illegal cofradías proliferated beyond their control.[4]

The sodality was confused frequently with the community fund. Technically, the *caja de comunidad* was a secular fund, administered by Indian town officials with funds gathered from community land and labor and used to pay tribute and to support the financial burden that visitas from bishops, corregidores, and presidents brought. In many areas, however, the cleric was the town leader, the only trusted figure who administered the two funds, or, as occurred frequently, administered them as one. It is difficult to estimate how much was contributed per capita to either fund. Much depended upon the wealth of the town (and, indeed, in some areas sodalities became so affluent that they were self-supporting), the product it produced, and its proximity to Spanish settlements. Eighteenth-century account books reveal great differences in the wealth and power of various pueblo sodalities.[5]

Strong community and sodality funds strengthened the town by providing economic defenses against the demands of colonists, bureaucrats, and clerics. Much of the prelate's income from community and cofradía funds was dispensed within the town (Friar Thomas Gage had to pay forty people: "this I found wearied much my brain and hindered my studies").[6] The intra-pueblo economy was stimulated and the scarce capital in land and coinage was enlarged. In the case of wealthy pueblos, money was lent to non-Indians with interest, increasing the town's support.

Control of pueblos was disputed frequently among clerics. Secular bishops claimed that regular friars abused the administration of wealthy sodalities and suggested that the funds should be controlled by the dioceses. Creoles claimed that peninsular clergy tried to accumulate large sums to take back to Spain. On the other hand, a growing Creole participation in orders through the colonial period led to the installation of friars with close familial ties to local Creole landed interests in nearby pueblos, which, in turn, led to the destruction of community funds and lands.

Controversies within the ecclesiastical structure over Indian labor policy represented the basic schisms within the church and society. Different clerics represented different interests, serving all levels of society, the Spaniard in the city as well as the Indian in the pueblo. Peninsulares rivaled Creole friars. High clergy fought low clergy. The orders were not united: a Dominican administering a wheat farm might employ Indians illegally to provide food for the Spanish in Guatemala: Dominicans in the highlands living in Indian towns protected their charges from officials and colonists and established local industry for the benefit of Indian communities. Controversies over bishops' visitas and disputes over ecclesiastical jurisdictions occurred constantly throughout the Hapsburg period.

In reality, the loyalties of clerics and friars were divided among the needs of the state, the colony, and the Amerindian. They served the state as the quasi-military sustainer of the conquest, guarding and protecting the Indian, insuring fidelity to the Catholic religion, fighting idolatry and other heresies, and reporting to superiors about the strength of the pueblo, its respect for the dominant religion, and its ability to survive. Dominicans, Franciscans, Mercedians and Propaganda Fide friars provided labor for the colony through *reducciones* or expeditions to gather and "reduce" Indians into pueblos. On the other hand, clerics protected established pueblos from abusive officials and colonists, preserving their cultures, albeit within a Christian context, and maintaining their autonomy through cofradía and community funds. Some clerics closely connected with Creole families abused their wards, but others did not. Where church control was strongest, in Chiapas, Verapaz, Quezaltenango, and Güegüetenango, Indian populations and cultures were more likely to survive.

This division in loyalties between colonial and Indian was marked in the church's policies towards reducciones and *entradas*, the conquest of unsettled Indians for labor purposes. In Honduras, Chiapas, Verapaz, and Costa Rica, unsettled Amerindian tribes lived dispersed outside Spanish control. They were havens for Indians and black slaves who sought escape from disease or European abuse. Generalizations about these tribes are difficult; the Lacandones and Itzás in Chiapas and Verapaz preserved many Mayan customs; the tribes in Honduras often served as intermediaries in trade between colonial Spaniards and English merchants on the Caribbean and lost much of their heritage. The Talamancan Indians in Costa Rica preserved their relatively primitive customs, remaining hostile to all outsiders. These groups all presented temptations for Spanish society. Whenever epidemics caused widespread death or new mines needed manpower, Creole Central America looked to the church to find new labor. Many clerics resisted—entradas were less frequent here than in Mexico in the seventeenth century—but others did not. Other friars performed reducciones for purely religious purposes: to establish Indians in towns under ecclesiastical guidance.[7]

Thomas Gage provided us with the best testimony of how seventeenth-century entradas were accomplished. Throughout the century attempts were made in Spanish Guatemala and Yucatan to link the two regions through the conquest of Verapaz. As early as 1622 prelates traveled from Yucatan as far as the island kingdom of Itzá on Lake Petén (which Cortés had visited a century earlier) only to be driven back. In 1629 Thomas Gage and the Prior of Cobán in Verapaz set out with some fifty men on the "hard and dangerous enterprise." From Cobán they traveled to two Christian pueblos and collected a hundred Indians. "We went up and down mountains amongst woods for the space of two days, being much discouraged with the thickets and the hardness of the way." The following day they came upon some poor cottages and found three women, two men, and five children. "We clothed them and took them along with us." As the conquistadores continued they found more villages with increasingly larger populations, but the climate, unhealthy for the Europeans, slowed their progress. Late one evening the Indians attacked. About a thousand "came desperately towards us, and when they saw they were discovered and our drums beat up, and our fowling pieces and muskets began to shoot, they hollered and cried with a hideous noise." The fight lasted an hour with thirteen Indians killed, ten imprisoned, and one Christian lost. "In the morning our soldiers began to mutiny and to talk of turning back." A debate ensued, "but that day nothing was agreed upon, for we could not stir by reason of the sick and the wounded." The following evening another attack came, and the next morning the party turned back. The Cobán priest entered the region alone the following year and was allowed by the Itzás to pass to Yucatan.[8]

A description of the uncolonized Indians by Franciscan friars in 1680 provides us with an excellent view of the manner in which the clerics viewed these "savages." The Indians, we are told, "lived a little more than fifty-six centuries as slaves of the demon" before Christianity was introduced. Now, many of them still "wander through the mountains making their settlements [*rancheras*] in one place and then another." They would stay three months to grow their corn before moving to another place. Confusing Amerindians with the Sambos and Mosquitos, the mixture of runaway blacks with other races, the Franciscans claimed that "there are many whites and reds; others more or less [are] black." Their language was a corruption of Mexicana or Pipil, whereas "others speak that of Angola . . . and others with such a mixture that it is impossible to reduce the tongues to any rules." The

Indians used lances and poison arrows to defend themselves or sometimes just run off. They practiced pagan dances though they were monogamous.[9]

The report shows the ignorance of the Franciscans of the unsettled indigenous populations. In reality, there were distinct Indian tribes that lived between the Spaniards in Comayagua and Nueva Segovia and the cimarrones, Sambos and Mosquitos on the coast. Peaceful in nature, these "Jicaque" Indians were often caught between the two groups.[10] Spaniards sent priests and soldiers into the mountains to reduce Indians in towns near Honduran mines. Cimarrones attacked the tribes and forced them to pay tribute in goods and slaves. Indeed, this two-front operation continued the depopulation of Honduras.

Throughout the sixteenth and seventeenth centuries, entradas were made into the vast region that covered three-quarters of today's Honduras—some by a single cleric, others with soldiers—only to meet with failure. One such offensive was begun in 1689, when a missionary with soldiers went to an area in the Valley of Yoro known to possess pacific Indians living in forty towns. "They live in good condition, with no idolatry nor any superstition, living in conformity with natural law." They were monogamous and wore cotton clothing. When the invaders approached the area, the Indians fled. The following year another attempt was made and "it was only possible to capture seventy-six persons using force." They were placed in a town, but some escaped, and some died, "from sadness," leaving a total of twenty-eight. Later, the missionary persuaded some one hundred people to join the reduced village.[11]

The results of all seventeenth-century reducciones in Honduras and Nicaragua were described in 1696 as five pueblos with 700 or 800 people. Although theoretically under Franciscan care, no missionary had visited them, a pestilence of smallpox and measles had killed many (muchisímas), and the Indians had begun to drift back into their original state.[12]

These entradas were expensive. They required soldiers and supplies. The crown and most of the clergy opposed them. In retrospect they were not productive. At the end of the century a general decline in population coincided with large mineral discoveries and the sorties began in earnest, more organized and better financed.

While the church spread the word of Christ on the frontier, it served as the bedrock of society in the Spanish city. Seventeenth-century Central America, isolated from changes in European thought, held a pre-Reformation mentality, perhaps more conservative than that in Spain itself. The Creole sought salvation. His daily life revolved around the church, its processions, masses, and festivals. The church schooled him as a youth, provided him with sustenance for his industry, charity in his poverty, and care in illness. He gave his sons as clerics and his daughters for protection. He donated funds for pious works and purchased bulls to fight the infidel. In death he provided for masses to be said in perpetuity in his behalf. Although the church, under the Patronato Real, was free from taxation and amassed great wealth that elite Creoles could use for their economic well-being, one should not underestimate the religious character of the society and the Christian charity of sixteenth- and seventeenth-century Creoles and peninsulares. More than a few gave large fortunes to the church to save themselves from purgatory; many devoted their lives to the cloth, working in orphanages, hospitals, or alone in Indian villages for twenty or thirty years.

Santiago de Guatemala was as much a religious as a business and government center. In a city that, in 1700 numbered perhaps 40,000 people of which 2,000 were Spanish, there were an opulent cathedral, twenty-four churches, eight *ermitas* or small monasteries, and fifteen convents. Next to the bishop of Guatemala, the Dominicans were the most influential, the most numerous, and the wealthiest order, bridging both the Spanish and Indian "nations" of Santiago. In the earliest days Dominicans had administered the artisan Mexican Indians who had come with Alvarado in the conquest. Many of the slaves freed by Cerrato were also put under their protection in the barrio of their monastery. The Dominicans organized the linguistic and nationalistic melange created by the conquerors into a coherent administration. From their haciendas the order provided the city with food, lumber, and sugar, and the necessities for religious observance. Franciscans and Mercedians, Betlemites, and the brothers of Propaganda Fide rivalled the influence of this order. The Franciscans, poorer and more zealous, saw the Dominicans as serving the Spanish populations to the detriment of the Indians. The Mercedians, more closely aligned with elite Creole interests, rivalled the Dominicans in providing food to the city.[13] And the Jesuits, who controlled most Creole education, fought against Dominican incursions in this realm.

The rivalry between secular and religious clergy in Central America was not as sharp as it was in other colonies, which indicates the dominance of the orders. Secular clerics were limited in the main to the bishoprics in the dioceses of Chiapas, Honduras, Nicaragua, and Guatemala, and to some Spanish parishes. Clerics had to learn Indian dialects, which the orders taught and the seculars could never learn. The crown favored the regulars as well. Their rules insured tight discipline rather than the loose atmosphere that tempted secular, and usually Creole, priests to corruption.

A critical role of both regular and secular clergy was the defense of local elites, economies, welfare, and institutions using the wealth of the church. The church received its economic support from three principal sources: the state, which supplied some funds from its own coffers for the support of religious functions; the tithe tax on most agricultural commodities, which paid for the upkeep of the diocesan administration and some charities; and most important, the continuous accumulation of money from donations, funds for perpetual masses, and dowries for nuns and priests. These funds were used in local economies, providing capital for the Creole society, absorbing most losses caused by natural disasters, and, in a curious manner, stabilizing in an anti-inflationary sense. Church boards manned by parish laymen controlled the resources, loaning them for investment locally. The secular Hapsburg state was concerned more with exporting capital from the colony in the form of tribute payments, but the Hapsburg religious institution buffered and insured the colony against losses by maintaining sufficient capital within the colony's economy. This vital institution was attacked by the Bourbons and their intellectual heirs, the liberals. The relationship of the local economy and church power requires close analysis.

Ecclesiastical institutions provided the mortar for society, serving important social needs and integrating the diverse sectors of the colony into one functioning unit in a manner that the secular government could not. Nuns and priests in Spanish cities and towns worked in hospitals and orphanages as well as in homes for wayward women. Convents provided havens for the daughters and widows of Creoles who were protected against the fragile economic fortunes of their families by the church. The cloister of Concepción contained a thousand women in 1630, "not all nuns; but nuns and their serving maids or slaves, and young children who were brought up and taught to work by the nuns. The nuns who are professed bring with them their portions, five hundred ducats the least, some six hundred, some seven and some a thousand, which portions after a few years (and continuing to the cloister after the nun's death) come to make up a great yearly rent." Whenever natural disasters or over-farming of land destroyed the cloisters' capital, the state had to intervene in support of the sisters. Such was the case in 1664 when the convent of nuns of Chiapas was granted 1,000 pesos in Indian tributes a year, for being "daughters of conquerors." The money was still being paid a century later.[14]

The church assisted towns and cities whenever famine occurred, importing food given in tithe from other areas. Prelates were the sole source for education as well, maintaining private schools in their homes in outlying Spanish settlements, and colegios in major cities. The Colegio de Jesús and the University of San Carlos in Guatemala trained future prelates and became the center of the Enlightenment in Guatemala.

The complex role of the church as guardian of families' capital and provider of social services is illustrated by the establishment of rival Jesuit and Dominican educational institutions. The Colegio de Jesús, founded in 1607, was the first such institution in Central America, rivaled only by individual private instruction of other orders. Fourteen years after its establishment, the Jesuits founded the Colegio Universitario de San Lucas, the first to grant advanced degrees. The schools lacked sufficient financial backing until 1646 when a regidor of the city and a graduate of the Jesuit system, Nicolas Justiniano Chavarría, gave 30,000 pesos to them with the obligation that the Jesuit fathers perform annual masses in his behalf after his death. The Jesuits used the money to purchase a hacienda between Amatitlán and Escuintla, the fruits of which—in 1647 it yielded 4,000 pesos—supported their work. In addition, Chavarría enlisted the aid of other Creoles who donated crosses and images of gold worth 1,000 pesos, a small piece of land in the city to provide firewood and grazing land for the Colegio, 1,000 pesos with which to build a well, and an encomienda of Indians worth 400 pesos annually "at the least." Why this sudden burst of generosity? Probably the fierce epidemic of 1646–47 in which over a thousand people died in Santiago contributed. "This is a time of plague," a Jesuit reported in 1647, "in which there is much loss of life. There are many forgivenesses for past injuries and reconciliations between enemies. The old, public scandals have ended. Those who have regained their health have, with many tears, given great amounts of charity seeing so much illness and repeated deaths."[15]

The Dominicans attempted to stem the rise of Jesuit influence in Santiago. They educated the children of families allied with the order, but the popularity, effectiveness, and resources behind the Jesuit's institutions undermined their power. Around mid-century the Dominican families began to amass resources and petition the crown for the establishment of a Dominican university. The Crespo Suarez and González families were the main benefactors. Their connection with the order dated back at least to 1624 when Pedro Crespo Suarez and Melchor González married wealthy sisters who had a considerable fortune and a sugar mill in Amatitlán. Melchor González held title to the land and Crespo Suarez the mortgage on the land's cattle and houses. The Dominicans operated the mill, free from government restrictions and taxes. The proceeds from this mill founded the university. Other funds were gathered from allied families so that by 1679, when the crown granted the charter, the institution had an endowment of 173,000 pesos, or more than double that of the Jesuit schools. Still the Jesuits held the respect of most of the Creole elite. Despite the great funds, Dominican schoolrooms remained empty while those of the Jesuits regularly had at least three hundred students. The strength of the Dominicans and their allies enabled the university to continue to exist until, in 1767, it became the most important institution with the expulsion of the Jesuits.[16]

Donations (*limosnas*) and the succession to estates that lacked written wills swelled church coffers. But by far the most important institution was the *capellanía*, funds deriving from land and housing destined to finance the celebration of masses. The capellanías were usually established by provisos in the testament of the benefactor to insure that descendants of the donor supported masses in his behalf, by what was, in effect, a perpetual "mortgage" on the property. The capellanías established by Antonio García y Gálvez of Guatemala in 1665 provide a notable example of how the practice functioned. García was a moderately wealthy man for the period. He placed a capellanía worth 1,500 pesos on a wheat farm of two *cavallerías* extension to celebrate masses for his parents, his wife, and himself, and another capellanía of 1,350 on a cattle ranch for masses for his parents. His heirs had to pay 75 and 67 pesos annually from the day of his death to support the masses in his behalf. Failure to do so meant the loss of the land to the church, which, in turn, would sell the property for the value of the capellanía to insure the continuation of the memorial.[17] When Manuel Cracía Candoso of San Raymondo lay upon his deathbed, he declared himself "a miserable sinner," having sired an illegitimate daughter and having other weaknesses. He gave most of his wealth including a cattle ranch, two corn fields, and two sugar works, to the church for the celebration of masses. After his death the church rented the property for the value needed to celebrate the masses for his immortal soul.[18]

Dowries for the support of nuns were another source of church wealth. The nunnery was a refuge for women and an institution of religious and social service. A woman who entered the convent paid a substantial dowry, the interest from which went to her upkeep. The nuns of the convent of Santa Catharina each paid 2,000 pesos to enter. Over the years the money purchased control over large areas of land. Indeed, the sisters held more money in mortgages and loans than the Dominicans, Mercedians, and Franciscans together. The convent of Purísima Concepción alone had more than three times the wealth of the Dominicans in Guatemala City. The difference lay in the fact that the friars had other sources of wealth as well.[19]

Family wealth could be dissipated by contributions to the church by pious family members. The Cura Pedro de Lara, for example, owned a house in Guatemala worth 5,000 pesos and a hacienda worth 3,000 pesos. The house was mortgaged for some 2,000 pesos to support the dowry of his sister, a nun, and an additional 2,000 pesos for a capellanía for a deceased nephew. The hacienda had no loans or mortgages on it. Upon his death in 1732 Lara gave the hacienda to the church for capellanías in his behalf, adding the additional 1,000 pesos that was clear of loans from his house. He thereby turned over all his possessions to the ecclesiastics.[20]

The church provided loans and mortgages with which to buy or improve holdings at the interest rate of 5 percent. Church boards, cabildos eclesiásticos composed of prominent parishioners, oversaw the operation. Because most land outside urban regions had little inherent wealth, loans were granted only for physical improvements (buildings or machinery) or the purchase of cattle, and the value of the land was determined by these physical possessions. Failure to pay the annual interest led to foreclosure. New tenants assumed the old mortgage at the same rate. Rarely did the price of land rise during this period except to reflect the number of cattle, buildings, and machinery, with profit in land holdings limited to the agricultural areas around Guatemala.

By financing land improvements the church protected its capital and supported local industry in a manner that the secular state did not or could not. At the same time it insured its importance within the secular society by being a power center where credit and land could be obtained. It maintained interest levels and land prices at the same level over a period of one hundred fifty years, serving unwittingly as defender of the colonial economy against inflation. In essence, it guarded the soul of the barter economy. But it did not at any time profit exorbitantly from its economic position. The church maintained its traditional practices, preserving its wealth, but protecting the economic health of the colony as a non-profit institution.

This guardian of capital also protected the colony from losses due to natural disasters: cattle under mortgage to the church were killed by disease; floods and hurricanes destroyed agricultural holdings and houses. The church absorbed these losses and used its wealth to restore damaged property, reconstructing towns and cities, importing new cattle, or purchasing agricultural equipment. This ability was, of course, limited to the wealth of each church. The Creole elite in Santiago possessed far more resources than, say, the mestizos of Nueva Segovia. But the function of guardian of community resources existed in all areas.

Because the church was an arm of the Hapsburg state, it faced little risk of losing its property to the secular government. Indeed, much of its "wealth" could not be expropriated. It was based upon housing and agriculture, with the liquid money received in interests and loans recirculated into the economy almost immediately in church functions, ecclesiastical salaries, supplies, and charities. This ecclesiastical arm thus reinforced local economies as compared with the secular state, which withdrew capital to the metropolis.

The intricate connection among local economies, social maintenance, church wealth, and state power was based upon a stable, economically strong church. Through the Hapsburg epoch, it gathered and controlled significant amounts of resources. The question of church wealth is complicated: ecclesiastical institutions controlled far more of the economy than they owned, and local civilian church boards controlled far more of church economic power than the church hierarchy. Still, its wealth indicates the power of localities, of elites, and of that Hapsburg institution the Bourbons sought to destroy.

At the end of the seventeenth century, Fuentes y Guzmán observed that "the most and best haciendas were in the power of ecclesiastical individuals." The wealth and power of each church institution varied greatly. The Dominicans were the most powerful and numerous of all the orders. Within the jurisdiction of the Guatemalan diocese, they administered almost three times as many Indians as the Franciscans did. Their land holdings and mortgages were much wealthier than those of the other orders.[21]

We can gain an indication of ecclesiastical wealth and power from a report prepared in 1740 that traces the resources of the regular orders, from government fiscal records that show state contributions to the church, and from tithe accounts. Church holdings in 1740 were less than those of the seventeenth century, diminished by the earthquake of 1717 that destroyed many urban dwellings.

The power of the Dominicans was still strong (see table 3.1). They owned large amounts of land and held mortgages on many privately-owned ranches, city houses, and businesses. The most impressive Dominican holding was the sugar hacienda of San Geronimo in Verapaz. Dating back to 1579, it was run by the friars with 150 African slaves and about a thousand Indians and produced in the quinquenne 1736–40 an annual average of 12,500 pesos, or almost a fourth of the total regular income accruing to the order. The hacienda provided Guatemala City with 12,500 pounds of sugar monthly in 1769, with a value ranging from 36,000 to 73,000 pesos, and was said to contain in addition 50,000 head of beef cattle. Another site near San Geronimo, called "el llano grande," had been used for cattle for a century, but was being used in mid-eighteenth century for sugar cane also. It was rented in 1735 for 600 pesos, but since returns had fallen, the sum was lowered to 320 pesos annually five years later.[22]

Near Guatemala, the order possessed a large hacienda (El Rosario) of cattle and sugar cane that had cost 22,430 pesos, which was "borrowed from various individuals . . . because this convent has no funds." It supplied between 400 and 600 pesos a year for masses for the deceased, invested to maintain the capellanías. A wheat mill worth 1,700 pesos financed five masses annually, and a small ranch worth 3,000 pesos was rented for 300 pesos. With mortgages on urban housing paying 5 percent interest, the annual income to the order was 2,920 pesos on some 58,400 pesos in capital.

Outside the region the order owned a hacienda of cacao, "lost because of the age of the plants," a cattle ranch, and one sugar plantation in Chiapas. In Salvador, haciendas worth 20,710 pesos annually produced 2,071 pesos, which, together with loans, a wheat mill, and a small farm gave the convent in that city 4,635 pesos. In other regions the value of holdings are unspecified: in Cobán, a hacienda; in Comitlán, some cattle ranches and farms and a sugar cane works; in Tecpatlán, a ranch and small holding of cacao; and in Amatitlán, some indigo holdings.[23]

This minimum estimate of value does not include all of the money received from the government to pay for salaries and wine and oil employed in the administration of Indian pueblos (of which the 8,192 pesos listed in table 3.1 as doctrinal fees is only a fraction). Unlike the practice in Mexico, a large part of church expenses was met by the government, especially in areas too poor to support a cleric.

The income of all of the orders was greater than that shown in table 3.1. Doctrinal fees for the Franciscans and pensions, which provided for the hospitals and nunneries in Guatemala and Ciudad Real as well as mortgages and loans held by the Mercedians outside of Guatemala, are not listed. The Jesuits still held the Chavarria ha-

Table 3.1 Partial Church Wealth in Central America, Ca. 1740

| | Convents | Clerics[a] | Income (pesos) | | | | | Total Annual Income (pesos) |
			Loans, mortgages	Land	Rented propty	Doctrinal fees[b]	Donations	
DOMINICANS								
Guatemala		81	2,920	12,788[c]	1,050	3,850	3,090	23,698
Ciudad Real			633	4,051		3,959		8,643
San Salvador			4,635		200	383	300	5,518
Cobán								4,735
Comitlán								3,693
Tecpatlán								3,541
Amatitlán								2,460
Sta. Cruz de Quiché								3,219
(Subtotal)			(8,188)	(16,839)	(1,250)	(8,192)	(3,390)	(55,507)
FRANCISCANS								
Guatemala	1	90	4,137			600	3,050	7,787
Chiapas	1	?	500				1,050	1,550
Comayagua	1	?	202			183	220	606
San Salvador	1	?	225				838	1,072
Quezaltenango	1	?	75				1,400	1,475
Other convents[d]	7	?						7,709
Chief pueblos[e]	20	?						14,906
(Subtotal)	(32)	(245)	(5,139)			(783)	(6,558)	(35,105)

MERCEDIANS								
Guatemala	1	100	2,571				1,770	4,341
Interior Guat. & Salv.	45	45						12,878
Chiapas	1	8						742
Nicaragua	7	31						3,400
Comayagua	8	25						3,932
(Subtotal)	(62)	(209)	(2,571)				(1,770)	(25,295)
OTHER MISSIONS								
Capuchines (Guat.)[f]	1	28						0
Carmelites (Guat.)[f]	1		5,285					5,285
Sta. Catharina (Guat.)[f]	1	50	6,939					6,939
P̄ssma. Concepción (Guat.)[f]	1	81	10,244					10,244
Hospital-Ciudad Real	1		450					450
Hospital-Sta. Catharina	1		191					191
Sta. Clara[f]	1	33	1,272					1,272
Colegio de Christo Señor	1	35						0
Cong. de Sn Felipe Neri	1	7						0
Total All Orders			40,279	16,839	1,250	8,975	11,718	140,288

SOURCES: A. G. G. Al. 18, Leg. 211, Exps. 5022–5029, Testimonio de las diligencias hechas en la Cura Eclesiástica de Guatemala. . .

[a] Includes choristers and novices.

[b] "Doctrinal fees" for wine and oil paid by the government.

[c] 12,500 pesos from Hacienda San Geronimo.

[d] In Guatemala, Almolenga, Comalapa, Tecpan, Sololá, San Miguel, Totonicapán, and Zamayai.

[e] *Cavezeras de pueblo.*

[f] Nunneries.

Table 3.2: Annual Average Government Support Given to Guatemalan
Churches and Missions

	1671	1694–98	1715–19	1731–35	1744–48
Doctrinal expenses[a]	25,310	17,724	21,658	18,804	45,591[b]
Wine and oil	n.a.	9,492	16,129	16,727	9,873
Bonds (*juros*)	0	0	10,729	11,854	12,095
Nuns of Chiapas	n.a.	654	476	821	n.a.
Hospitals of Guatemala	1,654	2,664	18,094[c]	n.a.	n.a.
Total for Guatemala	26,964	34,072	67,086	48,206	67,559
Honduras		10,059			9,132[d]
Nicaragua		11,184			2,022[d]
Sonsonate					2,216
Total for Central America		55,315[e]			80,926

SOURCES: *1671*: A. G. I. Guatemala 639; *1694–98*: Guatemala 419; *1715–19*: Contaduría 977 Los Ramos de Que se Compone La Real Hacienda; *1731–35*: Contaduría 977, Año de 1738: Testimonio del. . . todo el Ingreso de Caudal. . . que corresponde hasta fin. . . de 1735; *1744–48*: Guatemala 724, Razón de todos los Sueldos . . .

[a] Includes money chiefly given for salaries (*doctrinas*: 50,000 maravillades for every 400 tributaries by law), and support of missionary activity, the latter a very small amount annually.

[b] The Dominicans received 35 percent of the total, Franciscans 26, Mercedians 6, and the Colegio de Cristo Crucificado 6 percent. Secular clergy received 25 percent.

[c] An increase possibly due to the effect of the 1717 earthquake.

[d] The funds that these interior regions paid in support of clergy did not go through the central government administration.

[e] Nicaragua and Comayagua in turn remitted all tithe receipts to Guatemala, which amounted together to 5,888 pesos.

cienda, but its income, it was said, "hardly covered the costs of the hacienda." Most holdings in Nicaragua are missing.[24]

But the amounts shown in table 3.1 do provide a basis to establish the minimum income and wealth of the convents as well as the sources of support of the church. The two most important amounts given annually to ecclesiastical institutions came from the secular government and from loans and mortgages. The orders and secular clergy received an annual amount from the state based upon the formula of 50,000 maravillades for every 400 tributaries under the clerics' jurisdictions as well as the regular salaries of clerics in Spanish areas (see table 3.2). The government also financed the wine and oil used by the clerics for religious services.

On the other hand, the church provided support to the state in time of need. During the seventeenth century, to meet defense needs the state borrowed over 200,000 pesos from the church, issuing bonds (*juros*) that paid the clerics the same 5 percent interest that private sources (mortgages and loans) did. The Carmelite nuns held the largest amount in government bonds, having loaned the Hapsburg government some 60,000 pesos in 1700. The Bourbons continued and expanded upon the practice of issuing bonds as a method of furthering its anti-clerical policies, "taxing" orders by taking their capital and using ecclesiastical wealth to develop secular state commercial interests (i.e., minting and tobacco production). The state's use of church moneys culminated in 1803 with the calling in of all outstanding ecclesiastical loans to private individuals with the receipts transferred to the state.

The level of governmental support to clerics outside the bishopric of Guatemala is difficult to ascertain although some money [table 3.2] was from time to time passed to interior areas when those regions lacked sufficent resources. All tithe income in Chiapas and Honduras was collected by the state, which, in turn, undertook the responsibility of paying all ecclesiastical expenses. Local civil taxes in those areas became confused, as some towns' sales taxes were used to pay clerics' salaries, for wine and oil, or for masses.

The earthquake of 1717 destroyed much of the financial foundation of the Guatemalan church. Razing a large part of the city, it wiped out many holdings upon which the orders and the diocese held mortgages. The convent of the Sisters of Santa Clara lost 29,774 pesos of the 55,225 pesos it had in capital in mortgages. That of Nuestra Señora de la Concepción suffered "notable losses" when its ranches were ruined. In all, the sisters of Santa Catharina concluded in 1740, "it is public and notorious that the ranches of this kingdom do not have the value nor circumstances of those of New Spain nor do the houses of this city sustain [the church] as those in that capital."[25]

Other, less natural occurrences affected the well-being of the orders. When the congregation of San Felipe Neri was founded, it was promised 25,000 pesos by Juan Gonzales Carabello, the discoverer of a mine at La Corpus. But after the disasters that destroyed that holding, the congregation had to rely upon some capellanías, which were, in turn, lost in the earthquake of 1717. Its holdings consisted solely of a wheat-grinding mill in 1740.[26]

Whereas the orders and some of the secular church functioned with the proceeds from their investments, the metropolitan church had outstanding expenses that required the taxation of its followers. The diocese received its income from the tithe, 10 percent of most agricultural goods produced by non-Indians. However, there were some important subtleties: Indians in repartimiento to produce the

Table 3.3: Tithe Collection in the Diocese of Guatemala, 1712

Sacapa and Acasaguastlan	675 pesos
Escuintla	700
Indigo of San Salvador	8,800
Valley of Chaletenango	275
San Miguel	900
San Vicente	925
Valley of Guatemala	3,800
San Antonio	400
Chiquimula	1,200
Santa Ana	550
Guëguëtenango, Quezaltenango, and Tecpanatitlan	2,000
Guasacapán	1,200
Valley of Rabinal and Cobán	550
City of San Salvador	300
Sonsonate	850
Total	23,125 pesos

SOURCE: A. G. I. Guatemala 245.

grain, had to pay the levy, whereas Indians who farmed wheat as a cash crop and sold it to Spaniards did not. A plea from the bishop of Guatemala in 1712 concerning the effect of natural disasters during the previous decade urged that Indians pay the tithe on all wheat produced. "Indians farm the fruits and grains of Castille whose trade they have taken from the Spanish," the cleric claimed. "The Spaniard used to farm these fruits and grains from which the tithe on wheat of this church produced annually 11,000 to 13,000 pesos and today the sum doesn't reach 300 pesos." The crown upheld the Indian exemption from the tithe, however, and it wasn't until the 1720s that the Creoles regained their production capacity.[27]

Table 3.4: Annual Average Income from the Tithe in the
Diocese of Guatemala, Diverse Years, 1626–1820 (in pesos)

1626–1631	20,633	1714–1718	25,404
1644–1653	28,083	1724–1728	20,504
1654–1663	25,784	1730–1735	22,504
1664–1673	24,960	1743–1748	27,090
1674–1683	29,014	1752–1764	22,482
1684–1693	25,330	1772–1783	87,213
1694–1703	28,397	1790–1794	165,426
1704–1713	25,633	1805–1820	85,810

SOURCES: See appendix A.

Because of the inefficient manner in which the Hapsburg tax-farming system operated, there were repeated attempts to eliminate it in the collection of the tithe. The Guatemalan church took over control of the tax for one year, in 1712, and failed in its efforts to improve receipts. What the clerics did, in essence, was to remove only the middleman, the tax farmer in the capital, while they licensed collection in the interior to the traditional authorities (see table 3.3). Whereas the previous year the tithe was licensed and earned the church 28,000 pesos, now the clerics collected only 23,125 pesos. The next year the tithe was licensed again for 27,000 pesos and the practice continued until mid-century (see Table 3.4).

Once collected, the tithe was distributed for use in church administration, with portions going to maintain the cathedral, the bishop, and social services. Two-ninths of the tithe went, theoretically, to the crown, under the agreement of the Patronato, although this money was reverted customarily to the ecclesiastical authorities to assist in the maintenance of the cathedral and churches. This was important in Central America, where periodic earthquakes destroyed the temples, which either had to be rebuilt or repaired periodically when such a disaster struck. In Santiago the cathedral was reconstructed between 1651 and 1682 and had to be substantially repaired after the 1717 earthquake. In the cases of poorer provinces, such as Honduras, the whole tithe was given to the government, which, in turn, supported all ecclesiastical functions.

In conclusion, the bonds and mortgages and government subsidies to religious orders taken together with the tithe furnished the archdiocese of Guatemala (i.e., Guatemala and Salvador) some 105,000 pesos in 1740, this not including the indigo and wheat farms of the Mercedians and Jesuits about which we lack data. With the ranches that each prelate possessed, the annual upkeep paid by Indians to maintain all pueblo clergy, and fees paid to the clergy for ceremonial functions, the income from Guatemalan and Salvadoran parishes exceeded that of the civil government itself.

Aside from regular annual income, the clergy possessed great economic influence in Spanish towns and cities through its administration of Spanish sodalities and of funds from the sale of bulls. As in the Indian pueblos every Spanish settlement formed cofradías, which were centers of business activity throughout the colonial period. The patronato relieved all ecclesiastical activities from taxes and the cofradía fell under this protection. Involved in the ownership of large amounts of land and in production ostensibly to support its functions and governed by the major Creole families of the area, some cofradías became the predominant economic power. They ran mines, sugar works, and farms, sometimes for profit, and sometimes to protect the holdings of powerful families from foreclosure for failing to pay debts (the community holding the land until the debtor gathered sufficient resources). The crown had to guard against excesses of the cofradías, frequently issuing orders against excessive numbers of them in small communities. The problem of the sodality's freedom from secular control became aggravated later in the eighteenth century when the Bourbon reforms attempted to eliminate cofradía abuses.[28]

Perhaps the greatest church incursion into the secular realm of life was the use of funds gathered from the sale of church bulls (*Bulas de Santa Cruzada*). Sold as indulgences to Spaniards and castes, bulls could not be legally sold to Indians, although in Central America Indians did purchase the largest share of them. Receipts were sent to the metropolitan church in Mexico, where they were either used or sent to Spain, the only church moneys that were formally sent out of the colony.

The export of tax-free church goods created a device that allowed merchants to evade alcabala taxes. The administration of the bulls was, by law, closed and outside the jurisdiction of secular authorities. Money derived from the sale of bulls was used to purchase indigo, which, in turn, was shipped to Mexico and sold, with the proceeds reverted to the administration of the bulls. In this manner the indigo escaped the alcabala sales tax in Central America as well as the entry tax in Mexico. Merchants and producers in Central America received more for their commodities and the lay "administrator of the bulls" earned large profits. In 1665 and 1668, the administrator sent some 125,000 pounds of indigo worth 95,000 pesos and 17,175 pounds of cacao north to Mexico. Fourteen years later it was estimated that the indigo shipped north defrauded the fiscal administration of 43,000 pesos in taxes annually, with additional frauds in Guatemala and other regions. The practice continued into the eighteenth century, with the trade expanded to include the dye, cacao, pita thread, cochineal, and other goods.[29]

In summary, the church worked closely with the Hapsburg monarchy to maintain all areas of the empire within the control of the Catholic monarch, while the crown supported and financed ecclesiastical activities. The Hapsburg state was, in fact, composed of two parts: secular authorities and clerical officials, and the crown used both to further its aims. This secular role given the church combined with the spiritual control maintained over Spaniard and Indian alike to make the church the single most powerful institution in the empire, more powerful than secular authorities, who were divided by provincialism and greed, stronger than merchant groups that rivalled one another for commercial power, and, ultimately, more powerful than the crown itself, which depended upon all the interest groups in the empire to maintain its sovereignty. True, regionalism and rivalries did exist within the ecclesiastical institutions, but at the local level the power of the village clergy far exceeded that of an alcalde mayor and the voice of that prelate could command loyalty to or inspire revolt against secular officials. Finally, the church controlled (but did not necessarily own) the largest amount of economic resources in the Americas. It gathered more money than the secular state's own fiscal administration.

To the Hapsburg monarchy, the power of the clergy was the power of an agent of the crown. But with the ascension of the Bourbons to the Spanish throne the view of the church was changed. The new rulers sought to destroy Hapsburg institutions and the philosophy of decentralized power that had dominated the empire since the conquest. And the church represented such a Hapsburg institution. Thus, ecclesiastical institutions were seen by the eighteenth-century Spanish monarchs as rivals to the Bourbon efforts to centralize control. But before any attack could be made against the church, the crown had to build its own strength within the empire, first during the War of the Spanish Succession and then through measures that increased the power of the state first in the metropolis and then in the colonies. It was only at mid-eighteenth century that the Bourbons could commence the expansion of the state's authority at the expense of the religious bodies. The "Hapsburg" church thus maintained its power until long after the Hapsburg monarchical line had been ended.

CHAPTER FOUR

Colonial Society

IN SPAIN the crown was forced to mediate between its needs and those of the empire, of Castilian merchants and Aragonese lords, and of the bureaucracy. In the New World an equilibrium was equally difficult to achieve. Municipal cabildos and royal and ecclesiastical officials vied with one another for privilege, labor, and wealth. Amerindians struggled to retain their rights. A society developed outside the official structure that differed greatly from the royal dictates, one that could not be circumscribed by the categories and doctrines transferred to the New World after the conquest. A complex social structure was erected—American, perhaps even Central American, in character—which was not encompassed in *limpieza de sangre* (privilege based on pure Christian blood) or the medieval legal concepts that gave authority over the countryside to cabildos, or the theory of the "two republics," Moslem and Spanish in the Old World and Indian and Spanish in the New.

Hapsburg legislation did not reflect the new society. The crown's attempt to maintain a "two republic" policy, which separated Spanish and Indian populations and guaranteed their distinct rights, was undermined by the birth of a new people, mestizo, the union of Indians and Spaniards, who lacked the prerogatives of the colonial elite and the royal protection afforded the Amerindians. Another group emerged from the importation of African slaves. Some blacks and mulattoes remained slaves, others were freed and joined the mestizo in the political limbo, and some escaped to the Caribbean coast and to new tribes outside Spanish sovereignty. Indian and black blood entered the elite Creole population, and if the citizenry continued to claim pure blood, its physical appearance belied its political pretense. The Spanish who came to America in the seventeenth and eighteenth centuries saw the great physical differences between themselves and their Creole cousins. Language and education had changed as well. Rivalries between peninsulares and the traditional Creole elite developed, based upon the privilege of the Spanish officials and merchants as much as upon these social adaptations.

A dichotomy developed between the social reality and law. Theoretically, the *alternativa* system established in the late sixteenth and early seventeenth centuries alternated power between Creoles and peninsulares in certain positions, but mestizos, mulattoes, and ladinos were barely recognized in law. Most rural populations, Spanish or other, were not. Creoles with legally pure blood, whose faces showed African or Amerindian heritages, ruled in the cabildos that protected family privilege based on a supposed lineal descent from the original conquering armies. Reality and legislation did not coincide. Later, in the eighteenth century, it was transformed somewhat into a seat of merchant, rather than traditional family, power, and in the nineteenth, its authority rose and then collapsed completely under attack by rural elites, and then by the mestizos. Under the Hapsburgs and the early Bourbons, however, law and legal institutions were important despite the fact that they failed to encompass all of the new society. The center of traditional legal privilege was the cabildo of Guatemala.

When Pedro Alvarado established the first settlement of Santiago de Guatemala, like the other conquerors he formed a cabildo of members whose authority reflected their rank, in this case, their positions in the conquest. He petitioned the crown for recognition of the municipal council's de facto power. The most powerful received the richest encomiendas and the best parcels of land, both in the city and the countryside. The *regidores* (members) and alcaldes ordinarios of the cabildo held cacao encomiendas in Soconusco and then Isalcos.

Wherever the Spanish established towns cabildos were formed, in Gracias a Dios, in Sonsonate, in Chiapas, but the most powerful was in Santiago, center of *El Reino de Guatemala*. Even at the end of the seventeenth century, the Guatemalan chronicler Francisco Antonio de Fuentes y Guzmán would reaffirm that "all the other provinces [of Central America] are with this province of Santiago de Guatemala like the lines on a clock, all go to stop at the center, and that which the city produces and nourishes the others, as its principal body and head."[1] Law reenforced this dominance of the Guatemalan cabildo over the colony as did the crown.

By the end of the seventeenth century a seat on the cabildo was no longer merely a sign of military power or even great wealth as it had been 150 years earlier. It was a symbol of authority rooted in tradition. If the members were no longer wealthy in encomiendas, pensions, and lands, they were descendants of the conquerors, "hijos de los conquistadores," which supported their authority. The seat on the cabildo was power that was more important than wealth. Handed down from generation to generation, from ally to ally, the purchase price of the seat was returned in privileges and influence in the municipality. The privileges of tax collecting, butchering meat, selling liquor or water, and dividing the Indians for labor, all resided in the cabildo. Although few Creoles at the end of the seventeenth century could legitimately call themselves the descendants of the conqueror, the use of the words in pleas to the crown had some weight. Through tradition Creoles were linked to the authority created by the conquest. Spanish merchants or government officials wishing to establish themselves in the colony had to marry into the Creole elite to gain access to labor, economic privileges, and social standing. The Guatemalans, in turn, welcomed this new and rare "pure blood" from Spain as well as the new money to restore family properties and, perhaps, a connection to the court with its possibilities of pensions or favorable judicial decisions.

The legal authority of the cabildo evolved through the sixteenth century. After the abolition of slavery and the elimination of some encomiendas the surviving Indians were freed, but remained under the repartimiento obligation to contribute one-fourth of their manpower to the colony. Within the valley of Guatemala, roughly seventy-five Indian pueblos as well as urban Indian barrios, the city's cabildo and its two alcaldes ordinarios supervised the distribution of the labor force to the wheat fields and to work on public projects (the construction of churches or the maintenance of roads, for example). Periodically, complaints were received that officials rented out Indians to independent private contractors for the officials' own profit, but this was not a prevalent practice. The city was too small, the oligarchy too aware of the consequences of a dearth of agricultural labor, and the political factions too well entrenched to allow much deviation from custom.

Creole authority was established as well through the Dominicans, Franciscans, and Mercedians who administered the Indian barrios of Santiago and the valley's pueblos. These friars, many of whom were the children of the Creole elite, bridged the "two republics," ensuring a continued supply of labor for the city's existence.

Like the Spanish community, each Indian pueblo and barrio had a cabildo with two alcaldes ordinarios responsible for gathering the crown's tribute and labor. In line with the Hapsburg "two republic" policy, the Indian cabildo maintained the peace and order of the separate Indian community. If it failed, its officials were imprisoned, fined, or whipped until they fulfilled their obligations to the creole community.

Pueblos and barrios specialized in particular activities: some were farmers, others servants. The Indians of Santa María de Jesus provided timber to the city. Those of the barrio of Santo Domingo de los Hortelanos were gardeners. Jocotenango provided artisans. Indians from the Pacific hotlands of Escuintla, the highlands of Amatitlán, and the immediate surroundings of the city furnished salt, fish, meat, and wheat, thread and cotton, lime, and wood as well as the labor that produced and transported these goods and built public projects. There were many "free" Indians—not in repartimiento—who farmed freely, bringing their produce to market. Pueblos provided the city with building materials and corn without compulsion, profiting greatly from their enterprises, particularly toward the end of the century. But repartimiento guaranteed the city's supply and survival and the elite's authority.

The city grew, from 150 Spanish citizens or *vecinos* in 1529, to 500 in 1575, 700 in 1585, and a thousand in 1620. No other Central American town or city had more than 250 vecinos in 1620.[2] The total population of Santiago de Guatemala—vecinos, mestizos, slaves, and Indians—expanded consistently from the earliest days until the city's destruction in 1773, although the greatest growth was in the sixteenth and seventeenth centuries.[3]

As the city grew, so too did its power over the entire colony. The crown's quest for fiscal resources was directed through Santiago de Guatemala, the commercial and bureaucratic center of the colony. And as taxation increased, so did the power of the cabildo.

The major fiscal measure for taxing non-Spanish populations, the alcabala, was theoretically a sales tax, but, in practice, was a colonial tribute. Creoles in the city and the countryside gave an annual amount regardless of the levels of commerce. In 1602, for example, merchants in Santiago gave 10 pesos each, farmers 6 pesos, and cattlemen and wheat millers, between 3 and 4 pesos each.[4]

Through the first half of the seventeenth century the crown pressured for increased resources from the colony and the Santiago cabildo in particular. Between 1601 and 1612, Central America gave less than 2,000 pesos annually in alcabala. In 1614, the crown determined that the colony had to contribute at least 8,000 pesos annually, with the principal responsibility resting upon the city. In the event that the interior could not pay its alloted tax, the cabildo was compelled to make up the difference as the price for its privileges. In the eleven years that followed, from 1615 to 1625, trade declined and the province's share of the tax with it. Thus the city's contribution rose, reaching 8,000 pesos in 1624.[5]

As a result of the increasing fiscal burden the cabildo revolted. The alcalde ordinario was imprisoned in 1625 for failure to fulfill the city's obligations. After four years of adjudication, the crown compromised, reduced the total sum to 5,000 pesos, and awarded the tax farm for the entire colony to the Santiago cabildo. But it also ordered the city to contribute to the war effort by paying an additional 4,000 pesos annually for fifteen years from a tax on wine, cacao, and indigo.[6]

For the next thirty years, new taxes were added, all through the aegis of the cabildo: the barlovento tax paid 2,000 pesos annually, principally from indigo and cacao commerce; in 1639, a forced loan of 60,000 *ducados* in *juros*, bonds upon which the government was to pay 5 percent annual interest; the introduction of the sale of official paper, or *papel sellado*, in 1644, its first year, brought 17,500 pesos from the licensee, the cabildo; and a tax on government and clerical officials of one-half of the first year's salary.[7]

The right to collect these taxes enforced the cabildo's power throughout the colony. It was challenged, unsuccessfully, by the Viceroy of Mexico in 1639, but the crown reiterated its support for the municipality. Thus, even though encomiendas and trade with Spain were declining, the most powerful Creoles were able to collect taxes from the weakest, and the city from the countryside. As long as the crown received its annual tribute, for that is what it was, from the Kingdom of Guatemala, it did not disturb the process.

The presence of royal officials in Santiago also enforced the power of the city's elite. Here, important commercial and political alliances were made, which could not be done, say in Granada or Salvador. A Guatemalan who became an agent for an oidor could profit greatly as long as that official had sufficient power within the audiencia. Similarly, Creoles sought connections with alcaldes mayores and corregidores to serve as their agents in the selling of goods obtained through repartimiento, with regidores who provided licenses for commercial enterprises and labor forces, and with ecclesiastical institutions where credit and property were available.

The sixteen other cabildos that existed in the first half of the seventeenth century were subservient to Santiago de Guatemala. But each also had local authority to tax, to provide food, and to control Indian labor. Cabildo offices were sold but were worth less than those of the capitol. The value of cabildo offices in 1646 in Santiago de Guatemala was three and a half times that of the next powerful cabildo,

San Salvador. San Miguel (Salvador), Ciudad Real (Chiapas), Granada and León (Nicaragua), and Sonsonate each paid about one half the amount of Salvador. And Gracias a Dios, Comayagua, and San Vicente de Austria (Salvador) paid one half again. Seven others paid lesser amounts. As the century progressed, six cabildos were extinguished, most of them in Honduras where Spanish power was declining.[8]

In all the councils, regardless of size, the regidores oversaw the necessities of their settlements, the policing of streets, the supplying of food, and the day-to-day necessities of town life. Cabildos used their resources to contribute to the construction of churches, the repair of public buildings and roads, and the assistance of needy Creoles. The municipal corporations based on traditional authority also provided the legal framework of colonial society. Finally, the cabildos were the spokesmen of the Creoles before the crown, defending local prerogatives against greedy officials, abusive clerics, and other cabildos. They argued for Creole power against peninsulares and against Central American rivals. San Miguel complained about San Salvador, Granada about León, and all about Santiago de Guatemala. Under the Bourbons their prerogatives would be attacked; in the independence era cabildos aired local grievances and led their areas in the break with Spain.

Severo Martínez Peláez discerns in seventeenth-century Central America a "nation of Creoles," a group of elite Guatemalans who defended the colony's interests against Spain and its officials in an early nationalism.[9] As we have seen, Creoles frequently expressed anger at the favoritism the crown showed to peninsulares in royal appointments and in pensions. From time to time they fought the peninsular audiencia over the control of Indian labor. But we should not stress the point. Peninsular presidents, alcaldes mayores, bishops, and priests worked closely with Creoles. Spanish officials and merchants frequently married into colonial society. Most conflicts occurred across "national" lines. Creole society, on the other hand, was much more diffuse, divided between wealthy and poor, between neighborhoods, orders, regions, and even races within the "Creole" title—not all Creoles having the purest blood. When Central America fell into a series of disputes and revolts at the end of the seventeenth century, the factionalism across "national" lines was marked. The idea of America, of the Central American nation, had not yet developed. Colonials and peninsulares saw themselves within the context of one Spanish monarchy, ruling over the other republic, the republic of the Indians. And if we can see differences between the two dominant groups in the cabildo, they were only a part of a much more divided society.

Marriage reflected this fluid society. It was the most common mode of social mobility, of gaining access to the elite for Spaniard, poor Creole, or mestizo. Pure blood and prosperous mates were rare. In small Spanish villas the choice of a husband or wife was limited, and a man or woman either had to marry someone of different economic standing within the city or go to another area for a partner. Pressure was greatest upon unmarried women who needed protection for their wealth, a service that under the law only men could provide unless a woman entered a convent, giving her property as dowry to the ecclesiastical institution. In the countryside, her position might be less vulnerable because widows allied with brothers and sisters, children, or other widows in order to preserve their holdings. Wealthy men sought marriage with women who were not perhaps of their same status to provide legitimate heirs for their fortunes. In Guatemala a scarcity of Spanish women meant Spanish men married mestizos. The part that emotion, a less identifiable motive for marriage, played in making society more fluid cannot be measured.

Both men and women provided dowries, negotiated and contracted at marriage.[10] Generally, the family of the bride was required to provide funds sufficient to maintain her during the marriage and after, while the man gave a dowry of 10 percent of his wealth in "honor of the virginity of his wife." The funds received by each partner became his or her personal property (women had the right to own property), although the woman regained what remained of her dowry if the husband died or abandoned the marriage. The husband's responsibility from the moment of marriage was the safe investment of the funds in a farm or a house that would provide for his family in the event of his death. Poorer colonists gave little or no dowry, and thus in this sense the custom served to stabilize social classes by the ability of prospective mates to contribute equally. Nevertheless, marriages between individuals of different classes with unequal dowries were quite frequent in the late seventeenth and early eighteenth centuries, more often than in the late Bourbon epoch. Alonso Alfarez de Vega, for example, married twice, receiving 17,700 pesos from his first wife, to whom he gave only 2,500 pesos, and 4,000 pesos from his second, to whom he promised 10,000 pesos, his wealth having been increased by the proceeds from his first marriage.[11]

Two examples suffice to indicate the manner in which marriage could change social position. Josepha Inez de Asperilla's dowry brought 2,000 pesos in coin and 2,000 pesos in slaves, silver, and pearls to Phelipe Leonarde de Colonna, a man much poorer than she. With these funds, Colonna purchased an indigo farm in Salvador, although he needed an additional loan from the administrator of church bulls, Bartholomé Gálvez, to complete the sale. When Colonna died five years later he left his widow with two children and the large enterprises. But she could no longer sustain the farm and maintain the payments because of "growing expenses," so Gálvez took it over. Josepha was forced to move to Guatemala for protection and there sued Gálvez unsuccessfully in an attempt to recover her dowry. She died penniless twenty-two years after her marriage, owing a servant 60 pesos "that she loaned me so I could sustain myself."[12]

On the other hand, Juana de Osegueza was born poor, prospered through her marriage and that of one of her daughters, but died impoverished. An illegitimate daughter of a Tegucigalpa woman, she came to Guatemala where she married Don Antonio Xirón de Alvarado and brought as her dowry an offering of "twelve mules carrying salt." Their marriage produced nine children including a daughter, Sevastiana, who married Gregorio Carillo, an oidor of the real audiencia of Guatemala and, later, of Mexico. Sevastiana thus supported the family, providing it with a house, slaves, and some money. Unfortunately, Sevastiana died young, returning Juana's family to poverty. "With the industry and work of my husband and myself, we sought some capital," she testified on her death bed, "but we are now so poor that we had to sell a straw hut in Comayagua to support ourselves."[13]

Equality in marriage was not uncommon, especially among lower economic levels of Creole society where social restrictions and political prohibitions were not enforced, or in rural areas where the common hard work of the countryside was shared. "When we were married," Juan de Aguilar testified in 1731, "neither I nor [my wife] brought a dowry because we married poor, and with our own work and industry we maintained ourselves and raised our children." Similar statements in similar phrases indicate that rural Creoles, husband and wife together, without repartimientos of Indians or without slaves, had to work to sustain themselves.[14]

Wealth once obtained was not secured because a natural disaster or economic problems could wreck the fragile standing of most individuals. Locust plagues, diseases, and earthquakes destroyed the capital of Creoles as it did that of the church, and many had to forfeit their holdings because of debts. The only safe existence, theoretically, was in church institutions, where a dowry for a nun or sufficient capellanías for a cleric supported their lives. Should a loss in property eliminate the dowry as the capellanías' capital, the ecclesiastics still could rely upon the church for their existence.

There was a sharp distinction between the Creole of the city and of the countryside. Guatemala and Granada, devoted to commerce and living off of the production of the interior, offered an existence less dependent upon natural forces, because families could preserve their positions through creating a series of alliance or "protection" could be gained within the monasteries. However, a family could more easily lose its social standing within the city than in the countryside, where land, cattle, slaves, and repartimientos of Indians were subject only to the vicissitudes of nature. Farmers in need had to go to ecclesiastical institutions in the cities in search of credit, and, later in the eighteenth century, to merchants in the city. The life of commerce and government in the cities contrasted sharply with the basic agriculture of the rest of Central America. Daily masses, church and public functions, and communication with the outside world were a part of life in the city; farming and market days were countryside customs.

In both the seventeenth and eighteenth centuries, the great differences between the city and the countryside in Central America led to the regionalism that eventually caused the political dismemberment and internecine warfare of the area. The fundamental distinction between the two areas was economic, specifically the manner in which wealth was obtained and held. The urban centers were, of course, the focal point of power in the colony. Here, wealthy Creoles owned slaves who were servants and sometimes artisans such as carpenters and masons. City Creoles held either pensions or tributes in encomiendas until 1720 and received special favor through their participation in municipal or national government. They also owned and worked land, usually hiring agents (*mayordomos*) to supervise their holdings, or renting their land.

The chief problem of urban areas was centered around the collection and marketing of foodstuffs. Although well supplied with native labor for personal service and public projects, city residents were vulnerable to shortages caused by natural disasters, hoarding, and speculation. Leading Spanish officials and Creole families maintained storage areas outside the cities, allowing food to enter the marketplace only when the price was high. Attempts to establish government graineries (*alhondigas*) to control supply and prices as in Mexico, failed, powerful forces destroying all initiatives.

Until the mid-eighteenth century control of tribute payments made in food was essential to maintain the profits of speculation. Twice a year auctions were held in city stockhouses (*almonedas*) to convert Indian goods to money. The purchase of foodstuffs by any citizen who was not part of the monopoly would have destroyed the system, but the auction was controlled so that only agents of royal officials (the treasurer in Guatemala City, the governor in León, or the alcalde mayor in Chiapas) won the bid. Encomenderos, it was said, "were content" to sell their goods to the same official at the same price. Those who were licensed to collect the tithe cooperated in the arrangement, which kept prices and therefore profits artificially high.[15]

There were, however, sufficient sources of food to prevent monopolistic scarcity. The Creole elite may have controlled meat supply and sales in the five licensed slaughterhouses of Guatemala, but black marketeers undercut the monopolists' prices. Cattle rustling was a problem. Caste entrepreneurs purchased beef from licensed butchers and sold it to the city's poor. If meat was unavailable or too expensive, fish was plentiful and sold door to door by Indians and mestizos who brought it from Lake Atitlán. A few of the city's families controlled the "Spanish" grain, wheat, but monasteries owned considerable land and the orders represented different sectors of the population. Monopoly was impossible. In times of utmost scarcity the bishop could release stores of tithe wheat. In times of famine Creoles condescended to eat Indian corn. Throughout the epoch castes smuggled and sold corn, wheat, cheese, milk, eggs, fish, salt, sugar, and vegetables.

The agrarian nature of Central America, the relatively small urban population, and the subsistence trade economy of the seventeenth century mitigated against the severe food shortages and riots that plagued central Mexico. Food crises did occur, but the excess of foodstuffs in most times meant merchants could not withhold their commodities too long or they would be unable to convert them to scarce silver coinage. Only in times of natural disaster was famine a concern. During the famine of 1694 the Guatemala cabildo complained to the president that the auctioning of Indian-produced grains in tribute should be suspended until the needs of the city were met through distribution of the grain. Regional competition was a factor. Granada depended upon León wheat for subsistence and remonstrated periodically against high prices. Although if food did become scarce in the cities, urban dwellers could escape to the nearby countryside, where food was plentiful.[16]

The weak position of Guatemalan food merchants, compared to that of the Mexican monopolists, is apparent in the rise of Indian competition with Spanish producers at the end of the seventeenth century. Firewood, milk, and vegetables from Dominican and Mercedian monasteries at the outskirts of Guatemala were sold along with those produced on pueblo land. Fuentes y Guzmán complained that Guatemala's five textile workhouses that had been manned by vagabonds, thieves, and fugitive slaves had "disappeared from our eyes" thanks to the "harmful liberty" that the government afforded the Indians in textile production. Sugar and grain farming on monastic and private lands was reduced, he said, because "Indians have introduced themselves to these industries."[17]

Free competition pervaded Santiago de Guatemala, violating Hapsburg privileges and cabildos' power to license food, textile production, and trade. Spaniards provided manufactured goods to mestizo women to sell. Indians sold blankets door to door. Indians and free mulatto women baked bread in their homes.[18]

Populations were fluid, and this fluidity was linked to the growth of free and sometimes illegal trade outside the Hapsburg framework. Children from Indian barrios, rural haciendas, and encomiendas were hired as servants in Spanish homes or as aides to artisans. They learned Spanish trades. Young girls bore mestizo children. Their presence and their cheap labor was enough to reduce the demand to import slaves. Mestizo and mulatto populations rose through the entire period, according to Christopher Lutz's description of the increase in caste numbers through the mid-eighteenth century. Mulattoes tended to marry mestizos in preference to Indians, and mestizos married with all classes. Indeed, in the late seventeenth century, the Creole population accepted the offspring of mestizo-Spanish unions as vecinos.[19]

The complexity of race mixture in Guatemala is exemplified by the family of the chronicler Francisco Antonio de Fuentes y Guzmán. His older half-brother, Felipe, was the product of the union of his father, Francisco, and a free servant, María de Alvarado, who traced part of her descent to Bernal Díaz del Castillo. The light-colored Felipe was apprenticed as a saddle-maker, joined and rose rapidly in the army, and petitioned the crown in 1680 to allow his legal sons to attend the university.[20]

African slaves had existed in Central America since the sixteenth century, serving in urban areas as domestic servants, traders, mule drivers, and craftsmen. They were allowed to marry free men or women, though their offspring were born into servitude. Africans were able, however, to buy their own freedom, and the prevalence of this practice indicates considerable independent commercial activity by them, as in Havana. Serving as carpenters, masons, street merchants, or porters, they earned sufficient funds to free themselves even in times when their price was high. Antonia Rosales, for example, owned a slave, Sevastiana, who had five children of whom two died. Sevastiana purchased freedom for herself and one son for 350 pesos. Another of her daughters, María, who had a son and daughter, purchased her own and her son's freedom for 400 pesos, while María's daughter later paid 150 pesos. This left only one of Sevastiana's children, Manuela, enslaved, although married to a free mestizo. On her deathbed in 1722, the slave-owner Antonia declared in her testament that Manuela should not be sold to anyone and that she could purchase her freedom for 150 pesos "because of the great fidelity with which she has served me."[21] Other slave owners were more generous, granting freedom to their slaves upon their own deaths or that of their wives or husbands. Some installed female slaves in convents until their thirtieth year when they were free to leave or remain. By and large, manumission was practiced because of the domestic nature of urban slavery, which was less profit-oriented and involved closer relationships than that in the countryside.

There was wide variety in the types of labor institutions and patterns of landholding in the Central American countryside throughout the century. Cacao plantations with African slaves in the Matina Valley of Costa Rica and cacao plantations with free mulatto and mestizo labor in Soconusco contrasted with the small subsistence plots (*hatos*) of poor mestizos, mulattoes, and Creoles that spotted the Guatemalan highlands in increasing numbers as the century progressed. Indians worked pueblo-owned corn and wheat *ejidos* in those highlands under the supervision of clerics or in indigo and sugar haciendas held by Dominicans and Jesuits. They labored on private wheat farms, either freely contracted in salaried labor, under repartimiento obligation, or as debt peons. Spanish governors ordered entire Indian pueblos to gather pitch and sarsaparilla in the mountains of Nueva Segovia or individual Indians to carry goods along the royal road from Guatemala to Oaxaca. In Salvador, small and large indigo holdings attracted free labor from castes and, illegally, from Indians.

Vast cattle lands spread over the landscape, worked by Creole owners, perhaps with a few mestizo and mulatto hired hands and only rarely with Indians in repartimiento. Throughout Chiapas, Honduras, highland Guatemala, Nicaragua, and Costa Rica, cattle herds roamed freely or on large haciendas.[22] They were butchered for fat and hides for export to Panama and Peru and for food for urban consumption.

Mules and horses were raised alongside the cattle, destined for the overland pack trains south to Panama or north to Mexico. In Chiapas, Indians and Spaniards alike raised horses for the Mexican market.

Only wheat haciendas or perhaps a few indigo works fitted the stereotype of wealthy Spanish haciendas with Indians working in re-partimiento, and these declined as well at the end of the century. Spanish wheat haciendas near Santiago and León were, in fact, an extension of the city, quite different from the poor Creole farms in the highlands of Chiquimula and Sacapa that had few, if any, Indians to work the land, perhaps some salaried help, and some cattle herds in mortgage to the church. Survival was as precarious for most of these colonial herders and farmers as it was for many Indians. A sign of its availability, land in most of Central America had little intrinsic value; its worth was based upon physical capital, housing and machinery, the grazing cattle, and the available labor, preferably from repartimientos. Large landholdings were not a sign of wealth, for wealth could never be gained from their sale.

A fragmented survey taken in 1682 provides a glimpse of Central America's population and land tenure patterns, which, though we cannot be sure that they prevailed throughout the century, would seem to have continued, according to the findings of Murdo MacLeod on urban emigration,[23] from the 1580s onward (see table 4.1). Roughly, the survey shows three demographic patterns: the Pacific hotlands, the northern and western highland provinces, and the southern and eastern regions. The hotlands along the Pacific coast extended from Soconusco through Escuintla, Salvador to Bagaces, and Esparza in Costa Rica, with relatively sparse Indian and growing caste populations and haciendas of cattle, cacao, and indigo. In Soconusco, for example, 101 haciendas of cacao and beef evolved from the cacao encomiendas of the early sixteenth century. In 1682, however, only 800 tributaries survived, less than half the number of 1613. In their place were mulatto communities.

There were at least 200 farms in Salvador throughout the seventeenth century and, relative to the highlands, the indigenous population was low. Indians cultivated their ejido land for indigo or rented it to nearby farms.[24] A description of the indigo holdings in San Salvador, San Miguel, and San Vicente de Austria indicates one very large hacienda, 79 large (*mayor*), and 282 smaller holdings (*menor*). There was no great tendency towards latifundia, most of which were held by separate individuals.[25]

As we have seen, Indians were illegally used in indigo works throughout the century in repartimientos of labor and goods and by forced purchases and sales. Creoles and castes kept Indians on their lands in debt or made arrangements with pueblos to have a continuous supply of laborers during harvest season. In visita after visita, officials collected fines for the abuse of Indians in obrajes. In 1658, for example, eighty-four farmers were fined between 17 and 22 pesos each. In 1687 sixty-one producers paid a total of 963 pesos.[26]

The effect upon local populations is hard to measure. Doubtless the indigenous population was much smaller than that of the highlands because of the effects of sixteenth-century cacao production. In the 1680s producers requested permission to import slaves because of the epidemics that struck the colony in that decade. A cleric claimed that "the population is more diminished here than anywhere in the kingdom."[27] Later, in the eighteenth century, when government control over labor declined and free labor became more prevalent, the population of Salvador expanded rapidly in relation to other areas. Indigo was produced in other hotland areas as well as in Chiquimula and Comayagua, but intermittently and in smaller quantities. The effect upon the economy and demographic patterns in these other areas was much less than in Salvador.

To the south, on the Pacific coast of Costa Rica, a similar pattern of depopulation and latifundia existed throughout most of the seventeenth and eighteenth centuries. In 1662, in the Franciscan Thomas Calvo's description of the cattle lands running from the Nicoya Peninsula toward Cartago, 250 vecinos lived dispersed. Fifty years later the Bishop of Nicaragua observed much the same scene: "The vecinos live in naked paganism because of their abundance in the countryside. They go out to live there, leaving the cities and pueblos like deserts." Cattle was a source of food and suet and was traded whenever mule trains passed or small frigates called at Esparza. "Even the governor has to grow his own food," an observer wrote in 1719.[28]

In contrast to the Pacific coast (see table 4.1), the western and northern highland region was the largest and most densely populated Indian area. The Spanish islands of Ciudad Real and the Valley of Guatemala possessed large wheat, cattle, and sugar farms. Castes cultivated untitled land in their hatos. But here Amerindia flourished, despite the presence of the cities, of the abusive officials and their repartimientos of goods and labor, and of abusive clerics. Indians lived in their own pueblos, maintaining their culture and subsistence in a fragile partnership with the dominant Creole class. The possibility of revolt mitigated abuse; the cities feared the indigenous multitude and

Table 4.1: Demographic Composition in Central America, ca. 1682

Provinces	Indian Presence		Spanish Presence	Castes' Presence
	Tributaries	Pueblos		(Free Black, Mulatto, Mestizo, Ladino, and Lavorio)
WESTERN HOTLAND				
Soconusco	800		101 haciendas[a]	"4 mulatto towns with 259 people that come from other provinces"
Guazacapán	1,036 1,411 2,447	15 3 18	150 Spanish and mestizo[b] other Spanish owners in Santiago	"A multitude of mulattoes and other types that wander from one province to another"
Chipilapa	167[c]	4	24 vecinos per 99 total population in villa[d]	est. 84[e]
Santiago Cosumago	680[f]	9	2 Spanish	4 mestizos
Escuintla	2,500	3	6 haciedas with 6 Spanish[g]	63 mulattoes
Sapotitlán: San Antonio Suchitepequez	564	1	77 Spanish	71 mulattoes, 10 mestizos, 3 blacks, and 7 lavorios
24 other pueblos	5,229	24	48 Spanish	46 mulattoes, 13 mestizos, 1 black, 26 lavorios
Sonsonate: Izalcos	640	1	No information	No information
Pueblos	1,260 1,900	18 19		
San Salvador	2,724[h]	86	1 Spanish and "30 vecinos campesinos who live on their ranches"	6 mulattoes, 2 blacks
Nicoya	141	1	55 Spanish	
Esparza (de Cartago)	200[i]	1		29 mulattoes and blacks

NORTHERN & WESTERN

Chiapas:				
Ciudad Real	239	6 barrios	50 families	150 mestizos and mulattoes
Pueblos	18,429	97 pueblos	50 "Spanish, mestizos, and mulattoes"[i]	See other columns
Verapaz	10,753	27	18–20 Spanish, mestizos, and mulattoes[l]	See other columns
Guëgüetenango	6,446[k]	76	7 families[l]	
Sololá	2,632	20	33 Spanish and castes	One hacienda de campo with free Indians and mulattoes, and see other columns
Quezaltenango:				
Quezaltenango	992	1	53 Spanish, mestizos, and mulattoes	See other columns
San Juan				
Ostuncalco	431	1		
San Pedro				
Sacatepéquez	317	1	6 Spanish and mestizos	
Others	1,170	20		
	2,910	22	59 Spanish and castes	
Santiago Atitlán	2,394	14	2 Spanish	5 mestizos
Valley of Guatemala:[m]				
San Juan Amatitlán	1,896	1	413 Spanish, mestizos, and mulattoes[n]	
San Christoval Amatitlán	1,500	1	No information	
San Miguel Petapa	1,689	1	540 "non-Indians"	
San Ignes Petapa	251	1		
Santa Cattharina	618	1		
Mixco	984	1	81 ladinos	
Santa Cruz Chiantla	190	1		
Total, all Indians in the valley, including Santiago de Guatemala	41,413			

Table 4.1: (Continued)

| Provinces | Indian Presence | | Spanish Presence | Castes' Presence |
	Tributaries	Pueblos		(Free Black, Mulatto, Mestizo, Ladino, and Lavorio)
SOUTHERN AND EASTERN				
Chiquimula de la Sierra	540	1	60 families	43 families
Mita	182	1	9 "owners of haciendas"	53 families
Other pueblos	1,257	15	18	51 families
	1,889	17	87	147 families
Comayagua (city)			144 families	177 families
(prov)	3,376	126		mulattoes[o]
Tegucigalpa	No information		135 families	blacks and mulattoes[p]
Gracias a Dios			72 men	40 people
Santa Cruz de Yoro				167 men
San pedro			24 vecinos	
Itenco	?	10	26 Spanish in ranches	See other columns
Trujillo			Depopulated[q]	30 mestizos, 64 mulattoes and black men
Olancho			30 Spanish men	
Olancho el nuevo	1,180	137	9 vecinos	24 mulattoes and 2 mestizos
Jerez de la Choluteca	740	18[r]	50 Spanish	130 of all castes
León (Nicaragua)	1,241	8	220 Spanish	150 castes, 51 lavorios
Masaya	194	1	No information	
Granada (city)[s]	537	5	687 Spanish (140 families)	658 mulattoes (122 families) 270 mestizos (42 families) 45 adult male slaves 80 adult women slaves 29 boy slaves ? girl slaves 84 lavorios
Granada (jurisdiction)	1,138	24	No information	34 lavorios
Managua	178	1	60 Spanish[t] with ranches who live in Granada	
Sevaco (Matagalpa)	613	11		
Nueva Segovia	49	1	202 people known vulgarly (*conocen vulgarmente*) as Spanish	71 mestizos, 133 mulattoes
Cartago (city)			475 Spanish vecinos	
Puebla de los Angeles				16 mestizos and 100 mulattoes and free blacks

Note: This table does not include clerics or clerical holdings. *Lavorios* are Indians free from the tribute and pueblo-labor obligations.

a Cacao and beef cattle.

b On small indigo haciendas.

c "and 2,000 Indians from all over Guatemala on the hacienda of Antonio Botello."

d 8 haciendas of cattle, indigo, and cacao, 1 trapiche and 2 ingenios.

e On the Hacienda San Geronimo of Dn Juan de Gálvez there are two or three fishermen and twenty men who herd cattle to the sea (for drinking). There are also salt flats.

Cimarron cattle are herded on the Hacienda El Bonette of Doña Cathelina de Gálvez.

One slave and four *mozos* (servants) gather avocado on the Hacienda of Dn Fernando Bonilla. A trapiche of the Corregidor has one slave and five mozos.

An ingenio of the Dominicans has slaves and ten to twelve free people.

An ingenio of Dña Cathalina de Gálvez has slaves and twenty free people of all castes and some women.

f 680 tributaries is my estimate from "3,445 persons of all ages"—M. W. The Town of Magdalena Malacate had 34 persons of which 22 were blind and 4 were living dead ("*muertos en vida*").

g The Haciendas of Dn Sebastian Aguilar and of Dña Magdalena de Aguilar also held slaves.

h From Guatemala 159: Datos que se remiten . . . tocantes . . . (a) . . . los indios del pueblo de Esquintenango (1685).

i Fragmented, a minimum number.

j On some cacao haciendas.

k Fragmented, 9 pueblos' tributaries are missing. The pueblo of San Miguel Totonicapán had 860 tributaries.

l Sheep raising.

m Information for the Valley of Guatemala derives from a 1682 Padron, quite possibly the Contaduría 815 document, as reported in A.G.I. Guatemala 354, "Expediente de la Ciudad de Santiago sobre la cobranza de tributos y otras rentas del Valle de dicha ciudad . . . , fols. 166–227. Also see "Cuenta y Liquidación de la Importanza de los Tributos . . . in the same *legajo*.

n "Although some come and go."

o "Three leagues away is a villa of mulattoes."

p "Within 30 leagues live 300 blacks and mulattoes."

q "Six Spanish vecinos and 5 free mulattoes live in a valley 9 leagues away."

r Three pueblos depopulated for "having died."

s In 1679, the Bishop of Nicaragua reported that "Granada is depopulated because of the presence of the enemy." A.G.I. Guatemala 162, April 12, 1679.

t With ranches, live in Granada.

Table 4.2: Ranchers in Guëguëtenango, 1712

	Cavallerías[a]	Sheep	Cattle	Pigs	Horses
Domingo García Moscos	69	10,000			
Domingo García Moscos	?	4,000			
Martinez de Vega	7	1,100			
Juan Antonio de León	"less than 7"	400	50		
Isidro López de los Ríos	17	2,000	200		70
Michaela de la Parra	18	1,500	100	100	
Six smaller haciendas	?	1,030	90		"some"

SOURCE: Guatemala 224: Año de 1712: Testimonio de los Autos Fechos Sobre el Donativo de los Dueños de Haciendas de Campo de la Provincia de Guëguëtenango . . . .

[a] One cavallería equals 105 acres.

the crown made sincere efforts to defend Indian integrity. Escape or armed uprisings occurred only when nature or Creoles increased the pressure upon Indians.

In Guëguëtenango the indigenous population of as many as 20,000 surrounded a few, large, sheep-raising ranches. In 1712 (see table 4.2), the pattern of Creole land tenure in this Amerindian sea is clear. One family, that of Captain Domingo García Moscoso, held more land and

Table 4.3: Land Holdings in Sacapa, Chiquimula, and Verapaz, 1712

	Sacapa	Chiquimula	Verapaz
No. of Farms	36	31	22
Families[a]	69 (17)	67 (6)	43 (2)
Cavallerías[b]	?[b]	77	32
Sugar works	14		42
Cattle	7,784	1,240	294
Horses	2,377	314	77
Mares	386	227	48
Mules	487	94	62
Burros		5	27
Oxen (teams)			34
Value (in pesos)	22,773	?	12,607

SOURCES: A.G.I. Guatemala 224, Año de 1712: Testimonio de los Autos Fechos Sobre el Donativo de los Dueños de Haciendas de Campo del Partido de Sacapa . . . . A.G.G. A3.1, Leg. 19, Exps. 5239 and 5245, Año de 1712; Auto Sobre el Donativo de Los Dueños de Haciendas de Campo del Partido de Verapaz (y) . . . de Chiquimula.

[a] Figures in parentheses represent number of families headed by women.

[b] Twenty of thirty-one farms have a total of 108.5 cavallerias.

sheep than all the other settlers combined. Of the ten remaining lesser haciendas, five were owned by women, four of whom were widows and one, an orphan. One hacienda could not be sold for the lack of buyers, with the one thousand head of sheep on the land helping to "pay the salaries of the mozos that guarded the land" and some of the ewes' milk used for cheese.

Land tenure in Verapaz also reveals the slight effect of the colonial economy (see table 4.3). Sugar works predominated. The largest of all the holdings, the Dominican's hacienda at San Geronimo had 250 slaves and about a thousand Indians working in and around it. Only five of the farms listed in these 1712 tax records had more than two cavallerías (the largest having four), with three of the holdings held by multiple families. It is quite possible, by the way, that these farms developed after the 1682 census when the process of movement to the countryside increased in the economically depressed epoch.

The Valley of Guatemala had the greatest concentration of population, over a fourth of all tributes came from there, although it was not so great as in later years. There were constant complaints that "many Spanish, mulattoes and other castes have gathered in the valley's pueblos . . . and commit many crimes." Haciendas were beginning to surround Indian pueblos, particularly in the Amatitlán area, cutting Indians off from their lands.

To east and south of the valley, this trend was even more marked. Because of the geographical position of Chiquimula de la Sierra and Sacapa (see table 4.3)—between Salvadoran indigo fields, Santiago, and Honduran mines—the indigenous populations were drafted for labor more often and mestization developed faster. They raised horses and mules to carry indigo from Salvador to Oaxaca or the Honduran coast and cattle for Santiago. Some landholdings predominated. In Sacapa some thirty-six farms and ranches were owned by sixty-nine individuals who subsisted with a few cattle fattened for Santiago or horses and mules and some sugar cane works. Of the two, Chiquimula was far wealthier than its neighbor. As in Verapaz and Guëguëtnango one hacienda dwarfed the rest, that of a widow Juana Ruíz de la Estrella and her three sons. It was twice as large as any other, some thirty-one cavallerías (3,255 acres). But we do not know how much was mountain land (*tierra de la sierra*). The number of animals listed on the Ruíz de la Estrella holding—410 cattle and 232 horses—does not compare with the much smaller holdings of, for example, one of two cavallerías (210 acres) that held 500 head and 125 horses. And in Sacapa wealth was limited to cattle, because the area was not suitable for wheat production.

Chiquimula was an area of small ranchers. Only nine farmers held more than two cavallerías (the largest having nine), five of which were held by multiple families, and in Verapaz only five farms had more than two cavallerías (the largest having four) with three of the holdings held by multiple families. Indeed, multiple ownership was not unusual. The leading Creoles of Sacapa owned lands by themselves, although they were under heavy mortgages to capellanías or sodalities, but other holdings were usually held in common by more than one family. The San Francisco Río Jondo pasture was owned by thirteen people (six with common last names), led by the corregidor of the area.

In all of Guatemala widows in the countryside seemed strong enough to resist remarriage through alliances with nearby farmers or with the assistance of their children. In Sacapa the largest landholders were women and women held almost 25 percent of all land. However, some lived in abject poverty; one María Roldán had to support thirteen minors on land that held only twenty cows and twelve horses, while María de Victoria had nine minors with some ninety cows and thirty horses. The most unusual possession in the province was the hacienda Chispon owned by six widows together. In Verapaz and Chiquimula women held 4.5 percent and 9 percent of the land; in the indigo producing areas of Salvador they controlled a little more than 10 percent and most were listed as widows. In Guëguëtenango, the second largest rancher was a widow.

Beyond Chiquimula and Sacapa, into the mining and cattle regions of Honduras and Nicaragua (see table 4.1) Indian populations were small and dispersed. Pueblos declined whenever new mines were discovered or whenever Spanish governors issued harsh repartimiento orders to gather pitch, sarsaparilla, and honey in the mountains. Indians fled into the mountains to escape the labor drafts and there lived in small groups, vulnerable to Spanish entradas and to attacks from either Sambos and Mosquitos or from the forces of nature.

Like Sacapa, Chiquimula, and Costa Rica, cattle raising was the principal agricultural activity of Honduras. The cattleholdings were moderate in size (see table 4.4), with 4 percent of the ranchers owning 50 percent of the cattle, although many of these herds were wild, closely resembling those that roamed the mountains of Honduras.

As Central America gradually lost sovereignty over its territory and commerce these areas were the most unsettled in the seventeenth and early eighteenth centuries. Pirates repeatedly sacked Trujillo, Granada, and other regions. Sambos and Mosquitos pushed inland against Spanish and mulatto settlers, kidnapping Indians and selling

Table 4.4: Cattle Holdings in the Province of Comayagua, 1714

Number of Head per Holding	0–9	10–99	100–499	500–999[a]	1,000–5,000[a]	Total
Yoro	55	41	5		3 (6,000)	104 (8,170)
Trujillo		7	4			11 (750)
Olancho and El Viejo	11	79	26	6 (4,400)	3 (5,500)	125 (15,640)[c]
Gracias a Dios	6	42	5	1 (600)		54 (2,826)
Comayagua	24	48	5	4 (2,300)		81 (4,882)
San Pedro Sula	5	35	15	1 (500)		56 (3,618)[d]
Totals	104	285	73	13 (8,400)	6 (11,500)	481 (39,669)

SOURCE: A.G.G. A 3.1, Leg. 4, Exp. 58: Año de 1714, Autos Sobre la Cobranza del Donativo de la Jurisdición de Comayagua.

[a] Figures in parentheses denote total cattle owned.

[b] Olancho and El Viejo comprise a partido apart from the Villa of Olancho.

[c] Plus one farmer with no cattle but 1,000 mares.

[d] Plus sixteen farms with 3,890 cacao trees worth about one-fourth of the value of the 3,618 head of cattle in San Pedro Sula.

them to Jamaica. Indeed, Creoles and Spaniards installed mulattoes and free blacks with towns, land, and rights in the hope that they could guard this frontier area. Antonio Roque, a black who served in Nicaragua at the end of the seventeenth century, was one such guardian. After loyal service defending Granada, Roque gained fifty men— morenos and mulattoes—and the title "Captain of the Conquest" and was located in an outlying region of the Province of Nueva Segovia, "where neither Spaniards or Indians come for fear of Mosquito Indians." He established a settlement where he produced and traded wood, pitch, and beeswax to Granada. He reduced some ninety inland Indians into a pueblo and guarded over them. At the outbreak of war in 1700 he protected Segovia against intrusions by the English and the Mosquitos. It was suggested in 1704 that the crown ratify his settlement and autonomy.[29]

Roque's Nueva Segovia represented the greatest mestization in the colony in 1682, a portent of later developments. The tax report frankly says that the Spaniards there have no right to that name. The caste population was four times that of the Indians. Mestization was more advanced throughout Nicaragua, Granada, and León than it was in Santiago or in Ciudad Real. The slaving raids of the sixteenth century had depleted the province's Indian population, who were by 1682 mostly held in encomiendas to finance pensions in Guatemala and military expenditures. Mestizo labor was supplemented with slaves imported for personal service and military duty. In the mid-seventeenth century a shortage of slaves in Nicaragua led to a practice of breeding Africans with whites to produce mulatto slaves for sale. African women were kept solely for breeding purposes, it was repeatedly charged, and a trade of their offspring developed with Peru.[30]

Throughout the colony there were more blacks and mulattoes than mestizos. Slaves existed in the Pacific hotlands and in the Dominican sugar haciendas in Verapaz. They were domestics in the cities. The growth of a large mestizo population was not as yet as great as after 1680. Certainly there were mestizos in Santiago and elsewhere, but they did not become significant until the great epidemics at the turn of the century and later on with the invasion of the western economy and its wage system.

Just as the land tenure and labor system was diverse and complicated, there was a diffuse commerce, a fluid economy responding to the demand of ships appearing in the Pacific or Caribbean, of Mexican traders with Spanish cloth, or of mule trains crossing to Panama. In the first third of the seventeenth century, Central America's connection with the Spanish metropolis weakened as the empire's naval power declined. As buccaneers gained control over the region, goods were sent through other channels, down the San Juan River to Portobelo or Cartago and north to Mexico. But as the pirates' power expanded, fleets stopped sailing regularly from Vera Cruz, Nicaraguan commerce was stifled by pirates from Jamaica, Providencía, and Henrietta, and the Caribbean became too hazardous for commerce with only small boats able to take risks. Any large vessel that attempted to trade with Guatemala on the Atlantic faced innumerable difficulties. Aside from the exigencies of the Caribbean weather and pirates, a vessel that arrived in the Bay of Honduras had to sit at dockside for two or three months. Word was sent to Guatemala that a ship had arrived while the unloading took place in the Bay. Merchants in the capital gathered goods, traveled to and made commercial transactions in Salvador for indigo, and sent commodities via mule train over tenuous roads to the sea. In rainy season the pack had to wait until the road became passable. In the meantime the boat sat exposed, vulnerable to pirate attack, sometimes as long as six months. When a Spanish ship arrived in Trujillo in 1668 and began to unload the cargo, pirates appeared and the vessel was forced to take to sea without receiving any products in return for those it had left. It was captured at sea nevertheless.[31]

Still, along the Caribbean coastline, small boats sailed between the Bay of Honduras and Granada, and Yucatan, Havana, Portobelo, and Cartagena, repeating the commercial pattern of the Mayans before the conquest. Small vessels were built to handle this trade, and if a fear of pirates existed, these boats could hide more easily, and the risk was less than that of the grand Spanish galleons. Indigo, suet, sarsaparilla, and cacao were sent to the Yucatan, New Granada, and the Caribbean islands in exchange for wine, tobacco, salt, and cloth. The Atlantic or Pacific trade supplemented this economy—Spanish cloth and Peruvian wine showed up frequently as barter items—but the trade occurred continuously with or without these commodities.[32]

The commerce was active, vital, mostly illegal, and supplied and supported a developing, insular economy in the Caribbean region. The trading ventures of the interim governor of Honduras, Lorenzo Ramírez de Guzmán, illustrates both the adversities and the nature of this economy. Soon after his appointment Guzmán installed an agent next to his dwelling in Comayagua to sell clothing, organized a repartimiento of Indians to build a frigate in the nearby Río de Ulua, and sent an aid to Gracias a Dios with goods and clothing to barter with Salvadorans who "usually" brought their indigo to this Caribbean town. Guzmán's agent took the indigo to Puerto Caballos and traded it with a waiting boat from Campeche for clothing, wine, and tobacco from Havana. The tobacco was sent to Guatemala, while other goods were returned to Gracias a Dios to purchase more indigo. When the Guzmán ship was completed, it sailed to the port of Trujillo where it was loaded with 20,000 pounds of indigo, 2,000 pounds of sarsaparilla, and 1,000 of cattle suet with a total value of 30,000 pesos. Unfortunately for the governor, an English vessel came and seized his ship together with another in the same harbor that held much grain. Two other frigates, one from Cartagena and one from Trinidad, escaped the English, having earlier exchanged tobacco for indigo and suet.[33]

The trade between Central America and other Caribbean settlements was both considerable and irregular. As can be seen in this one instance a barter economy developed (nowhere in the testimony is the exchange of silver mentioned) and thriving trade routes linked Salvador, Guatemala, and Honduras in the last third of the seventeenth century. But this traffic was undependable; war, piracy, and specific local problems in the Caribbean areas disrupted commerce for years.

Far more important than the Caribbean trade was traffic on the Pacific, which absorbed much of the commerce that the metropolis had commanded earlier. Central America had left the "Atlantic world" and looked towards the Southern Sea. Nicaragua became tied to the Lima-Panama-Cartagena nexus serving as an alternative route for the transfer of capital between the Atlantic and Pacific from that of Panama. León wheat helped to feed Lima, Segovia pitch was needed to build ships for the Pacific trade and to construct casks for Peruvian wine, and Salvador indigo was employed in the obrajes of Lima and Arequipa.

This commerce was partially interrupted at mid-century with the change in the geopolitical power relationship in the southern Caribbean and the English seizure of Jamaica. Pirates began to attack in the region with greater force than before and Granada itself was assaulted and sacked in 1648, an event that marked the beginning of the decline of the city. Nicaraguan trade shifted from the Caribbean and Granada to the Pacific and Realejo with its León merchants and commerce with Peru expanded. In 1647 over a million pounds of pitch were sent from Nueva Segovia, it was said. "In these provinces," the Nicaraguan Bishop commented in 1679, "there is not a *real* that has not come from Peru. . . . The commerce that we had by the Rió San Juan . . . has been taken by the enemy." Some thirty years later it was proclaimed that "this province of Nicaragua came to be the conquest of Peru and to have been united [with it] . . . one cannot survive without the other."[34]

Thus, the Pacific became the principal source of trade for Central America. Commerce did, however, still continue with Mexico. Notary records reveal large shipments of indigo north to Oaxaca and Veracruz in the 1660s. The treasurer of the church bulls (Bulas de Santa Cruzada) sent at least 22,000 pounds of indigo in 1666 and 70,000 two years later. The total commerce is impossible to discern.[35] The general estimates of production in the forty last years of the seventeenth century ranged from 400,000 to 600,000 pounds annually. These figures, however, do not take into account the effect of locust plagues that halted production for years. No indigo was produced between 1659 and 1663, and 1683 and 1689, because of the insect assault.[36] Because of the fluctuating quantity and demand for the dye, the price of indigo changed frequently, ranging from three to six reales with two reales used as the constant rate for tax purposes until 1667, and then four reales. But, here again, the use of silver was limited and the value of indigo was related only to that in barter with other commodities. Oaxaca merchants traded clothing rather than pesos to earn a profit on the two commodities, and Peruvian shippers used wine.

In conclusion, unlike New Spain or Peru, Central America never achieved commercial unity. No Lima, Mexico City, or Buenos Aires existed through which most trade flowed. Instead, Central America was an amalgam of disparate trade routes whose activity fluctuated with the relative fortunes of the markets they served. Salvador indigo producers and León wheat farmers found better prices offered by Pacific ship captains (and paid in silver coin) more frequently than they did from Oaxacan or Guatemalan muleteers who offered cloth in exchange. Spanish alcaldes traded indigo gained in repartimiento to Oaxaca for cloth they sold to Salvadoran laborers. Salvadoran and Guatemalan Creoles cooperated in smuggling Guayaquil cacao through the colony and north to Mexico, competing against the Central American cacao producers of Soconusco and Suchitepéquez.

There was one other important seventeenth-century trade from Central America in which the Spanish colonists were not involved. Early in the century the abandoned Caribbean coastline attracted English loggers in search of logwood (*haematoxylon campechianum*) for the developing textile industry. The dyewood was cut principally in two areas, in Campeche and in northeast Guatemala at the mouth of the Belize river. The former area was occupied by Spanish settlers who traded directly and openly with the English.[37] In Belize, where there was no Spanish population, the English established their own settlement, the first European, non-Spanish settlement within the confines of Guatemala. The intrusion produced some beneficial results for Central America. The trade pacified Caribbean pirates who channeled their efforts in the profitable logging operations, and, perhaps more important, the Belize settlement and the regular flow of ships between it and Jamaica in the eighteenth century created an easily accessible market for Central American goods.

The English recognized the future of logwood as well as indigo. In negotiations which led to the 1670 "American" Treaty, the English ambassador proposed to the Spanish crown either an English monopoly in slaves, a monopoly [*estanco*] over Campeche for dyewoods, or a monopoly over all of Honduras [sic] for indigo. This latter suggestion was "so novel that it was never bespoken again," rejected because "God created the naturals of those provinces free and not to be monopolized [*estancados*]."[38]

The logwood trade and the existence of Belize were tolerated by Spain after the 1670 American treaty that temporarily ended territorial disputes between the two countries. It was agreed that all settlements established in America up until that date would be recognized by the two nations with no future expansion by the British to be allowed. The pact had the tacit result of semi-legalizing the logwood trade from the Spanish Main, attracting more loggers and expanding the British encroachments, particularly along the Belize river. As the trade grew, so too did contraband traffic with Central America. Central America was thus beginning to regain commercial ties with Europe, although not with Spain.

As the English re-export trade grew, the price of logwood in Europe more than tripled between 1670 and 1680, with imports rising 25 percent between 1669 and 1770. At the turn of the century and the outbreak of war, one English merchant worried that logwood was "so essentially necessary in dyeing [British] manufactures that it would be of the last and worse consequence to be deprived thereof." Indigo was not yet as highly valued, although a market existed. Still, a basis for future expansion was created in these early years.[39]

In conclusion, Hapsburg Central America was a decentralized society, decentralized in economy as well as bureaucracy, in loyalties as well as culture. The decentralized nature of government militated against effective fiscal measures necessary to create a strong defense against the empire's enemies. The commercial and military power of the English, together with their allies the Sambos and Mosquitos, was clear in 1680. The Hapsburg Empire was, on the whole, weakening. In the last twenty years of the century this empire and Central American society fell into crisis.

CHAPTER FIVE

Crisis and Continuity, 1680–1730

WAR DRAINED the Hapsburgs' lifeblood. Throughout the seventeenth century the Dutch, English, and French tested Spain's ability to amass resources for war. In the test the very strength of Hapsburg rule, its ability to balance the interests and traditions in the disparate regions of its empire, was the source of its weakness. The clergy, nobility, and merchant class, each resisted the royal bureaucracy's moves to increase remissions to finance the military. The power and territory of the empire declined. Charles II's inability to sire a legitimate heir to the Spanish throne was the perfect symbol of the impotence of Hapsburg rule.

In the last years of their rule the Hapsburgs attempted reforms. Anticipating their Bourbon successors, they tried to control the privileges of each region, taxing pensions, limiting ecclesiastical establishments, and reforming the bureaucracy. But the attempts were ineffective, often withdrawn before they were enforced. The entrenched interests upon which their rule relied resisted Hapsburg incursions; the bureaucracy was too corrupt and too closely allied with the elite to effect significant change. Still, when the Bourbons ascended to the throne in 1700, they did not initiate reforms, rather they expanded upon and repeated the earlier Hapsburg attempts. Their victory in the War of Spanish Succession (1701–1712) confirmed their rule, defeating those Spanish interests—the church and the nobility—that supported the Austrian Hapsburgs' claim.

A new Spanish bureaucracy developed, based upon the experience of the French Bourbons as brought to Spain by Philip V and his ministers. But Philip encountered sufficient resistance from traditional groups to impede change. Hapsburg traditional society was too well entrenched to initiate quickly a Bourbon absolutist state, especially in conservative colonial areas such as Central America. After the War of Spanish Succession some attempts were made. Encomiendas and pensions were eliminated. The establishment of new church orders was halted. But the bureaucratic structure remained; so did the fundamental weaknesses.

The turn of the eighteenth century was one of crisis in rule as well as continuity in tradition. In Central America Hapsburg institutions maintained the elites' authority though wealth was diminished. That this epoch was also one of crisis in the colony, as in Spain, was both related and coincidental. The erosion of encomiendas and pensions and the changes in repartimiento rules deprived Creoles of government support. Rivalries, shootings, and civil war in Central America were a sign of the collapse of Hapsburg bureaucratic rule. Simultaneously nature wreaked havoc with disease, earthquake, drought, and insect infestation, which struck, one after another, during this period.

By 1730 the fundamental nature of the colony was altered, foreshadowing the greater changes to come in mid-century. The Santiago elite and its cabildo lost authority. Disease diminished Amerindian labor forces upon which they depended. They lost their pensions. The total urban population stagnated and perhaps declined as poor urban Creoles and mestizos migrated to the countryside, to the mines and indigo farms.

New dynamic forces were supplanting traditional urban privilege. As the old elite declined, new Spanish migrated to the colony bringing fresh infusions of capital and perceptions of the world. As the world economy and the first impact of the English industrial revolution was felt, Central America was drawn in. The British increased their commercial activity along the Mosquito shore in league with the Sambos and Mosquitos. Contrabandists came to Honduras in search of dyes and minerals. Trade between Mexico and Spain increased and consequently Central America's trade drew away from Peru and shifted to Mexico. These trends become clear later with the establishment of a mint in Guatemala in 1733, with regular shipping between the Bay of Honduras and Spain after midcentury, and with the expansion of Salvadoran indigo production about the same time. But the beginnings of these developments had taken place in the 1680s.

The city of Santiago reached its greatest height around 1680 with the establishment of the University of San Carlos and the construction of the fountain and Plaza of La Alameda—"second only to Lima,"

Fuentes y Guzmán tells us. As the urban population reached its apex in this decade, the water system was expanded: it would not resume expansion until the mid-eighteenth century.[1]

Then, in 1683, disease and insects struck Santiago and its surrounding valleys. Locusts descended upon the region and remained for five years, devastating crops. The population, both Indians and Spanish, had to flee to the countryside to search for root food. There was hoarding and speculation in food. In December of 1686 an epidemic of either typhus or pneumonic plague broke out in Santiago. One-tenth of the urban population died during the next year, the disease affecting the poorer mestizo and Spanish populations more than the wealthy classes. Five thousand Indian tributaries, perhaps twenty thousand Indians, succumbed in the Guatemalan valley. Two years later an earthquake struck central Guatemala. Additional Indian repartimientos were ordered to help repair the damaged structures and rebuild pueblo churches. In 1693 a new wave of disease swept through, virus, measles, and smallpox, and then there was poor weather, a drought followed by excessive rain. Hard times continued into the eighteenth century: a general epidemic from 1703 to 1705 killed "many of the naturals"; locusts in 1706 and additional famine; smallpox in 1708–09 almost completely depopulated many towns near Santiago. Food speculation was rife. Wheat and corn tripled in price. Then, in 1717, a major earthquake struck Central America, destroying most of the capital, and new repartimientos were created for reconstruction. For the next twenty years locust infestations (in 1723–24, 1732), smallpox (in 1725 and 1733), measles (in 1728), and drought (in 1734, 1736, and 1739) struck throughout Central America forcing the reduction of tribute in most regions; in some years, it was not paid at all.[2]

Regions such as Amatitlán and Escuintla, which had flourished in 1680, reported that their population in 1735 dropped to a fourth of its earlier amount. In Guatemala City between 1680 and 1700 mulattoes and blacks declined some 40 percent and then rose 20 percent by 1740. The number of Spanish marriages in the capital that had risen or stabilized until 1680 declined from that date until 1760. Only mestizos seem to have increased, as Indians sought to escape their status and the labor drafts that became increasingly harsh as their numbers declined.[3]

This summary does not include other, regional natural disasters that afflicted various pueblos. Salvador suffered terribly from the 1680s locust attacks and epidemics. The bishop of Honduras reported many deaths from smallpox and measles. Tribute payments in Nicaragua declined precipitously in the first twenty years of the eighteenth century. Indians of Chiquimula de la Sierra suffered from the "sterility of the soil" during the first three years of the eighteenth century, an occurrence that also afflicted Isalco (Sonsonate) two years later. Intestinal illness, local diseases, and a great variety of other ailments considered normal by contemporary standards contributed to keep population down throughout the colony.[4]

Why, suddenly, forty years of natural disaster? Fuentes y Guzmán wrote that the large and important pueblo of San Juan Amatitlán had been "healthy and free from contagious diseases until 1682 when this region was infested with chills and fever." Perhaps the climate changed. Or perhaps the population had expanded beyond its capacity to produce sufficient foodcrops to maintain resistance against disease. One expert claims that the colonial Indian population of Guatemala reached its highest point just before the outbreak of these diseases.[5]

Whatever the reason, natural disasters were aggravated by the actions of humans. The disease-caused reduction in the work force led to increased food prices and speculation that, in turn, furthered the malnutrition of the poor. Earthquakes increased the pressure on laborers. Corregidores, alcaldes mayores, and encomenderos insisted that Indians pay tribute on traditional head counts. Underaged Indians were forced to marry so they could count in the tribute. Pueblos were required to contribute the same number of Indians in repartimiento. Sometimes the pressure was too great. When mineral production began to expand in the 1720s, the Indians of Chiquimula and Sacapa rose, escaping into the mountains with the corregidor giving chase. Brought back, they fled again and continued to resist until the 1750s.[6]

The late seventeenth-century disasters and the Hapsburg reforms coincided. Both combined to produce the greatest unrest among the colonial population since the conquest. Unlike the later Bourbon measures, the Hapsburg reforms were haphazard, seeking tax resources wherever they might, rather than a policy to strengthen fiscal administration. They lacked the long-range planning and government philosophy of the Bourbons. They were frequently tainted by the self-interest of officials. For example, in 1671 the Bishop of Guatemala, Juan de Sancto Mathío, who ruled the colony as inspector (*visitador*) of the president of the audiencia, found the three repartimiento judges earned 8,000 pesos annually from the fee of one-half real for each laborer they distributed. The bishop seized the funds, contributing them for the construction of the Santiago cathedral. The Council of the Indies approved, going one step further to annex the tax in the future for the royal coffers. The measure deprived the judges of the incentive to distribute workers. Farmers paid the tax without receiving laborers and were forced to pay additional bribes, increasing their costs. Combined later with the locusts and diseases, many food producers were destroyed. With rising prices of food and declining sources of production, Indians began to produce on their common lands for Guatemala's sustenance, competing with the Creoles.[7]

With the controversy over the repartimiento fee and its effects still fresh, the audiencia moved to increase its authority and the personal income of the *oidores* and the president by seizing control over Indian labor in the Guatemalan valley. Since the late sixteenth century Creole alcaldes ordinarios of Santiago's cabildo had divided labor to haciendas owned mostly by the cities' elites. The president of the audiencia tried to remove the alcaldes ordinarios and place in their stead corregidores under the president's jurisdiction. The fiscal explained the rationale behind the move: the valley, the richest area in the colony, could be a source of profit. "Spanish, Negroes, and other castes have settled in such great numbers [that they are] establishing haciendas of wheat farms, sugar farms, and mills." "Surrounded by Spanish haciendas [the Indians] lacked the ground to grow their own corn [and] firewood has to be brought from other regions." Indians were powerless to evade abuses being perpetrated against them, as mestizos, mulattoes, and Spaniards lived lawlessly in their towns and lands. The alcaldes ordinarios were powerless or unwilling to counteract these practices. It was impossible for one man to cover the nine leagues that encompassed the valley and to carry on his own and the city's business. Separate corregidores were needed for efficient administration.[8]

The cabildo and its allies denied that any great abuses occurred and argued that the city needed the Valley for subsistence. Didn't most *corregimientos* in Central America encompass twenty or thirty leagues? the cabildo asked, overlooking the particular population density of the Guatemalan valley. The fiscal ordered a survey; the Jesuits and Augustinians held sugar works, and the Dominicans, an indigo plantation, the remainder of the land was divided among private wheat farms and cattle ranches that relied upon the Indian towns for labor. The local indigenous population was large, with many non-Indians living among them. San Juan Amatitlán, for example, had 1,896 Indians and 413 Spaniards, mestizos, and mulattoes.[9]

The crown took control from the cabildo, dividing the valley into three regions, two administered by alcaldes mayores and one by a corregidor.[10] But no sooner was the order enforced in 1683 than serious disturbances occurred. Areas that had in the past permitted Indian free labor or where accomodations existed between colonists and Indians now came under the authority of repartidores appointed by the president. The customary rhythm of work was disrupted by the introduction of an alien system. Pueblos revolted against the new repartimientos, food shortages developed in the capital, and within six months the new jurisdictions were suspended. Control over the valley reverted to the city in the interest of peace and loyalty of the kingdom.

The Creole victory led to yet another controversy. Since Mencos' transfer of the alcabala to the audiencia, there had been little problem with its collection. But in 1688 the oidor in charge of it, Pedro Enriquez, doubled the assessed value of the indigo taxed, from two to four reales per pound, thereby doubling receipts. The city's merchants refused to pay, appealing the evaluation to the Council of the Indies. Enriquez resorted to the extraordinary and illegal impounding of all dyes until Spain's decision was made—a process that usually took years. The customary practice in such a situation was to get a financial bond. The city was enraged. Commerce would halt if the oidor's decision stood. The Spanish bishop Andrés de las Navas y Quevado supported the Creoles. There was an attempted assassination of Enriquez which killed his servant instead. Finally, the crown upheld the Creoles and ordered Enriquez arrested for disturbing the peace of the colony.[11]

There is no doubt that the attempts of the bureaucracy to challenge the Guatemalan elite over the distribution of labor or taxes at the time of natural disasters upset the colonial order. After the Enriquez affair rivalries among the bishop, the oidores, and the president of the audiencia divided the colony, resulting in virtual civil war in 1700.

The discovery of large silver deposits at La Corpus, Honduras, and the struggle for control intensified the rivalries. Juan González Caravello made the initial find in 1682. Discovering the worth of the mine, Caravello arranged his daughter's marriage to a Catalan merchant, Bartolomé Garacho, who had connections in Guatemalan business and government. The Catalan invested heavily in the enterprise, bringing Indians in repartimiento through his connections in government. He discovered "extremely fine [finísimo] gold in such quantity that each person who came out of the hold carried on his shoulders eight, ten, or twelve castellanos of gold, easily separated from the sand and earth without need for screens or ingenios." The discovery provoked a gold rush. Others came to sink holes near the original mine and angle into the lode. Merchants established a town, while an alcalde mayor was named to oversee repartimientos of Indians and to maintain "law and order."[12]

Within a few years, jurisdictional and property disputes arose among miners, townspeople, and government officials. Alliances were formed involving local officials and miners, the different cliques in the audiencia in Guatemala, the bishop, and various merchants and officials throughout the colony. Bishop Navas y Quevedo allied with the oidor of the audencia, Joseph Descals, against the president, Jacinto de Barrios Leal. Descals formed an alliance with the alcalde mayor at the La Corpus mine and with merchants who smuggled illegal mercury and traded other valuable commodities between Honduras and Guatemala. The president, on the other hand, allied with the other oidores and the alcaldes mayores of San Salvador and Sonsonate. He appointed Francisco de Valenzuela as his representative and "judge" at the mine to resolve all disputes, to collect the quinto, and to supervise the draining of rainwater from the mines. When Valenzuela arrived at La Corpus and called all parties together, two miners allied with the alcalde mayor and Descals and other "Spaniards and mulattoes," in Valenzuela's words refused to accept his authority.

When the dispute was sent to the Council of the Indies it ruled for president Barrios Leal and against oidor Descals and his ally, the alcalde. But the issue was far from closed. The defeated oidor wrote the crown in retribution that the "gold production of Corpus is immense with little or no fifths going to Your Majesty." For six years there had been contraband in gold, he claimed, "the fifths from these mines [worth] more than all the tribute that all the towns of these provinces pay." Descals accused the president of installing allies and relatives in various Guatemalan provinces as alcaldes mayores, the president's brother-in-law was alcalde of San Antonio Suchitepéquez, the fiscal's brother served in the same position in Chiapas, and the uncle of another oidor was the judge of Nicaragua. The president extorted money and labor through repartimiento and illegal jueces de milpas. He took 40,000 pesos in bribes, raped a married woman, and jailed the only *abogado de credito* (lawyer of credit), Lorenzo de 'La Madriz. He also attacked the president's allies. The merchant Juan de Bustamante sent 15,000 pesos of untaxed gold to Mexico, while the alcaldes mayores of Sonsonate and Salvador engaged in contraband mercury trade and forced Indians to accept clothing in exchange for labor from which the president earned 80,000 pesos. The dean of the cathedral in Guatemala defrauded the church of tithes.[13]

The controversy was not limited to the Spanish. Indeed, it involved many Amerindian peoples as well. The decline of population in the Guatemalan highlands and the rise in demand for repartimiento in the capital and in the mines disrupted the rhythm of labor between farmer and Indian. Both Descals and Barrios Leal sought repartimientos throughout Central America for the miners allied with them at La Corpus. There were entradas into the mountains of Honduras, Chiapas, and Verapaz. In 1695 Barrios Leal led a general offensive against "that great walled city as large as Sevilla" in the Petén Lagoon. From both Yucatan and Guatemala forces invaded, easily conquering the Itzá peoples. The city was renamed "Pueblo de los Dolores," and a permanent military force established. Escapees were rounded up and sent to the mines. But the conquest was not complete; some were able to resist this and other later entradas from Cobán, Campeche, and the Petén presidio.[14]

In Chiapas, however, the Dominicans ruled, supported by the bishops in resistance to the labor drafts. Descals retaliated with a visita. He decried the number of sodalities and the great amounts that every Indian had to pay, criticizing the bishops of Chiapas and Guatemala for allowing these practices. He ordered them to cease. The clerics resisted, appealing to allies in the archdiocese of Mexico where the Court of the Inquisition indicted Descals for interference in religious matters.[15]

The Hapsburg colonial government had reached its weakest point. Smuggling pervaded the colony. Mercury was shipped from Peru along with illegal Guayaquil cacao, and silver. Silver was smuggled to Mexico on the Pacific and then exchanged for Asian clothing and cloth. Accusations were tossed between officials as each profited in his own way from the silver boom. This weakness extended to Madrid. Four months after Descals assumed the interim presidency, a replacement, Gabriel Sánchez de Berrospe, arrived. Descals and his allies in the audiencia inhibited the new official until two years later when the crown permanently removed Descals and ordered him to return to Spain. His allies, however, remained in the audiencia.[16]

The president of the Council of the Indies, the Count of Adanero, gained the appointment of Francisco Gómez de la Madriz as visitador to Guatemala. The visitador, also known as Tequelí, arrived in late 1699, assumed the leadership of the Descals faction, and attempted to take power from President Berrospe. It was civil war. "There was no father for son nor son for father, wife for husband, nor husband for wife because all were divided in discords, hatreds, and enmities," a contemporary wrote. "There was no house without fighting and yelling every day, vituperations were cried at each other without any other reason than to proclaim 'I am Berrospísta,' or 'I am Tequelí' "[17] Berrospe's military compelled Tequelí to take refuge in the chapel of the Jesuit colegio. The bishop, Navas y Quevado, supported Tequelí, as he had Descals, providing him with sanctuary and excommunicating Berrospe and his allies. Nevertheless, Tequelí and his supporters were driven north to Soconusco to gather additional forces, the Berrospistas giving chase, defeating them definitively. Tequelí was later arrested in Campeche and sent to Spain to face a new and unsympathetic Bourbon monarch. The Guatemalan bishop resigned. In Soconusco, the alcalde mayor of Corpus unsuccessfully appealed to the crown for the release of his impounded wealth.[18]

The La Corpus and related Tequelí affairs affected the entire Central American society. The movements of Indian labor, the new entradas, the illegal smuggling of Peruvian mercury to the mines and Honduran silver to Mexico, and the involvement of ecclesiastical and secular officials in Guatemala as well as in Mexico and Spain testify to the wealth that the La Corpus mine must have produced. In Honduras new populations came in search of other riches. In 1713 Julien Izquierdo discovered a new vein near La Corpus and other finds followed. A rich mine was opened at Alotepeque near Tegucigalpa the following decade. Most of these exploitations escaped taxation. No mint existed in Guatemala. Miners and their mercantile allies shipped their minerals to Guatemala for stamping and on to Mexico for coining, which was costly in taxes and bribes. Subterfuges developed, such as a silver-working industry in Guatemala that converted illegal, unstamped minerals into religious artifacts of fine quality for export to Mexico and Spain. English smugglers on the nearby Caribbean coast traded untaxed silver for cheap clothing. It was so profitable that a permanent English settlement under William Piche (Pitt) was established in 1729. The clergy of Honduras and the officials of that province, Nicaragua, and Costa Rica became notorious for their smuggling. Indeed, in 1703 Peruvian silver smugglers tried to use the route to smuggle 349,000 untaxed pesos from the Pacific through Costa Rica to the English.[19]

The very moment that Central America's export economy was expanding the Hapsburg bureaucracy was too impotent to gather fruits from it. This was the ultimate weakness of the Hapsburgs from the Central American perspective. Greedy officials who were paid insufficient salaries fought among themselves for the wealth of La Corpus. In desperate need of funds, the crown was unable to collect its legal share or control its bureaucracy in Guatemala or in Spain, in either the secular or the ecclesiastical hierarchy. Heretofore the Hapsburgs had ruled by balancing the different sectors and interests throughout the entire empire. We have seen their method in tax collection, rewards, commercial policy, and bureaucratic structure. But this balance was unable to provide the fiscal resources for the destructive European wars. This structural crisis was evident in Central America, where from 1650 to 1720 nine cabildos, primarily in Honduras, ceased to operate because they were unable or unwilling to gather the traditional fees for the crown. About the same time the alcaldes mayores in Honduras excused their smuggling with their need for funds to pay for their *residencia*, the inspection that followed their tenure. In 1699, for example, one inspector was paid over 15,000 pesos for his inspection in Honduras.[20]

As in the metropolis, there was a crisis forced by increased military expenditures in the colony. Levies to finance a military capable of defending the empire's frontiers against contraband trading and foreign invasion were resisted by colonials throughout the Hapsburg era. Most income derived from Indian tribute with only a nominal amount coming from Creole-licensed sales taxes and forced loans and contributions. The government borrowed over 200,000 pesos from the church throughout the century.[21]

When Honduras, Nicaragua, and Costa Rica fell under attack from buccaneers and Sambos and Mosquitos Indians, Guatemalan and Salvadoran Creoles fought efforts to raise funds for defense. Beginning with Martín de Mencos, Guatemalan presidents reported repeatedly to the crown the need for fortifications at Trujillo and on the Río San Juan in Nicaragua and for funds to supply soldiers. In order to overcome this resistence the Hapsburgs taxed Guatemala's Creoles where they were most vulnerable, in the pensions and encomiendas that the crown granted them and that were administered, by and large, by royal officials. At first the crown followed the suggestion of Mencos, assigning Indian tributes from vacant or expired encomiendas (*situados*) for military construction and upkeep. For those colonists who still held encomiendas and were strong enough to have them renewed, the crown attacked their overall value. In 1663 it ordered the media anata tax, one-half of the first year's value. In 1685 it seized a year's pension to finance war efforts. For fear of losing future pensions, the encomenderos acceeded. After 1688 the crown taxed pension income heavily; an additional 50 percent levy was a usual occurrence. Encomenderos received at that time 80,900 pesos, of which 15 percent went to the government annually for its *escudería* or quinto tax and 22.5 percent to pay for clerical salaries and church expenses in Indian areas, leaving 50,500 pesos in real income. When the Bourbons came to power they ceased to renew pensions and in 1705 forced encomenderos to donate another year's income to the war effort. With the war's end and the consolidation of Bourbon power, the encomienda was finally eliminated in 1720. Encomiendas of certain privileged families—called pensions but supported by the tribute of Indians—were maintained and continued to exist until the 1760s. In the main, however, the institution had been removed and most encomenderos lost their means of support.[22]

Pensions of Indian tribute that once came into the city were directed either to Spain in taxes or to the interior for supplies. But the fiscal problem that faced the Hapsburgs and early Bourbons was still not solved. They relied on Indian contributions, unable to levy Creole and caste direct contributions. With the epidemics in the last years of the century, income from tributes and thus income to situados declined. In the areas around the capital Indians began to "hide" their race and escape the tribute by migration to cities, calling themselves soldiers, according to the custom of mulattoes and blacks. Others went to other Indian towns, claiming to pay their tribute in another jurisdiction, or went to cities to marry mestizos or mulattoes. Some took refuge in the church or on haciendas. Mestization increased.[23]

While income declined, military needs increased. The incursions against the Itzás and Lacandons and the establishment of the Petén lagoon presidio in the 1690s cost over 200,000 pesos. Companies of mulatto guards created in 1700 in Guatemala during the Tequelí affair and the civil war cost 27,000 pesos and the guard remained after the disturbances. With the onset of the War of Spanish Succession the Sambos and Mosquitos attacked Indian and Spanish populations in Honduras, Nicaragua, and Costa Rica. Military expenditures increased for at least fifteen years, costing at least 10,000 pesos annually. In 1712 an Indian revolt in Chiapas caused a reduction in tribute payments and an increase in expenses for a permanent force in that area. Finally, in 1717, a major earthquake struck northern Central America, destroying the royal palace and other official buildings in Guatemala as well as numerous Indian towns. Tributes in Suchitepéquez, Escuintla, and Chiquimula were diverted for building new churches and reconstructing town facilities.[24] Defense appropriations in Central America between 1715 and 1719 were eight times that of the period from 1670 to 1674.

The fiscal problem was critical. At the beginning of their reign the Bourbon rulers perceived that Central America could not support additional expenditures. When the empire became embroiled in the War of the Spanish Succession, the monarchy ordered the merchants of Guatemala to assume a debt of 171,460 pesos, which it contracted with the Seville Merchant Guild (consulado) at 8 percent interest in

1700. The loan had yet to be repaid by 1711, the interest then doubling the amount owed, and the crown took steps.[25] Ordering a visita of the fiscal administration in Central America, the crown requested the senior oidor to perform the task, but his inspection in 1717 was considered incomplete. In 1719 the president, Francisco Rodríguez de Rivas was ordered to review the situation, but his report also left the metropolis unhappy. These first, tentative inspections of the tribute collection system raised questions that forced Rivas to make an additional inspection six years later that uncovered widespread fraud and malpractice. Those in control of the treasury used funds for their private commercial dealings. The *contador* owed the government more than 30,000 pesos, and the treasurer, more than 5,000, "not counting the many extra-judicial debts that either man has incurred with the 'fruits' that enter the royal coffers in tribute." The officials lent money in exchange for help in tribute collection or "for reasons of family ties and friendship." Among the some 80,000 pesos owed to the government, the preceding president owed 4,000 pesos, and five different oidores, 10,415 pesos. Rodríguez de Rivas alleged that these loans were made to insure that nobody would inform against the illegal enterprise. Others refused to testify because of the political power of the officials involved. "It seems," the president commented, "that these voluntary actions have more force than law."

Other irregularities were uncovered. Private individuals were loaned tribute goods and paid interest to the officials. Those who could not repay the loan either lost their collateral or, if they were closely connected to the official, the loan was forgiven. Lesser bureaucrats also partook of the scheme; the alcalde mayor of San Salvador owed all tributes collected in that province for three years and other alcaldes and corregidores withheld portions of tribute every year.

Rodríguez de Rivas claimed that between 1711 and 1717 some 200,000 pesos in debt were incurred, although he confused the fraud with the legitimate debts resulting from the Indian revolt in Chiapas. The amount was, indeed, excessive, in a colony where total annual income was roughly 200,000 pesos.[26]

Who was to support the increasing government expenses as the number of tributaries declined? Although other measures could be taken to force greater income from non-Indian groups, tribute could not be allowed to decline. The pressure was passed from the president to the treasurer and from the treasurer to the corregidores and alcaldes mayores. At the lower level, these minor officials were compelled to maintain annual incomes. During the first two-thirds of the eighteenth century new head counts were refused for most areas and officials called on Indian alcaldes to furnish the old numbers.

The Indian woman was a partial answer to the dilemma. In the late sixteenth century the crown had permitted the levy of one-half a peso for single Indian women. Despite a ban the practice continued and was corrupted further. At the end of the seventeenth century complaints were sent to Spain that unmarried girls and widows were forced to pay full tribute of 2 pesos. During Indian rebellions, or whenever a single male Indian fled, the woman was expected to assume responsibility. By 1725 the practice was widespread and generalized to include all women, abandoned or not. Little or no action was taken against this illegal practice throughout this period. It was not until 1759, on the eve of the great fiscal reforms, that a definite ban was announced.[27]

Tribute continued to decline in relation to other taxes. The fiscal difficulty was, in part, a demographic problem. The tax system established in the late sixteenth century was designed for a colony with few Spaniards and many Indians, a situation made archaic by a population trend toward more and more non-Indians. The Indian's descendant who married a mestizo or Spaniard was permanently lost as a tributary. The colonial fiscal system that imposed most of its burden upon indigenous populations ironically encouraged the Indian to escape his status, thus reducing its income.

The interior's inability to provide major funds to the central administration increased the fiscal burden upon the valley and highlands of central Guatemala. Without many Indian tributaries, and with major defense expenditures, regions like Honduras and Nicaragua perpetually drained the resources of the northern part of the colony. The settlers and militia in these regions participated in the very contraband trade that made government expenditures necessary.

Indeed, the interior best illustrates the reliance upon tribute to support expenses and the weakness of the policy. In Nicaragua (see table 5.1) during the peacetime years between 1731 and 1735, 71 percent of all income from within the province derived from Indian tributaries, while only 7 percent came from direct taxes upon the non-Indian populace (*embarcaciónes*, an export tax). The remaining income came from media anata, mesada eclesiástica, and ecclesiastical taxes and immediately reverted to the church for its expenses. The low Indian population, provincial poverty, and a poor tax structure meant the central colonial government annually sent a situado—comprised of money from Guatemalan tributaries—to support the defense

Table 5.1: *Tax Income and Outflow, Nicaragua, 1731–1735 (in pesos)*

Income		Outflow	
Tribute	15,103	Church expenses	5,218
Church taxes	2,338	Salaries and pensions	7,295
Embarkations	2,530	Military expenses	20,479
Misc. taxes	1,256		
Money sent from Guatemala	14,000		
Total	35,227	Total	32,992

SOURCE: A.G.I. Guatemala 724, Año de 1737: Testimonio del . . . todo el ingreso de caudal que tiene . . . la real caja . . . .

Note: The church taxes derived from the episcopal fourth, and the two-ninths.

needs of the colony. This pattern existed from the 1680s until the reforms in the later eighteenth century.

The decline in tribute and the corruption in its collection was not the only cause of the fiscal crisis. When, in 1656, Martín de Mencos transferred control to royal officials of the collection of the alcabala, income had risen dramatically. After 1680, when income declined again, the Bourbon rulers perceived that the bureaucracy they inherited was unable to collect taxes efficiently or honestly from the non-Indian population. Fifteen percent of the income due the state between 1706 and 1726—about 60,000 pesos over the period—was never collected. Internal squabbling among corrupt oidores divided the audiencia, which was unwilling or impotent to deal with the problem.

To gain additional funds the Bourbons retreated from centralized rule. In 1728 the crown assigned the collection of the alcabala and barlovento taxes to the city's merchants. In the first contract the businessmen guaranteed the government 18,500 pesos annually, plus 11,000 pesos for every vessel (*nao*) that arrived in Honduras. A comparison with the previous fifteen years of audiencia collection reveals that in the former period the alcabala and barlovento produced 270,997 pesos (the numbers are reduced by 24,274 collected from two boats in Honduras), which is an annual average of 16,448 pesos from internal commerce. Income in the first eleven years of the reform was an additional 2,000 pesos annually.[28]

The merchants' monopoly violated the Bourbon philosophy of strong and absolute centralized government. The merchants' tax power provided them again with the power to tax articles at will and for their own profit. The city's commercial powers delegated the taxing power to business allies in the interior, extending their control in areas such as Salvador and León where Peruvian and Cartagena traders competed. Nevertheless, the crown, which needed time and additional resources to build its political power, was compelled to ally with local interests. In contrast, in Lima the merchant monopoly on tax collection ended in 1721, reverting to the royal treasury. The measure was intended to end the pervasive contraband commerce. In Guatemala the crown was unable either to reform the entire fiscal apparatus or to eliminate merchant participation in tax collection.

In essence, the Hapsburg fiscal system continued until 1763 and lasted in most interior areas until the 1786 Intendant reforms. For almost two hundred years Indian tribute supported colonial government and income was collected in the same manner. There was, however, one major difference between the late Hapsburg and early Bourbon governments. The seventeenth-century monarchs expected the regular remission of tribute from the Kingdom of Guatemala to Spain; the Bourbons maintained tax income within the colony, using it to expand government control and resources, and thereby strengthen sovereignty.

The Bourbons' renewal of Creole authority over alcabalas did not end the crisis for the city and its elite: the valley's labor remained scarce; encomienda pensions were either reduced or eliminated; the valley's production was reduced. The church, bank and bulwark of both city and countryside, suffered when Creoles forfeited loans on capellanías and sodalities. For twenty years vacant lands fell to the church. Then the earthquake of 1717 in Santiago destroyed many houses that were mortgaged to central ecclesiastical institutions, and while some were rebuilt and their mortgages continued to be paid, many were not. The colonial system upon which the social order and economy had relied—the repartimiento of goods and labor and the encomienda rewards—either no longer existed or was declining in importance. Indians traded agricultural goods freely, competing with traditional families. Repartimiento of labor had become important for commercial commodities, for mining and indigo, rather than for wheat and corn. Peninsular officials fought among themselves for mineral wealth rather than live by the trade of labor and the goods of Indians. And when the new Bourbon monarchy attempted to limit the legal commerce that Santiago did control, the wine trade to Peru, the city had rebelled. The city lost control over trade. "Goods from Castile are under the authority of the merchants of Mexico," it was said in 1709. Spanish alcaldes traded dyes and silver directly to Oaxaca, not through the hands of Guatemalan agents. Honduran and Salvadoran producers no longer sold their goods to Guatemala. Instead, they traded to Pacific ships and to Englishmen in the Caribbean. The reduction in urban authority was apparent in the city's cabildo; once prized seats had lost their value, their price, too high to be earned back through labor drafts or other monopolies. By 1720 the cabildo, at one time nineteen regidores, was only five. Between 1674 and 1698, the price of the *Alférez Real* office dropped from 5,000 pesos to 1,000 pesos, and regidores seats from 2,000 pesos to 500 pesos. When President Rivas asked for the names of vecinos who could serve on the body, he was told there were only thirty or forty families who could qualify. In 1734 the municipality decided that it was preferable to elect the regidores rather than sell the offices as in the past.[29]

The old, urban Creole families might find themselves adrift in the Bourbon era, but new Spanish merchants arrived who, over the course of fifty years, became naturalized Creoles through marriage into old families. The Arroyaves, the Urruelas, the Landivars, the Pavóns, and the Larrazábals—their names would become important—changed the nature of the colony. And while this new elite formed, the old left for the countryside, for the mines, wheat farms, cattle ranches, and indigo plantations, or was subsumed through marriage.[30]

This change was gradual, masked by the tumult of the times. Increased pressure upon Chiapan Indians for labor and tribute and the seizure of valuables from Chiapan cofradías by a zealous bishop and other less identifiable factors led in 1712 to the largest indigenous revolt since the conquest of Central America. Along the Mosquito Coast from Honduras to Costa Rica, the Sambos and Mosquitos terrorized Indian, mulatto, and Spanish populations. In Santiago itself, after the civil war of Tequelí, unrest continued. Presidents Cosío y Campo and Rivas overruled the Bourbon's interdict on trade with Peru, which stemmed the unrest, but order was not achieved.[31]

The 1717 earthquake symbolizes both the upheaval and the change in colonial life. It destroyed many of the buildings and much of the urban wealth of Santiago. The mortgages that the church held in league with the traditional elite were lost. The temples of San Felipe Neri and Santo Calvario were totally destroyed and had to be rebuilt. It cost 25,000 pesos to repair the Dominican convent, while 9,000 pesos in annual rents was lost to the order from other razed buildings. The church of Nuestra Señora del Carmen cost 40,000 pesos to rebuild.[32]

When a movement developed to transfer the site of the city to another "safe" location, the king asked "Who would build the convents, churches, royal and episcopal palaces at the new site" in the event the move occurred? "How would the lost rents of the convents, hospitals, and cofradías be made up?" The attempt to transfer the city caused another upheaval. The bishop supported those who favored it, the president, Rivas, did not. When it appeared that Rivas had lost control, he formed a new company of mulatto soldiers and then ruled that the cabildo had to finance any move that was made. Lacking any funds, the move was cut off.[33]

The earthquake marked the decline of the cabildo and the beginnings of absolutism, but it would be wrong to suggest that peace and government authority were restored. Just a decade later, two oidores of the audiencia caused "part of the plebe" to revolt against the president, who, in turn, used the mulatto militia to suppress the revolt. Twenty years later the president was removed from office for "many and serious charges." Stability emerged very slowly as the colonial social and political order changed.[34]

In conclusion, these years of tumult showed the collapse of Hapsburg rule in Central America. The Hapsburgs had attempted some reforms, but the nature of the system that rewarded loyalty through encomiendas or through taxation of only the subjugated Indian peoples militated against change. When the Bourbons came to power, however, they rejected such traditionalism and built on the first Hapsburg measures. Until 1730 their attempts were tentative, only slightly more effective than those of their predecessors. The encomienda was abolished. Fiscal income was kept within the colony, rather than sent to Spain, building bureaucratic strength. But repeated visitas did not alter the basic problem of reliance upon Indian tribute for government funds and a change in the collection of the alcabala sales tax was actually a retreat from absolutism.

After 1730, however, reform increased. In that year the crown seriously entertained the idea of transferring control of the central valley from the cabildo to the audiencia, but appeals and then war intervened, until finally the move took place in 1751. In 1733 the mint was established in Guatemala and an economy of coinage was born. For the moment, however, this period from 1680 to 1730 was one of transition, in which traditional families were losing their power, the traditional city as well as its indigenous population were in decline, and new bureaucrats and commercial forces were emerging.

PART TWO

The New Order

CHAPTER SIX

The Transformation of the Colony

THE CRISIS of demography and bureaucracy and the transformation of commercial patterns in Central America coincided with the Bourbons' accession to the Spanish throne, with their struggle against Hapsburg allies both within and without Spain in the War of the Spanish Succession. As a new commerce developed in Central America, a new bureaucracy and philosophy of rule took shape in the metropolis. And, about the same time, there was a discernable quickening of pace of industry in England, the Netherlands, and perhaps even France.

The change in government deeply affected Central America. The Hapsburgs had done little to foster economic growth. The crown was concerned chiefly with maintaining empire, annual payments of mineral wealth, obedience to basic legislation, and religious fidelity. Colonial defense and economy were considered important, but, because of other priorities and impotence, they were poorly financed or totally ignored. By the time that reform was instituted, it was too late. In the seventeenth century, the Kingdom of Guatemala defended itself and promoted whatever commerce it might, despite royal policy.

Under the Hapsburgs government involvement took three forms: First, the church served as banker and co-producer in a quasi-public manner that continued capital support of production through periods of economic decline in dispersed regions of the colony by integrating the national capital within the church's administration. Second, the state controlled labor, both providing work forces in developed regions and limiting abuses. It never insisted that Indians pay their tribute in silver and thus tacitly reenforced a subsistence level economy based upon limited barter. Third, the Hapsburgs established marketing restraints that prohibited intra-empire traffic in certain goods (Peruvian wine, Guayaquil cacao) as well as access to international buyers. The state was unable to enforce some of these commercial interdicts and tacitly accepted violations of policy.

Hapsburg policies and practices at the turn of the century and the diffuse commercial activities failed to satisfy the demands the Bourbons made on the state, their sense of the exigencies of absolutism. So, too, of course, did the weak, corrupt bureaucracy fail. As Colbert had propounded in France, a strong state required royal stimulation of the economy through factories and monopolies of key crafts that could be easily taxed. A strong economy could not rely solely upon the New World's mineral wealth; a strong, privately owned agriculture was equally essential. These ideas were expounded in Spain by Gerónimo de Uztáriz in *Theórica y práctica de comercio y de marina* (1724). Bernardo de Ulloa and José de Campillo y Cosío elaborated on these thoughts around 1740, but their implementation took place slowly, awaiting the end of the War in 1712, only to be interrupted by war from 1739 to 1749. But slowly, through the eighteenth century, the Bourbons altered and modified the attitudes and institutions they had inherited from Hapsburg Spain. Institutions more directly involved in stimulating commerce developed, providing the opportunity for the private sector to profit and these profits to be taxed. A Hapsburg institution as it was constituted, the church and its privileges were attacked and their financial holdings placed under control. Colonial authorities continued to supply labor as their predecessors had done, and, indeed, increased draft labor for mines and indigo fields, but they were now complemented by debt peons.

Hapsburgs and Bourbons differed as much in style as in substance. The indirect government control that was exercised by the seventeenth-century government through clerics was replaced with direct and secular bureaucratic administrations. Creole merchants, supported by encomienda and other privileges, were supplanted by merchant-immigrants who brought new capital from peninsula "companies." They invested in colonial enterprises and supplanted the church with relative ease. At first the new business elite focused upon the extraction of minerals. Government and business worked together to expand the mining industry under the control of the crown. Agricultural investment and growth occurred later, delayed by the effects of rural diseases and insect invasions that plagued indigo- and food-producing regions through the 1730s. The War of Jenkin's Ear closed commercial export channels partially until 1750, postponing change further. At war's end a heightened economic vitality flowed into international commerce. The economic expansion created the basis of modern Central America.

As commercial production changed, so did labor practices. At first there were greater drafts of repartimiento labor for the mines and later the indigo fields. As commerce grew and local production became more specialized, lands that had been used for food production were converted to money crops. The shortage of food led to increased debt peonage and a credit system that forced the dependency of interior producers upon city merchants.

The effect of the western commercial revolution that brought Central America within its expanding network at mid-century must not be underestimated. A dramatic rise in price reflected the demand for indigo in English textile mills. Questions of war and peace with Spain were discussed in London in terms of the availability of Central American dyes. New trade routes formed at mid-century throughout the western world, and new institutions had to be developed in Central America, regardless of government philosophy, to deal with the changing eighteenth-century world.

If we look at Central America at the end of the eighteenth century, we see a radically different colony from the one a hundred years earlier. Guatemala City was a major center of commercial activity linked directly with Spain through regular sailings of boats to the Bay of Honduras; Salvador, a major producer of indigo for the metropolis; and all the areas of the colony, integrated into one economic framework, under the domination of the capital city. New commercial organizations and government bodies administered this transformed colony, while the Enlightenment philosophies provided intellectual underpinnings for the society. How much of seventeenth-century Hapsburg Central America remained and how strong the new Bourbon institutions were could not be determined until the process was complete, until Central America was independent from Spain and these institutions were tested.

Honduran silver attracted a new wave of immigrants and English boats and settlements to the Bay of Honduras. It brought direct government involvement. It drew local Hapsburg barter economies under its influence and integrated the colony within the world trade system. Without adequate silver, Central America had existed with a semi-barter economy in the seventeenth and early eighteenth centuries. The government had suffered by its inability either to convert Indian tribute commodities into silver for export to the metropolis or to tax adequately any trade that existed in barter.

In 1724, Bourbon activism attempted to stimulate silver production. The quinto, which had been 20 percent in Central America, was lowered to 10 percent, and the price of mercury, reduced by half, from

60 to 30 pesos the pound for ten years. To remedy the chronic labor shortage in Honduras the president of Guatemala ordered new reducciones of Indians, resettlement of towns to mining areas, and release of those Indians who worked the mines from the obligation to pay tribute. All encarcerated criminals were sent to the mines to work, the mine owners paying the government twelve reales a month for fines and judicial costs. The salary was said to be a fourth of that which was paid Indians in addition to food and upkeep.[1]

There was an immediate expansion of mining throughout Honduras. In 1712 only one mine was working. Twenty-five years later Tegucigalpa alone had seven silver and two gold exploitation regions with thirty-three mines. Comayagua had six sites with at least twenty-five mines with "title" and many without. Gold panning in the province's rivers became more prevalent. The growth of the mining industry attracted population, which, in turn, led to new discoveries and the exploitation of less productive deposits of alluvial minerals. Between 1729 and 1736 a reported 462,655 pesos of silver were mined.[2]

Production and control was less than optimum for lack of a mint. All silver was sent to Guatemala, where taxes were paid before it was made into bars and stamped with the royal seal. Then silver was traded to Mexicans for goods or given to the government for transportation to Mexico City for minting. The system perpetuated the shortage in coin in Guatemala and added to the cost of silver production. It also provided an incentive for smuggling silver to foreign boats along the coast or hoarding untaxed minerals as many clerics did. The crown ordered a mint in Guatemala in 1733, and sent 80,000 pesos to Honduras to purchase silver at the mine site, eliminating the profit-leeching middlemen and stimulating mineral production. The results of these moves were dramatic (see table 6.1). Minting in the last five years of the decade was one-and-a-half times that of the first years. The increase in coinage created new commercial possibilities and provided the government with the first sizable income in taxes on minerals since the sixteenth century.

The authority and wealth of Guatemalan merchants were not cut off, however. Guatemalan merchants bought up the cheap mercury provided by the government, selling it illegally to Honduran miners at higher prices. When war erupted in 1739 and the crown withdrew funds for purchasing silver at the mines, merchants moved in, providing capital to purchase mercury, gunpowder, food, and government influence for labor allocation. They gave loans to the miners for purchases of supplies which they sold. They purchased silver at the mine site for transport back to the mint. They set prices on materials and

Table 6.1: Output of the Guatemalan Mint, 1733–1757 (in pesos)

1733	136,715	1741	209,174	1749–1753	187,983[a]
1734	191,423	1742	199,583		
1735	177,865	1743	232,478	1754–1757	166,388[a]
1736	249,521	1744	178,063		
1737	290,162	1745	153,559		
1738	281,184	1746	139,354		
1739	327,750	1747	164,186		
1740	190,733	1748	142,166		

SOURCES: A.G.I. Guatemala 236, President of Guatemala, 12/22/1749; Guatemala 243, Report of the Chief of the Casa de Moneda: "Razón de Oro y Plata, 4/1/1733–6/30/1736; Guatemala 234, Año de 1746: Testimonio del Real Orden . . . todo el Oro y Plata que se ha labrado el Real Casa de Moneda . . . ; Guatemala 795, Consejo de Indias, 3/3/1761; García Paláez, *Memorias*, 2: 147.

Note: Based upon 1 Marc of silver = 8 pesos, 5 reales.

[a] Annual average.

interest rates for loans. In short, the profits from mining went to Guatemala. In the first six months of 1745, for example, of some 60,185 pesos of silver sent to the mint, 22,783 were controlled by a regidor of the Guatemalan cabildo, Ventura de Arrollave y Beteta with some 10,000 pesos more owned by another prominent Guatemalan, Cayetano Pavón. Both were first generation immigrants, *nouveaux arrivés*.[3]

The hoarding of mercury by powerful merchants and miners created shortages which caused a decline in production in the 1740s (see table 6.1). Many mines could not be worked for the complete lack of quicksilver. The crown ordered 50,000 pesos to be sent to Honduras to purchase silver directly from the mine site, eliminating the merchant control over production. Officials in New Spain were ordered to ship mercury to Guatemala. Still, the power of the Guatemalan businessmen was sufficient to counteract the royal legislation by controlling credit and other supplies.[4]

The scarcity of labor imposed the most severe limits on silver production. Creoles in the Guatemalan valley and highlands and officials opposed the movement of indigenous labor and royal legislation forbade it. Indigo production and trade, gathering momentum towards mid-century, increased pressure on labor. Miners pushed for greater production; abuse and illness led Indians to flee to the mountains, creating an even greater shortage.

The regions of Chiquimula and Sacapa were the most affected by silver mining. When the mines of Alotepeque were discovered, the corregidor brought some seven thousand Indian families into mining towns and nearby agricultural areas. He spent his four-year term from 1732 to 1736 roaming the hinterland and capturing runaway Indians for the greatly increased demand.[5]

Chiquimula and Sacapa suffered a five-year famine in the next decade (caused by "sterility of the soil") that further reduced the numbers of laborers. Indians "fled the towns to look for corn in San Salvador, Sonsonate, and Guatemala." Towns were unable to fulfill tribute payments based upon antiquated head counts. The governor of Comayagua invaded the province of Chiquimula—ostensibly looking for runaway workers—and carried off families "delinquent" in tribute payment. Once placed in the mining areas, families that lost their men either through escape or death were obliged to work. Boys and girls were whipped into submission.[6]

Indians were reduced to mining areas in previously unsettled regions of Honduras. A major conquest of the Paya tribe was organized—they were said to be English allies—which resulted in two small settlements of a total of 197 Indians "big and small." Once "reduced," the Indians tended to flee. "Since 1728, Indians are returning to the mountains," a friar reported twenty-three years later. One entry by Spaniards led to an encounter with Sambos, "who were many and very expert in the handling of arms." The expedition captured thirteen—wrapping and tying them in hides—before retreating in canoes up river. But the boats carrying the captured overturned and the Indians drowned.[7]

In contrast to the inertia of the Hapsburg epoch, this pattern, which would later be repeated in other industries, was significant. Summarized briefly: Bourbon fiscal and labor intervention stimulated an underexploited industry; as the industry developed, Guatemalan merchants, by virtue of their strategic position at the center of the legal trade and their control of capital, siphoned off the greatest profits. Amerindian populations were either compelled or induced to labor, their numbers were reduced and their cultures weakened. Other indigenous populations in the Guatemalan and Chiapan highlands were drawn into the commercial net of silver production, producing food and cloth for the mines' support. The growth in production and taxation created a stronger bureaucratic presence at the mine sites and ultimately enabled the establishment of a mint.

Under the Hapsburgs, traditional societies were protected, Amerindian populations expanded, and the Creole elite maintained. The crises at the turn of the century weakened them. Now the mining industry strengthened centralized government and the position of the new Spanish merchants at the expense of the Amerindian population and the old Guatemalan families.

The expansion of silver production stimulated other commercial ventures. Following the lessons of Colbert, the Spanish Bourbons organized factories under royal patronage to stimulate, channel, and tax production. The first manifestation of this policy in the New World was the Real Compañía Guizpuzcoana, a private Basque company— with shares given to the crown—that financed cacao production in Caracas. In exchange for its investment, the company was granted the monopoly over exports and the responsibility for its defense against contrabandists. The company created a merchant marine and an efficient trade network. These nouveaux-arrivés, however, antagonized the old Creole producers who sought for the remainder of the century to break the peninsular monopoly.[8]

The success of the Caracas enterprise led Guatemalan merchants, most of whom were also nouveaux-arrivés, to imitate. They petitioned the crown in 1741 to establish a private company of colonial and Spanish businessmen (whose share cost up to one million pesos), which would have the right to trade with Mexico, Peru, and Spain and to supply mining areas with mercury and other goods. The crown received a portion of the company, but its efforts were short-lived. Construction of boats at Realejo for Pacific commerce was expensive. Competition for Peruvian mercury increased with the exploitation of San Luis Potosí, Pachuca, and other New Spain mines that were wealthier and much more efficient than those of Honduras. Perhaps most important, by 1760 Peruvian commerce had lost its importance for Central America, as trade expanded into the Caribbean and Atlantic centered upon the export of indigo to the metropolis. With Spanish capital competing in the Guatemalan dye market and Spanish boats in the Gulf of Honduras, the infant company died prematurely.[9]

Still, such organized commercial vitality had not been seen in Central America for at least one hundred years. Capital was flowing into Central America. Both external and internal traffic increased. Goods came from Asia via the Manila Galleon, Acapulco, and Mexico, engulfing the colony particularly during the (European) war years of 1739–49. It was estimated in 1746 that 150,000 to 175,000 pesos of Asian goods entered Guatemala City annually, "the principal commodity of all the goods that are purchased in Mexico." Trade expanded with Campeche and Havana from Honduras. Small vessels sailed between Cartagena, Portobelo, and Granada via the Río San Juan. The mule trains from Costa Rica to Panama became larger and more frequent.[10]

The commercial dynamism was not confined to the empire. The lure of Honduran silver led to increased British presence on the Honduran coast and a reduction in Spanish sovereignty. During the War of the Spanish Succession contraband trade was prevalent. The Peace of Utrecht (1713) granted the English a thirty-year *asiento* (monopoly) over the slave trade to Spanish America and the right to keep a vessel off Portobelo for trade.

England's increased commercial presence on the Central American Caribbean coast, together with the Sambos and Mosquitos renegade peoples, posed a significant threat to both Spanish territory and the Bourbons' attempt to direct the economy.

The slave monopoly met some of the demands of the growing Central American economy. For most of the seventeenth century slaves had not been imported; the offspring of those imported in the sixteenth were the sole source of supply. After 1700 slaves were smuggled into the region. With the British monopoly there was a new influx; the price within Central America dropped from 400 to 500 pesos to half that amount. Their cheapness made domestic slavery fairly widespread among the elite in urban areas. In 1739 the asiento ended and war erupted.[11]

In 1740, the Council of the Indies dispatched an engineer, Luis Díez Navarro, to appraise the situation in the Central American coastline. One of the new generation of Bourbon administrators who reported loyally and honestly his estimation and proposals for reform, Navarro remained through the 1770s, directing the construction of Caribbean forts, influencing defense policy, and conveying domestic colonial conditions to the crown. His report (summarized in table 6.2)

Table 6.2: Summary of Caribbean Settlements in Central America, 1743

Region	Remarks
Gulf of Honduras	(Castle with 63 men) Castle is ruined and soldiers unable to handle arms.
Motagua River	Canoes come from Sacapa and Vera Paz to trade.
Port of Omoa & Port of Caballos	Should be developed.
Río Chamalecon	Canoes from San Pedro de Sula; "Sambos and Mosquitos have invaded this river more than fifty leagues and robbed the pueblos."
Río de Ulua	Desagua for most of Honduras. The Sambos and Mosquitos have invaded the rivers to rob the five pueblos on the shore.
Port Sal	Monastery with Jicaques Indians.
Río de Leones	Entry only 30 leagues, a good port that serves for contraband commerce.
Trujillo	"Looking to the east, a small port called Puerto Escondido," where English boats come to trade every year, January through April.

Table 6.2: (Continued)

Region	Remarks
Island of Roatan	Populated by the English since June 1742.
Río of Aguan	Canoes enter and ascend up to 40 leagues inland to San Jorge Olanchito without difficulty for contraband.
Río Limosnas	Canoes come from the mountains of Olancho el Viejo; two leagues from the coast is an English settlement.
Río Tinto	English seat of government. William Piche lives here.
Río Payas	Canoes can go up to 20 leagues where Patucas and Xicaques Indians live.
——	Farther south of Rio Payas are many rivers where the land is very low. Sambos live in small islands in this region. Subjects of William Piche.
Río Platanos	English settlement with a lieutenant named by Piche.
Puerto Cartago[a]	Populated by "English thieves and wanderers who live through contraband and the gathering of hardwood in Belize.[a]
Cape Gracias a Dios	Populated by English and mulattoes. Inland live Patucas and Xicaques Indians, and along the coast, Mosquitos.
——	Between Gracias a Dios and Río San Juan is a "wide point," the Río de Mais, a large Bay, and the Pearl Islands, all populated by English, Sambos, and Mosquitos.
Río San Juan	Three mouths of the river all join together 6–8 leagues inland. 25 leagues inland is the fortress and from here to the lake, 12 leagues.
Río Reventezon or Ximenes	
Río de Suerte	
Río de Mainao or del Carpintero	Haciendas of Cacao (30 leagues from Cartago, Costa Rica).
Port of Moin	Embarkations of small boats.

SOURCE: A.G.I. Guatemala 872B, *Descripción de toda la costa del mar del norte y parte de la del sur . . . en este año de 1743.*

[a] The Port of Cartago has no relation with the capital of Costa Rica by the same name.

indicates the extent to which English commercial houses had invaded and to which the Spanish had receded from the territory. The center of English-Sambo-Mosquito power was Río Tinto, some 102 leagues from the nearest Spanish outpost on the Gulf of Honduras. Since 1729, an English governor, William Piche, controlled trade throughout the coast and its interior regions, as well as governing the Sambos and the Mosquitos. "He is well esteemed by all the inhabitants of these provinces . . . and has various armed canoes of Mosquito Indians for his guard and many black slaves who manage armaments well." Spanish merchants, Díez Navarro claimed, sent the English, through Tegucigalpa, "gold, silver, indigo, and sarsaparilla in exchange for goods that are sold in outlying regions throughout the Kingdom." All sectors were involved. "The inhabitants of the whole territory," the Captain General claimed in 1737, "including the clergy and the highest government officials," were interested solely in illicit trade. Even the forts were used as warehouses for goods. Piche traded with the colonials, but also directed the attacks of Sambos and Mosquitos in time of war—sometimes aided by English forces—against Spanish settlements. The schizophrenic existence of Spaniard and Englishman fighting and trading alternately continued until late in the nineteenth century when the pro-English Sambos and Mosquitos were finally conquered.[12]

The revitalized trade drew off much of the newly minted money of Guatemala. All commerce in imported merchandise was exchanged for silver and some indigo and cacao. It was claimed in 1746 that some 500,000 to 600,000 pesos "leave" for New Spain annually.[13] Only the growth in value on the world market of an agricultural commodity could attract rather than deplete capital. This is precisely what occurred at the end of the War of Jenkin's Ear with the rise in demand for indigo.

Indigo had served as the basic trade commodity since its export in the late sixteenth century. With the decline in the Atlantic trade it was still produced and sent to Peru and Mexico for use in the textile works. It remained in demand in Europe, but the costs of production, transportation, middlemen, and taxes, as well as the negative effects of Caribbean pirates, corrupt officials, and the intermittent European wars militated against the Atlantic trade. English interlopers from Jamaica farmed dyewood at the Belize river in Guatemala and in the Campeche lagoon in the Yucatan to meet Europe's demand. Toward the end of the seventeenth century the growth of English textile production and its re-export trade made indigo much more important, but indigo introduced into India had limited potential. Demand grew dramatically throughout Europe in the first third of the eighteenth century. Bordeaux became a center for its re-export to the continent. In Spain, the Bourbons organized textile and tapestry factories. The War of Jenkin's Ear between 1739 and 1749 put pressure on the market—Carolina, Brazil, and Santo Domingo responded, but Guatemalan indigo was preferred for quality.[14]

Demand grew in the Pacific as well as the Atlantic. In Sonsonate and Realejo indigo brought between 2.5 and 3 reales a pound between 1750 and 1753, and 2.5 and 3.5 reales for the next two years. Then,

Table 6.3: Spanish Vessels in the Bay of Honduras,
1730–1765

Year	Number	Total Tonnage	Taxes Paid
1730–1736	0		
1737	?	275[a]	9,901 pesos
1744	2	124	4,547
1752	1	94	3,470
1754	3	386	14,149
1755–1756	3	335	12,325
1759	?	318[a]	11,657
1760	1	171	6,233
1761	1	120	4,400
1763	4	539[a]	19,721
1765	3	460	16,866

SOURCES: Deduced from A.G.I. Guatemala 680, Expediente Sobre hallarse enteramente cubierta la Real Hacienda
del Arrendamiento de Alcabala . . . ; and A.G.G. A3.5, Leg.
2407, Exp. 35432.
   [a] Estimated tonnage.

in 1756, the price of *corte*, the cheapest commodity, shot up to 6 reales
and maintained that level throughout most of the rest of the century.
In that year merchants received almost as much money as they had
in the six previous years.[15]

Poor shipping channels presented the most serious obstacle to
expansion of the indigo trade. Indigo could be sent to Vera Cruz, but
Mexican middlemen and taxes then cut into the profit of both Guatemalans and Spaniards. Boats traveled between Havana and Guatemala, but faced a double danger because the British watched both
ports. One boat filled with indigo was captured in the Bay of Honduras
during the War of the Spanish Succession, while another was seized
in transit to Havana. The construction of a fortress at Omoa offered
only a partial solution. Spanish merchants had to finance boats to
make the trip directly as well as to provide capital for the purchase of
the dye in Salvador.[16]

The slow process involved in the changing trade patterns is seen
in table 6.3. During the first half of the eighteenth century most indigo
destined for Europe traveled overland to Vera Cruz. Only one vessel
called in the Bay of Honduras in the first 35 years of the century.
Then, after war ended in 1749, commerce expanded with more tonnage carried from Honduras to Spain during the 1750s than in the past
half century. Trade was regularized in the next decade with vessels
arriving biannually.

The indigo boom attracted a new generation of Spaniards to Central America, men with strong commercial ties with the metropolis or powerful allies within the government, men who usurped the position of the old Creole establishment. Immigrants had come before. They had married into the traditional elite and become a part of the colonial leadership. But they had always been absorbed by the traditional colonial order, values, and institutions. Now, these new eighteenth-century "conquistadores" dramatically changed both society and government. Military officers, who defended Granada, and businessmen in the forefront of the commercial revolution came, married into established families, and quickly assumed control of major economic and political positions. By the end of the eighteenth century they had created a Central America within a world commercial system that bore scant resemblance to what it had been only a century before. By the time of the independence movement the descendants of these nouveaux-arrivés would constitute the national leadership.

The Vidaurre family is a case in point. José de Vidaurre, a native of Vizcaya, came from the peninsula with commercial connections in Cádiz already established. He married the daughter of a Granada trader and sister of the dean of the León cathedral, linking an established mercantile family with new capital. The union yielded a powerful and diversified clan. Bartolomé, the son, was a leading merchant, regidor, and alcalde ordinario of Granada. His wife, Juana de Carrión y Mendoza, came from one of the most powerful families in León, her brothers were alcaldes ordinarios, assistants to the governor, and the master of the León cathedral, representative of the office of the Inquisition in that city. Her mother was said to be a descendant of "one of the first conquerors." A number of Bartolomé and Juana Vidaurre's sons were clerics. José was Dean of the León Cathedral and served as interim bishop of that diocese. Francisco, the primogenitor, was a regidor and, more important, the lawyer of the real audiencia. In 1793 he was called "a legitimate son of the descendants of the conquerors" and accepted as a member of the Creole hierarchy. Francisco's marriage to the daughter of the protomédico of Guatemala, José de Medina, yielded sons who numbered among them Diego, one of the leading officials in the Comayagua diocese, and Felipe, a leader of the cabildo in the indigo-wealthy region of San Vicente. By the time of independence, the Vidaurre clan was one of the most powerful factions in Central America. A Vidaurre served as alcalde ordinario of Guatemala and was chief official of the merchant guild.[17]

There are many other examples of the creation of the new colonial elite. Simon Larrazábal came in 1725 as a ship captain and merchant working for Pedro Carrillo of Cádiz; his grandson was a leader of the liberal movement at the beginning of the nineteenth century. Gaspar Juarros came as a merchant in 1752; his son Domingo was a prominent liberal and wrote the first extensive history of Central America. Martin Barrundia and Gregorio Urruela came in the 1770s; their sons were prominent in the independence movement and national politics. José Piñol came from Cádiz to serve as the first factor of the Barcelona Company in Central America. He linked the fortunes of those Guatemalan merchants who had organized the Pacific Company, the Irisarri-Arrillaga group, with those of his allies in Spain. After developing trade connections with the Guatemalans, he left the Catalan company and on his own became an international merchant with his brothers in Cádiz. His widow linked the fortunes of the Piñol clan with those of the most dynamic of the nouveaux-arrivés, the Aycinenas.[18]

The most important new arrival was Juan Fermín de Aycinena. Born in 1729, he migrated to Mexico in 1748 where he became involved in the mule trade. Moving to Guatemala in 1754, he began to accumulate a fortune through a series of propitious marriages, which also created the powerful clan that led Guatemala's commercial sector through the national period until contemporary times. Soon after arriving in Guatemala Juan Fermín de Aycinena married the daughter of the alcalde ordinario of the cabildo, which placed him in line for that office four years later. After his first wife died in 1768, he married the widow of Piñol, creating the alliance with the Cádiz-Piñol family that continued until the end of the century.[19] With money and influence, Aycinena accumulated land in Guatemala and Salvador and acquired a major part of the indigo trade. His rise to dominance over Central America culminated with the purchase of a *marquesado* in 1781—the only such titled nobility in Central America—and the construction of his house on the central square next to the cathedral and government offices. By the end of the century his wealth was said to be more than a million pesos, with indigo plantations and commercial houses or strong connections in Lima, Mexico City, Cádiz, Jamaica, and Britain itself.

The history of the Aycinena family in many ways is the history of Central America after 1750. The clan's commercial policies created the economic pattern for the colony, controlling trade in most regions of the colony as well as capital, serving as the banker for government and private citizen alike. With the decline in Spanish power the Aycinenas switched their trade to Britain, becoming a leading force in the move for independence. Once freedom from Spain was achieved, the Aycinenas were the single most powerful family during the federal period. The Aycinena name is still prominent in commercial and political affairs in Guatemala.[20]

The impetus for the familial and commercial revolution came in part from Spain and the activist Bourbons. The monarchy established textile and tapestry factories with royal financing. It chartered the Barcelona company with the right to trade to Honduras. It allowed the 375 members of the *Cinco Gremios Mayores*, who dominated retail trade in Madrid, to finance vessels for the New World. These ships frequented the Honduran coast from the 1750s onward, and their representatives established a commercial house in Guatemala. In 1763, Charles III chartered a privileged merchant company, which had as shareholders only members of the Cinco Gremios and the king. Their representatives became some of the most powerful businessmen in Guatemala.[21]

New capital flowed into the colony and with it new families who assumed control of trade, production, and labor. However, their invasion was not limited to the cities. Rather they moved into the countryside and usurped the traditional position of colonial farmers as well. The fights were particularly violent in Salvador, the center of indigo production. At mid-century the Creole population in Salvador was small and well-integrated. In the city of Salvador in 1740 there were but fifty-eight vecinos who defended their privileges against all outsiders. When peninsulares attracted by the indigo wealth arrived, the Creoles attacked. Disputes erupted over the right of the peninsulares to buy offices or to sit in the cabildo of Salvador, or to purchase land through the administration of the tax on land purchases. The peninsulares accused the most prominent Creoles of forming anti-Spanish groups, of harassing and assaulting them.[22]

The tension came to a head in April 1755. In the middle of the night three Spanish merchants came to the corner of a house owned by a prominent Creole family and began to sing and play their guitars. When the men of the house came out to complain, the peninsulares attacked them with knives. The aggressors subsequently fled and took refuge in the Dominican convent. The Creole alcalde ordinario began to prepare charges against them, while the Spanish alcalde mayor attempted to placate the aggrieved Creoles. Tension between the two sectors grew until May 23rd, when a group of prominent Creoles together with over a hundred mulattoes met at the house of Thomas de Arce to plot the "murder" of one of the above aggressors, Juan de Otero. They sought out Otero and approached him "carrying firearms and naked swords" and yelling "now has come the hour of the dogs." Otero fled towards the Dominican convent, followed by the group yelling "kill the dog." At the door of the convent Otero was injured in the foot, but made sanctuary safely. Still, three days later Arce returned with three hundred men, claiming that Otero did not possess sanctuary, but the Spaniard was able to escape over the mission walls unnoticed.

The conflict between Creoles and peninulares had reached a critical point: "the republic is tense and moving against the Europeans," it was said. It was understood that the underlying cause of the disputes was that "the Creoles do not wish the Europeans to settle (*avecindarán*) in the land." The president of Guatemala explained that "various European merchants had gathered in the city of San Salvador and had bid for vacant offices of the cabildo with the aim of settling there; the Creoles believed that the Spanish would monopolize all commerce, obtain the judicial posts, and not allow them to live in liberty." A *cabildo abierto*, a general vecino meeting, was organized by the Creoles of all nearby areas, which the peninsulares attempted to attend, but they were repulsed "with fists." The meeting denounced the aggressions of April and May as well as various peninsular merchants, officials, and military personnel who had participated or aided the Spaniards involved. The meeting was the climax of the affair, and the dispute was later relegated to the courts.[23]

The 1755 dispute was a dramatic representation of the tension between groups in what had become a valuable commercial area of exploitation. Spanish businessmen continued to come from Spain or Guatemala to gain a share of the profits of the valuable indigo trade. The overt tension of 1755 was replaced by more subtle hostility: the usurpation of trade and profit by merchants through the manipulation of credits and prices and the seizure of land during poor years. The peninsular Spanish "became" Guatemalan, rather than Salvadoran, Creoles by settling in the capital city. In the end, this new moneyed class won out and gained control of most of the profits and created the schism that led to the post-independence wars and the dissolution of Central America. We shall see, in the period between 1810 and 1840, Salvador under the leadership of an "Arce" fighting Guatemala partially under the direction of an "Aycinena."

The Creoles were not completely without power. As long as they maintained control over the Salvadoran cabildo they could control labor and production. This gave rise to rivalries between regions and individuals deprived of labor and those Creoles in control, producing an alliance between the "weaker" Creoles and the "new" peninsulares against the Salvadoran cabildo.

"The alcaldes ordinarios are the highest [primeros] subjects of the province and owners of the richest haciendas," it was said in the 1750s, "dividing among themselves and their creditors Indians for work." During the early part of the decade the alcalde ordinario claimed that Vicente Molina took laborers to his three haciendas "leaving many without workers." Molina, however, claimed that he offered better salaries and "never used force to take workers." In 1755 the alcalde ordinario Joseph Arce accused the Spanish alcalde mayor of making private arrangements with Indian leaders, as well as selling goods to them "at prices higher than those sold by the merchants of the city." The alcalde mayor claimed that because of him the repartimiento of the city was made in common for "all classes of people, equally serving Spaniards, republicans as well as mulattoes, negroes and mestizos."[24]

The rise in the value of indigo increased the demand for labor. In 1757, for example, the cabildos of Salvador, San Vicente, and San Miguel denounced the alcalde mayor in the audiencia for excesses in the use of Indians, dividing them among "a few of the most powerful families." Although the official was never conficted, he was removed. His successor (as interim alcalde), Christoval de Gálvez, a citizen of Guatemala and the "principal protector" of the cabildos in the audiencia guaranteed the labor force.[25]

The growth of internal markets accompanied the rise in indigo and mineral production. Labor forces devoted to mining and indigo farming needed foodstuffs and clothing. Now, with the pressures on workers rising and with land diverted from food to dye cultivation, trade grew between Oaxaca, Quezaltenango, Salvador, and Honduras, with dyes and silver exchanged for clothing. The owners of mines and indigo fields purchased cattle from Costa Rica and Nicaragua and corn and wheat from Guatemalan highland areas. What had been fairly local economies with minor trade between areas now mushroomed dramatically into an extended commercial network. A system of dependency developed in many regions. Indigo, silver, and cattle areas became attached through merchant channels to cloth and wheat producing regions, which, attracted by the rise in prices for their commodities, in turn became dependent upon the commerce.

Guatemala grew in importance as the new merchant elite established its houses and organized its trade along roads that ran through the capital. Roads were built or repaired, creating the physical commercial network through the merchant center. Mestizos and mulattoes became as numerous as indigenous populations, and debt peonage was widespread. A new Central America was formed, dramatically different from its economically isolated Hapsburg predecessor, more integrated within its confines and within the European trade network.

As the Central American commercial network expanded, so too did the powers of Guatemalan merchants. But the new prosperity was a mirage. Responding to the rise in prices of indigo, producers expanded their works, borrowing more from Guatemalan businessmen to finance the growth. As indigo prices rose with the growth in trade, so did the rate of inflation. Beef cattle that cost 2.5 to 3.5 pesos a head in 1730 rose to 4 pesos in 1758, 5 to 6 pesos at the end of the century, and 6 to 7.5 pesos in 1805. Wheat brought 4 reales the *fanega* in 1723, 7 reales in 1750, and 16 reales in 1800. The rise in taxation on most goods produced throughout the same period also contributed to the inflation.[26]

Natural disaster and warfare struck encumbered producers particularly hard. Major infestations of locusts struck indigo regions between 1769 and 1773 and 1800 and 1805. Alcaldes mayores could not collect from producers for repartimiento Indians. Nor could farmers continue to make payments on loans to the Guatemalan merchants.[27]

Warfare disrupted the export of indigo to Europe, causing a drop in Central America, so that the market price was insufficient for producing expenses and debt payments. The Seven Years War (1756–1763), the War of the American Revolution (which involved Spain 1779–1783), and the diverse conflicts after the French Revolution intermittently between 1793 and 1815 created an unstable situation which, over the long run, concentrated capital in the hands of creditors who seized most of the land in forfeiture.

The power of the Guatemalan merchant was thus aided by the effects of locust plagues and warfare. This was apparent between 1760 and 1775 when war and locust infestation occurred simultaneously. Farmers had to turn to businessmen for support. The prelate Benito de Castilla, for example, owned the hacienda Yaguatique in San Miguel devoted to farming indigo. Purchased at 18,000 pesos, he improved the property by introducing some 2,000 cows, 100 mules, and 250 horses, which raised its worth to 36,000 pesos. He borrowed 32,630 pesos at 5 percent annual interest from the house of Aycinena, promising to pay annual installments of 3,000 pesos in times of war or locusts and 4,000 pesos in normal years. Because of locusts, he failed to pay in 1774 and 1775 (which the Aycinenas allowed him through their "spontaneous goodwill"), the next year he owed the usual installment of 4,000 pesos plus 4,894 pesos for three years of interest. Unable to pay, the hacienda was taken by the Aycinenas. Between 1780 and 1785, the house of Aycinena, in a similar manner, took five additional haciendas, whose total value represented 156,000 pesos. Thus, slowly, the merchant house dominated production as well as trade in Guatemala and Salvador.[28]

The credit power of the Guatemalan merchant was also extended to mining and, later, cattle. As seen above, businessmen supplied miners with quicksilver, food, and clothing, while taking the silver at the mine site from the producers. Government efforts to intervene in favor of the miner by forwarding money to mineral areas in Tegucigalpa and Comayagua only partially succeeded. Once in debt to the merchants, miners had difficulty escaping their power, and thus fell into greater debt. During wartime, government funds were diverted from the mining regions for use in colonial defense and thus provided an opportunity for businessmen to reassert their commercial authority when goods and credit were difficult to attain.

The cattle industry was controlled in a different manner. With plentiful herds in Honduras, Nicaragua, Chiapas, Costa Rica, and Salvador, the business of importing beef to the urban Guatemalan market was dominated by the city purchaser, who controlled the distribution of meat in the city through cabildo license. The producer brought his herds over treacherous roads and through potentially torrential rivers to get his meat to market to face competition from cattlemen from other regions. The buyer could thus select his cattle and price. Because of the risky business, the cowboy became indebted to the Guatemalan for the purchase of supplies, with the businessman determining the future price of cattle and the right to select quality beef from herds.

The merchant extended his dominion into the Guatemalan highlands as the century progressed. Through familial alliances and the control of important government offices, city businessmen came to dominate the production and marketing of cloth and foodstuffs with repartimientos of labor in the highlands, which continued to supply the work force required to support the economic structure. But here resistance to the intrusion by outsiders was relatively weak. The labor system was by now traditional, and the few Spanish populations in the highlands could not muster sufficient voice to oppose business and government intrusions. The old Hapsburg institutions of repartimientos of goods and labor were thus continued in the highlands, with few modifications (for example, Creole alcalde mayores with familial connections to the Guatemalan business community) to adapt to the new economic structure until the end of the century.

CHAPTER SEVEN

The Bourbon Reforms in Central America

CENTRAL AMERICA HAD changed dramatically in the first two-thirds of the eighteenth century. The foreign market for its goods had shifted away from the Pacific and from Mexico to the metropolis. New populations came to assume the control and direction of the developing economy from their center in Guatemala. The producer, who had subsisted throughout the seventeenth and early eighteenth centuries with erratic trade, now found his products in demand but his land and labor under assault by merchants who sought direct access to producing regions, while the farmer became dependent upon these same businessmen for goods and credit. The essential nature of labor changed from one that depended upon government administration to one of a free market. The economic and political character of Central America was altered from local to central control, with the major decisions concerning production and prices being dictated by creditors in the city, and rulings concerning tax collection and labor administration from Guatemala being enforced in the interior.

As the new merchants consolidated control via Cádiz and Guatemala, so too the new Bourbon monarchy worked to unite the colony politically and bring it under greater control of the metropolis. Bourbon rule commenced in 1700, but Bourbon authority did not begin to take hold until after peace was achieved fifteen years later. Then, the government began to attack the localism—the semi-independence of Central American internal matters—that Hapsburg rule had sanctioned and, by its ruling philosophy, promoted. The new rulers promulgated a series of measures that sought to eliminate the vestiges of Hapsburg rule and to consolidate power sufficiently to enhance the authority of the State.

The intellectual champion of the Bourbon revolution in government was José del Campillo y Cosío, whose 1743 manuscript, *Nuevo sistema de gobierno económico para la América*, suggested a mercantalist policy in the manner of the French and English. More important for Spain, he suggested, was the government promotion of economic growth by allowing the Indian to act as a free peasantry for an agriculture-export economy. The Indian would be treated as "Spaniards [were] of the same social class." Once a free peasantry developed, free trade between Spanish and Spanish-American ports would cause economic growth in the colonial market and in the producing metropolis.[1]

Campillo's recommendations represented the advanced economic thought of France, England, and Spain. It would later be shaped and reinterpreted by other Bourbon thinkers, Pedro de Campomanes, José Moñino, and José de Gálvez, in particular. However, conditions in each region differed and officials like Gálvez responded to these variations by instituting individual, regional measures.

In Central America the Bourbon strategy had six aims, all in the spirit of Campillo: 1) a stimulation of both communications and trade in an effort to promote greater traffic between all Spanish cities and colonies; 2) a limitation of ecclesiastical power through an attack on church property and privilege; 3) the partial support of interior producers in their grievances against the power of the Cádiz-Guatemalan merchant class; 4) government reform with the institution of Intendancies to replace the "corrupt" officials in the interior; 5) the reform of the tax structure that would provide greater revenue to finance increased government power; and 6) increased military activity aimed against both the economic and physical presence of the British in Central America.

There were two distinct periods evident in the Bourbon offensive. First, the state allied itself with the new merchant families, using their force to eliminate Hapsburg institutions, the encomenderos, the church, and "old families" whose wealth and productivity had dissipated. Second, after weakening the power of the Hapsburg sectors the government turned its assault against the new merchants who had developed power during the first two-thirds of the eighteenth century. Antiquated Hapsburg fiscal institutions had remained essentially intact, allowing most of the important economic sectors of Central America to go untaxed. The government began to institute reforms in the 1760s that changed the tax structure dramatically, altering the centuries old reliance upon the Indian for fiscal support and providing the state with sufficient funds to expand its power. The measures

Table 7.1: *Total Revenue Sent from Central America*
to Spain, 1647–1750 (in pesos)

	Total Sent	Prorated Annual Income
Jan. 1647–Feb. 1666[a]	1,478,975	101,998
Feb. 1666–Jan. 1685	1,925,321	101,333
Jan. 1685–Sept. 1706[b]	1,099,554	55,910
July 1707–Feb. 1726	463,745	24,955
Feb. 1726–Jan. 1750	1,171,733	48,822
Total	6,139,328	59,174

SOURCES: A.G.I. Contractión 4730 A and Contaduría 981
(for diverse years, 1635–1724); Guatemala 335 (1724–1750).
[a] May 1655–May 1658 and April 1659–Jan. 1661 missing.
[b] April 1693–April 1695 missing.

precipitated tension and minor violence and created the antagonism between merchant and government official that continued until, and created one of the basic, underlying causes of, the movement for independence.

Unlike their predecessors, the Bourbons did not depend upon remissions from Central America as a sign of the loyalty of the kingdom to the metropolis but viewed the colony as an integral part of the Empire from which earnings could be better extracted through commerce and more efficient government. Fiscal revenue could better serve the crown through investment in defense, road networks, and ports within the colony. Looking back, remissions of money to Spain under the Hapsburgs in the last half of the seventeenth century averaged more than 100,000 pesos a year (see table 7.1). During this time Spain's enemies gained strength. Central America's defenses were left to local residents aside from the fortress on the San Juan river and weak efforts in the Matina Valley (Costa Rica) and at Trujillo. Without a strong military presence, contraband trade flourished. Still, the Hapsburgs continued to remit tax funds to Spain rather than use them to build an adequate colonial defense. Remissions home declined at the end of the century, in part because of defense needs in the colony but also because of the decline in Indian tribute during these crisis years.[2]

The Bourbons, on the other hand, kept fiscal wealth in the colony. They didn't, or couldn't, ever extract 40 percent of the amount taken to Spain by the Hapsburgs. After 1763 and the great fiscal reforms, remissions ended and the increased revenue was used to expand bureaucracy and defense within Central America and strengthen the sovereignty of the Empire. Indeed, at the end of the eighteenth century the Bourbons imported capital into Central America for defense.

Using the taxes that had been remitted to the metropolis in the seventeenth century, the government developed the colonial bureaucratic infrastructure that the Hapsburgs had neglected. Fortifications were constructed, the military establishment expanded, defense expenditures rose, and new offices were created. Inspectors arrived to examine defense and bureaucratic needs, which led in the 1780s to a major military offensive along the Mosquito Coast for the first time since the conquest. It led as well to government expansion using a system of intendants.

Bourbons built their structure slowly and consciously, whittling away at localism and old traditions with new laws and ideas. Policies of fiscal reform and defense manifested the power of the crown in a direct rule that contrasted with the weak combination of tradition and legislation and the balancing of different colonial sectors that was the basis of Hapsburg rule.

Hapsburg rule had been based in part upon the organizational and spiritual power that the church maintained. The Dominicans, Franciscans, and other orders possessed the best-financed, most powerful, most loyal, and most united bureaucracies in the Spanish Empire. In the civil sector they collected taxes, preserved loyalty through the Inquisition, and reported conditions to the crown from throughout its vast domains. In the Americas in particular, the cleric was sovereign in the isolated communities; civil authorities relied upon him to maintain the conquest.

With the decline of their power at the end of their reign, the Hapsburgs' reliance upon the church increased. Most ecclesiastical appointments in the peninsula were made in Rome, and the church provided loans to finance the war efforts. Any attempt to limit its power was too weak. For example, in 1687 the crown asked the audiencia of Guatemala how best to diminish the number of convents in the realm ("because they burden the temporal republic"), but never took action and indeed approved new establishments later on.[3]

The Bourbons arrived in Spain with an anticlerical bias derived from their French experience, a tendency that increased with the pope's support of the Hapsburg pretender during the War of the Spanish Succession. In 1713 the crown broke off relations with the Holy See; they were not restored until 1753. But regardless of political maneuverings between church and state, Bourbon absolutist ideology ran basically against church power. Thus, Pedro Rodríguez de Campomanes' 1765 work, *Tratado de la regalía de amortización*, proposed that the "idle lands" the church controlled would be better developed if in private hands. Religious charities encouraged mendicancy in their hospitals and among the 200,000 clerics and 3,000 ecclesiastical institutions in the peninsula, which had a population of only ten million. The church's amassing of real property ran against the interests of the state and the well-being of the people.[4]

If church power ran against the absolute state's interests in the peninsula in the thought of Bourbon reformers, in the Americas, and in Central America in particular, the church represented not only a rival bureaucracy but also the local and regional interests of the colonial and Indian populations. Traditional families and Indian cofradías amassed and defended local wealth in the banking institutions of the church. Regular orders dominated the economic and social life of Indian and non-Indian alike, while they continuously gathered power at the expense of secular authorities. If the Bourbon state were to stimulate private economic development with ties to the metropolis, the church's control of labor and capital had to be broken. If taxation to develop state power were to be increased, the ecclesiastical credit institutions had to be destroyed and replaced by private individuals whose primary aim was profit from an increase in commerce.

Any effective erosion of church power also implied the destruction of vital colonial institutions. Regional Creole economies relied upon the church's credit institutions to defend them against natural catastrophes and to support local subsistence economies. Community funds and cofradías financed all pueblo obligations, tribute, and church services and guarded the economic boundaries of the pueblo. Clerics dominated Amerindia for the crown and colony, preserving the conquest to such an extent that any state attack against its power had to proceed with caution.

Conflict between cleric and crown developed, inevitably, over the control of Indian funds. In times of trouble, when death or drought limited pueblo resources, the crown continued to seek its tribute, while the cleric guarded scarce resources for himself, religious practice, or the pueblo. Whose claims to the community funds—the alcalde or the cleric—had priority was debated endlessly. The tendency throughout the eighteenth century was a slow erosion of the pueblo cleric's authority over church resources as greater power flowed to the Creole alcaldes and pueblo defenses crumbled.[5] In the beginning, the Bourbons moved slowly with somewhat ineffectual measures that increased the antagonism between state and church. Clerics and clerical organizations were inspected and criticized. Bourbon officials decried bishops' visitas to cofradías, saying their principal aim was to collect three pesos for each sodality they visited with 5,000 sodalities in the diocese of Guatemala alone. The canonic visits "are reduced to no other purpose than dances, music, dinners, games, and the [Indian] hosts must play [cards] with the visitors with large amounts of money." Sodalities under the administration of *curas* were charged with abuses in the collection of money through labor or commodities. Royal orders were issued which were supposed to limit the power of priests in the administration of the church funds, but these had success only in areas where the Spanish population was strong.[6]

Long-standing abuses were described: Creole friars with close family connections in nearby areas used Indian labor on their personal properties, paying money into community funds which they controlled. Trading the commodities that were produced on the farm, the ecclesiastics escaped taxation. This "blurring" in church role was seen by the state as both a challenge to its authority and an abuse of ecclesiastical privileges under the patronato. Missionaries were accused of conquering new lands and peoples to establish farms for themselves with a source of labor. The practice was described in 1772 as existing "since the beginning of the century when missionaries began their despotic manipulation against the purity of the mission rules."[7]

Perhaps the most irritating "abuse" of clerics was their involvement in contraband trading. Priests in Honduras were accused of doing "nothing less" than trading in illegal commodities during the War of Jenkin's Ear and after. One cleric, for example, Diego Rodríguez de Rivas, "very close to those ecclesiastical and secular subjects that communally are classified as contrabandists," requested permission to travel from Tegucigalpa to Guatemala and "went to the settlement of Guillermo Piche where he met and traded with a Frenchman established there." Such activities were said to be destroying the "independence of this Captaincy General and that of the Royal Patronato."[8]

Tentative moves on ecclesiastical power marked the first half-century of Bourbon rule. Cédulas were issued repeatedly to limit the power of regular orders in favor of secular clergy, to restrict membership in convents, and to reduce the number of cofradías. A cédula of 1717 prohibited the creation of new convents, but eight years later the crown approved the Capuchin convent in Guatemala. Another royal order in 1732 transferred the administration of Indians in Chiapas from the Dominicans to the secular clergy, an unenforceable command, because the seculars could not match the Dominicans' knowledge of the province, its people, and its languages.[9]

The crown's offensive took hold around mid-century, after peace was restored, and it had sufficient force to sustain any action. A royal cédula in 1751 prohibited the collection of tribute by ecclesiastics and ordered civil authorities to administer community funds. When enforced, the power to control labor and protect local Indian wealth from incursions by outsiders was taken from the church, so that sixty years later most community funds were bankrupt.[10] Viewing the regular orders as administrative and political rivals, the crown issued another cédula for all the American empire, declaring: "Since the reasons that existed at the time of the conquest to charge the curing of souls to the regular prelates have ceased . . . all regulars who leave their posts will be replaced by secular priests."[11] Enrolling noviates in convents was banned, except for those necessary to maintain the convents.

In the valley of Guatemala regular clerics were replaced or secularized. But elsewhere the resistance of the powerful regular orders deterred action against them. The secular clergy's ignorance of the diverse indigenous languages or customs of Central America and their reluctance to organize entradas into unsettled areas to conquer or retrieve souls forced the maintenance of the orders in the pueblos. Who would replace the Franciscans in Quezaltenango or the Dominicans in Chiapas? The frontier status of Central America forced the crown's retreat, and it subsequently ordered that the regular clergy continue to serve Central America "until such time that sufficient secular priests can be trained" to replace them. By the time of independence, however, they had not yet been replaced, and they remained dominant if weakened. The orders continued to maintain the conquest of Central America in the Indian towns of highland Guatemala and in Honduras. The friar maintained control over his Indian flock, a symbol of religion as well as stability in the changing world.[12]

Still, the crown possessed sufficient power to limit the strength of the regular clergy. Peninsular friars, unlike secular priests, were restricted in travel to the Americas. Many posts stayed vacant for years, because the number of noviates allowed entry into the convents was limited in Spain as well as America. Central America was forced to turn to New Spain for replacements for peninsulares. A similar process took place in Mexico, and by the end of the century there was a scarcity of prelates in both regions.[13]

Why didn't the church resist this erosion of its authority? Rome lacked sufficient power. Pressured by Enlightenment attacks on the faith and hierarchy and by anticlericals in France, Hapsburg Austria, or reforming despots in Central Europe, the church looked to Spain and its monarch for support. The concordat of 1753, in essence, was Rome's recognition that the Bourbon monarchy ruled the Spanish church.

Within the Spanish church there was no unity. Indeed, two distinct and rival opinions coexisted concerning Bourbon absolutism: one, supported by the Dominicans who saw the growth of royal power as contributing to a strong, Spanish church, and the other, "ultramontanist," supported by the Jesuits. Rivalry between the orders subsumed the debate over ultramontanism and absolutism. The Jesuits made alliances in their universities with the nobility supporting students of noble blood and using the Inquisition to restrict publication of absolutist and Dominican works. In between the two parties the secular clerics supported the erosion of the orders' authority.

The issue came to a head in 1766. With anti-Jesuit resentment spreading throughout Europe, the Jesuits were rumored to have instigated the revolt or *Motín de Esquilache* against royal absolutism. The next year, the crown expelled the order from all of Spain's domains.[14]

In Central America the Jesuit's presence was felt mainly in the education of an elite. In all, twenty friars were expelled. Unlike Mexico, where some were the children of the Creole elite, here only two were Guatemalan, lessening for Central America any feeling of the resentment that the exile of the sons of the elite to eastern Europe caused in New Spain. Indeed, the tense, furtive arrests and deportations, which were common in most areas of the empire, were not repeated here. In June the friars were notified, but they didn't depart until the following month.[15] The Dominicans in Guatemala assumed the position of educators of all the Creole elite. The University of San Carlos reached its height in the years following the expulsion as a center of Enlightenment and absolutist ideas.

After the Jesuit expulsion the Bourbon monarch reached its goal of absolute sovereignty over religious institutions. The economic power of the orders was seriously curtailed by the limitation upon the collection of tribute and the control of community funds by ecclesiastics. Government support for clerical administration of pueblos was reduced. The state ordered the investment of church funds in public monopolies, forcing the church to finance the growth of government. Curtailing the economic strength of the regulars, the state created an opening for private capital. In the past, ecclesiastical institutions served as banks, financing farms and rural production, but now Creole merchants entered the market using their commercial power and connections with Cádiz to cut the church out of the important production of indigo and silver, in particular, and, in some cases, of cattle.

The economic authority of the church was not completely destroyed however. Its credit institutions were maintained until the early nineteenth century, competing with merchant economic power, a rivalry that was a significant impetus for the anti-ecclesiastical sentiment held by businessmen. The merchants joined the state in attacking church influence, but the church maintained an economic role. Finally, in 1803, the crown ordered the consolidation or the payment of all outstanding loans held by the church into government coffers. Centuries-old loans and mortgages were called in, shocking unprepared farmers and home owners. Pueblo cofradías, Spanish churches, and capellanías lost their wealth at one stroke; in the future, the state would finance all ecclesiastical activity.[16]

By independence, the economic power of the church was curtailed. It still possessed some haciendas: the Dominican convent in Chiapas had 23,000 head of cattle that produced almost 7,000 pesos in 1806; the San Geronimo hacienda still supplied sugar to the capital; and there were other lesser holdings. Tithe collection rose through the eighteenth century (see appendix A), but so had the population. With the economic collapse at the turn of the nineteenth century came a reduction in church income, especially from indigo. The immense power the clergy had possessed under the Hapsburgs and the first years of the Bourbons was gone. Community funds that had been under friars' control and went for their upkeep were exhausted, drained by secular officials. Indigenous labor was now under the control of either haciendas or officials.[17]

The decline in the regular orders was severe. Of the eighty Franciscans in Guatemala before independence, twenty-seven were "old, useless, and ill." In all, 177 regulars were in Central America. The 276 secular priests were poorly trained; most were more loyal to their Creole families and farms than to the pueblos.[18] Bourbon absolutism had weakened church power significantly. Spanish liberalism among the merchant class in particular, with its anti-clerical bias, would leave heirs who would continue the offensive against church power through the nineteenth and, with Marxism, into the twentieth century.

With the power of the church limited, the Bourbons turned to attack the prerogatives of that class of merchants that benefited the most economically from the destruction of clerical power. The new merchant class had come from Spain and merged or took control of the old elite through marriage or commercial power. Cádiz capital was united with the traditional authority of the cabildo. The right to distribute urban labor forces, the licensing of slaughterhouses and sales, the distribution of water, as well as the granting of permits for shops and taverns fell under the control of the same men who traded indigo and silver to Spain. When, in 1728, the crown granted Guatemalan merchants the right to collect the alcabala, barlovento, and *almojarifazgo* (import) taxes, it gave it the fiscal authority over all of Central America, and with it most commercial decisions. Its members could ensure that they did not pay taxes, whereas competitors within and without the city might. Reporting every nine years to the audiencia, the cabildo manipulated records to show annual losses which, given the nature of the expanding economy, seems unlikely, but kept taxation at low levels.

Through their control of taxation and alliances with peninsular commercial interest, the Guatemalan merchants financed officials in the interior, using power to subsume political to business interests. In the past, local officials took loans in Spain to repay creditors: now, these same officials were supported by merchant houses in the metropolis and acted as their business agents in the diverse regions of Central America. As Central American commodities gained in the world market the practice developed. The alcaldes and corregidores administered government business as well as serving as inspectors for peninsular (and their agents, the Guatemalan) merchants. The conflict in interest led to fraud in tax collection, trade regulations, and reports on labor conditions in local areas. Nevertheless, this "corruption" was the price the crown paid to regain control of the interior areas from local and clerical power.[19]

Ultimately, the domination of capital, legal trade, taxation, and the rural bureaucracy enabled the merchant community to finance interior producers, gaining control over agriculture. Farmers, who heretofore looked to the church for assistance, now turned from a much weakened church to Guatemala and the Cádiz business community. Producers, who had looked to the community church for aid, now lost their farms to Guatemalan merchants.

The influence of the city reached such proportions that the crown took measures to stem the tide. The first attack was, of course, over the control of the valley of Guatemala and its Indian labor force. In 1730 the president of the audiencia revived a fifty-year-old controversy suggesting that the collection of tribute and administration of Indians in the jurisdiction ought to be taken from the cabildo and placed in the hands of royal officials. A number of facts had led to the recommendation: there were many tribute debts in the valley; Indian justice was impossible to administer with the limited resources and personnel of the cabildo; there had been a jail break in Amatitlán, thievery in Paxera, and abuses on haciendas and trapiches that had all gone unpunished.[20]

The cabildo argued that the debts were the result of the fifty years of epidemics since 1680 and a decline to a fourth of the earlier population. Indeed, the valley was easier to administer than before. Clerics supported the cabildo. They reminded the crown of the food shortages that occurred when the audiencia temporarily took control in 1680. Food prices would rise, the Mercedians, who owned wheat haciendas, declared. The Bethemites testified that Indians brought building materials to the city in free trade and were paid a "just price," a practice that would not continue under the Spanish corregidores.[21]

Inquiries and appeals continued until 1740 when the crown supported the city's control, perhaps to maintain imperial unity for the duration of the War of Jenkins' Ear. With peace, however, the crown ordered the division of the valley into three corregimientos in 1751, ending the city's domination. Food prices did rise in the city; the expansion of trade caused the inflation as much as the new corregidores.

Indeed, by that time, the dispute had lost its importance. The new Spanish commercial class was overpowering the old oligarchy, expanding the trade of Guatemala throughout Central America and into regular international markets. The production of foodstuffs in the highland regions to supply the city and indigo regions diminished the role of the corregidor as provisioner. The control of the valley was lost to officials at the very moment that the valley lost its monopoly as provisioner of the city with the expansion of the colonial economic infrastructure.

The reform of the fiscal system was a much more crucial move in the war on the traditional merchant class authority. Some sixty-three years after the Bourbons took control, the Hapsburg tax structure in Central America remained virtually intact. Most income derived from Indian tribute, although the demographic importance of indigenous populations vis-à-vis other groups had declined. Income from sales and import taxes had remained stable—because collection was farmed out—during a period of great economic expansion. Only taxes on minerals reflected economic reality to any degree, because the crown maintained control of collection of silver levies. Indigo, now Central America's most important commodity, was scarcely taxed.

The Bourbon offensive against the merchant class in Central America was a series of brilliant measures that we might call a bureaucratic revolution. Under the control of the visitador to Mexico,

José de Gálvez, the power of the colonial government changed dramatically. There was a precursor to Gálvez' measures in 1758 when the crown moved to establish a government monopoly (*estanco*) over the production and sale of *aguardiente* alcohol. The control over the sale of this commodity was held by the cabildo in Guatemala. The Guatemalan merchant class appealed the royal order in the municipal body, claiming that if the monopoly were given to "some private individual," he would become a "sponge" that would absorb money and encourage the spread of liquor consumption throughout all of Central America. The opposition of the cabildo was strong enough—or the resolution of the crown weak enough—so that the liquor monopoly was established, but it was awarded to the cabildo. The municipality then offered subcontracts to the interior provinces that produced "strong revenues" for the council's coffers.[22]

The Gálvez-led attack began in early 1763 with the arrival of two visitadores, Agustín de Guiraola, serving as inspector or a sub-delegate of the Mexican *Escribanía de Camara* (criminal tribunal), and Manuel de Herrarte, appointed as the first Guatemalan *Contador de Cuentas* (inspector of accounts), a position which heretofore had been located in Mexico. Their reports and actions during the next decade were to disrupt the peace and privilege of the colony, and fundamentally change government rule in Central America.[23]

The reports of the officials described the most flagrant abuses of the merchant class and their allies, the alcaldes mayores, in the collection of taxes. Major areas in Central American "have not been matriculated nor head counts taken for twenty and sometimes thirty or more years, and some, since the beginning of the century." In those areas with old head counts,

> the alcaldes mayores seize, imprison [sic] or embargo the amounts that in reality these pueblos need not pay, with the alcaldes mayores making a profit from the goods taken. . . . And if the pueblos have grown, the Indians must charge every individual the tribute [of the new count], resulting that since the quantity [listed] is much less, the officials are left with the excess. The alcalde mayor violates the royal patronage in that he can not charge more than the amount of the last head count.[24]

The fraud was customary, done by every alcalde mayor "without exception," except when the royal treasury was in its worst danger. There were other abuses in the tributary system. A reduction in tribute payments caused by the crown's pardon of women tributaries joined with pressure from alcaldes to force the payment of tributes in goods not native to areas compelled "Indians to flee from their towns . . . and live in Spanish haciendas, protected by the Spanish so that they could have labor at hand."[25]

The abuses of the tributary system were particularly important because this tax contributed more to the royal treasury than any other. The manner in which the tribute was allocated to situados—tribute of specific towns allocated for defensive needs, pensions, or the upkeep of clergy—was particularly prejudicial, because the treasury automatically gave the funds to the budgeted areas even when tribute from the pueblos was lowered because of disease or famine or without considering whether the tribute for the specific year had been paid. The situado which financed the fortresses at Granada and Petén (*situado de castillos*) was financed in part by one-half a real that the wheat farmers of Guatemala paid for the weekly labor of each Indian from some twenty-eight towns in the Guatemalan valley since the seventeenth century. But by 1763 the wheat farms were either "lost," or "lacked owners." Because the budget of the situados was based upon seventy-year-old estimates, it was constantly "in debt," because payments due the situados were never received. "The administration of the tributes must be made with greater clarity . . . excusing those responsible [in the past] for being without guilt but resulting in permitting excesses."[26]

The reliance upon tribute to sustain the needs of the government was antiquated. If the crown was to achieve its goal of an efficient administration of fiscal income that would lead to greater resources for the state, it had to reform old practices in the collection of the sales tax that did not represent real commercial trends and devise new methods of collecting income. Guiraola viewed the method employed by the Guatemalan cabildo in the administration of the sales tax as corrupt and inefficient. "The citizens are accustomed to pay a little more than 1 percent on taxes upon merchandise and fruits," Guiraola asserted. Other abuses resulted because each item or piece that entered or left Guatemala paid four reales, "whether that item weighs ten *arrobas*, or five, four or three," (one arroba equalling twenty-five pounds), or whether the item was worth "three hundred pesos or thirty, forty or fifty." Under the old system it was difficult to ascertain the value of each commodity because the crates or sacks were never opened or taken to the treasury for inspection, but were stored in private homes.[27]

Following secret orders from the crown, Guiraola directed the suspension of the contract that farmed out the collection of sales taxes to the Guatemalan cabildo and established a new, independent sales tax administration apart from the audiencia with a Spanish bureaucrat,

Francisco de Valdés, to direct it. Valdés immediately raised the alcabala and barlovento taxes. The additional charge of four reales on
the import (*entrada*) and export (*salida*) of commodities regardless of
the value of the shipments was dropped as Valdés doubled the alcabala
and barlovento levies to a total of 6 percent. He charged the alcabala
on goods that heretofore had never been taxed. All meat and byprod-
ucts were charged, as was aguardiente which the cabildo distributed
under license from the king. Valdés also instituted alcabala taxes on
individual shopkeepers in Guatemala City.[28]

These measures ended two centuries of bureaucratic practice.
They were all enacted within a four-month period. Unable to oppose
the suspension of the cabildo's tax-farm contract, the city's merchants
attacked the subsequent measures instituted by Guiraola and Valdés.
They complained to the crown about Valdés' inexperience. He
charged the barlovento levy on all goods leaving Guatemala City,
whether destined for markets outside or inside the colony, when the
tax was meant solely for exported goods. The suspended entrada and
salida taxes were levied on goods deriving from or destined for areas
outside of Central America. The doubled alcabala and barlovento
taxes, which were meant to replace the entrada and salida, were
charged on all commodities, whether internal or external commerce.
Valdés changed practices "held since time immemorial," forcing merchants to open crates and sacks for inspection for value, an action the
merchants claimed would limit commerce. But, most important, the
increased taxation would lead to increased contraband and decreased
commerce during a period when it seemed that Central America's
economy was on the rise.[29]

Despite Guiraola's assessment that the attempt by the merchants
to return to the old tax system was meant "for the convenience of
those four vecinos in the Ayuntamiento and Deputation of Commerce
opposed not only to the opening of the crates of indigo but also to the
inspection of the shipments that they receive for others," the merchants' appeal succeeded in part. The crown agreed with the businessmen's assessment of the effect of higher taxes and ordered the
return of the alcabala and barlovento taxes to the old levels. The real
cédula disapproved of many of Guiraola's methods, and reminded him
of the 1762 instructions that barred any change in the manner in
which taxes were collected.[30]

The crown wished to proceed at a moderate pace, taking control
of Central American tax collection without disrupting significant sectors of the colony. The zeal of the visitadores had threatened the royal
offensive and thus the need for retreat. Then an accident occurred

which again disrupted the equilibrium of government. The private report of Guiraola of 1763 was sent to Spain where indictments were issued against "royal officials, their families, and persons of character" in Guatemala and sent by secret dispatch to the newly-appointed president of Guatemala, Joachim de Aguirre, for implementation. However, before the charges reached the colony in 1765 Aguirre died and his predecessor, remaining in his position, received the indictments and made them public. To escape persecution Guiraola fled to a convent, where he remained for three years. Only a stern order from the audiencia allowed him to leave his sanctuary and the colony safely.[31]

The crown reacted strongly to the quasi-rebellion against Guiraola's authority. It ordered the Guatemalan members of the Deputation of Commerce and royal officials to cease resistance and transfer the control of all collection to the administration of alcabala, reiterating its full confidence in the measures taken by its appointees in the implementation of the reform measures. A sub-visitador was appointed by the visitador to Mexico, José de Gálvez, to enforce the royal decrees, while a new president and captain general was named to supervise the institution of more radical measures.[32]

With the first reforms implanted, the crown moved to extend its fiscal power. A royal order was issued in Guatemala on November 4, 1765, establishing a government monopoly of tobacco, and removing those of gunpowder and playing cards from Mexican control to direct administration in Central America. The move exacerbated an already tense situation. Tobacco had been traded in Central America since at least the early seventeenth century. Imported from Cuba, it was cultivated in Honduras for the first time probably in the early eighteenth century. It became a source of easy profit for producer, requiring little care, and for the storekeeper, who could acquire it from many producers.[33]

The tobacco monopoly was to become an essential part of the fiscal structure of the colony. As has been seen, prior to 1763 most taxes were paid by Indians through tribute. With the reforms of the sales tax in that year, the Spanish merchant and the Creole producer were compelled to pay significant amounts of taxes for the first time since the conquest. Although some mestizos and mulattoes and those Indians classified as ladinos were indirectly affected by the sales tax reform, the major proportion of the income from that tax came from the export of indigo and the importation of European cloth. Those castes still did not pay taxes, by and large. The introduction of the tobacco monopoly completed the general reforms in that all classes of Central America now contributed to the royal coffers.

Under the provisions of the monopoly, only the crown could license production, purchase raw tobacco from legal farmers, and then sell it through licensed stores throughout Central America. The government selected areas in Honduras, Costa Rica, and Guatemala where tobacco was to be cultivated, with all of Chiapas, Nicaragua, and Salvador forbidden production. When the government took control in March 1766, it immediately raised the price, which had been low in the old free market economy. From this point, whenever the government needed additional funds, it raised the cost of tobacco to the consumer. The first year tobacco was sold at one-half to three reales the pound, depending on quality. Prices were raised 25 percent in 1779 and again in 1793. Nine years later prices were raised an additional 20 percent. On the eve of independence in 1820, the monopoly paid licensed producers from one-half to one real per pound and sold it at market for six reales.[34]

The announcement of the tobacco monopoly was made simultaneously with an order applying the alcabala to resale. Technically, all goods had to pay the tax whenever they were sold, with shops keeping records for the tax collector. Under the cabildo monopoly, this, of course, was never done. Now, Francisco Valdés ordered the measure implemented and sent inspectors through the streets of Guatemala to insure compliance.

Together, the two reforms caused turmoil. "Since the beginnings of '66, public announcements of sedition and the most demonstrable acts revealing a lack of subordination and respect due to superior authority" occurred in Guatemala. The president was forced to take precautionary measures. "The universal disgust . . . [with] which the resale tax was received" was cause for rebellion, the Guatemalan cabildo reported. When, in October 1766, the crown revoked the monopoly of the Guatemalan cabildo on the production and sale of aguardiente and established a royal administration in its place, all sectors of the population were united against the measures. The chief enforcer, the oidor Don Sebastian Calvo de la Puerta—who functioned as sub-visitador—was driven from Central America, but the reforms remained.[35]

All sectors had grievances. The rise in taxes and the cost of tobacco enraged the townspeople; the loss of the right to sell aguardiente and tobacco angered small shopkeepers, and the removal of the profitable tobacco crop hurt small farmers. The merchant class, which had once dominated and had kept taxation to a minimum, was now controlled by the government, which deprived it of the profitable aguardiente monopoly. The repeated attacks on local and merchant power for the past five years drove the colonists to the point of rebellion. A petition was sent to the alférez real, Manuel de Batres, by Guatemalan artisans in November 1766 protesting the policy of the king of "taking from each individual what is his, by means of monopolies, custom duties, and taxes." The city was at the point of rebellion, and the cabildo feared violence in support of the public's demand for the "extinction of the monopolies and other expressions of poverty." The mulatto militia was ordered to turn in its rifles, and all military training of locals was suspended. Fiscal receipts were transferred to the royal palace where loyal military forces were gathered and the authors of the artisan petition were arrested. The archbishop and cabildo attempted to intervene, requesting that the captain general conciliate the rebellious factions. The president, in response, suspended the collection of taxes on all resales and distributed grain to the poor areas of the city. The "humor of the multitude," in the words of the Guatemalan president, sunk to its lowest point on December 31st, when the official wrote the king expressing fear of a great "popular uprising."[36]

The revolt never occurred. The measures of the royal officials quelled the upheaval. The Bourbon state was successful, for the moment, in implementing its reforms and its control over what had been in the past a virtually autonomous state. Attempts at government centralization exacerbated the antagonism between Creole and peninsular.

Under the tax-farming system that the Bourbons had abolished, businessmen had collected the state's revenue and tried to dominate fiscally those areas that colonial authorities could control only partially. Previously, the merchant had worked with the state to collect revenue and expand royal power; now the interests of the two diverged. Three distinct, antagonistic factions were created: the state, the merchant, and the producer, with the church now a vestige of the past and under the control of the government. The tensions between these groups continued until the independence period, causing much of the friction that led to freedom from Spain and the later dissolution of Central America.

At stake was not merely the fiscal structure of the colony but the whole social network. Under the Hapsburgs, tax reforms were piecemeal, with income increasing immediately after enactment but then levelling off. Under the Bourbons, income to the state continued to rise for forty years in some areas and until the separation of the colony from the metropolis in others. Whereas tribute had contributed at least 80 percent of all income for the Hapsburg and most of the Bourbon period and more than 63 percent from 1760 to 1763 (see table 7.2),

Table 7.2: The Relationship of Major Sources of Fiscal Income, Annual Averages, 1694–1768 (in pesos)

	Indian Tribute (%)	Quinto (%)	Alcabala & Barlovento (%)	All Other Income (%)	Total
1694–98	172,518 (73.0)	795 (0.3)	16,881 (7.0)	45,914 (19.5)	236,108
1713–17	159,171 (80.0)	640 (0.3)	11,002 (6.0)	13,461 (7.7)	184,274
1723–25	152,311 (77.5)	9,152 (4.6)	15,081 (7.4)	20,079 (10.2)	196,623
1731–35	193,888 (81.0)	4,946 (2.0)	18,349 (7.6)	21,711 (9.0)	238,904
1744–48	202,968 (80.0)	12,402 (5.0)	18,500 (7.3)	18,990 (7.5)	252,860
1752–56	173,941 (67.6)	23,949 (9.0)	23,137 (9.0)	36,098 (14.0)	257,125
1760–63	136,822 (57.1)	21,665 (9.0)	23,663 (9.9)	57,420 (24.0)	239,570
1764–68	140,139 (41.3)	16,003 (4.7)	98,989 (29.0)	83,789 (24.7)	338,920

SOURCES: A.G.I., *1694–98:* Guatemala 419, Los Ramos de Que Se Compone La Real Hacienda . . . 6/20/1698; *1713–17:* Guatemala 977, Cartas Cuentas; *1723–25:* Contaduría 976, Cartas Cuentas; *1731–35:* Guatemala 724, Testimonio del . . . todo el Ingreso de Caudal . . .; *1744–48:* Guatemala 724, Cartas Cuentas; *1752–56:* Guatemala 725, Cartas Cuentas; *1760–68:* Guatemala 726, Cartas Cuentas.

after 1763 and for the first time since the conquest, it fell below 50 percent, never to rise again. This trend continued until independence, as new reforms aimed to increase income from the non-Indian population by the sales tax and the tobacco monopoly. The tribute paid only 36 percent of the government revenue from 1771 to 1775, and, for the first time since the conquest, income from the sales tax in 1777 surpassed that of the tribute. The 1763 measures laid the basis for the abolition of Hapsburg labor practices within the next fifty years, a change that affected radically the structure of Central America.

The reforms continued until the end of the century, as the government used the resources gained from the new measures to expand its power and thus its ability to increase tax revenues. The Bourbon monarchy established its sovereignty and will—to a degree the Hapsburgs never dreamed possible—until that point in the early nineteenth century when warfare crippled the metropolis and economic depression caused a collapse in fiscal income in bureaucracy.

Once the reforms of 1763 took hold and the administration of the sales tax had been firmly established, the government attempted to extend its authority. Although meant to encompass all of Central America, the collection of the sales tax in the interior failed because the alcaldes mayores "either did not understand the literal sense of the measures or for other reasons . . . did not follow orders." A report by the sales tax administration, in 1776 determined, that the *receptorías* maintained as collection centers in the major towns throughout the kingdom were insufficient to deal with the widespread and blatant fraud. The annual average income from the alcabala tax in the capital between 1770 and 1774 was 102,524 pesos, while the product of the entire interior annually averaged but 37,803 pesos. This was extremely irregular, according to the report. Receipts (*libro de guías*) collected at the exit points (*garitas*) from Guatemala City ascertained that almost five million pesos of clothing and merchandise were sent from the capital to the interior during the quinquennial. This, combined with the tax on cattle, should have brought in much greater funds. The fraud, according to the administrator general, was due to the "bad faith" of many of the merchants, who introduced their effects secretly without consulting the guards (*resguardos*) or using receipts. In addition, there was a lack of soldiers, and, perhaps most important, "little zeal shown by the alcaldes mayores, and corregidores."[37]

Typical of the common fraud was that which occurred in the mining region of Tegucigalpa. It was reported in 1774 that the sales tax administration was missing reports from the alcalde mayor of that city, Laudio de la Vega, for the years he had been in office, since 1769. Notices had been sent since 1770 without any response, and a fine of 200 pesos was levied against the official in 1772 for his refusal to reply to a registered letter. Ordered to come to Guatemala, he failed to respond; the fiscal of the audiencia demanded that an example be made of the alcalde and that troops be sent to bring him back, shackled and at his own expense. De la Vega escaped to Nicaragua where, despite repeated demands from the central government, he was sheltered and protected by the local authorities.[38]

To establish a more efficient tax collection system, four sub-administrations, under direct royal control, were proposed for Salvador, León, Chiapas, and Comayagua. Merchants and some royal officials objected to the changes, claiming that problems would develop over jurisdictions. Who, for example, would maintain control over the valuation of indigo upon which so much of the sales tax was paid? Nevertheless, despite these weak appeals, the sub-administrations were established.

This second reform was equal in importance to that of 1763. Then the power of the central merchants was challenged and weakened; now, for the first time, the force of the Spanish monarchy was extended into the interior, employing the most sensitive and significant measure of its control, the authority to tax. Inspectors traveled to areas where officials may have visited, but never enforced royal authority. Questioning Creole and mestizo farmers in Honduras and Nicaragua about the paying of taxes, "they all responded that they never had to pay his majesty on that which they sold."[39]

The establishment of the sub-administrations was important for the future, for it defined the jurisdictions of regions, drawing lines that were used in 1786 when intendancies were established. These lines were a major factor in the definition of areas that became independent nations after the dissolution of Central America in the 1830s. District lines were defined in 1777 based upon diocesan jurisdictions, but some variations were made to accommodate areas whose trade patterns fell outside the districts. The Guatemalan areas of Quezaltenango, Totonicapán, and Sololá sent much of their cotton goods north to Chiapas and Mexico and, along with San Antonio Suchitepéquez, were placed under Chiapas control. Chiquimula and the Caribbean port of Omoa were given to Comayagua and the indigo-producing region of Sonsonate to Salvador. Modifications continued to be made until the intendancies were established. Control over the administration of Chiapas was switched from Ciudad Real to Tuxtla because the latter city was on the royal road and cacao from Soconusco passed through it. The tax collection in Honduras was more efficient nearer the mines, at Tegucigalpa, than at the seat of the church in Comayagua. All of the Guatemalan areas subsumed under other jurisdictions were returned to the authority of the general administration in Guatemala with the intendant reforms.[40]

These reforms were not, of course, implemented immediately. It took time to establish offices and authority and to develop an effective bureaucratic structure within the sales tax administration. Once established, there were administrative problems complicated by an inconsistent application of tax rates in different regions, indecision on the part of authorities or conflict between officials over the rate to charge, and the constant series of appeals by merchants that delayed the implementing of higher tax levies for years. An attempt was made in 1773 to raise the alcabala and barlovento tax (now called simply the "alcabala" tax) from 3 to 4 percent, but it was delayed for four years by numerous appeals. When the general administration of taxes decided to enforce the higher rate, the president overruled it and was subsequently upheld by the king. A year later, however, the 1778 general decree of free commerce again raised taxes, this time successfully.[41]

The general decree of free commerce also revived the almojarifazgo tax, which was rarely collected in Central America, though it had been in effect since the sixteenth century. The almojarifazgo—

to be charged at 5 percent on "goods deriving from outside the empire"—threatened the commercial progress of the Guatemalan merchants. Years of appeals delayed its implementation. The audiencia ruled in December 1785 that the levy be cancelled permanently, but changed its mind the next June. Attacks on the tax from "representatives of various commercial enterprises" in August led to a temporary one-month suspension, but, when word arrived the next month of the king's approval of the December 1785 suspension, the litigation was further confused. The collection of the almojarifazgo was not begun finally until the next year.[42]

Because of the fluctuations in tax rates, commodities were taxed at different levels in different regions of Central America, with appeals of tax rates forestalling for years the collection of many levies. The new administration of taxes was overwhelmed by its role. Because of increased trade, incoming goods flooded tax offices, making it impossible to inspect all articles immediately, and delaying their delivery to merchants. The businessmen appealed to the crown, suggesting a return to the old manner of taxing per item rather than per value and weight, but this was not allowed.[43]

The new fiscal science that was flourishing at the court of Charles III and the influence of Jovellanos led to a change in the method of tax reporting within the government in an effort to develop a more ordered system. Tax offices were told to send monthly reports to Guatemala in 1784 and to give a general accounting at the end of the year. The report was to contain the income from each tax, that which was charged, was due to be charged, or that which had not been levied. The figure from smaller, local towns had to be included in each report. Repeated appeals delayed the introduction of the system and it wasn't until 1786 that an attempt was made to begin it. But its complexities and the inability of bureaucrats to comprehend the novel system led to another suspension and the "new system" was not installed permanently until 1796.[44]

With the establishment of a colony-wide, national fiscal administration, the basis was created for the 1786, empire-wide intendancy reforms in which Central America was included. Intendants were installed in Comayagua, Salvador, and Nicaragua, with control of tax collection, police power, and police authority over their respective regions. The general political effects of the establishment of this office will be discussed later, but the effect of the reform on fiscal policy was to establish a supreme authority and a powerful representative of the crown over lesser officials (alcaldes mayores and corregidores as well as cabildos).

Table 7.3: Annual Average of Funds Sent to the Royal Coffers by Jurisdiction, 1781–1819 (in pesos)

	Guatemala Central Administration	Interior Guatemala	Salvador	Nicaragua	Honduras	Chiapas	Totals
1781–86	126,071[a]	13,257	60,650	28,520	15,835	19,818	264,151
1787–89[b]	169,466						270,278
1790–94	111,178	20,292[c]	87,453	32,557	8,730	10,068	271,163
1795–99	129,438	32,971[c]	54,780[d]	33,785[e]	8,967[f]	11,222[g]	228,594
1800–4	85,324[a]	36,358	42,544	31,313	19,448	13,607	189,194
1805–9	80,806	16,085	51,997	20,761	11,910	7,636	194,008
1810–14	91,861	18,395	45,385	19,687	7,778[f]	10,902[g]	137,138
1815–19	61,442	16,005	30,759	15,761	5,965	7,206[g]	

SOURCES: See appendix B.

[a] No data for 1782, 1786, 1801.

[b] Receipts from all interior areas missing.

[c] No data for 1793, 1795, and 1796.

[d] No data for 1796.

[e] No data for 1796

[f] No data for 1796, 1812, and 1813.

[g] No data for 1796, 1812, 1813, and 1816.

Once established (see table 7.3), the sales tax furnished sizable returns from most areas of Central America. Whereas prior to 1763, the government received some 18,000 pesos through the tax-farm to the Guatemalan cabildo, from 1780 onwards the royal coffers never received less than 100,000 pesos, even during the depressed economy of the days prior to independence.

The income shown in table 7.3 reflects economic trends of the colony in the forty years prior to independence. The central tax administration in Guatemala, by far the most important in terms of percentage of receipts, mirrors the international commercial pattern, affected by war between 1790 and 1794 and, later, 1800, and finally reduced in value in the days before independence to a half of what it had been forty years earlier. The great increase in income from Salvador from 1780 until 1794 coincides with the last, great expansion in indigo production before the collapse in the trade after the turn of the century. With substantial commerce with Peru and, illegally, with Cartagena, Nicaragua also experienced a significant economic boom in the same period. But the wars of South American independence eliminated much of its commerce, and the decline in indigo trade affected also parts of its jurisdiction. Receipts from this region were, in the days prior to independence, one-half of what they were in the eighteenth century. Honduras' income, on the other hand, did not follow the predominant pattern. With a fluctuating economy based upon mining, its production fell in the second half of the eighteenth century as capital was diverted to Salvador and as minerals became more difficult to mine. In Chiapas the economy declined constantly as a result of a population crisis and then the War for Mexican Independence that closed its nearest markets. Income from the Guatemalan receptorías in the interior area of the province reflected much of the economy of the entire colony, because of its trade in food and clothing. When production in indigo declined in Salvador, trade with that province in manufactured materials and corn and wheat from interior Guatemala also fell, resulting in a decline in fiscal revenue.

The general trend in tax income is important in that it reveals the extent of money available to the bureaucrats to finance state authority. If the Hapsburgs depended upon one constant sum coming into their coffers, the Bourbons relied upon a constantly rising income to establish new offices and expand their authority. Since the enlarged bureaucracy depended upon income based on levels established in the last twenty years of the eighteenth century, when income fell off for the subsequent twenty years, a crisis in rule developed. This was crucial to events that occurred both before and after independence in that it hampered the control of interior regions under colonial and federative rule alike.

Government policy in the implementation of its monopoly on tobacco production and sales affected every area of Central America and revealed the strong rivalries throughout the colony. Tobacco is a prolific weed that, once cultivated in a tropical climate, exists without cultivation, although, to be sure, high quality tobacco needs much care. Growing in a semi-wild state in most of the hotland regions of the colony, the cost of cultivation and harvesting was limited to labor itself and to transportation to the cities. When the monopoly was established, the crown determined that its production should be limited to Honduras, Costa Rica, and Guatemala. As production grew, other farmers and areas appealed to the government in vain for permission to grow the weed. Regions with the capability of cultivating tobacco had to purchase it from government outlets that imported it from elsewhere in the colony. Thus, Guatemala City—where the bureaucrats controlled the monopoly—and Verapaz, Gracias a Dios, and Costa Rica all earned substantial funds, and wealthy areas such as Salvador and Nicaragua were taxed heavily.

The position of the licensed producers, however, was not enviable either, as the monopoly maintained a low price of purchase. The government sometimes suspended permission to grow the product, thus causing hardship. When this occurred in Costa Rica in 1813, Creole rebellion forced the governor not only to allow cultivation, but also to permit its sale outside of government auspices.[45]

Whatever the problems of production, the tobacco monopoly was the foundation of the fiscal system, growing in revenues continuously throughout the sixty years of its existence (see table 7.4), financing much of the Bourbon government's operations. Because of its crucial importance, the state compelled ecclesiastical institutions to invest

Table 7.4: *Annual Profits from Tobacco by the Government Monopoly, Diverse Years, 1766–1819 (in pesos)*

1766–71	71,894	1800–5	192,612
1779–84	98,329	1806–11	276,273
1785, 1787–91	131,683	1812–17	263,024
1794–99	132,888	1818–19	338,250

SOURCES: See appendix C.

Table 7.5: Annual Average Income from the Sales Tax, Tribute, and Tobacco Monopoly, 1771–1775, 1805–1809, 1815–1819 (in pesos)

	1771–75	(%)	1805–9	(%)	1815–19	(%)
Sales Tax	123,094	(36.6)	189,194	(31.1)	132,973	(22.7)
Tribute	124,003	(36.9)	111,762	(18.4)	135,030	(23.0)
Tobacco	89,096	(26.5)	307,080	(50.5)	318,890	(54.3)

SOURCES: 1771–75: Deduced from A.G.G. Guatemala 744, Demostración o Resumen General de el Ingreso i Salida de la real hacienda en el reino de Guatemala en el Quinquenio Corriendo de enero de 1771 a fin de diziembre de 1775; 1805–9: A.G.I. Guatemala 835, Guatemala 530, Estado Que Manifiesta La Renta de Tabacos; for sales taxes see appendix B.

some 125,000 pesos in 1781 to assist in the expansion of production and sales administration. Part of the substantial profits earned were reinvested; the rest were used to finance defense, colonization, and the support of indigo prices.

The alcabala receipts depended upon the colony's economic health; tobacco apparently resisted the effects of the early nineteenth-century depression. A comparison of income in the first years of the new Bourbon administration, from 1771 to 1775, and the 1815–1819 pre-independence epoch (both peaceful years) is striking (see table 7.5). Tobacco gave 26.5 percent of the revenue in the earlier period, and some 54 percent between 1815 and 1819. The royal monopoly on aguardiente did not yield as much substantial revenue, although its use was as great. Annual income from it averaged 43,629 pesos between 1812 and 1816 or less than a sixth of that received from tobacco. Unlike tobacco, contraband traffic in alcohol was rife because it was impossible to ban the growth and transportation of its basic ingredient, sugar cane, although the monopoly interdicted private production. The existence of tobacco without a license was illegal and, therefore, more easily controlled.[46]

The two monopolies were, in fact, taxes against towns and cities. Tobacco and aguardiente production and consumption could not be controlled in outlying regions, but inspection was possible to some degree in urban areas.[47] However, in the last years of the colony, as state power began to collapse, so did the policing power of colonial authorities in the cities, and contraband traffic in the two commodities developed. Once independence was achieved, when regionalism caused the partial dissolution of Central America, urban areas seized control of the two monopolies, depriving Guatemala of its customary funds.

With increased revenue from all regions of Central America, the crown undertook to expand its authority and seal its frontiers. Soon after the beginning of the War of Jenkin's Ear, the government sent Luis Díez Navarro to Central America to survey the needs of the colony in order to halt the infiltration of English settlers and contraband trade and to establish strong defense perimeters. He toured the Caribbean coastline and recommended the construction of a fort in the Bay of Honduras at Omoa. Begun at war's end, it took some twenty years to complete, and then, in 1777, fell to the British during the War of the American Revolution. But a counterattack by Spanish forces under the leadership of Matías de Gálvez not only recaptured the fortress but also established hegemony over most of the English settlements on the Mosquito Coast (with the exception of Belize). The treaty of Paris of 1783 confirmed this sovereignty, although Spain was forced to grant settlers from Belize logging rights south of the British colony.

After peace was restored, the crown ordered the establishment of new colonies in Trujillo, Roatan, Río Tinto, and other coastal towns, to be populated by immigrants from Galicia, Asturias, and the Canary Islands. The treasury of Guatemala was to pay the transportation for the colonists' upkeep until they became settled and for military expenses for their defense against Sambos and the English. In this manner, the vacuum that had plagued Central America along the Caribbean coast since the early seventeenth century would be eliminated.[48]

With the conquest of the Mosquito shore and the effective implementation of many of the Bourbon reforms, the state power of the Spanish monarch was greater in 1790 than at any time since the conquest and yet, within twenty years most of these accomplishments were destroyed. There were many reasons for this dramatic collapse: the European wars, the ideology of the Age of Enlightenment, and a decline in trade. But in Central America the chief cause can be traced to an overextension of fiscal resources for bureaucratic and defensive purposes, which, when retrenched because of a decline in fiscal income, led to a collapse in central authority.

Government outlays in the first two-thirds of the century were fairly constant. Expenditures for civil and ecclesiastical salaries and expenses ranged from 119,000 to 140,000 pesos between 1693 and 1761 (see table 7.6). The only increasing expense was for the military, from 32,190 pesos annually in 1693–1702, to 151,751 pesos in 1757–1761. Most of the outlay in the latter years was caused by the construction of the fortress in Omoa.

Table 7.6: Annual Average Salaries and Expenses in Guatemala, Diverse
Years, 1693–1761 (in pesos)

	1671	1693–1702	1744–1748	1757–1761
Clergy	31,074	71,053	76,790	63,826
Civil salaries and expenses	29,570	68,405	60,660	55,424
Military salaries and expenses	4,052	32,190	68,760	151,751
Secular and ecclesiastical salaries of Nicaragua and Comayagua		21,743	37,368	

SOURCES: A. G. I. 1671: Guatemala 639, Informe of Real Hacienda; 1693–1697: Guatemala 419, Los Ramos de Que se Compone La Real Hacienda . . .; 1698–1702: Guatemala 679, Relación de todos los tributos, rentas . . .; 1744–1748: Guatemala 724, Año de 1748, Testimonio sobre todos los sueldos . . . 1757–1761: Guatemala 726, Año de 1761: Testimonio de . . . lo que importan anualmente los sueldos . . .

But after that date there was a general rise in civil as well as military expenditures. Civil salaries in 1783 cost the government 163,463 pesos. That and the intendant reforms three years later caused an increase ranging from 50 percent to three times the earlier cost in different areas of the colony. The colonization scheme became a burden on the crown's resources despite the fact that this was the most prosperous period of the colony's history. Originally, the plan budgeted 80,000 pesos for settlement costs and 20,000 pesos for the construction of boats. Failing to support itself, the colony was maintained until the end of the century, along with a constant military presence. The treasurer of Guatemala claimed that between 1782 and 1798 almost a million and a half pesos were invested in the project.[49] The colonies never took hold and, after the Spaniards departed, the government placed a large number of blacks from Haiti in the settlement.

During the last twenty years of the eighteenth century the Spanish empire was at war for almost half the time, and in the first fifteen years of the new century warfare was virtually constant. Military costs ran well ahead of income. Average annual costs between 1780 and 1800 were 231,772 pesos, of which roughly half was financed by loans from the treasury of New Spain. Expenses exceeded income by more than 50 percent annually during the depressed economic and war years between 1805 and 1809, although annual measures were taken to gain new revenues. Despite the fiscal reforms of 1763, Central America could not support itself. It could turn to Spain or Mexico for help, but when the former was invaded by France and the latter involved in a long revolutionary war, assistance ended.

As a century earlier, government reforms were inadequate. True, the Bourbon reforms were more dramatic than those of the latter Hapsburgs. Jurisdictions were realigned. Political and social hierarchies were rearranged. But the major goal of fiscal strength eluded the reformers.

This failure was critical, for what had been the strength of the Hapsburg "Reino" was now undermined, replaced with a new colonial order, society, and government whose structure was deficient. And when Spain itself came under attack in the nineteenth century, the fissure became a fracture, the center gave out, the colony became independent localities, and order was destroyed.

CHAPTER EIGHT

~~~~~~~~~~~~~~~~~~~~~~~~~~~~

At the Mercy
of the World Market

WHILE BOURBON AUTHORITY expanded, the world economy invaded. Together the two forces transformed the colony. The trade network reached out and into Central America; capital was dispersed into the interior, financing trade not just for export but within the colony as well. As high prices stimulated indigo production, land was converted from food to dye farming. High wages attracted laborers and secondary merchants to the boom regions. The Guatemalan highlands and the Honduran and Nicaraguan tablelands were drawn into the network, supplying grain, cloth, and meat for the growing laboring population of the indigo regions.

Because of the dependent network, Central America was more integrated than at any other time in its history. Before, Salvadoran farmers had traded their dye to a variety of markets, directly to Pacific shippers and Caribbean boats or through Guatemala to Mexico and Spain; now they were linked to the capital, where merchants used their control of credit and food and their political influence to join all regions. The demand for the dye, the high prices it brought, and the active shipping that purchased other goods, all drew areas other than indigo-producing ones into the monoculture.

The new order created tensions as well. Subsistence economies that had depended upon nature for prosperity became dependent upon European demand for dye as well as fluctuations of nature in their regions and the indigo zones for survival. Localities lost their communal defenses against disaster that had existed in church funds, and more subject to economic fluctuations, lost their lands to outside creditors. Monopolistic tendencies had existed among grain and meat merchants, but producers could avoid them in the informal market place. The eighteenth-century credit relationship enforced price control and merchant dominance. Rivalries had existed between families and regions, but they became more intense as the economic forces became more rigid. Earlier, Guatemalan families were closer to internal elite groups, either through family relationships or friendships. The new and dominating forces were clearly foreign, peninsular, with access to capital, with new ideologies, and entrepreneurial attitudes that violated the traditional ethic.

Government intervened to promote the expanding enterprises as well as to protect producers in the interior from merchant credit abuses. abuses. But if for a time it succeeded in channeling the commercial boom, it failed in its attempts to control credit. Business had become far too strong for the absolutist monarchy.

As long as government was strong, it could control the tensions of the new order. The strong administration was, however, linked to the economic boom. Unlike in Hapsburg times, an end to prosperity would mean a collapse of the credit system and foreclosures, heightened antagonisms, and a collapse in government power.

Still, in the late eighteenth century, the new merchant group and Bourbon absolutist bureaucracy together reached their greatest power. Like the Madrileños' full-length capes and wide soft-brim hats, the Central American traditional elements were shunted aside. The dominant families lost their social as well as their political positions. Elite, snobbish, and often better educated Bourbon officials and merchants inspired the same hatreds and prejudices that the *gachupines* suffered in Mexico. Some Creole families compromised and merged their fortunes with those of the newcomers through marriage, but others resisted and were overcome.

A series of natural disasters coincided with this economic, political, and social disruption. A major earthquake in 1751 destroyed many Guatemalan buildings, and lesser quakes occurred in 1757 and 1765. The measles epidemic of 1769 affected the Spanish as well as the Indian population. Between 1769 and 1772 locusts caused severe shortages of foodstuffs, disrupting trade and bankrupting many small farmers. The capital was in a constant state of insecurity and tension, aggravated by feuds between old and new merchants and conflict between commercial and governmental sectors.[1]

A natural disaster ignited the passions of the citizenry, beginning a seven-year battle that revealed the depth of the schisms in Guatemala. A series of earthquakes struck the city of Guatemala on July 29 and 30, September 7 and December 13 of 1773, destroying a large part of the capital as well as many other areas. With many interior walls of government buildings, churches, and merchant homes fallen, and the wood-beamed and straw houses of the working classes collapsed, the people of Guatemala were forced to evacuate the city and live in the countryside until each quake subsided. In the days immediately after the first disaster the colonial leaders met in a farm and decided to transfer the capital to a safer region in the Valley of La Hermita. There was a precedent for such a move. The original Guatemala (city) was destroyed in the sixteenth century and the settlement moved to this same location. But through the centuries this site had also proved dangerous. The volcano "fuego" that towered over the capital had erupted ten times since 1700 and three major earthquakes had occurred in the century preceding 1773. Indeed, repairs of damage to government and church offices caused in 1751 had only recently been completed.[2]

A bitter controversy ensued over the decision to move Guatemala City. The majority of the populace reacted against the transfer, the poor and the artisans as well as the landed interests surrounding the old city, led by the clergy and the archbishop. Favoring the move were the new elite of merchants and Bourbon officials, who had made and were attempting to enforce the decision. They were headed by the president, Martín de Mayorga, and those merchants whose names would remain prominent into the national period, Manuel Gonzáles Batres, Juan Fermín de Aycinena, and Simon Larrazábal.

The fundamental issues were clear: if those who wished to remain in the old location were permitted to stay, the new capital would be deprived of population and vital services. Did the cabildo of Guatemala, the audiencia, and the president have the right and power to force compliance with their decision and compel the populace to move? There were other complications as well. The church had large holdings in the old city, and although the cathedral, many churches, and missions were severely damaged, they were repairable at much less expense than building new edifices. Perhaps more important, these ecclesiastical institutions held substantial mortgages on the land and houses of most of the important Creoles and peninsulares. The transfer of the city would leave the clerics with vacant and worthless property. As was later borne out, the financially declining church could no longer offer mortgages, thereby forcing colonials to turn to the Bourbon merchants for credit.[3]

The new city would be created along the same lines as the old, with each family given a plot of land equal in location and size to that it had occupied in the destroyed capital. In the view of the populace this apparent justice was offset by the expense and burden of moving and construction. Although the crown made provisions for the economic assistance of the poor in the transfer, bad administration and corruption meant that most of the funds aided government personnel and prominent private individuals.[4]

A royal grant of the sales tax receipts collected in Guatemala for ten years following the earthquake was to finance the move. The ecclesiastical institutions were to be financed with 10 percent of the resources of all sodalities in Guatemala and Salvador. This was the first instance in which large scale projects directed by secular authorities used church-controlled funds. It was part of the general Bourbon offensive against ecclesiastical privilege, one which met with immediate clerical resistance. The audiencia ordered an accounting of all sodality resources preliminary to computing the 10 percent figure, which the church opposed as an obvious intrusion into ecclesiastical governance. The crown granted its share of the tithe (the *dos reales novenos*) to finance the construction of the cathedral, but the cost of the other missions and churches was met through the sale of church property and mortgage receipts. Added to the fiscal reforms that had depleted ecclesiastical income, these sales deepened the impoverishment of the missions.[5]

Clerical resistance became an open rebellion joined by much of the populace. There was, of course, a fundamental conservatism that preferred the traditional location to a move that offered no hope of change in the conditions of everyday existence. The poor were settled in their city; the artisans were dependent upon goods and labor from nearby Indian towns; and the old Creole families who held land near the old capital profited from provisioning the city and faced the loss of those profits to the new aristocracy in Nueva Guatemala. The Indians in Jocotenango who had worked as masons refused to move their pueblo and were forced to transfer to a site near the new capital. The Spanish residents of Antigua Guatemala with more rights resisted forcibly. After a cédula was issued by the king in July 1775 the opposition became open rebellion. From its site in La Hermita the cabildo of Nueva Guatemala reconsidered its earlier support "the major sector of the inhabitants do not wish to move . . . and remain determined in Antigua Guatemala." Only government officials, Indian laborers in repartimiento, and those who were to become the new aristocracy of the capital resettled.

The new city faced severe difficulties. Food and labor were short, and water supplies had to be carried until a water system could be built. Nevertheless, the crown stood firm in its resolution that the city should be moved and ordered President Mayorga to take all action necessary to enforce its legislation. The official transferred the military guard, removed all police protection, and ordered the closing of stores, forbidding the sale of any article in the old city. The archbishop, at the head of the resistance, compared the transfer of sites of the cathedral to that between Antioch and Rome and claimed he was powerless to act without license from the pope. When the president and audiencia persisted in their order that ecclesiastical officials move, they were excommunicated. In April 1778 major demonstrations for three days demanded the return of the capital. The two sides were stalemated—one with official power, the other with popular support— until 1779 when the archbishop was ordered home to Spain by higher church officials and the president resigned "for reasons of health." The outbreak of the War of the American Revolution, which involved Spain, brought about a compromise that allowed those who wished to remain in Antigua to do so though the capital was removed to the new city.[6]

The Indians in repartimiento bore the brunt of the construction. In the early days of resettlement there was an insufficient supply of labor and workers were abused, compelled to work four days each week without food or pay. Indians and criminals who were used in draft labor suffered many fatalities. As the construction proceeded throughout the remainder of the century, Indians as far away as Chiapas were forced to furnish goods for constructing public buildings and monasteries.[7]

Other Spanish areas were affected negatively by the construction. The city of Comayagua suffered earthquakes that destroyed public buildings in 1773 and 1774, but its restoration was neglected because all available resources of the colony went to Nueva Guatemala. Comayagua's cathedral remained in ruins despite appeals in the 1790s and thereafter, and it was never rebuilt. Salvador was destroyed by an earthquake in 1776 "that did not leave a house standing,"[8] but its labor drafts and tithe also went to Nueva Guatemala.

The establishment of Nueva Guatemala ratified Bourbon and merchant power that had been developing throughout the century. The merchant city, with new families tied directly to the crown and to business allies in Cádiz, was built to serve as the seat of power, dominating all areas of Central America. At the head of the new order was Juan Fermín Aycinena, whose reward for his support of the crown was the title of "marquis." He was the only such noble created in Central America during the eighteenth century. He was given the most prominent plot of land in Nueva Guatemala, on the central square across from the presidential palace and cathedral and next to the customs house. There he built a house of fifteen rooms, seven patios, and twenty-four stores worth 75,000 pesos. From this position the marquis and his descendants controlled much of the economic and political life of Central America until well after independence.[9]

The Guatemalan merchant elite, which the Aycinena family led, reached its greatest prosperity between the end of the War of the American Revolution and the Napoleonic struggles. The great expansion of the British textile industry combined with the scarcity of dyes of the world market—the result of the loss of indigo-producing areas in the Carolinas—forced prices to their highest levels. The British government reduced tariffs on indigo as demand in Bordeaux and Amsterdam created a seller's market.

But if the city prospered, few in the countryside enjoyed the fruits of the demand for indigo on the world market. The dye producer, dependent upon the merchant for credit and goods, was compelled to sell his produce for less than market value. Theoretically, the producer and merchant met at an annual fair in which a just price was determined, but the economic power of the businessman was too strong and the farmer remained constantly in debt. Unlike the small, cohesive merchant class, indigo producers were socially and geographically disparate. Indian pueblos, poor mulatto and mestizo farmers, and wealthy Creoles all farmed the dye. With most production derived from small or medium-sized farms (see table 8.1), no commercial unity could be formed against the monopolistic Guatemalans. Even the wealthiest farmer in 1771, the Cañas family, produced about one-half of one percent of total production. Thus, at market, the indigo grower "had to sell his goods for a fourth of their real value—which he never knew—to provide for the needs of his house and family." When there was sickness, or when the members of the family found it impossible to work, he was ruined forever. During the boom years it was said that most farmers remained "reduced to their old miserable existence, mortgaged for more than their intrinsic value." Most of the profits from indigo fell to Guatemalans and their mercantile allies in Cadiz.[10]

The same colonial-merchant-producer connection was repeated in most other sectors of the Central American economy. Funds were needed by Honduran miners to purchase mercury and powder to exploit their domains and to acquire and sustain beasts of burden. Mercury and gunpowder were brought to Honduras by the Guatemalan merchants who exchanged them for silver. Excluding that profit earned on goods sold to miners, and on interest on credit, Guatemalan

Table 8.1: Relative Size of Indigo Producing Farms in
Central America.

Farms	1748	1771
Small	121	191
Medium	83	117
Large	16	31
Total	220	339

SOURCES: Deduced from tithe records of 1748 in A.E.G. Diezmos de San Salvador, 1680–1811, fols. 12–19, and of 1771, Cuenta del Añil Que Entró Perteneciente al Diezmo, A.G.G. A 3.22, Leg. 2122, Exp. 32075. See Rubio, *Historia del Añil*, 1: 67–76, and 2: 325–63, where these documents can also be found.

Note: I define small farms as having tithed 0–10 pounds of indigo in 1748 and 0–10 pesos of indigo in 1771; medium farms, 11–100 pounds in 1748 and 11–100 pesos in 1771; and large farms, over 100 pounds in 1748 and over 100 pesos in 1771.

merchants earned from 10 to 20 percent on the silver minted in the capital.[11]

The merchants dominated provisioning in much the same manner. They purchased cattle from Honduran and Nicaraguan cattlemen at fairs held in Salvador or Guatemala with prices theoretically controlled by the government. The power of the purchaser to control credit often negated state intervention. Cattlemen, given loans at 6 percent interest, were contracted to produce a number of cattle in good condition at a predetermined price. Their risks included cattle diseased, lost, or injured on the way to market. Loss of weight on the drive meant that they had to be fattened before being sold. In 1797, out of 14,134 cattle brought from Honduras, it was said that 2,637 died of illness, 186 were lost on the road, 114 eaten by the herders, and 1,593 sold on the road with only 8,614 head—about 58 percent—arriving at the fair. Two years later a cattleman claimed that it cost 121 reales to raise and bring a steer to market and the final sale price was 127 reales—a profit of six reales *excluding* the loss of cattle on the road.[12]

Merchants maintained their economic domination through other methods as well. As Creole producers in the interior fell within the money and credit economy of Guatemala and the world, they concentrated on trade goods to the exclusion of subsistence crops so that food was actually imported. A Guatemalan wrote in 1808 that Salvadorans work with such dedication in the indigo works that "they forget to cultivate food for themselves." Partial crop failures from locust infestations or from a paucity or overabundance of rain created famine and dependence upon traders. In addition, all cloth for clothing and blankets had to be imported from the Guatemalan highlands.

The great demand in the south encouraged the alcaldes in the highlands to expand repartimientos of Indians to produce and transport clothing and food. Towns near Quezaltenango and Antigua Guatemala devoted their energies to cotton. Guatemalan regions such as Chimaltenango and Mixco often sent food to Salvador and Honduras as well as to Guatemala City. The merchants thus came to dominate much of the intra-colonial trade in both exportable money commodities and necessities.

Only one major product seems to have escaped the control of Guatemala's merchants and Bourbon bureaucrats. Cacao plantations flourished in Rivas (Nicaragua) and in the Matina Valley of Costa Rica on the Caribbean coast with the commercial expansion of the late eighteenth century. Rivas exported almost 800,000 pounds in 1777. In 1768 an English official reported some "300 Spanish of all colors" from Cartago tending 180,000 trees (probably an overestimate) on 120 haciendas, spread out over eight miles. Production was expanding daily. The cacao was traded to Cartagena legally and, illegally, with Providencia, Jamaica, and Curaçao, as well as with the English-allied Mosquito Indians. In peacetime this illegal traffic infuriated Spanish traders and government officials in León, who attempted to tax and control the trade. Merchants in Granada were implicated in the traffic as boats from this port exported Rivas cacao or went to the Matina Valley to collect Cartago cacao and then to English colonies to affect the trade. Thus, a similar antagonism between regions in Nicaragua and Costa Rica existed as in the north.[13]

But indigo was the chief factor in the expanded colonial economy. As long as prices continued high for the dye, Central American merchants would possess sufficient capital for credit for producers. But a decline in demand or production would inevitably lead to a decline in profits, which would affect all areas of the colonial economy.

As part of its general offensive against merchant power the Bourbon government attempted to limit the control of credit of the Guatemalan business community. Flush with the success of resolving the earthquake controversy and of opposing British power on the Caribbean coast, President Matías de Gálvez issued a series of orders that aimed to usurp the credit monopoly. He appointed an official to impose fair prices and supported the establishment of an organization of indigo producers. More importantly, he oversaw the creation of a revolving fund to finance indigo production at lower interest rates than those charged by the merchants. This fund, the *montepío de añil*, was supported by an initial government loan of 100,000 pesos from the tobacco administration and was to be financed subsequently by a four peso export duty on every *zurron* (214 pounds) of indigo.[14]

The Gálvez reforms were inadequate to break the merchant monopoly. Loans granted to the farmers went to the largest and most powerful producers in Salvador and were not repaid. Thus, the "revolving fund" did not revolve. Within a decade the organization of indigo growers was in a "state of uselessness," with growers being "ruined by the monopoly and usury of the merchants." The *montepío* fund was virtually bankrupt by 1801, with all the fund's assets (some 340,000 pesos) in outstanding debts. The following year only twelve people received loans totalling 17,625 pesos, and within five years the fund ceased its activities. Similarly, the government's attempt to control prices failed. "The only reason for the setting of prices," it was claimed in 1802, "was to [form a basis for] the paying of taxes." By that date indigo production had diminished, with many farmers bankrupt, their lands taken by Guatemalans. The merchant remained all powerful.[15]

Other Gálvez reforms involving producers and merchants suffered a similar fate. He established a bank in Tegucigalpa that allowed silver miners to exchange their silver for coinage at the local level but prohibited merchant dealings with the bank. Theoretically, the institution removed the major expense to producers of getting silver to the mint in Guatemala, but this did not deal with the problem of credit. Miners still relied on Guatemalan financiers and commodities to survive. The bank reform was moribund and, in 1792 merchants were permitted to use the bank. Thus, Guatemalan commercial power survived the Gálvez reforms and was restored to full status within a mere decade.[16]

Gálvez also tried to control prices in the cattle trade. Cattle were usually sold at annual fairs, brought from Honduras, Nicaragua, and as far off as Chiapas and Costa Rica. As with indigo, Gálvez attempted to regulate prices at the fair, but again the merchants resisted by using the power of credit in illicit deals. Dependent upon the businessman for their supplies, cattlemen were compelled to negotiate sales outside the fairgrounds, and failure to do this left the producer with unsold stock that had been transported at great cost over long distances. "The fair," it was claimed, "far from meriting that name, has been a site for oppression, monopolies, and violences." As with silver and indigo Gálvez's price fixing of cattle failed. It was suspended in 1791 and permanently eliminated nine years later. Later on, with the decline of indigo production in the early nineteenth century, Salvador became a prime area for cattle raising, and this, combined with the consolidation of debts owed the church, destroyed much of the Honduran cattle industry.[17]

The tension between rural producer and urban merchant continued and exacerbated the rivalry between regions and families. Some interior families prospered, to be sure, but wealthy families tended to move to Guatemala, leaving their lands to agents to do their work. Most farmers, ranchers, and miners had lived at subsistence levels, and when prices rose with the increased commercial activity, interior producers could not keep pace with expenses and fell into debt. And when war and locusts damaged the Guatemalan indigo trade, first in the 1770s and then, more seriously, between 1800 and 1808, the interior producer went bankrupt. The failure of the eighteenth-century economic structure thus reinforced regionalism, with the interior producers blaming the failure on the merchants. The consequences of these recriminations will be seen after independence with the collapse of national sovereignty.

The Bourbon offensive against merchant power and interior weakness culminated in 1786 and 1787 with the establishment of intendancies in Salvador, Chiapas, Nicaragua, and Honduras. The offices were given control over the administration of justice, police, war, and taxation. Within their jurisdiction, intendants were to be the chief judges of appeals in judicial and commercial matters, with appeals concerning taxation to be resolved by a *Junta Superior* of finances in Guatemala and, beyond it, the monarchy. The reform established royal authority at a more local level, depriving "corrupt" alcaldes mayores and corregidores of their force. At the same time the intendancies centralized rule. In Honduras the alcaldía mayor of Tegucigalpa was abolished and placed under the direct control of Comayagua; in Nicaragua the corregimientos of Realejo, Matagalpa, and Nicoya were eliminated, while the city of Granada was placed directly under León's control; and in Chiapas the gobierno of Soconusco was also eliminated and placed under the jurisdiction of Ciudad Real. In all, some thirty-two provinces or jurisdictions were reduced to fifteen by the reforms.[18]

The intendancy reforms were the last move in the Bourbon attempt to control prices and credit as well as the culmination of the reform of fiscal administration in Central America. By creating a tax-collection agency independent of the merchant class and its allies, the alcaldes mayores, a firm foundation was laid in the attempt by the crown to develop its sovereignty in the interior of Central America. Using increased revenue from the tobacco monopoly and higher taxes, bureaucrats were paid better and did not have to rely upon merchants' financing. Because they did not work closely with the central merchants, intendants tended to ally themselves with local families against the power of the Guatemalan merchant, and they jealously guarded their prerogatives against Guatemalan business practices and even unfavorable decisions made by the president of the audiencia.

The Bourbon offensive thus succeeded only in that it broke much of the hold the merchants had over the interior's bureaucracy. But the commercial power of Guatemala remained intact. The interior still had to rely upon credit for production and upon the merchant class to export its merchandise to the exterior.

The "victory" of the merchant class was symbolized by the establishment of a consulado or merchant guild in Guatemala. Like their counterparts in Caracas, Buenos Aires, Havana, Cartagena, Guadalajara, Vera Cruz, and Santiago de Chile, the businessmen petitioned the crown to establish a consulado that would give them judicial control over all commercial traffic as well as the maintenance and authority over roads and ports. Almost all of the signatories were new, eighteenth-century merchants. With the coming of the French Revolution and the subsequent European wars, Charles IV was forced to concede the establishment of the guilds in these cities, but he refused to allow the new organizations to collect all taxes as they had requested.[19]

Thus, ironically, a decade after President Gálvez attempted to restrict merchant power, merchant power was now predominant. The guild ruled over trade throughout Central America. A tribunal named and composed by the consulado judged all commercial disputes, though protests from farmers led the crown in 1803 to exempt producers from the merchants' decisions. A 5 percent import tax, the *avería*, financed guild operations, the functions of the commercial tribunal, and the maintenance of all roads and ports. In practice, however, the funds were sufficient only to maintain the road to Omoa.[20]

The guild symbolized the power of the merchants of Central America, but the Guatemalan businessmen were not a unified group. Despite the preponderant position held by the Aycinena family in the last forty years of colonial rule, there were other factions in the business community. Struggles for control of the guild reflect these schisms. Article twenty-six of the consulado charter prohibited its officers from holding any other public office, thus preventing leading business figures from serving on the guild and the cabildo. A faction arose composed of newly-arrived Spanish merchants who rivaled the Aycinena group much in the same manner as the Aycinenas had when they fought the old Creole merchants at mid-century. The sectors exchanged power in the consulado until 1808 when the new peninsulares gained control, sustained after 1810 by a conservative president of the audiencia, José de Bustamante.[21]

The power of the Bourbon state rested upon its ability to stimulate trade to bring Central America into the economic expansion of the late eighteenth century, to control the merchant community, and to tax the profits of the growing commerce. With the greater fiscal income, an expanding bureaucracy could better control and stimulate additional commerce. But merchant and official were pitted against one another as businessmen sought the most profitable trade openings through licit or illicit channels, which forced the Spanish government to take strong measures against contraband. Only as long as Spain could control the empire could it be secure in the benefits of high taxation. An English (or any non-Spanish) article had to pay, at a minimum, a duty of 35 to 40 percent to enter Spain. Another 7 percent was levied for the right to send foreign goods to the New World, and still another 20 percent was charged to enter the Spanish colony. At a minimum, the tax on English goods was 65 to 70 percent. Added to the expense of shipping goods via Spain, rather than directly between Britain and the Caribbean, the costs made contraband traffic far more profitable than legal commerce.[22]

But contraband traffic was not constant. Its importance rose and declined with the power of the Spanish state as well as other commercial factors. Illegal trading had its risks and additional costs as well. Spanish officers had to be bribed and then might seize a valuable shipment anyway. Trade often went through the lands of the Sambos and Mosquitos, who were unpredictable at best, although ostensibly the allies of the English traders.

The eighteenth-century British contraband trade had political as well as economic motives. Depending upon the English government in power and the governor of Jamaica, policies, more or less deliberate, were aimed to attract more trade and to destroy Spanish hegemony in the Caribbean. During the War of Jenkin's Ear, for example, the governor of Jamaica sent an agent to the Mosquito shore, one Robert Hodgson, to carry out both policies. Hodgson arrived by chance a few years after Luis Díez Navarro, the Spanish engineer, came to Guatemala. The two were rivals for the next forty years. Hodgson directed Mosquitos raids against Spanish settlements and contraband trading, while Díez Navarro reconnoitered the coast, designed the defense of Spanish sovereignty, and directed the construction of the fortress of Omoa.

Hodgson's secret dispatches about the western Caribbean contraband,[23] together with Díez Navarro's reports, indicate the extent of English penetration into Central America throughout most of the eighteenth century. The Englishman's letters of the 1740s reveal that the English wanted dyewoods—not indigo—from the Mosquito Coast and that the chief problem for the English was not the Spanish but their own contraband trade. English production at Belize of dyewoods was substantial; they exported to Jamaica some 13,672 tons worth £109,376 (sterling) in the war year of 1745 alone, or half the value of the annual indigo exports from Central America. But what the English regarded as illegal was considerable; Dutch boats from Curaçao brought "goods from India, wine and aguardiente, all much cheaper than we [English] can sell." When, in 1755, the woodsmen complained that the Bay of Honduras area they farmed was logged out and that they needed to expand into Spanish territory, Hodgson replied they had to "make some proof of restoring the trade to our country" before the English would assist them. Ironically, Hodgson's solution to the contraband problem was to imitate the Spanish-Caracas establishment of a company to guard the trade and to exchange goods and slaves for dyewood.[24]

Spanish merchants as well as officials aided and abetted the trade that flowed between Central America and the English on the Mosquito shore. Every Jamaican merchant who visited the Matina shore paid 150 pesos annually to the Spanish lieutenant, who, in turn, passed along 500–600 pesos to the Governor of Cartago for his employment. Hacendados in the area maintained storehouses which were constantly luring the Mosquitos. Hodgson, for example, sent an English-educated Spaniard named Ruíz to Central America in 1751, where he enlisted a brigadier in León who believed that he was soon to be named president of Guatemala. The Central American official met with Hodgson and claimed that "he marvelled at the great risks the English took to trade in a little wood, Sarsaparilla, and Carey when they could gain licenses to cut the wood and buy whatever they needed easily." The brigadier suggested 50,000 pesos as a price for protection for the trade; the plan failed when the officer was not appointed president. The plot, however, anticipated similar schemes enacted under independent liberal governments eighty years later.[25]

　　　The steady flow of contraband from Central America to the Mosquito coast declined dramatically after 1750. "The number of English inhabitants on the Mosquito Shore have declined during these years," Hodgson reported in 1768. "There are but 150 dispersed throughout the country." Spanish officials continually overestimated the English trade; Hodgson reported the trade skimmed only a portion of the total indigo produced. In 1775 some 100,000 pounds of indigo were exported illegally (about a tenth of that produced), together with 700,000 pounds of dyewood. The following year some 300,000 pounds of sugar went through the Mosquito coast. The latter two products were not in demand in the metropolis and could not find any outlet through legal channels.[26]

　　　Why the decline in commerce? With the Omoa fortress there was a Spanish presence on the coast. But the fort served more to guard the Guatemala-Cádiz trade route than to extend Spanish sovereignty over the shore. More importantly, the interconnected trade and credit network kept indigo within the empire. Loans from Cádiz to Central America and Guatemala to Salvador were paid with indigo; taxes and tithes were paid in indigo; Guatemalan highland grain and cloth for Salvadoran workers were paid with indigo.

　　　Other Bourbon legislation aided the growth of this network. In 1765 Charles III authorized legal commerce between Caribbean ports and Central America. Thirteen years later he broke the Cádiz monopoly and allowed Peninsula ports access to America. Still, these measures were not of critical importance for Central America, although they may have weakened contraband channels in Jamaica. Eighteenth-century trade from the Bay of Honduras went directly through Cádiz, which re-exported indigo to northern Europe. Credit, merchant representatives, and the authority of the *Cinco Gremios de Madrid* reenforced the Guatemala-Cádiz connection.[27]

　　　Contraband trade was reduced not so much by military action as by the creation of the interrelated trade network, a network that the government encouraged. Still, there was a military danger on the Mosquito shore. Hodgson was first sent to the region during the War of Jenkin's Ear to explore the possibility of a conquest of Guatemala with "two or three thousand" Mosquito Indians. Forty years later, in the War of the American Revolution, the English planned to seize Omoa, attack Nicaragua, "divide the Americas and take control of the Pacific commerce." But their expedition was crippled when half the soldiers sent to Jamaica from Britain died before the Central American attack could be organized. When the British took Omoa disease struck again and Gálvez's counterattack drove them out. The Gálvez offensive eliminated dyewood loggers from the Bay of Honduras, and proceeded down the Mosquito Coast to reduce English power to its weakest point in a century. "The Spanish have won the confidence of numerous tribes," in the vicinity of Bluefields, Hodgson wrote, "and they fortified the mouth of the Río San Juan.[28]

The Treaty of Paris in 1783 later restored the rights of loggers south of Belize in the Bay, the English recognizing Spanish sovereignty, and the Spanish guaranteeing the protection of the loggers and settlers. Spain named Robert Hodgson as its representative on the coast, the very man who had been attacking them for forty years. The English presence, albeit under Spanish authority, guaranteed contact and created the potential for expanded commercial interchange.[29]

Still, the 1780 battles mark the zenith of Bourbon strength in terms of fiscal income, economic power, and national defenses. The English "are almost exterminated," Hodgson lamented, "the rich commerce in dyewoods ruined for now and Great Britain is at the eve of losing the Mosquito Coast and the Honduran territory forever."[30] In contrast to the Hapsburg fiscal and military weakness of eighty years earlier, Bourbon absolutist measures and the new western economic expansion had seemingly solidified Spanish rule in Central America.

CHAPTER NINE

The Indian Under the Later Bourbons

MORE THAN ANY OTHER group in the colony, the Indian resisted the great changes at the end of the eighteenth century. Pueblos remained outside colonial culture and maintained their amalgam of Christian and Amerindian religions and customs. Still, the centralization of Bourbon power and the change in the economic structure of the colony profoundly affected the Indian, in some ways positively, and in others negatively. The expansion in trade and integration of Central America into the European commercial sphere accelerated the demand for Indian labor, and labor practices that heretofore were illegal—such as the use of Indians in indigo obrajes or forced labor in the indigo fields—were now permitted by legislation. Land that had been devoted to growing foodstuffs for the barter economy was converted to money crops, and food had to be imported from distant areas and purchased with specie. Valuable Indian common lands in indigo-growing areas fell before the colonists' assault. When tribute was ordered paid in coinage in most areas, Indians were forced to leave their pueblos and work in cities and haciendas. Debt peonage developed as a major form of labor, first complementing and then supplanting the repartimiento.

The state invaded the sovereignty of the pueblo. The attack on church power was, to some degree, an attack against its autonomy in the Amerindian pueblos. With the decline in the number of friars in Central America and in the wealth of the orders, clerics could no longer protect their wards, and the authority of the alcaldes and corregidores grew. The insatiable demand of the state for fiscal resources led to the "conquest" of pueblo community and sodality funds, which were shifted to the public treasury and to the control of Spanish officials. The change deprived the pueblos of resources to defend themselves against outside invasion, against debts incurred for food or for tribute, and this too contributed to the rise in debt peonage.

There were some benefits too. Money was now earned in international commerce and officials and merchants did not have to rely as much upon the Indian pueblo for their upkeep. At the end of the century, the crown banned the use of the repartimiento and, with the power of centralized government, the legislation was enforced. Once the demand for indigo ended, British textiles began invading the Central American market, destroying the local cotton trade and reducing the demand for indigenous labor. The Indian was able to return to subsistence farming.

The Amerindian population increased. There were terrible epidemics, particularly in Chiapas, but after smallpox vaccine came to Central America and, concommitantly, the demand for labor lessened, the Indian population increased to the highest point since the conquest.

Still, the pueblo's defenses were weakened. Hapsburg rule had been based upon a two republic policy that guarded the sanctity of the Indian village. Although the Bourbons continued to bar non-Indians from the pueblo, they sought to create an agricultural, wage-earning class, a free peasantry. If the encomienda and repartimiento were abolished for the benefit of the Indian, the subsistence economy and the common understanding between colonial and Indian of the Hapsburg period were also lost. The institution that defended the pueblo, the church, was now attacked by both the state and modern thinkers. The Enlightenment and Bourbon ideas of free peasantry may have theoretically recognized the Indian as the equal to the colonist, but it also led to essays on Indian mendicancy and alcoholism, and in the end provided the justification for the destruction of the pueblo's sovereignty. The thought of the Enlightenment was also alien to indigenous religions. Once independence was achieved and the Creole became colonial ruler of the Indian, the two greatest champions of the Indian's prerogatives—the church and the Spanish crown—were eliminated. Common lands could be invaded and abusive labor systems could develop without fear of state intervention. With independence, the Indian pueblo lost its authority.

Under the Hapsburgs and early Bourbons, the Indian provided the state with most of its financial resources through the payment of tribute to alcaldes mayores and corregidores. These same officials, together with local Creole producers, worked in turn to use Indian labor in repartimiento for their personal profit. Tribute collection and repartimiento of labor and goods were so interrelated that the state was not able to abolish one without the other. All efforts to ban the repartimiento of labor met with stubborn resistance from colonists, who saw the act as a threat against the society as a whole. Legislation that prohibited alcaldes mayores and corregidores from profiting from their position through repartimientos of goods was ignored by all levels of the state, where it was understood that officials could not sustain their position in the Indies without this income.

Similarly, the power of the cleric within the pueblo was also connected to the tribute/repartimiento system. As the town leader with the strongest ties in the colonial society, the priest controlled the community and sodality funds that were frequently used to pay tribute. As the representative of the crown, he saw that the Indians remained loyal and sufficiently industrious to provide their annual tax to the officials. The village priest commanded more respect for his spiritual function than the alcalde mayor or corregidor or any other secular official could.

The crown's antipathy toward the repartimiento, together with the Bourbon attempt to limit ecclesiastical power in all areas of society, led to measures that altered these pueblo institutions. New legislation attempted to change or abolish the repartimiento, the tribute, and the role of the pueblo cleric, and, in turn, changed the basic nature of the indigenous labor system and the position of Creoles who depended upon it.

Unlike the Hapsburgs, the Bourbons attempted to integrate Indian pueblos into colonial society by compelling them to enter the money economy and by bringing village institutions under the control of secular authorities. Legislation in 1747 ordered that tribute heretofore paid in goods should be paid in coin. Although the order was enforced irregularly throughout Central America, it nonetheless brought pueblos into the colonial money system. Drought that had destroyed corn and bean crops could no longer be offered as an excuse for failures to pay tribute, because Indians could earn pesos from other work. Pueblos lacking sufficient funds fell into debt peonage. The structure of the pueblos was undermined. As Central America became more integrated into the western European economy through indigo, the Indian became more dependent upon the colonial society, particularly in those areas (such as indigo-producing Salvador and Nicaragua) where the money economy was strongest.[1]

The commutation of tribute institutionalized great differences in the amounts each pueblo paid. The inflationary economy of the late eighteenth century caused some Indian goods to rise in price while others retained their earlier value. Goods worth two pesos in 1747 sometimes cost as much as three, forty years later. The amount of tribute paid was expressed in terms of commodities (for example, "two fanegas of corn"), but had to be paid in coin. The difference in relative values of commodities changed the amount of tribute each pueblo paid. A survey of tribute paid by the pueblos of Nicaragua in 1787 showed fourteen pueblos paying less than a peso annually, eleven between one and two pesos, twenty-eight, two pesos, and eighteen, more than two pesos. In San Salvador, only twenty-four pueblos paid two pesos, with nineteen paying less and eighty-seven paying more, and in Chiapas, most pueblos gave three pesos annually.[2]

Some pueblos were unaffected by the measures; those nearest to Spanish populations had already adapted to the colonial economy; others possessed a strong enough internal structure to resist. But weaker pueblos were destroyed, with Indians "living divided in different types of haciendas and many not knowing their pueblos." Some Indians became wanderers (*forasteros*) who earned their living roaming from ranch to ranch.[3]

Within those pueblos that maintained themselves, village leaders and clergy preserved the custom of contributing time and labor to work in community fields for the benefit of community funds. This source of revenue came under attack in 1776 when the control of community funds was given to the alcaldes mayores and corregidores. Every Indian was required to work a specified amount of land, the proceeds to supply the cleric's wine and salary and the remainder controlled by a government fund that would finance pueblo expenses. By destroying the communal nature of the work the state encountered resistance. Indians complained in Central America, as well as in Mexico, that their work supported the government, not the pueblo. Their sense that their work no longer benefited them meant that Indians avoided communal labor, with the result that the government introduced a tax on every Indian of two reales (¼ peso) to sustain the fund.[4]

The attack on pueblo resources yielded substantial funds for the crown. Whenever the government needed money, it used community funds (called "*hechar mano*" or "put the hand in"). After the French invasion of Spain, a contribution of over 100,000 pesos was sent to the metropolis from the community funds. A review of the community funds existant in the Intendancy of León in 1815 showed 76,000 pesos in loans to the government and private individuals, only 8,800 pesos owed by Indians. Only 25,000 pesos of available resources remained in the royal coffers. By independence, Central American pueblos no longer had financial resources for a time of need.[5]

There was one other source of pueblo wealth, the sodalities. Many were involved in the cattle trade and indigo production, competing with Creoles with the double advantage of being Indian and ecclesiastical, free from taxation and secular control. Aware that these organizations had lost much of their original significance and were used either to sustain communities or to finance fiestas that at best were irreligious and at worse heretical, the crown issued orders repeatedly in the last half of the eighteenth century to bishops and archbishops to report on the state of these organizations.[6] The most extensive examination of the sodalities was made by the archbishop of Guatemala, Cortés y Larraz, between the years 1769 and 1777. Sodalities were divided into two types: cofradías under the control of clerics and theoretically licensed by the diocese and the crown, although many were not; and *guachivales*, "exactly the same except they [were] administered by private individuals without books or accounts." The archbishop asserted most abuses occurred in guachivales. Cofradías' and guachivales' funds financed masses for saints and the fiestas that followed, most of which lasted "for the next day and night." Their money paid the priest and maintained the pueblo, with interest, or usury, charging 20, 30, or as much as 50 percent for loans. Cortés y Larraz concluded that the sodalities were "a pure pretext for dishonesty, drunkenness, and disorders." The government's attempts to end or reduce their power had caused revolts, and when the archbishop ordered a review of all sodality accounts by alcaldes mayores and corregidores, the Indians resisted. Yet to eliminate the cofradías would remove "almost the sole source of support for the priest."[7]

There were some very wealthy sodalities. Some in Salvador held valuable indigo lands, which were usurped by colonists in the late 1750s with the growth in demand for the dye. Cortés y Larraz described others in 1770: an Indian cofradía in Guatemala City had 12,000 pesos, which it loaned to the government and received annual interest upon; the sodalities in San Pedro Petapa had 14,725 pesos invested in Creole property and about 15,000 pesos in its own cattle; those of San Miguel had some 21,000 pesos outstanding in loans; and the indigo and ranch lands of the sodalities of Chalcasapa were said to be wealthier than the holdings of Creoles in the region. There were extremely poor pueblos as well; some sodalities based upon agricultural holdings had lost their capital through natural disasters or fraud on the part of administrators (mayordomos).[8]

In all, the cofradías of the archdiocese of Guatemala (Guatemala and Salvador, excluding Chiapas, Honduras, and Nicaragua) held minimally some 291,883 pesos in coinage, mostly loaned to Creoles, about 225,000 pesos in beef cattle, 60,000 pesos in horses and mares, and about 5,000 pesos in other livestock for a total value of 581,883 pesos. This did not include the lands they controlled, which in indigo regions or near cities were quite valuable.[9]

Although the government tried to eliminate unlicensed sodalities, it was unable to do so within the pueblo. The Indians resisted incursions, helped, in part, by the clergy itself.[10] The state was able, however, to tap cofradía financial resources invested in the Creole society. In 1802, pressed by wars and economic recession, the state ordered all the funds held by sodalities to be "consolidated" in a general consolidation of debts owed the church and given to fiscal authorities. The ramifications of this policy were many, but, immediately, the effect was the cancellation of outstanding loans from sodalities and the seizure by the government of their principle, which forced many local farmers who held the loans into bankruptcy.

In exchange, the state agreed to finance legal sodality rituals, in effect giving it, through its fiscal power, authority within the pueblo. In times of trouble, the community and sodality funds had been used to pay tribute and were a defense against the incursions of officials and Creoles who compelled Indians to produce goods or to work on their farms to pay off their tribute debt. The funds had guaranteed the pueblo some prosperity and protection from the outside world and preserved the tradition of communal ownership against the market economy. With the financial defenses of the pueblo eliminated, the town had to look to the outside, to the haciendas, and, in some cases, to debt peonage for aid. In the last twenty years of the colony, the government was bankrupt, using all of its funds to finance the European struggles. The needs of Indian communities and sodalities were forgotten. The Bourbon policy furthered the three-hundred-year-old conquest of the Central American Indian.

While Bourbon legislation destroyed the fiscal sovereignty of the pueblo, forcing the Indian into the colonial economy, it also attempted to alter the Hapsburg system of repartimiento. But although the enlightened despots sought to create a free peasantry, they faced obstacles that had plagued reformers since Cerrato himself. Alcaldes mayores and corregidores depended upon repartimientos, as did Honduran miners and Salvadoran dye farmers. The crown's own effort to promote trade would have been stymied by any ban on repartimiento labor in the indigo fields.

On the other hand, the invasion of the western economy worked to support a growth in free labor, as Indians and castes were attracted by high prices either to produce food and clothing or to work for a salary on indigo farms. In the early eighteenth century a decline in population, an expansion in mining, and then a rise in demand for indigo led to labor shortages, which increased, rather than lessened, forced labor drafts and competition between regions and industries. Indians in repartimiento, criminals, and Indians who failed to pay tribute were sent to the mines. In order to avoid the dreaded drafts they fled to Dominican and Jesuit haciendas, to other pueblos, to the mountains, to the city, or even to indigo haciendas. When the crown permitted Indian labor in indigo obrajes in 1737, alcaldes began to issue repartimientos. And as the price and demand for indigo rose, Indian pueblos licensed their ejidos for indigo production to Creole farmers and then provided the labor for its exploitation. After mid-century the forced labor demands increased with the construction of the fortress at Omoa and of a royal road between the capital and the Bay of Honduras.[11]

Rivalries between regions and officials increased. Friars were accused of keeping too many Indians on their lands; alcaldes mayores and corregidores increased their demands upon their wards in labor and goods; private indigo haciendas incorporated Indian pueblos and their ejidos; Indian forasteros were more prevalent. Indian pueblos caught by their proximity to Honduras or Salvador suffered greatly, in particular, those of Chiquimula and Sacapa. They sent repartimientos to the Honduran mines in the thirties, to indigo works in the forties, and then for the construction of the Omoa road in the fifties. After the road was completed, they were compelled to provide beasts and their own backs for the transport of goods and men to and from the port. These obligations depopulated the towns, converting them into centers of non-Indian population as the survivors became ladinos, functioning within the Spanish money economy.[12]

Not all Indians in Salvador suffered. Some owned, through their cofradías, valuable indigo lands and cattle ranches. In the valley of Guayabal, very poor (*pobrecísima*) Spanish families produced "very little" (*cortíssima*) indigo, cattle, and sugar, and Indians held haciendas that were "the best, most developed, and magnificent in this province."[13]

Debt peonage developed on prosperous indigo haciendas, but the repartimiento remained a major force for the far more numerous and poorer dye farmers. In one noteworthy incident, the decision by the President of Guatemala to grant a miner two hundred Lenca Indians in repartimiento in 1780 was resisted successfully by the Indians, supported by the indigo planters in northeastern Salvador who depended upon them for their labor.[14]

Still, indigo areas were consistently short of laborers as demand for the dye and for exports rose through the century. Salvadoran Indians and ladinos were accused of "scandalous idleness," of making loans, of promising to work and then leaving for other areas. Essays on mendicancy explored the best ways to encourage Indians, castes, and poor Spaniards to labor. One suggested a clash between subsistence agriculture and the export economy: "They do not need our [Spanish] commerce nor our work. . . . They need nothing more than their women, who farm and prepare corn and live with them in a contemptible hut, without any civility. . . . They have no need for money; it would be foolish to interrupt their idleness." Father Goicoechea argued that the monoculture of indigo actually caused mendicancy because hacendados preferred to have a surplus of labor available.[15]

In an attempt to muster additional labor, the government altered repartimiento to include castes in draft labor for the first time. Alcaldes mayores and indigo growers were ordered to draw up a list of growers and available manpower. Friars were warned not to protect their wards against labor drafts unless they were involved in indigo production. All ladinos, mulattoes, mestizos, "sambos," blacks, "and the other castes" were required to work in obrajes. Only those who owned or leased farm land were exempt. In 1785 ninety-nine haciendas received draft labor of 1,026 Indians and 3,284 caste peones. The wealthiest hacendado, Pedro Castilla, used 484 peones and 116 Indians on his four haciendas. Haciendas that had workers living on their grounds had arrangements with pueblos, had a regular supply of salaried labor, and did not draft labor. Smaller farmers were too poor or too weak to get laborers.[16]

Outside of the indigo regions, repartimientos continued, although their importance declined toward the end of the century. The earthquakes that struck Comayagua, Salvador, and Guatemala in 1773 and 1775 created a need for draft labor for urban construction, for the transport of construction materials and food from areas as far off as Chiapas. In the highlands of Quezaltenango and Güegüetanango repartimientos gathered and processed wool, around Guatemala they supplied food; they were even used to farm contraband tobacco in Chiapas. In Nicaragua, the intendant divided goods worth one peso to Indians for nine pesos.[17]

Still, outside the mining areas, government legislation and other forces worked to destroy the repartimientos. Unlike the seventeenth century, Central America in the late eighteenth century possessed a large, non-Indian class that worked for wages or under debt peonage and ladinos and Indians who had taken refuge in haciendas. There were more and larger haciendas, as small indigo plantations and cattle ranches in debt to merchants were merged to create great landholdings owned by a few, wealthy families. There was, overall, a decline in the use of repartimientos.[18]

In 1793 the government banned repartimientos of goods and labor with the exception of those areas dependent on them for food and essential public services. The Hapsburgs and early Bourbons had issued such interdicts, but they were too weak and the practice too important to the survival of the colony to be effectively enforced. Alcaldes mayores and corregidores had ceased to resist. In the past, they had borrowed funds to purchase goods and their offices, now they paid only to gain the office. In 1765, for example, the alcalde mayor of Güegüetanango needed 25,000 to 30,000 pesos to purchase wool from farmers and distribute it to Indians for weaving. In the five years of his office he could earn a profit of 30,000 pesos or more, but if an official had to borrow to begin, his profits could be cut in half. Now, as collectors of alcabala and tobacco taxes, the alcaldes mayores earned commissions of 4 percent upon all receipts; they were fiscal officers over the colonists rather than over the Indians. The farmers suffered however. The textile trade declined as costs rose and cheap contraband English goods entered. The cabildo of Quezaltenango, arguing for the farmer, asserted that "by trying to protect the Indian, the government has impoverished him. Not only should [the repartimientos] not be prohibited, but they should be promoted in all areas." The Güegüetenango trade collapsed; by independence no commerce remained and "the pueblos only work to subsist."[19]

Repartimientos continued in some areas, in the cities and in the indigo fields. The mines of Gotera caused "much illness and the death of some, while others escape and desert their pueblos" to avoid drafts. As late as 1820, the governor of Tegucigalpa issued orders to pueblos to supply mines with sufficient labor.[20]

Overall, the repartimiento had diminished, replaced by peonage. Simultaneously the western economy, the intracolonial market economy, large landholdings, and government centralization, all grew in importance as well. With these transformations there was an increase in the mestizo population. Disease and labor pressure, which forced Indians to flee pueblos for cities, also pushed them to become ladinoized and their offspring to intermarry. Some fled to the countryside and to haciendas where mestizos flourished. Cortés y Larraz reported forasteros, Indians and castes in transit from one hacienda to another, absent from their pueblos and families. Pueblos were in a marked decline in the years of the first impact of the western economy. Forasteros from other provinces wandered to San Antonio Suchitepéquez, while the natives vanished. "I understand that many go begging in haciendas and trapiches, many hide in the mountains. Others go to the Lacandones." Here, as in Sonsonate, Escuintla, Guazacapán, Sacapa, Santiago Atitlán, and elsewhere he saw the same phenomenon: "It is impossible to know how many people live in the haciendas. . . . Today they are here and tomorrow, elsewhere." Indeed, his observations of the Guatemalan highlands provide a striking contrast with the 1682 report. Now the men of once cohesive pueblos with strong local economies wandered to earn a living. Rather than subsistence, Amerindia was a money economy. In the pueblos of Guëguëtenango "only a third of the families live," the rest go elsewhere, "and only return to hear two or three orations before leaving again." The priest of Alotenango couldn't provide an accurate account of his wards, because "some are mining, others have gone off to work and others died in a measles epidemic." Chipilapa, "that used to be a pueblo of Indians," was now ladinos; only one-fourth of the entire province was Indian; Santiago Atitlán, once with thousands of Indians now had merely hundreds. The archbishop observed of the entire archdiocese "it is a wonder how fast the most flourishing provinces are ruined."[21]

Many Indians labored on indigo plantations, while others dispersed to cattle haciendas. The five haciendas in San Pedro Sacatepéquez had five to eight families each and the eight in Santa Cruz de Quiché had nineteen families in all. Elsewhere, in Comalapa, Totonicapán, and Textutla, Indians lived dispersed "outside the pueblo in their milpas." The strongest pueblo civilizations remained in Verapaz where there were few haciendas. Even there, Cortés y Larraz described an impoverished soil which forced some to go elsewhere to survive.[22]

The western economy was not the only disruptive influence on indigenous life. Disease continued to take its toll. After mid-century smallpox struck the colony in 1752, 1761, 1780, and 1789. The period 1768 to 1770 was "the time of the plagues," a measles epidemic leaving "stiff cadavers lying about [city] streets and royal roads." In Amatitlán and Santapéquez "the flower of all families were carried off, up to 10,000 children." In the curate of Alotenango 74 percent of all infants died, while 8 percent of the adult population succumbed. Chiapas suffered a terrible epidemic in 1771 and 1772, with the bishop claiming that at least 20,000 Indian tributaries died. If this estimate was accurate, the fatality rate was probably 75 percent. Local epidemics destroyed whole towns. San Juan Naqualapan, an annex of San Antonio

Suchitepéquez, was annihilated in 1764, while the latter pueblo was scarcely touched by disease despite being just a league distant. In 1796, 441 tributaries out of a total of 775 died in San Francisco el Alto together with 1,000 women and children as a result of a localized disease, and two thirds of Jacaltenango was destroyed by disease. A "terrible pest" decimated Quezaltenango in 1798.[23]

The diseases were stemmed in part due to the efforts of the protomédico, José de Flores, who distributed smallpox vaccine to most of the settled population of Central America. Also the greater authority of the government enabled it to localize disease—a notable success of the 1780s when a viral epidemic from the Yucatan through the Lacandon mountains was contained with a *cordon sanitaire*. The alcalde mayor of Güegüetenango, Sebastian Chamorro, overcame the Indians habit of "fleeing to the mountains" in order to halt the spread of the disease.[24]

These successes led to a remarkable growth in the indigenous population. The total number of tributaries went from 99,156 in 1788 to 115,935 in 1802, and 138,505 in 1811, or a 38 percent increase. The fluctuations in Indian population, which had plagued Central American since the conquest, ended, and from this moment onward the population of the area continued to rise, although specific pueblos did continue to suffer periodic diseases and famines.[25]

Indians revolted periodically in the late eighteenth and early nineteenth centuries, but most revolts were local, against specific authorities or abuses of established labor or tribute customs. (One small uprising resulted from the attempts by Flores to administer vaccine.)[26] Perhaps the most significant and yet least known was the peaceful but widespread revolt in highland Guatemala that was sparked by the Guatemalan earthquake of 1773. The revolt was not caused by the excessive labor draft or the dispute among colonials and the president, Martín de Mayorga, over the city's transfer that marked the following years. The Indians rose in October only two months after the earthquake. The disaster itself signalled the revolt. The alcalde mayor of Mazatenango saw "various movements of people without permission towards Guatemala City. Even the employees of the church are leaving without saying anything to their curas." A ladino, Antonio Barbarena, heard from various Indians in their language that "a king had come from Spain, he whom they had been waiting for, who was an Indian but had been taken as a youth to Spain by the Franciscans and had risen to honored positions and now was coming to free them from tributes and other obligations and restore to them that which the

Spanish and Ladinos had usurped." Manual Antonio Montana, a Spaniard of San Sebastian married to an Indian, reported that the Indians were saying that God had sent a king named Martín who had destroyed the capital. Before they were conquered, the Indians "had a prophet named Martum that in Spanish means Martín and he had prophesied that he would return in a long time to destroy all Spanish and they would be alone and free from tributes and labor drafts and return to primitive life." The movement was widespread. In Soloma, the Indians were unruly, claiming that the president was an Indian. The Indians of Quiché "are cleaning the Palace of the King of Kiché." Throughout the entire highland area Indians left their pueblos, traveling to the president in the capital, because "he knows their language and dresses like that . . . and has made the earth move to destroy the city." The officials faced great difficulties persuading the populations to return to their pueblos.[27]

And so, coincidentally the earthquake of 1773 in Guatemala, which sparked the upheaval between new families and old oligarchy, also ignited perhaps the most widespread Indian agitation in the Bourbon epoch.

The drift toward independence did not, of course, involve the Amerindian population. It was a movement of Creoles. Once independence was achieved, the Indian lost his authority to protest against abuses at the national level, through the church, the fiscal, and to the crown. For the Indian independence meant increased subjugation.

CHAPTER TEN

The Economy Collapses

FROM THE END of the War of Jenkins' Ear until the wars of the French Revolution, the western economy expanded. The early industrialization of Europe required increasingly more and different primary materials, some of which Latin America provided, and most areas, like Central America, became tied to the world commercial system. Mexican silver mines were better financed and better supplied with needed materials, such as mercury and salt. Buenos Aires developed into an important port, an outlet for Peruvian silver as well as a provider of hides for the world's shipping. In Central America the indigo trade flourished. Commercial prosperity continued for Mexico until the War for Independence in 1810 and for Buenos Aires until long after independence. This was not true, however, for Central America. The collapse in the demand for indigo, and other important factors, led the well-integrated colonial economy to suffer severe depression from 1803 until the eve of independence. Highland Guatemalan cotton producers, Nicaraguan and Honduran cattle farmers, and Honduran miners all suffered equally. Many producers lost their holdings to their Guatemalan merchant creditors, increasing the animosity between the two groups that the merchants' control of prices had fostered.

The economic unity that indigo financed for the previous fifty years disintegrated slowly. If a century earlier one commodity had suffered a decline, the others would have been unaffected, and if a farmer had lost his land to a creditor, that creditor would probably have been the church—the community that is—and not an alien outsider. With the decline in the indigo trade and the collapse of the new economic unity, regional animosities were renewed.

There were other factors: the decline in Spanish power led to a rise in English and North American contraband trading, bringing cheap, manufactured textiles, destroying the local textile industry of highland Guatemala; Honduran silver and coinage were used to pay for the imports, leading to decapitalization; the process was furthered by extraordinary fiscal measures taken by the crown to finance the European wars. Although these factors were present elsewhere in Spanish America, it was the weakness of the primary commercial product, the *produit moteur*, indigo, that worsened the situation.

A number of factors, not all of which were perceived at the time, caused the collapse of the indigo trade. First, although trade was at its highest level from 1790 until 1797, when war erupted between Britain and Spain in 1798, most international commerce was suspended and the most important market for indigo was greatly reduced. Both merchants and producers relied upon the sale of indigo in Europe to finance the following year's harvest, but with the hostilities that money was not forthcoming. Within a year of the outbreak of war, indigo production was said to decline, leaving more than three million pounds of Guatemalan indigo in storehouses in Havana, Vera Cruz, and Guatemala. Although active contraband trade was developing, English resources were also scarce, and it took years before firm commercial arrangements could be established between Guatemalan and British houses.[1]

Second, almost immediately after the end of the war, locusts attacked much of the indigo producing areas of Central America. Attracted by the wet bagasse, as well as by the humid climate, these insects destroyed much of the harvest of 1802 and 1803. Locusts also devastated food harvests, leading to high prices as food speculators took advantage of the situation. The government prosecuted those who hoarded grain, gave tax relief and some financial aid to indigo producers, but almost three years of locusts overwhelmed the effects of government interference. The insects, it was said, "generally ruined everybody, transcending all classes."[2]

Perhaps the hardest struck area was the Salvadoran indigo region, where workers were forced to fight the insects "day and night" to try to salvage the harvest. Food shortages were so severe that people in the city of Salvador fled to the mountains to salvage verduras and other root plants. Indigo workers were forced to migrate to healthier regions, while farmers suffered because of the lack of workers.[3]

The war and insects were temporary phenomena, but the disruption they caused magnified a third, more fundamental problem in the indigo trade of the last twenty years of the eighteenth century. Merchants and producers, who blamed the decline of indigo on the war and on the locusts, ignored these fundamental problems and actually aggravated them.

The excellent position of Guatemalan indigo on the world market was based, in part, on its reputation. Indigo was classified in three categories: *flor*, the finest, *sobresaliente*, or medium, and *corte*, the ordinary cut. Flor brought the highest profits and the success of Guatemalan indigo depended upon quality production. In the 1780s merchants and producers quarreled about the labeling of the dye; the businessmen claiming that the quality of the commodity had declined, the farmers countering that indigo that had been classified as flor and sobresaliente was called corte at the local market and sold at flor prices in Europe. Farmers found it easier to produce the lesser quality indigo than to spend time, energy, and funds producing the higher-quality product without higher prices. Between 1779 and 1781 (see table 10.1), flor quality represented 21 percent of all indigo exports, yet in the bountiful years of 1791, '94, '96 and '97, prior to the war, flor represented only 3 percent of production. To encourage the production of the higher quality dye, the crown removed all taxes on both sobresaliente and flor in 1803, but to little avail. By 1810 the distinctions between the qualities of indigo were slowly eroding. In that year over 182,000 pounds of corte were produced, almost 3,000 pounds of sobresaliente, 1,800 pounds of flor, and approximately 374,000 pounds "without distinction." After independence the three qualities of indigo were rarely mentioned.[4]

As high taxes contributed to the increase in illicit commerce, they also raised the base price of indigo to such a level that it could not compete on the world market. Both merchants and producers decried levies that added an additional 25 percent of the cost to indigo imported into Spain, and 45 percent to that re-exported to other European countries. Producers claimed there were too many middlemen, each taking a share of the profits. "When this precious fruit is passed through three or four different people, leaving each rich, the foreigners must pay a price higher than the market [will bear]." The high price with the drop in quality was particularly damaging. Finally, the Guatemalan merchants' monopoly of all imports, together with high customs, increased the costs of foreign implements, thus raising the price of indigo, "the difference between buying [products] first hand, or third hand."[5]

With these problems, competition for the indigo market increased. In the Americas, indigo production began in Caracas. In 1775 the dye represented 0.8 percent of all exports from Venezuela, but eleven years later, 19 percent, and between 1793 and 1800, roughly 29 percent. During this latter period, Caracas produced little more than half of that exported by Guatemala, but the quality of the dye was much higher. A Guatemalan claimed in 1804 that "it wasn't many years ago

Table 10.1: Export and Production of Flor Quality Indigo, 1779–1810 (in pounds)

Year	Amount	Year	Amount
1779	133,666 exported	1797	7,982 exported
1780	111,352 exported	1798	19,780 exported
1781	111,254 exported	1799	21,000 exported
1791	79,546 exported	1802	56,640 exported
1792	24,500 exported	1804[a]	230 produced
1794	26,900 exported	1805[a]	26 produced
1796	19,780 exported	1808[a]	6,000 produced
		1810	1,804 produced

SOURCES: For 1779, 1780, 1781, 1796, 1797, 1798, and 1799 see A.G.G. A1.6, Leg. 6, Exp. 110; and A3.27, Leg. 1759, Exp. 28248, fol. 26; for 1791, 1794, and 1802 see Smith, "Indigo Production," pp. 185, 197; for 1792, see A.G.I. Guatemala 669, Estado que manifiesta el monto de la cosecha . . . de 1792; for 1804, 1805, 1808, and 1810 see *La Gazeta de Guatemala,* 26 de marzo de 1804, 8: 17, 20 de noviembre de 1808, 11: 153, and 17 de noviembre de 1810, 14: 346.

[a] These figures represent incomplete production figures, but show at least 75 percent of total annual production.

when this colony produced considerable amounts of flor and sobresaliente that were surely the best in the world, and was preferred by all the European markets. It was when poor corte indigo was farmed that we could no longer compete with that from Caracas."[6]

Merchants, producers, and officials debated the effects of the decline in quality, high prices, competition from Caracas, wars, and locusts. But one distant cause was not fully appreciated until it was too late. In 1780 the British began to promote indigo cultivation in Bengal, with sizable imports reaching England around 1800. From 1805 until 1814, India exported on the average some five and a half million pounds annually, easily five times Guatemala's peak production. Using cheaper labor, and creating a surplus of the dye on the world market, the English caused a drop in prices in Europe. As the Bengal commerce developed, Britain imposed high protective duties upon indigo coming from the Americas (see table 10.2), doubling those of preceding years. With an economy with inflated prices, Guatemala could not produce sufficient, cheap indigo to compete. The high quality of the Guatemalan product had protected it from competition, but now that quality no longer existed.

The transient problems of the turn of the century hid the long range one of increased competition, but once peace was restored and

*Table 10.2: Duty on Indigo Imported
Into Great Britain from the British
Caribbean, 1798–1819*

Date	Rate Per Pound
July 5, 1798	15s
Oct. 1, 1801	Free
May 12, 1802	18s
July 5, 1803	14s 3/4d
June 1, 1804	15s 7 1/2d
April 5,1805	15s 11 1/4d
May 10, 1806	16s 11 3/4d
July 5, 1809	33s 4d
April 15, 1813	39s 7d
July 5, 1819	41s 8d

SOURCE: Lowell J. Ragatz, *Statistics for the
Study of British Caribbean Economic History,
1763–1833.*

the locusts had fled, the truth became apparent. Central America
discovered it was impossible to sell the dye at a profit.

In the last quarter of the eighteenth century (see table 10.3),
indigo exports had reached their highest level. Although in total quantity the greatest exports took place in the last decade, the greatest profit
derived during the 1780s from the higher quality dye. At the turn of
the century exports dropped precipitously. With the wars and then

*Table 10.3: Average Annual Exports of Indigo from
Central America, 1772–1813*

Years	Pounds	Years	Pounds
1772–1776	561,000	1797–1801	1,006,000
1777–1781	834,000	1802–1804	637,227
1782–1786	884,000	1805	n.a.
1787–1791	1,016,000	1806–1810	719,648
1792–1796	1,035,000	1811	n.a.
		1812–1813	340,000

SOURCES: Smith, "Indigo Production," pp. 195, 197, and
Floyd, "Indigo Merchants," p. 487; A.G.I. Guatemala 668,
Fiscal of New Spain (1821) gives ten-year average figures
between 1772 and 1802 that confirm the calculations of Smith
and Floyd; Rubio, "El añil," p. 342; *La Gazeta de Guatelmala,*
19 de noviembre de 1804, 55; Rubio, *La historia del añil,* 1:
357–58.

Table 10.4: *Average Annual Indigo Production According to Dunn, 1791–1818*

Years	Pounds
1791–1795	989,260
1796–1800	761,252
1801–1808	n.a.
1809–1813	543,518
1814–1818	375,298

SOURCE: Dunn, *Guatimala*, p. 212.

insect attacks, annual production during the years 1801–04, and 1806–08 averaged 405,781 pounds, or less than 40 percent of the average annual production of the previous fifteen years. In the years 1809 and 1810, production somewhat rebounded, to be followed by another decline. The figures provided by Henry Dunn in the 1820s are inexact, but they are evidence of a contemporary view of the epoch (see table 10.4). Between the first and last quinquennial, production dropped some 60 percent.

In 1816 the town of Rivas (Nicaragua) had twenty indigo farms that produced virtually nothing "because of the cost of the harvest and the low prices." The following year the Guatemalan merchant guild complained:

> It has been years since we . . . harvested more than 1,100,000 pounds of [indigo] . . . but in these last years we could not export it at any price; nor do the harvests come to a half of what they were before. Large amounts, well stocked, exist in the warehouse of Cádiz, and in those of the Commercial houses of this city and others of the tax administration, without any demand for them. . . . In Zacatocularioa there are five haciendas deserted with 20,000 pesos worth of loans from the Montepío still outstanding.[7]

As the nineteenth century progressed, the decline in indigo production and prices slowly destroyed the small producer. Those farmers who had outstanding loans to Guatemalan merchants forfeited their farms. It was said, in 1816, that the Marquis de Aycinena was gaining control of "various haciendas" because of old debts. Three years later the Aycinena family produced one-sixth of all indigo in the colony as compared with one-tenth at the end of the eighteenth century. Although this dynasty also suffered during the declining years, it was able to gain control of land that would become more valuable after independence when prosperity returned. The seizure of indebted farms exacerbated the bad feelings between the interior and the capital's leading families.[8]

The producers in the interior, subject to the world market economy, and the Guatemalan merchants were also victims of the Bourbon state's hunger for resources. The combined assaults cut the bases of survival in many areas. The tobacco and sales taxes, which had been introduced in the interior with the intendancy reforms, proved effective sources of revenue. But the depletion of the royal treasury in war led the crown to order (for Spain in 1797 and for the Americas in 1803) all loans held by ecclesiastical institutions, including cofradías, called in, the proceeds to pay the state's debts. Hereafter, the state's tobacco and aguardiente monopolies would finance the masses and other rituals the interest on those loans was meant to pay. All loans had to be paid back within two to eight years, depending upon size.

Despite pleas from the Guatemalan cabildo and the University of San Carlos to exempt the colony because of the depression in indigo, the measures were enforced. Between 1804 and 1808 Central America sent more than a million pesos from the consolidation of debts to Mexico and Spain, the first such outflow of capital since the Bourbons took power. "The consolidation caused the gathering and export to Spain of the wealth with which this Kingdom functioned," the Guatemalan fiscal claimed in 1817. A series of patriotic and "voluntary" donations to aid Spain against the French invasion, which sent another million pesos to Europe, complicated the problem further.[9]

The immediate effect of the consolidation was strongest in the agricultural regions of Central America. Most of the urban mortgages held by the church in Guatemala were destroyed by the 1773 earthquake; thereafter loans were made by businessmen. In the countryside, where cattle were financed by church loans, consolidation caused economic upheaval. Cofradías and ranchers in Honduras were forced to sell their herds to pay their debts. "Beef and horse cattle are the principal patrimony of the inhabitants of Honduras and the only article for commerce," the ecclesiastical cabildo in Comayagua decried. "If the cattle are sold for the consolidation, the church will receive no tithes whatsoever." The church pleaded in vain for a ban on the sale of cows to maintain some stock in the region. Again, to no avail. Eleven Spanish cofradías in Olancho sent 5,000 head to San Salvador to sell for indigo. The seven cofradías of Danli sent 3,000 to San Miguel. In all, the stock of Honduras fell some 40 percent when the few farmers with capital, mainly in Salvador, purchased the herds, moving them onto lands once occupied by indigo. With the decline of silver and the depletion of cattle the last source of wealth for Honduras was destroyed.[10]

The consolidation was condemned by a Guatemalan Creole as a measure "which turns [the government's] vassals into a troop of slaves." By 1808 warfare disrupted the tax gathering efforts; Napoleon's invasion of the peninsula destroyed the metropolis' ability to enforce the unpopular measure. When the president of Guatemala heard that regions in New Spain had halted enforcement, he, acting on his own, suspended collection. These acts represented the first break in the power and policy of the Bourbon administrations in both colonies.[11]

The economic depression caused by the loss of capital, the decline in indigo production, and the destruction of the Honduran cattle industry affected the major families of the region, but the urban working class and the Indians near Guatemala City were plagued by other problems. With the advent of large-scale international trade and the economic advances of the late eighteenth century, and with a rise in population, prices became inflated and food scarce. Cattle, which had cost from 2.5 to 3.5 pesos per head in 1730, cost 4 pesos in 1758, 5 to 6 pesos in the late eighteenth century, and from 6 to 7.5 pesos by 1805. Corn cost half a peso the fanega in 1723, "less than a peso" around 1750, and 2 pesos by the turn of the century. The greater population and increased demand for food together with the weak pueblo structure made it possible for Indian communal lands to be seized and the Indians moved to distant regions. In Quesaltepeque, lands that had previously been devoted to cattle grazing and to small-scale farming "were closed." The towns nearest Guatemala complained the most. Villa Nueva claimed that they possessed "not even a small square of land." Amatitlán reported that "we need ejidos now for our agriculture." Communal lands in Cuidad Vieja were moved, so that Indians had to travel half a day to reach them. In Suchitepéquez, the alcalde mayor reported that the abuses of cattle owners, who left their stock to run loose in agricultural lands, was the cause of the lack of prosperity in the district. *La Gazeta* attacked the cattle owners' usurpation of lands, depriving men of work and causing vagabonds to roam the streets of the capital. Soon after independence, in the town of Mixco some three leagues from the capital, José del Valle reported that Indians had no common lands and were forced to pay rent for this milpas.[12]

There were numerous droughts and famines: the most devastating crisis occurred during the locust attack, but others took place regularly.

The president declared in 1805 that, "although in the greater part of the provinces of this kingdom there is an abundance of food, in the regions close to this capital there is a need for wheat and corn." Orders were issued in May 1809 to outlying areas to plant as much grain as possible, but there was famine only seven months later and provinces were ordered to send all grains to the capital. Later the same year, reports came in of other bad harvests in Jalapa, Quezaltenango, Totonicapán, and other areas. Similar situations existed in 1813 and 1817.[13]

The Guatemalan monopolists controlled and exploited the food situation. Unlike other areas of Spanish America, the institution of the alhondiga or government grain warehouse had little effect. During a famine the government controlled, theoretically, all grain flowing into the city and the price, by prohibiting the hoarding of grains to force the prices upwards. For most of the colonial period there was sufficient grain and the alhondiga served as a tax collection area. Guards at the edge of the capital gave traders receipts for the goods they brought into the city and, whenever a sale was made, the receipt was brought to the alhondiga where a tax was paid on the sale price. But with a sharp population rise toward the end of eighteenth century, hoarding became more prevalent. With the threat of famine, merchants forced prices up by holding grain outside of the city and then slowly releasing it to the marketplace. Repeated legislation against the practice could not halt it.[14]

The land scarcity in Salvador took on a different aspect. Salvador was the most heavily populated country per acreage in Central America. During the indigo boom in the last third of the eighteenth century, laborers were imported; as corn, wheat, and cattle fields were converted for the production of dyes, a shortage of foodstuffs developed. Trade with the Guatemalan highlands exchanged indigo for wheat and corn, but with the collapse of the indigo trade, this commerce halted. Indebted Salvadoran farmers lost their indigo farms to Guatemalan merchants, who either continued indigo production, allowed the properties to lie fallow, or imported Honduran cattle for the land. But grains were not farmed to any great extent and the corn and wheat that had come from the Guatemalan highlands were diverted to the food-short capital. Salvadorans, many of them landless, pressed on the Indian common land, the only available agricultural land. The Spanish colonial government and the church tried to protect the Indians, whose land was their only source of food short of debt peonage. After independence, these defenses against usurpation were gone, and with renewed demand for indigo, there were increased pressures upon the Indians.[15]

The rise in contraband trade contributed to the shortage of food and the drop in demand for indigo by drawing off the coinage and minerals the colony possessed. The capital's merchants—the Aycinena clique in particular—imported cheap foreign fabrics that, in turn, destroyed the cotton and wool industries in interior Guatemala and, particularly, the textile artisans in and around the cities of Quezaltenango and Antigua Guatemala. The repartimiento had been eliminated as a dependable source of labor just a decade prior to the beginning of large-scale imports. With more costly manual labor the producers could not overcome the industrialized foreign competition. Around the city of Antigua Guatemala there were some 2,000 artisans and some twenty towns in the highlands devoted to raising cotton for sale to the weavers, which also suffered. When a new president arrived in Central America in 1818 he saw that "everybody at my arrival [was] dressed the same—in English articles."[16]

Contraband trading opened markets for Central American products, but it also reduced the silver in the colony and destroyed much local industry. Local Creoles described the economy of Quezaltenango in 1810 as decayed, the result of "clandestine commerce and foreign trade" and the end of the repartimiento. Indians worked only to sustain themselves.[17]

In summary, Central America faced severe economic turmoil at the beginning of the nineteenth century as the Bourbon bureaucracy and the economy came crashing down. The houses of Comayagua were described in 1803 as "falling in ruins," the destruction caused by the 1773 and 1775 earthquakes never remedied. The Mercedian and Franciscan convents were destroyed completely, and the cathedral, "built to last eternally, was on the point of falling because it had not been repaired for a long time." The city of Gracias a Dios had been badly damaged with only one church still standing. Indigo farms "that at one time were the business of this city were half-abandoned since the war in 1795," and most inhabitants had moved to the nearby town of Los Llanos where tobacco was produced under license to the crown.[18]

Although Honduras possessed the colony's mines, it lacked sufficient capital to develop its holdings, and this, together with "the ignorance in mineralogy and lack of any work force," created a "miserable" economy. Fiscal weakness meant the government no longer sent money to the mines in exchange for silver. The merchants "make the hardest laws for the miners," paying them half in clothing and half in coinage for the fruits of their labor.[19]

Nicaragua also experienced an economic decline, though Granada was a center of commerce with foreign nations. At the end of the eighteenth century Nicaraguan cacao yielded annually 220,000 pesos, and the province produced 160,000 pesos in indigo, 100,000 pesos in cattle, and 89,000 pesos in diverse products. But war and locusts caused a drop as severe as that in Salvador, while strong competition from Guayaquil and Caracas caused cacao production to fall. When land in Salvador was converted to cattle haciendas, Nicaraguan cattlemen were deprived of their Guatemalan market.[20]

The beneficial economic effects of the Bourbon reforms were now eroded. Creoles in most of interior Central America suffered from the dislocation of local economies caused by the early dependence upon indigo and the trade network throughout Central America. Guatemalan merchants were despised for gaining from the impoverishment of farmers and miners by manipulating prices and credit and importing English textiles to the ruin of the domestic cotton and wool trades. The animosities of the depression era were released later, when independence removed restraints upon political action. León cattlemen, Salvadoran indigo farmers, and Honduran miners would, after independence, find a political voice free from the vestiges of loyalty to a Spanish king, a voice with which to express intense feelings of regionalism and separatism.

CHAPTER ELEVEN

José de Bustamante
and the Crisis
in Colonial Government

BOURBON AUTHORITY HAD reached its greatest power in 1790. Intendants were established throughout the empire, fiscal income was up, strong armies were created in most colonies, colonial trade was more active than ever before, and an intellectual ferment resounded everywhere. Within twenty years, however, imperial authority had been shattered, most of Spain occupied by foreign troops, and the American colonies either at the point of or in rebellion. By 1825 only the Caribbean islands remained of the three-hundred-year-old American empire.

The destruction of Spanish rule contrasted starkly with the situation a century earlier, when the seventeenth-century wars had debilitated Spain. Despite the weakness of the metropolis and its agents and the end of the Hapsburg line, Spanish-American colonies remained loyal, a loyalty intrinsic to the Hapsburg colonial system. To fight the sixteenth- and seventeenth-century European wars, to defend their prerogatives, and to rule an empire that reached from the Danube to the Río de la Plata, the Hapsburgs did not impose a single set of principles. A loose understanding existed among all the realms of the Empire, united under a crown whose sovereignty was based upon respect for local traditions and the prerogatives of a wide variety of groups. In the colony the Creoles, the Indians and castes, the merchants and producers, the noble and ignoble, the church, and the crown itself, each possessed privileges that the crown defended and balanced against one other. Royal sovereignty rested on the ability to maintain this balance; legislation that opposed too many of these factions remained a dead letter.

The church, the marrow of the structure, kept local institutions strong, defended the royal will, and reenforced Christian-hispanidad as the uniting ideology of the empire.

When the Bourbons took power in 1700, they understood that if Spain were to survive in Europe, it had to centralize power, stimulate industry, develop an efficient fiscal system, and establish a strong bureaucracy and military. To keep commerce under the authority of the empire, frontier and trade routes had to be patrolled and battles fought to maintain its borders. But reforms had to proceed slowly, in traditional Spain as well as in the empire's realms, with their specific rights. At least sixty years passed before major reforms were made in Central America and another twenty years before their effect was felt. By 1790 the reforms were installed, the government was strong, and it appeared that the Bourbons had indeed succeeded.

But such success proved illusory. The basis of the Bourbon state, the "veins of the empire," as one bureaucrat represented it, was the fiscal system, and it was here that the state was weakest. The crown required a large bureaucracy to maintain direct control over all regions and a large army to fight its wars. Fiscal reform had led to the growth of the bureaucracy and the army. But military expenses rose constantly, caused by the series of wars between 1790 and 1815. When the state had to sacrifice colonial military power for the metropolis, it began to lose control of the colony itself. Raising taxes to support larger armies led to even greater defections.

Royal bureaucrats, together with the new merchant classes and elements within the church, prepared the way for the entry of the Enlightenment and the destruction of the Counter-Reformation mentality as epitomized by the Inquisition. The ideas of Copernicus and Gassendi began entering Spain through the universities around 1690. The Benedictine monk, Benito Gerónimo Feyjóo, gave impetus to the new age, introducing Descartes, Newton, and Francis Bacon to the Hispanic world in his *Teatro crítico universal*. His attack upon Aristotelian thought was opposed by the Jesuits and the Tribunal of the Inquisition but gained royal favor in 1750 when the crown banned any refutation of the work. After the expulsion of the Jesuits, enlightenment thought emerged at the court of Charles III where enlightened despotism reached its greatest heights under the influence of Campomanes and Jovellanos and took form in the Bourbon reforms. French thinkers were translated into Spanish, published, and disseminated throughout the empire. Despite the resistance of the Inquisition, Montesquieu's *The Spirit of Laws* and Rousseau's *Emile* were widely known, read, and cited in discussions of political economy and education. Both *Emile* and Abbé Raynal's *Histoire philosophique* were burnt by the Inquisition, but the latter work was published openly just five years after the *auto de fé*. Even Voltaire was available after 1780. The Inquisition was virtually, if not legally, moribund, killed by the state itself, "a flimsy bulwark against the multitude of its enemies," in Jovellanos' words.[1]

The new ideas flowed to Central America along with the numerous bureaucrats and merchants who traveled between the metropolis, Mexico, and Central America. The vital Bourbon bureaucracy—personified in Central America by Díez Navarro, Valdéz, and Matías Gálvez—introduced enlightened despotism, stimulated trade, increased taxation, and improved defenses. But it was the Franciscan friar José Antonio Goicoechea who was the most influential, performing for the colony what the Benedictine Feyjóo had done for the metropolis. Goicoechea, educated at the court of Charles III, participated in the literary salons and scientific experiments that were fashionable. At the University of San Carlos he introduced many of the new ideas of the epoch to the children of the leading Creoles, the new merchants, those who were to become the leaders of the independence movement and of the national governments. At the same time he fought for basic reforms in the university's curriculum. Descartes, Locke, Nollet, and Linnaeus were taught by Goicoechea, much to the disdain of his superiors. A teacher of philosophy, he surreptitiously included botany, geometry, optics, astronomy, mathematics, and, heretically, experimental physics in his classes.

Goicoechea's most important contribution was the intellectual spirit he introduced into Central America. A force behind the republication of the newspaper, *La Gazeta de Guatemala* (in 1797), he contributed treatises on mendicancy and the cultivation of indigo to the reborn journal. He also was one of the prime sponsors of the *Sociedad Económica de Amigos del País de Guatemala* (founded in 1794), which instituted experiments and offered awards for inventiveness in the manner of the best economic societies of the age. After Goicoechea, all writing, thought, and argument in Central America were phrased in the manner of the French encyclopedists.[2]

Experimentation, progress, and economic growth were willingly accepted by the new Central America elite in New Guatemala. They financed the newspaper and the economic society. Their children were trained by Goicoechea and used his logic and ideas to express their views in later, more turbulent times. If the traditionalists had their foundations in the church, the new groups had their ideology.

The new currents of thought were limited, by and large, to the merchant city, Guatemala, and perhaps to Granada. They did not flow into the interior except to those children of the elite who were sent to the university. Lacking the intellectual heritage that had contributed to the acceptance of the Enlightenment in Spain, and to a lesser extent in Guatemala, poor Creole farmers, mestizo and mulatto laborers, and, of course, the Indians never understood or accepted the new ideas. The shift from Counter-Reformation Catholic theology to new definitions of natural law and the application of new ideas to government reform was too radical for the political inheritance of most areas and sharpened the existing differences between city and countryside.

The succession of Charles IV and of his first minister Manuel de Godoy and the virtually simultaneous French Revolution splintered the intellectual revolution. In Spain, the euphoria of Charles III disappeared into factions of traditionalists like those of Godoy, who looked to revolutionary and Napoleonic France for leadership, and of those who sought to establish a Spanish national liberalism, such as would emerge in 1812. "The critical turn in recent Spanish" as well as Central American history "revolved around the loss of faith in enlightened despotism, in the idea of a disabused monarch directing his people toward justice, prosperity and happiness."[3]

Almost immediately Bourbon absolutist successes became disasters, enlightened fiscal policies became oppressive tax burdens, and economic reforms, monopolistic polities. The center gave out with war, first, with revolutionary France and then with Britain. Taxes were raised. Trade was disrupted. Spain was invaded in 1794 and in 1807. The structure collapsed, as did the empire's defenses.

Republican ideas seeped into Spain. "Foreign gazettes, newspapers, books, and broadsheets came crammed with impious doctrines" carried by propagandists "engaged in diplomatic offices and among the members of the commercial and industrial missions." Rather than trust the ultramontanists of the Inquisition, Jovellanos suggested boards of censors or local bishops to create in effect a national ideological defense.[4]

If enlightened despotism ended in Spain, the Enlightenment continued in the minds of young bureaucrats, officials, and clerics, who looked to the French Revolution with mixed feelings, revolted by the violence, but admiring the end of commercial and governmental policies. In the Americas, the merchant classes willingly allied with them. The oidor Jacobo de Villa Urrutia protected *La Gazeta* from less sympathetic officials; another bureaucrat, Alejandro Ramírez, became its editor, providing a forum for radical dissent and discussion of science and philosophy. Ramírez became an important adviser to the president of Guatemala, González Mollindo, who was also sympathetic with the philosophy of the new age.[5]

In the space of a few years the Guatemalan elite evolved from loyalty to the empire to a liberal and national force, most of whom were trained by Friar Goicoechea, challenging the authority of the metropolis and its bureaucracy. Economic conditions played as much a role in this evolution as ideology. The collapse in the indigo trade because of locust infestation, warfare, and declining quality was followed by the consolidation of church debts, which forced many small farmers and miners into bankruptcy, making "the government's vassals into a troop of slaves." But most important was the growth of contraband trade and the commercial links between Guatemala's elite and the English, aided and abetted by Spanish officials.

A royal order was issued in Spain in November 1797 allowing trade with neutral nations, and, although the order was never "published" in America and seems to have been limited to the peninsula, it was interpreted to apply to Central America by Jacobo Villa Urrutia, the chief oidor of the audiencia, in the absence of a president. English and American ships openly called at the port of Omoa, the citadel of Bourbon power in Central America. Fiscal officials in the port and on coast guard vessels participated in the trade. In 1801 the official Alejandro Ramírez traveled openly to Jamaica and brought back a variety of plants for experimental purposes. In these first years Guatemalan merchants established contacts with Boston, Philadelphia, and Jamaican commercial houses. Under the presidency of González Mollindo (1803–11), the trading house of Irisarri was granted permission to trade in "foreign merchandise."[6]

Illegal commerce developed through a variety of channels. Guatemala sent its indigo and Honduras its silver to the Bay Islands (chiefly the island of Roatán) and to Belize. Nicaragua sent indigo and cacao through the San Juan River to Curaçao and Jamaica. Throughout the entire Mosquito Coast commerce was carried out with Mosquito and Sambos Indians, as well as with Jamaican shippers, as the defenses of the Bourbon system collapsed. In the Pacific, foreign whalers picked up goods at the Nicaraguan port of Realejo. The English bartered Manchester textiles.[7]

As illegal commerce grew and Spain's military fortunes declined after 1800, the cabildo's authority expanded. The center of traditional vecino rule under the Hapsburgs, now a center of merchant power, welcomed nationalistic ideas deriving from France and assimilated them to traditional institutions in support of their idea of sovereignty. When Ferdinand VII was captured in 1810, these rights, the cabildo asserted, devolved directly to them. This was no disloyalty, as in Mexico; it was an opinion that Guatemala represented by the cabildo had the right to ratify the succession to the crown.[8]

The Guatemalan cabildo's instructions to its representative to the Cortes, Antonio Larrazábal, is a critical document in Central American intellectual history. Authored chiefly by the regidor José María Peinado, a close associate of the Aycinena merchant house, it shows the fusion of enlightenment thought, Bourbon reforms, and the French Revolution in the ideology of the "new" Creole merchant class (now two-thirds of a century old). It argued for promoting diversified agricultural enterprise and free labor. It supported the right of Spain to monopolize commerce in those products she could supply. It recognized the Catholic church as absolute. But it also replicated the Declaration of the Rights of Man and spoke of natural law. "All human institutions have the stamp of the century in which they were made," it quoted Montesquieu. Change was inevitable.[9] Significantly, one of the four sections of the instructions concerned taxation, rejecting the Bourbon system as expensive and cumbersome and suggesting that a head tax be imposed on all, to be administered by cabildos and provisional juntas. This return to the fiscal structure of the old Hapsburg and early Bourbon periods presaged the head taxes that were the chief support of the liberal national governments after independence. Half a century later the fundamental Bourbon reform that had faced revolt in 1766 was still not accepted and would be replaced with independence.

The Spanish Cortes that sat after 1812 was the intellectual heir of the enlightened monarchs, continuing those policies that war, invasion, and the collapse of central rule had disrupted. The Cortes ban on repartimiento and the end of the tribute tax was consistent with the monarchical philosophy of promoting the Indian as a free participant in society. The Inquisition was abolished; the Bourbons had ended its authority long before. Legislation diminishing the power of convents and monasteries to recruit and retain minors reflected a century-old trend. The creation of a degree of freedom of the press had existed under Charles III, in fact if not in law.

The Cortes' most radical measure was the Provincial Deputation that removed much authority from the audiencia, providing a greater voice in political decisions to the local level in the various regions of the empire. The deputation introduced indirect election for officials who administered localities. Its members were chosen by cabildos with the president of the audiencia holding the only appointed seat, "political chief," with one vote on the council. The deputation was given power over finances, the judiciary, the royal patronage, and police affairs. Even more than under the Hapsburgs, then, the elite was to control the destiny of the colony.[10]

Creole and peninsular liberals were not united. The American idea gained strength among Creole deputies who had been loyal but who had become embittered by peninsular rigidity toward colonial representation and rights in the empire. The independent action of the Buenos Aires cabildo and the wars of independence in Mexico and Caracas inspired political divisions. Creoles themselves were divided; some derived their thought from the French Revolution, others from the enlightenment, some were clerics like Larrazábal, others were virulently anti-clerical.

And there was opposition in the colonies to the events in Spain. In Central America, bureaucrats, Creole merchants tied to peninsular commercial houses, clerics, and artisans threatened by English imports were all opposed to liberalism, although all retained some elements of enlightened thought. The liberal faction in Guatemala, headed by the Aycinenas, was a distinct minority, perhaps among the Creoles themselves. Indeed, the fight over Creole authority and Cortes power is reminiscent of the seventeenth-century dispute between cabildo and monarch, except that natural law rather than tradition was called upon, and the monarch or its regency was no longer thought to balance interests.

The authoritarian soldier José de Bustamante, who served as president of the audiencia from 1811 until 1817, represents the archetypal Bourbon bureaucrat, honest and determined to fulfill his role in maintaining centralist, royal authority at a time when the center was giving out. His role was as important as that of his arch rival, the Marquis Aycinena, who represented liberal merchant power assaulting the state. Bustamante is an example of a public figure, trapped by historical circumstances, who is considered a fool at best, a tyrant at worst, despite his efficiency and abilities. His role has been reviled by all Central American historians and ignored by the Spanish. "Hard, inflexible, suspicious, absolute, vigilant and reserved, his plans of government were a perfect reflection of his character," one of his contemporaries wrote.[11]

Bustamante arrived in Central America in 1811 with long experience in the colonial military. As governor-general of Montevideo, he had fought the vast contraband trade in the Río de la Plata. In 1806 he had commanded the unsuccessful defense of the town against the British and was repatriated to Spain. His experiences in Montevideo had hardened him to those who traded with the enemy or any other nation. After a decade of contraband trade that had enjoyed the protection of González Mollindo and his aide Alejandro Ramírez, the Guatemalan cabildo expected to continue its free hand in Central America's commercial and political affairs. Bustamante saw a depressed economy in indigo, cotton, wool, and in the trade of the artisans, and in the following years he faced sporadic Creole rebellions for independence throughout the colony and an invasion of revolutionary forces from Mexico. The Spanish political fluctuations handicapped his authority during the six years of his rule. Government orders that came from one government were later rejected and then reinstated. Judicial decisions could never be made final. The Aycinena merchant community openly defied his orders developing a state of passive resistance to his rule. His efforts to maintain order as well as to combat the enemies of Spain—be they Mexican revolutionaries, British contraband traders, or Guatemalan merchants—were further stymied by a fiscal structure weakened by the depression and by the suspension of the tribute payment by the 1812 liberal Cortes that eliminated a large portion of the colony's annual income. In constant conflict with the Guatemalan merchants and with liberal oidores in the audiencia, the besieged military commander was finally replaced in 1817. He was subsequently indicted by the restored, conservative government of Ferdinand VII, which sought to restore its ties with the Guatemalan merchant community.

The political fluctuations in Spain were the most important factor in weakening Bustamante's authority. Liberals controlled the Spanish government in 1808, were replaced by conservatives the following year, and were, in turn, overthrown by liberals in 1812. Orders from these different governments counteracted earlier measures, creating confusion within the colonies and causing unrest in an empire already disrupted by revolutionary movements. The 1808 liberal congress, for example, created a central junta with equal representation from all areas of the empire. Each cabildo was to nominate three individuals and choose one name by lottery. These victorious candidates' names were to be sent to the audiencia, who were to select three of the best, with one of these to be chosen by lottery. Of all the nominations made by the various Central American municipalities, perhaps three were not Guatemalan merchants and one of these was the bishop of Chiapas. The three candidates chosen by the audiencia were Antonio Juarros, José Aycinena, and Manuel José Pavón. Juarros was a cattle merchant with close connections to the Aycinenas, while Pavón had married into the family. In the end, Juarros was chosen, but the long involved process that took almost a year was all for naught, because the liberal junta was overthrown by conservatives who annulled the proceedings.[12]

The election process, however, did allow for the first "democratic" elections for representatives in Spain and further fortified the colonial liberals. The central junta had declared that "the vast and precious domains of Spain are no longer colonies like with other countries, but an integral part of the Spanish monarchy." Under the Hapsburgs, the Americas held "kingdoms," under the Bourbons "colonies," now, the region was united, if only temporarily, with the metropolis.

Spain and its colonies worked at cross purposes. In those places in which a strong president ruled (for example, Bustamante), suppressing periodic attempts at independence and attempting to maintain an absolutist state, the Spanish Cortes, established in 1812, tried to give Creoles more power within the government. Declarations came from Spain which Bustamante resisted and sometimes suppressed, while the Guatemalan cabildo, the leader among Central American liberals, appealed to the Spanish parliament for enforcement of its decrees. Paradoxically, José Aycinena, the son of the Marquis, served on the executive council of state in Madrid from 1812 until 1814, working for liberalization of the empire, while the peninsular Bustamante served in the colony attempting to preserve absolutism.

The liberals used every opportunity to pressure for greater power in Central America. Given the atmosphere of the period, with cabildo power in Buenos Aires and Caracas leading to strong, independence movements, and with Hidalgo and Morelos in nearby Mexico involved in bloody revolutionary struggles, a fine line existed between political maneuvering within the empire and revolutionary movements.

There were three attempts to enlarge Creole power during this period. The first commenced just nine days after word had been received in Guatemala of the appointment of Bustamante. The Guatemalan cabildo sent a request to the outgoing president González Mollindo to raise urban militias, "so that the Kingdom has the necessary training in the handling of arms." Before he could act, however, González Mollindo was deposed by his second in command, Colonel José Mendez, who assumed command because of the "illness of the President." He ordered the immediate transfer of troops stationed in

Granada to the capital and established a "Tribunal of Loyalty" under his control to ensure the allegiance of all citizens and to make sure that no illegal publications were distributed. A Guatemalan liberal later said the Tribunal employed "detention, spying, and other inquisitorial processes that were carried out in all regions [of Central America]."[13]

Bustamante arrived in March 1811 and continued many of the policies of Mendez. He repulsed efforts by Aycinena and other merchants to gain influence and ruled as a stern, military officer. With all avenues towards power blocked in the capital, a series of rebellions occurred in the interior. Beset by the severe problems caused by the decline in indigo production, with the drive towards liberalism throughout the empire, and the example of the Mexican Revolution, a group of conspirators, headed by the prelate Doctor Matías Delgado, seized the armory in San Salvador and deposed the intendant in 1811. All of the plotters were members of the leading families of the region and were later, after independence, to play significant roles in the Central American federal government. But in 1811 they lacked support among the populace of Salvador and the liberal cabildos. Only eight months in the colony, Bustamante was persuaded by the Guatemalan cabildo that its leaders could pacify the rebellious areas. A picket of troops led by José Aycinena and José María Peinado met with no resistance and peacefully suppressed the uprising. Peinado was appointed the region's new intendant.[14]

A series of factors had precipitated the rebellion. "The results of twenty years of war, of locusts, or ruins caused by earthquakes and from political calamities," a loyal Salvadoran group later explained, "this province has come to such a state . . . that the sad moment has arrived in which there is no work to be done [*no tener en que ocupar sus brazos*]." Peinado agreed with the assessment, claiming that there were innumerable people who came from all parts of the province each day asking for help with their debts, "both property owners as well as workers." To remedy the situation, the cabildo and Peinado suggested that tobacco be introduced into Salvador and higher than market prices paid to the growers so that a new money crop could replace the once profitable production of indigo.[15]

The Salvadoran upheaval had a ripple effect elsewhere in the intendancy and throughout Central America. The town of Santa Ana supported the Salvadoran rebellion. Government officials in San Miguel and San Vicente concentrated troops to aid the return of the region to Spanish control. A brief uprising, quickly suppressed, took place in the neighboring Guatemalan province of Chiquimula.[16]

When news of the Salvadoran disturbances reached León, a revolt broke out in December 1811 and the intendant was deposed. Peace was restored when the rebels were persuaded to turn over the government to the local bishop. Word of the insurrections in Salvador and León inspired the cities of Granada, Segovia, and Rivas to revolt and depose their "European leadership." Segovia and Rivas followed León's example, but the Granada rebels continued their fight in the bloodiest conflict of this early period. Their new government freed all slaves, reduced the price of tobacco, and lowered various taxes. Forces from León and Rivas beseiged the rebels for four months. The civil war ended with a guarantee of general amnesty, which Bustamante negated, ordering the arrest of the rebels.[17]

Small disturbances erupted in Tegucigalpa and Cartago. In the former city, the appointment of a "Spaniard" as the local chief by Comayaguan officials provoked rebellion and Bustamante sent troops. In Costa Rica there were brief uprisings in Cartago and other towns caused, it was said, "by the ill effects of the monopolies of aguardiente and tobacco." The governor of the area allowed the two products to be traded freely.[18]

The revolts indicate the animosities provoked by economic depression, centralized government, and regionalism. The Nicaraguan civil war and the violation of the peace fueled hatreds that lasted long into the national period. As Granada fought León, so too did Salvador oppose Guatemala, and Tegucigalpa fought during the following twenty-five years.

Within a year of his arrival, Bustamante had faced opposition and revolts throughout the interior. With the successful suppression of these movements, however, the 1812 liberal revolution in Spain established a government antithetical to his policies. For the next two years, until the counterrevolution in May 1814 in Spain, the efforts to maintain control by the soldier-president were opposed by both Central American colonists and his superiors. Specifically, Bustamante resisted the Cortes' establishment of the Provincial Deputation that gave colonials, rather than bureaucrats, control of local administration. Repeated controversies ensued over the censorship by the Spaniard of cabildo meeting minutes and orders concerning the treatment of the captured Granada rebels and, above all, Bustamante's censorship of all news concerning the Morelos rebellion in Mexico.[19]

Tension between Spaniard and Creoles reached its greatest point in 1813 when Bustamante informed the Guatemalan cabildo that the fall of Oaxaca to the Mexican Morelos rebellion meant he "must as Captain General and Political Chief take active and vigorous military measures to defend the nation." He would move mulatto troops from Omoa through the city to the north, a show of strength that terrorized the Guatemalans for racial reasons as well as for its demonstration of the military power he possessed. The cabildo stressed that troops should not enter the city, because they might attack local residents. Bustamante persisted and the Creoles issued their most blatant attack:

> Your Excellency has not dealt with this municipality with the union and harmony that one would expect from its chief. Ever since you assumed office, you have not related to the citizenry of this city, principally those most esteemed by the indigenous population of the country; you work for only yourself without consulting the most respected subjects. . . .[20]

When Bustamante rejected the diatribe, the cabildo ordered that no troops enter the city. The síndico of the municipality proposed that a "Provincial Governing Board" take control of the colony from the president (some six months before the Cortes established the Provincial Deputations), and the cabildo of Guatemala wrote the Cortes, requesting that the Marquis de Aycinena be named as *Jefe Político Superior*. The actions of Bustamante, the cabildo wrote, "have led to ruin, the character of this jefe is not suitable to lead in these very critical times and circumstances."[21]

Bustamante, who saw himself as defender of Spanish power in the Americas, interpreted Creole opposition to the movement of troops as support for the Morelos invasions. He intercepted correspondance that betrayed pro-rebellion feelings. "Manuel Aguilar has written to his brother Nicolas," Bustamante reported, "that Spain is completely lost and cannot resist the French; that the rebels in the Kingdom of Mexico are winning and will soon enter the capital."[22]

Military reverses complicated the resistance to Bustamante. He ordered the Caribe troops north to defend the frontier, but he specifically forbade an offensive into Mexico. The troops invaded Oaxaca, seizing a number of rebel towns. Lacking reserves and stores, the Spanish troops were forced back to Chiapas when the rebel commander Matamoros counterattacked. Matamoros pursued them as far as the gates of Ciudad Real, returning finally to Oaxaca because of his own tenuous military position.[23]

With rebel troops descending from Mexico and Creoles about to take power in a liberal Provincial Deputation, other members of the merchant community plotted a "revolution," in Bustamante's words, within the walls of the Belén convent. José Francisco Barrundia, who was later to become president of an independent Central America, José María Montúfar, who was close to the Aycinena family, and other

Creoles planned a Christmas eve revolt of the city's only battalion, the arrest of the colonial authorities, and the liberation of the Granada prisoners and a proclamation of independence. Representatives were to take control of the interior, uniting Guatemala and southern Mexico into one liberated area.[24] The Belén plotters were betrayed by one of their participants. Bustamante imposed martial law for two months and imprisoned members of the Guatemalan cabildo and some of the other leading Creoles. An abortive revolt took place in Salvador.[25]

Bustamante's general repression ended, for the time being, any Creole hope of taking power. He suspended all of the Cortes' liberal legislation, including permission of free speech and press and local autonomy. The Creoles appealed to the Cortes, but the counterrevolution of May 1814 restored the conservative Ferdinand VII to full power and the Cortes was dissolved.

Bustamante launched an offensive against the liberal merchants, taking control of the merchant guild, removing the Aycinena faction and replacing it with businessmen who did not deal in contraband trade. He ordered the restitution of all money paid to Cortes deputies by the treasury, some 500,000 pesos, with the heaviest responsibility placed on those who participated in the elections. "Now is not the time to protest," Bustamante reminded the Creoles, "but to pay without delay that which you owe."[26]

Bustamante also attacked the virulent contraband traffic that was sapping the strength of the empire and the colony as well. Since 1800, when liberal Spanish officials permitted the entry of English textiles, the trade had grown, promising Guatemalan merchants much greater profits than trade in Central American cloth. The trade had two damaging effects: destroying local artisans and sapping the colony's silver reserves. Further, in 1800 merchants exchanged highly valued indigo for English textiles, but a decade or so later only coinage could be traded because the dye had lost its value. According to the intendant of Honduras in 1815, Central America's principal economic problem was "the extraordinary extraction of silver of all classes by the English in exchange for merchandise and articles of luxury that are consumed quickly."[27] A decline in a cash crop leading to the sapping of silver wealth from Central America repeated the experience of two centuries before.

A sizable portion of the Guatemalan merchant community allied itself with Bustamante in his efforts to prosecute contraband traffic. The importation of English cloth destroyed their trade in Central American textiles as much as it hurt the colonial fiscal system.[28] Bustamante gave control of the consulado to this faction of the merchant community after the conservative 1814 revolution. It would form the conservative loyalist faction that opposed independence in 1821.

Bustamante attempted to restrict contraband traffickers by prosecuting them in the capital and by maintaining a coast guard in the Bay of Honduras, but he was only partly successful. He deprived the house of Aycinena of government business, and, after 1814, of its control of the merchant guild and the Guatemalan cabildo that held power over many important monopolies. He brought charges against the Marquis for failing to pay taxes on English goods imported during the liberal years prior to Bustamante's tenure, forcing Aycinena to place a large bond on deposit in the royal treasury. The harassment of the house had some effect by tying up its resources. A decade later an Aycinena, commenting on those troubled times, told of the fight "to conserve the reputation of the house, and provide means for the many credits that tormented us." Nevertheless, Bustamante failed in his ultimate objective of destroying the Aycinenas, and when the crown removed him in 1817, it cleared the commercial house of all charges in an effort to restore relations between the crown and the colonial business community.[29]

His guard of the Central American ports was also successful only in part. English vessels were seized periodically along the coast and Spanish vessels coming from Havana with English cotton goods were also condemned, but the trade continued unabated. The commercial route with Spain had lost all value with the decline in indigo commerce, and trade with Mexico created only additional expenses. Only Britain remained a viable trading partner. "The contraband trade that the [English] colonists of Wales [Belize] do along our coast is incalculable," the intendant of Comayagua reported in 1819. "Pirates" from rebel Cartagena sailed the Caribbean, plaguing Central American ports, which the Spanish were impotent to defend.[30]

In spite of Bustamante's desire to suppress contraband, the lack of fiscal resources severely limited his movements. The official could do little to halt the process of steadily contracting taxes. "Bustamante did not maintain a zealous guard in the ports," it was later said by an enemy, "and dismissed employees with the pretext of making [fiscal] savings." The decline in government revenue and Spanish power was inevitable and beyond the control of the soldier-chief. Even before Bustamante took office, the fiscal administration was pressured by growing war expenses and declining income caused by contraband trade and the depression in Central America's economy. The crown had ordered the treasury in Mexico to provide 100,000 pesos to support Central American defense, but the aid was cut off when the War for

Table 11.1: The Fiscal Situation of Central America, 1812 (in pesos)

Jurisdiction	Active Debts	Passive Debts	Firm and Eventual Income	Firm Expenses
Guatemala	543,321	4,011,287	619,628	1,004,335
León	20,745	235,141	75,368	180,700
Ciudad Real	24,901		61,780	25,325
Comayagua	36,698		265,704	200,799
San Salvador	17,390		318,680	242,357
Sonsonate	604		16,311	12,273
Trujillo			23,373	137,053
Omoa			103,694	100,609
Totals	643,659	5,146,428	1,484,538	1,903,451

SOURCE: A.G.G. A3.1, Leg. 2724, Exp. 39026.
Note: Active debts refer to those needing immediate repayment. Passive debts refer to those bonds or *juros* or loans that demand an annual payment of interest rather than repayment.

Independence erupted in the colony. Fortifying the coast and raising a militia against revolutionaries drained the treasury further.[31]

Bustamante found an impossible fiscal situation when he arrived; he reported in 1812 that the state was losing half a million pesos annually (see table 11.1) in military expenditures. The emergency situation was compounded when the Cortes suspended the Indian tribute, which theoretically cost the treasury 672,000 pesos during the period of its enforcement.[32]

Bustamante took drastic and extra-legal measures to meet the fiscal crisis. He reduced the interest paid on government bonds from 5 to 4.5 percent, a rate that had existed for at least two centuries, and compelled the Creoles to make "voluntary contributions" to the war effort. He depleted all of the Indian community funds by taking ("hechar mano") the moneys to meet emergency expenses, the money supposedly to be repaid in the future.[33] His most radical move violated the purpose of the suspension of Indian tribute by the Spanish liberals. He issued a proclamation calling on all Central Americans to "keep proving your loyalty and patriotism using the easiest means." Indians were reminded that they were expected to give "that which they voluntarily want for the expenses of the present war so that in this manner they can prove that they are good children [son buenos hijos]." A "patriotic donation and subscription" was opened in April 1812: "in each parish, the clergy with the respective [civilian authority] or a secular citizen will be in charge, so that there exists no individual who doesn't respond to this very sacred obligation." Indians remained "under the debt of being vassals;" they must "contribute to the maintenance of the religion, the return of the adored King Ferdinand VII, and the sustenance of the war in Spain."[34]

Forced contributions superseded the suspension of the tribute. During the year 1812 there were two requests for "donations" of a peso, which equalled the usual two-peso Indian tribute payments. One clergyman complained that this "quota" was impossible because of the "abject poverty" of the people and suggested that the authorities look elsewhere for the funds. In Honduras an official was notified that the Indians of one town refused to fulfill their quota because "they had already given that year."[35]

Despite Bustamante's extraordinary measures the treasury remained in debt, forcing a reduction in expenditures. He suspended repairs on the Omoa fortress and support for the black colonists who had been introduced there twenty years earlier. He halted construction on the presidential palace and the cathedral in Guatemala that had been proceeding since the city had moved. He reduced the number of civil officials, saving 25,600 pesos annually, and military posts, saving 70,000 pesos annually. In all, he estimated that he had reduced expenses about a million and a half pesos in his six years over the previous term.[36]

The treasury was pressed by the needs introduced by liberal Spain, measures which Bustamante held to be treacherous. Each representative to the Spanish Cortes had to be paid from 4,000 to 5,000 pesos annually, travel costs, and daily expenses (6 pesos per diem). The expenses were covered by a tax of one real per pound on tobacco. But when, in 1813, further Cortes reforms added representatives from each partido (or province) in America rather than from each intendancy, there were additional expenses.[37]

The pressure upon Bustamante to cover military expenses (and his judgment of the alien liberal government) led him to transfer the tobacco tax revenue to government expenses and to order the local cabildo to support the salary and expenses of the Cortes representatives. The municipalities appealed this repression to the Cortes. The Guatemalan cabildo did "not overlook that the reason for the present decision of the Supreme Government and the lack of funds in this province to sustain its deputies [is being used] as a reason to reduce its representation." Nevertheless, Bustamante's anti-liberal fiscal measures remained.[38]

When Ferdinand VII tried to restore good relations with America's liberal merchants in 1817, Bustamante was removed from office. As part of a general, empire-wide amnesty, the Marquis of Aycinena was pardoned, along with all the rebels who had taken part in the various uprisings in Central America. Bustamante was indicted for poor administration at the instigation of José de Aycinena in Madrid. He was subsequently cleared, due, in part, to a brilliant defense by a Spanish official, José Tejada:

> Bustamante served his term without the great bloodletting that other, less fortunate countries suffered, he suffocated the spirit of insurrection that developed in some provinces at their point of origin, and repelled the neighboring rebel insurgents [from Mexico] and received no decorations as did all other leaders in America. Perhaps no other chief in America left the royal treasury in the same [good] state.[39]

Thus, in 1817, centralist power came to an end in Central America. The Aycinena-dominated liberal cabildo of 1812 to 1814 was reappointed. Within two years open trade with foreign nations became a reality, and the president was unable to do anything to halt it. Within three years the provincial deputation took power and authority away from the president of the audiencia, and within four years Central America eased into independence, one of the few regions to achieve it peacefully.

PART THREE

The Center Gives Out

CHAPTER TWELVE

The Widening Gyre

THE SINGLE, MOST important result of the Acts of Independence of September 1821 was the end of the monarchy. For three centuries Central America had been a political entity under the crown, the "Kingdom of Guatemala." The valleys of Honduras, the Guatemalan highlands, the Salvador and Chiapas hotlands, the ports of Omoa, Granada, and Realejo, the cities of León and Guatemala, and the hundreds of diverse areas with hot, dense cacao plantations, or well-ordered sugar works, or the great, wild expanses of cattle haciendas, or the well-kept Indian common lands, all were united within this kingdom. Spanish merchants, Creole farmers, miners and cowboys, mestizo and black laborers, and the diverse populations of Indians speaking hundreds of dialects and doing hundreds of tasks, all recognized that they lived under the domain of a Spanish sovereign, who was the ultimate mediator and judge of the multitude of disputes over political jurisdictions, labor or business practices, or bureaucratic decisions, and whose representatives ruled in Guatemala. The monarchy was, indeed, the preserver, as well as the symbol, of unity and once independence was achieved, the cement that bonded together the fragile Central American entity dissolved.

The act of independence was the culmination of a slow drift away from centralized rule that had begun at the turn of the century with the growth of commercial contacts with foreign nations and continued through the destructive military embroglios of the metropolis. Free trade with England became a reality in 1817, more the result of Spanish frailty than any other cause. The cabildos of Central America grew in power as the authority of the audiencia declined. Control from the center gave out. As Central America grew further and further away from Spain, it divided more and more internally. As free trade became open practice, the internal regions gained autonomy. Honduran and

Nicaraguan towns rejected Guatemalan rule fully a year before independence. When independence was declared it was proclaimed by separate, independent cabildos, not by a national authority. Without a sovereign in Spain, most cabildos became sovereigns who ruled their territories independently, resisting central control. The result of the attempt at centralization, which the Bourbons had begun, was these separate political entities that were born in September 1821. Any attempts to preserve Central American unity thereafter went for naught. Out of the crucible of war and bloodletting that was the fifteen-year epilogue to the act of independence, weak, small states with new institutions were forged.

The impetus for the break with Spain came from the small but powerful group of Guatemalan merchants headed by the house of Aycinena. This minority group first pressured for free trade and later forced independence by allying itself with rebel leaders in Mexico in 1821. Most of Central America followed its lead reluctantly, hesitating to join a movement that by September 1821 was all so evidently succeeding throughout the Americas. This chapter will consider the growth in power of this small group, its efforts to supplant the declining Spanish central authority with central authority under Guatemala's control, and the resistance of the interior to it.

The first sign of the weakening of Bourbon authority was the end of Spanish control of trade. Illicit trade with the English had become common by 1818, with English cotton goods readily available in Guatemala. As trade with the English became normal, Spanish commerce was restricted, obstructed, and harassed by Caribbean "pirates" (as Central American officials called the independence fighters from New Granada), who plagued the Honduran coast, raiding Omoa for indigo and seizing frigates on their way to Havana. Guatemalan businessmen repeatedly petitioned the crown to allow trade with other nations "to foment industry, agriculture, and commerce that is in a miserable state because of the inability to export indigo." A group of Cádiz merchants even suggested the use of "neutral" ships to bring indigo to Spain. The pressure of the business interests and Spain's obvious inability to protect the coastline compelled a compromise with those who favored more liberal trade policies.[1]

"Free trade" with other nations became a reality as a result of these pressures and the inability of a weak captain general to resist the Guatemalan cabildo. Carlos de Urrutia Montoya y Matos arrived in Guatemala in March 1818 with careful instructions from the crown to make peace with the Aycinenas and others with whom his predecessor, José de Bustamante, had struggled. The liberal cabildo, dismissed in the 1814 counterrevolution and now reinstated, was given considerable influence over Urrutia's activities. The municipality demanded free trade, and these demands, combined with the other forces at work, compelled Urrutia to accede. The president attempted a minor reform, allowing British traders some entry to Central American ports while maintaining the prohibition on Guatemalan merchants traveling to Belize. This legitimized contraband traffic while it benefited the government through customs taxes. But the crack in the dam created by the order soon became a deluge, as the Guatemalans, at first surrepetitiously and then openly, traveled to the British settlement. Thus, the "free trade" of illicit contraband traffic was legitimized. Within a year, the Guatemalan cabildo informed Spanish authorities that "absolute liberty of commerce no longer is a problem as in earlier times."[2]

The opening of direct commercial relations with the British immediately created a surge in business. The Belize merchants, who had traded illegally with Guatemala for twenty years, gained entry and direct contacts with most of Central America. Cheap cotton goods flowed into the colony and were sold at prices so low that demand rose and the Central American economy was temporarily stimulated. The great profit margin the English enjoyed allowed them to exchange textiles for cheap indigo as well as silver. Mining and indigo production rose.

The spurt was, however, only a temporary phenomenon, limited by the resources of Central American merchants and the small demand for indigo in England's depressed textile economy. However, it did normalize trade relations with Great Britain and later, between 1821 and 1825, when the British economy expanded and demand for indigo rose, independent Central America was linked to Britain through Belize.

The expansion in Central America's economy benefited only a small part of the colony. The Aycinenas, who had gained control over a sizable portion of indigo producing lands in Salvador through farmers' defaults on loans and who had links with the English, profited the most and their economic power, which had appeared destroyed by Bustamante only a few years earlier, flourished once again. Other businessmen in the capital linked to the export economy also profited by trading silver coins and indigo for textiles.

But at the same time the English commercial invasion destroyed those involved in Central American textile production. "Thousands of workers in the southern [Pacific] coast know no other agricultural product than this one," it was said, while in Verapaz, highland Guatemala, and the regions around Antigua Guatemala "thousands of poor women were occupied spinning it into thread." In these regions as well as the capital, artisans made cloth from the thread. But as the English commodity deluged Central America, the price for the cloth fell 75 percent from twelve to three reales the *vara*. Before 1810, highland Guatemala was said to have sold Mexico from 35,000 to 40,000 in cotton goods at 30 to 35 pesos for a dozen pieces. With free trade, there was no commercial interaction, even though the articles were being offered at 12 to 30 pesos.[3]

A bitter controversy developed between those who prospered and those who suffered from free trade. José del Valle, a student of Goicoechea, became the spokesman for protectionist sentiment, advocating the support of artisan craftsmen:

> It is true what a philosopher once said: "Kings have States; the great have houses; the rich have money; and the people have virtue.
> Mortality exists in the workshop: it exists in the forge and the loom. [If they were here] Cienfuegos would meet artisans who are fit for his cantos, and Seneca would see virtue in hands grounded in work.[4]

To defend local industry it was necessary to abolish trade with the English:

> Prohibit the introduction of foreign goods, principally of cotton into all our ports, and on all our roads: attempt to extinguish their use in this colony: Burn the stockpile [of foreign goods] and, if it is possible, return them to their producers, then, in this manner, we will see the need to dress ourselves in our own national textiles, agriculture will prosper, interior commerce will become activated, the number of artisans will grow.[5]

On the other hand, the advocates of free trade pointed to the low prices of imported commodities, arguing the need to remove all government restraints in order to develop the natural economy of the area. To counter the idea of a prosperous past when government control over trade was strong, Pedro Molina, another student of Goicoechea and spokesman for the liberals, argued,

> . . . if somebody asks me, what opulence? The past will answer him, that in which we now live, that that began one year ago, in which the evil free commerce with Belize came to convert us to smoke and misery. Oh happy past times! Before, a vara of gauze cost six pesos in every store, if you could find it, now it costs four reales [½ peso]. Bad sign! A bottle of wine then cost two reales without deposit, and now it's a

good profit to sell it at one with deposit and everything. Lost is this world! Before, nobody ever went to look for goods outside of the Kingdom while Mr. So-and-so, merchant, with his counterparts in Cádiz, waited in his house for the boat to come from Spain, each year clothes and merchandise arrived, and [the people] would come to his house like flies to honey attempting to get a lot [of goods] at the price that the seller would give, and now whatever little boy can take his money and go and buy a hatchet. . . . What an injury for Guatemala![6]

The dispute reflected political differences between the economic and social classes, which were after 1820 the basis of Central America's first political parties. Highland cotton farmers and artisans joined together with the Spanish merchants and clergy to advocate a return to the centralized authority of Spain and an end to trade links with the British. Nicaraguan and other merchants from the interior allied themselves with these groups as commerce was drawn away from their region toward Guatemala and commodities moved to Belize rather than Granada.[7]

These groups felt the effects of the artificial stimulus to the economy that created a demand for indigo affecting a small sector of the colony while it drained Central America of silver. If Guatemalan merchants profited greatly from the textile trade, and if imported goods were cheaper, the local, interior Central American economies of highland Guatemala, in León, Granada, Tegucigalpa, and elsewhere were drained of their coinage. The demand for manufactured commodities from interior Central America also declined. Wealth continued to drain to the English and other nations through the federation period, the nineteenth century, and into the twentieth century.

As producers suffered, new crops were suggested for introduction to Central America, "agriculture and commerce being in a state of absolute decay and ruin." Cabildos proposed free trade in tobacco. Pedro Molina suggested: "the entire coastline of Trujillo, Omoa, and the Gulf of Honduras is adequate for the cultivation of coffee . . . and sugar, the two products that have made the island of Cuba prosperous." But the nation was losing its capital, and if some cochineal dye was introduced around Antigua Guatemala, by and large the merchant class was unwilling to invest in new projects that did not guarantee instant profit, such as importing British textiles.

Between 1819 and 1821 the political authority in Central America rested with the Guatemalan merchants who advocated free trade. Their move to reduce state control of their activities eventually resulted in independence. After independence, with central government authority shattered, the issue of government control of commerce was a moot point. Factional conflicts in Central America became public with the liberal revolution in Spain in 1820, when the restitution of the liberal Cortes and provincial deputations led to the formation of political parties and newspapers representing the opposing views. The *Cacos* favored free trade and Creole rule in the cabildos and deputations, and their opponents, the *Gazistas*, were primarily those groups who were hurt by free trade, merchants with close connections to Spain and the bureaucracy.

The crucial question for the interior was the structure of the new political process rather than specific issues. For them, the chief problem was the domination of the colony by the capital city, the control of commerce, the control of credit, and the inordinate influence of the Guatemalans upon Spanish rule. Each city and town, through their cabildos, fought for the establishment of local autonomy and disputed any attempt to supplant Spanish authority with Guatemalan power.

In the 1820–21 pre-independence period the political disputes between all the interests and the regions focused on the function and the power of the provincial deputation, the organ that served as the link between the colonial and independence periods. Resistance to the liberal Guatemalan body came from the Spanish authorites, the *Gazistas* and the interior regions who fought: first, the establishment of the body with full control over government institutions; second, the attempt to spread the authority of that body over interior areas; third, the usurpation of the remaining power of the president of the audiencia, now called the political chief (*jefe político*); and, fourth, after independence, the maintenance of the deputation's position as the central authority over the Central American state.

With the restitution of liberal rule, the deputation, which had scarcely functioned in 1814 before it was deposed, was reconstituted. It was controlled by the liberal *Cacos*, members of the Aycinena faction, and the Delgado liberals of Salvador who had revolted in 1811. José Aycinena informed Central American liberals of the March 1820 liberal revolution in Madrid and they were able to organize quickly a deputation before President Urrutia could take effective measures to forestall them. In August the deputation announced its intention to appoint civil judges (*jueces letrados*) throughout Guatemala, Honduras, and Salvador as its direct representatives over the interior, taking judicial responsibility from the audiencia. This insured Guatemalan "liberals" would interpret laws, not Spanish sympathizers.

Furthermore, the deputation would name the heads of the mint, the prison system, the post office, and the tobacco administration.[8]

President Urrutia, now political chief, resisted with the support of the old audiencia. At first, he failed to attend deputation meetings, pleading illness. Then, he refused to send government documents to the deputation, hesitated to enforce the legal decrees of the Spanish Cortes, and misinterpreted laws in an effort to delay "liberalization." He fought what was, in effect, the Creoles' attempt to take control over central administration that was, consciously or not, developing the infrastructure necessary for independence.[9]

The high church also opposed the deputation in what was the beginning of liberal-church antagonism in Central America. Archbishop Casaus was suspicious of the moves to erect a diocese in Salvador and of the general liberal tenor of the body. The deputation complained that the archbishop did not give it proper status in official religious celebrations. "It would not be strange," the body commented, "if the public interprets this omission as a sign of disagreement with the new system," and ordered the cleric to give it proper seating in the cathedral. The archbishop refused, remaining hostile to the liberal body.[10]

Disputes between the deputation and the Spanish officials became more significant in February 1821, with the important military revolt in Mexico led by Agustín de Iturbide. The Mexican independence movement merged the conservative, anti-Cortes faction with liberal pro-independence groups. Iturbide's *Plan de Iguala* called for the conservation of the Catholic religion, independence under a limited monarchy, and "union between all Americans and Europeans in Mexico."[11] The region was acutely sensitive to events in Mexico. With its southern borders exposed to the Bolivar independence movement and with the Iturbide rebellion in Mexico, only Havana remained loyalist, though a center of free trade and the scene of revolutionary plots. The deputation harassed Urrutia to force his resignation in favor of the second in command, Gabino Gaínza, a liberal Spaniard who was closer ideologically to the Creoles. After nine months of harassment, and in the face of the full force of the Iturbide rebellion, Urrutia resigned "temporarily" in March 1821.[12]

Spanish authorities compromised with the liberals because they lacked the forces to deal with any major rebellion in Central America. Little help could come from Spain; troops destined for the suppression of the Bolivar movement had rebelled and installed the liberal regime in Madrid, which eliminated the last major threat to the South American rebellion. There were garrisons of mulattoes and felons in Central American port towns who were not reliable. Despite the presence of these garrisons, nearly half a million pesos of indigo was taken from Omoa by a "rebel privateer" in early 1821, and later that same year "insurgent privateers" seized vessels from Nicaraguan ports.[13]

The Spanish government could not repress a major independence movement, but neither could the central government compel national cohesion. Only the creation of a strong bureaucracy in Guatemala could maintain central authority, but fiscal resources were just not available. The 1820–1821 liberal government faced the same situation that Bustamante had; with declining tax revenues, liberal changes in government were difficult to support. Two new deputations had to be supported, one each in Guatemala and León, civil judges, deputies to the Cortes, and, for a time, chiefs of local militias. "In a state of urgency" the treasury could not finance this; even local cabildos were unable to support their function.[14]

The revocation of the Indian tribute further complicated the situation. In 1812 Bustamante had converted tribute payments into a tax of another name, but now stronger resistance and weaker government negated this maneuver. As it was, there was a noticeable decline in tribute payments between 1815 and 1820, because some Indians believed government officials were stealing from them when the tax was reinstated in 1815. Many Indians assumed that the tribute was revoked with the restoration of the liberal government in 1820. In fact, the royal decree of April 15, 1820, ordered that "no change be made in the taxation system" when all the laws of 1812–14 Cortes were restored. Was the tribute a tax or a custom? An inconsistent policy developed throughout Central America. In Nicaragua, the governor of Costa Rica charged no tribute tax; in León, the political chief did. In Guatemala, highland Indians around the pueblo of Totonicapán rebelled against collection of the tribute by "different killings and sackings." Elsewhere, not only was the tribute charged, but the Indians' new status of citizen meant they were also liable for taxes that under the tributary system they had not paid.[15]

Should the government enforce the spirit of the constitution and eliminate the tribute or maintain it as a remedy for the shortage of funds? Everyone agreed that other servile obligations of the Indian, such as personal services and repartimiento had been abolished, but those acts did not affect the central government. But the deputation was powerless to enforce its decrees in the interior of Guatemala, where priests or corregidores ruled. A full year after the personal service requirement had been eliminated by both the Cortes and the deputation, protests of the failure of officials to comply deluged the authorities.[16] As late as August 1821 no decision on the tribute tax had been made. The deputation repeatedly put off its decision "to another season," avoiding confrontation with interior areas and Indians. There is no evidence of any decisive act prior to independence in September. It was not until the Mexican Empire, in February 1822, that the tribute was suspended in Central America.[17]

The central authorities procrastinated, but income from the tribute tax declined nonetheless. The government looked elsewhere for resources: an attempt to "hechar mano" in community funds found them generally bankrupt; a call to local cabildos, which unanimously pleaded insolvency. The municipality of Sanayaz replied, "we must restore the commerce we had in the past." Mazatenango wrote "it could not encounter any means because all the townspeople were daily laborers" and "the town needs water in the plaza and a primary school." Naxapa could not "see what the result would be of [supporting] a deputy to the Cortes" because the Guatemalan deputation had not honored a royal decree granting the town some abandoned land. There was unanimous opposition to extra funds that would yield nothing for the localities, and numerous grievances and economic difficulties were voiced as well.[18]

The responses indicated a tax revolt and the precarious condition of cabildo funds. The town of Anon (de Chimaltenango) declared:

> If the voyage of our deputies could be facilitated, we could loan beasts and workers with much pleasure. It would be easy for the town to conduct them from this town until the next, but nothing more. The cabildo has no funds. Neither the secretary nor the political chief are paid. The roads are in need of repair. . . .

Antigua Guatemala, the richest cabildo outside of the capital, added that it could count on only the *chicha* monopoly for any funds, and that these 9,000 pesos were not sufficient to pay deputies to the Cortes or to cover the salaries of the cabildo, tax administrators, and civil judges.[19] Immediately before independence a member of the deputation summed up: "A sad experience is occurring daily because of the empty state of the public treasury. While there are greater demands and new officials, income has declined."[20]

The Bourbon fiscal system had collapsed. Government was weak at both the national and local levels. The deputation could decree new fiscal measures, but it could not enforce them and it lacked an economic base to tax. Any government reforms requiring additional expenditures had per force to be weak and were resented by the populace.[21] This was particularly true in the attempt to institute civil judges throughout Guatemala. Like the Bourbon intendants of the eighteenth century, liberal civil judges were meant to extend and strengthen centralized power in Guatemala. The judges were to mediate disputes, represent the central government in the interior, oversee tax collection, and make political and economic decisions. Responsible to the Guatemalan deputation, they had little affinity for the region where they worked, representing an alien, liberal government. They challenged the traditional power figures of the area, either dominant families or, often, the clergy.

The new liberal institutions, like the judges, were Creole attempts to supplant Spanish authority with its unifying power of the king with an institutional framework for a locally administered colony under the authority of Guatemala City. After hundreds of years of rule by alcaldes mayores and corregidores appointed by and representative of the crown, the introduction of Creole judges appointed by Guatemalans created a crisis in authority and, indeed, in sovereignty.

Similarly, a crisis occurred when deputations tried to extend their authority to the interior. Lacking the power to enforce their decisions, challenges from Honduras to Guatemala authority and from Costa Rica to Nicaraguan authority could not be overcome. Comayagua rebelled against the decisions to transfer its profitable tobacco factory to the nearby town of Tegucigalpa and to permit mulattoes to vote in elections. The Tegucigalpan families had long rivaled the Honduran city. Less prosperous, but traditionally the dominant city of Honduras as the seat of the diocese, Comayagua's families had been fighting attempts by the wealthy miners of Tegucigalpa to make their city the province's political center for most of the eighteenth century. The deputation's order was the work of the economic and political alliance between the Aycinena faction of Guatemalan businessmen and Tegucigalpa miners. Comayaguan families would not permit the move. Nor would they allow the mulattoes they had feared for centuries to take political control of outlying regions where a small number of Creole families dominated. The racial antipathy between Spaniards and blacks was the result of class distinctions and the constant wars with black Sambo tribesmen on the Mosquito Coast. No decision from Guatemala could force Creoles to abdicate their authority over the larger mulatto population.

Comayagua thus became the first region in Central America to secede. In early November 1820 the political chief, and former intendant, of Honduras, José Tinoco, established a deputation provincial in Comayagua and assigned deputies to the Cortes from each Honduran region. He also announced his intention to send all future government reports to Havana, bypassing Guatemalan central authority. Tinoco was supported by the leading families and the ecclesiastical authorities of Comayagua. The town had been "sacrificing its rights, sitting in silence, suffering a true enslavement in order to conserve its loyalty to the crown [sic]." "Now is the time for this ayuntamiento to reveal the pitiful picture of miseries to which we have been reduced by the merchants of cattle and silver of Guatemala." The Comayaguans decried the lack of protection from Sambos and foreign enemies, the failure of Guatemala to deal with the problems of abandoned mines, and the exporting of cattle from Honduras for breeding closer to Guatemala. The colonial administration in the capital "ran and runs all of its offices with the lucrative taxes from the province of Honduras." The new Honduran deputation concluded that "the interests of Honduras are diametrically opposed to those of Guatemala. Nothing, nothing will the Guatemalan deputation do to benefit this land."[22]

The Guatemalan deputation denounced the Comayaguan revolt and suggested that an example be made of Jefe Tinoco by bringing him back to the capital in chains. But without military force, the Guatemalan authorities were powerless to bring Comayagua under control. Other pressures could be brought to bear. The rich mineral resources of Tegucigalpa remained under Guatemalan control as that city pledged its loyalty to Guatemala; and the central deputation threatened the transfer of the Honduran capital to Tegucigalpa. The threats continued between Comayagua and Guatemala. The Honduran city threatened to seize the port of Omoa, and, indeed, after independence, took a shipment of armaments that had been destined for Guatemala. Comayagua lowered taxes on minerals as a lure to all mining regions outside of central Tegucigalpa.[23]

As Tegucigalpa separated from Comayagua and Comayagua from Guatemala, smaller localities became involved in the dispute. When Comayagua dissolved the cabildo of Jutigalpa, placing it under the authority of Olancho, Jutigalpa turned to Guatemala and the deputation there authorized the old cabildo to continue in office. Other towns were merged by Comayagua and those that lost political power looked to Guatemala for assistance.[24]

These territorial and jurisdictional disputes continued until well after independence, with Comayagua asserting its sovereignty, Tegucigalpa, its loyalty to the central authority, and Guatemala, its supremacy. The wars that plagued Central America for the next two decades continued these pre-independence controversies. The dispute over the Comayagua deputation was never resolved. When independence was declared, the deputations of Comayagua and Guatemala each assumed authority.[25]

Nicaragua also rejected the authority of Guatemala. Given a provincial deputation by the Cortes, Creoles in León pointed out to Urrutia, Gainza, and the Guatemalan liberals that they had autonomy. When Urrutia requested contributions for the purchase and dissemination of smallpox vaccine, the León deputation refused on the grounds that it controlled all fiscal matters and all such requests had to "derive from the deputation by necessity."[26]

But regionalism also plagued Nicaragua. The placement of Costa Rica under León's jurisdiction heightened the historic rivalry between León and Granada. Granada rejected León's authority. Costa Rica appealed to the Cortes for its independence: "the antipathy that the province of Nicaragua has shown [toward us] is notorious." There was no immediate military action, but when independence came in September 1821, independent regions emerged amidst bloodshed.[27]

The Creoles tried to dominate all aspects of government administration. But here, as in their attempt to control the interior, their successes were limited. The merchant guild is a good case in point. When, in 1815, Bustamante purged from the guild those merchants involved in contraband trade, the control of commerce and commercial courts was placed in the hands of those who wanted to continue monopolistic trade with Spain, the group that later was called the Gazistas. The liberal Guatemalan deputation struck at this influence in late 1820, accusing the guild of "privately exercising the administration of justice in mercantile matters, and also in the determination of the route or roads and other objects of commerce." They charged that the administration of justice had been "put in the hands of only shopkeepers" and proposed to abolish the guild. Urrutia and other Spanish bureaucrats forestalled this move. They were unable to resist other assaults against the Gazista trading group, however. When the deputation established primary custom houses in the ports of Omoa, Trujillo, and Realejo, it removed the obligation to bring all goods via the capital to pay taxes before exporting them. The measure aided the economic position of the English traders, of interior families who wished to avoid the capital's merchants, as well as the house of Aycinena, which had developed sufficient enterprises in the interior to avoid Guatemala.[28]

The liberal deputation was less successful in controlling municipal government in Guatemala City. With "democratic" elections the declining artisan classes, who suffered from free trade, supported the Gazistas. The new municipal government, the last one to serve a full term under colonial government, was ironically, a conservative, loyalist body.[29]

But the movement for independence was growing too powerful to be halted by a conservative cabildo. Liberal Creoles made contacts with General Iturbide, whose victory was becoming more and more apparent with each month. Pedro Molina wrote, as early as May, that "now [we must] prepare the opinion for the future," and followed it with a seditious fictional story of a revolution in a land very reminiscent of Central America.[30] By July, it was apparent that Mexican independence would be realized. On the second, Puebla fell, on the sixth, Zacatecas, and the thirty-first, Oaxaca. In Guatemala, control of the cabildo returned once again to the liberals, as Molina wrote: "we must make ourselves more commodious to the circumstances of the time in which we live and to the matters with which we deal."[31]

Finally, news of Iturbide's victory came to Central America in September, and as it travelled from north to south, cabildos declared their independence. The strength of Iturbide's forces, combined with a sizeable number, if not a majority, of advocates of independence among the Creole population, compelled all to follow Mexico's lead. Failure to do so would have meant warfare and conquest, either by Mexico, Guatemala, or rival nearby towns. Ciudad Real (Chiapas) was the first to declare for independence, and Guatemala, the most important, with acting jefe político Gaínza supporting the move. Some cabildos hesitated when others declared independence, secretly pledging their loyalty to Spain, but, with an impotent metropolis, independence was assured.

Cabildos declared their independence not only from Spain but also from their rival cities or towns. The center gave out. Ciudad Real declared independence from Comayagua and union with Guatemala. When León (Nicaragua) declared "absolute independence" from Guatemala, Granada, Rivas, and Masaya revolted and pledged unity with Guatemala. Costa Rica chose complete independence.[32]

The Kingdom of Guatemala was destroyed. The economic and political domination of the capital, the centralization of power accomplished by the Bourbons, and the perception of one region under a monarch, all disappeared. If the event was dramatic, it was not precipitous; it was the culmination of a trend that had been developing since at least 1800, a drift away from Bourbon centralization and Spanish hegemony.

Nor was this event surprising to contemporaries. Although some

Creoles may not have understood the consequences of independence, many saw the slow dissolution of Central America. Four months prior to independence a representative from Salvador addressed the Cortes and expressed the feelings of the interior towards Guatemala. Criticizing the fact that there were only two deputations in León and Guatemala, 700 leagues apart, he discussed the long distances, "rough roads, crossing mountains, sierras, and torrential rivers that in winter make transit difficult, because of the abundance of water," that would make elections and representative government difficult. The political and commercial interests of Guatemala, he asserted, were opposed to those of the provinces. Under the current system, most areas were not represented. The creation of eight separate deputations would, however

> make for the common and general well-being that this representative system guarantees and obtain political and moral education; moreover, it will show those inhabitants [of the interior] the benefits and utilities that true liberty provides; . . . [without reform] neither agriculture, industry, commerce or the arts will be improved; the roads, bridges, and canals will not be built to facilitate the traffic and export of our fruits, and the same abuses that existed before will be continued under another veil. *In the end, the towns will become disgusted and will be provoked, exasperating the hatreds of everybody towards each other. . . .*[33]

With independence, the problems of the colony became the problems of independent regions. The king was gone. The Cortes was forgotten. There was no higher authority to resolve disputes.

CHAPTER THIRTEEN

The Republican Experiment: In Search of Order

CENTRAL AMERICA DISSOLVED in 1821 into a multitude of independent, autonomous cabildo governments reminiscent of Hapsburg localism rather than Bourbon centralism. Families controlled affairs in each region, without concern for a colonial government or the affairs of Guatemala City. But what of the unity that followed independence, the united Central America under Mexico, and then the independent federation? Did this perpetuate colonial unity until the federation dissolved in the 1830s, as the history texts tells us? Certainly not. Indeed, during the period following independence there were a series of complicated attempts to restore unity, all unsuccessful. The federation was not a force for national unity, but for regional unity, defending the local hegemony of "liberal" towns against "conservative" towns, and a defense against foreign invasion. There were those who hoped for centralized rule or a united and federal Central America, but the attempts of either form of government to enforce its will ended in war.

Independence had been achieved through the efforts of liberals in Guatemala, who followed rather than resisted Mexico. Mariano Aycinena and Pedro Molina packed the galleries of the general meeting that debated independence with supporters of independence. But if Aycinena and Molina agreed on freedom from Spain, they disagreed on the future of the nation. Aycinena viewed an independent Central America as much under the domination of Guatemala City as it had been as a colony and saw unity with Mexico under Iturbide as a means of preserving Guatemalan hegemony, given the political situation. From early September onward, Aycinena corresponded with the Mexican and his followers, informing them of all developments in Guatemala.

Molina, on the other hand, understood the political reality differently. Mexico was historically and culturally separate from Central America. Perhaps Guatemalan merchants could unite with Mexican, but the hegemony Guatemala had enjoyed for centuries was now and forever destroyed. A federation could maintain unity: "Compare all the advantages of a federal government, in which liberty reigns, and union with the problems that Mexico offers, with a modern monarchy. The plan of Señor Iturbide sets back political progress twelve years."[1]

Opinion in interior regions differed as to union with Mexico. Many cabildos and families preferred domination by the distant capital in Mexico to Guatemala. Ciudad Real, Comayagua, and, later, León, all believed that they could achieve political hegemony over their respective regions under Mexico, while Tegucigalpa, Omoa, and Salvador were allied with the Molina liberals.[2]

Iturbide resolved the political division. A month after independence, he wrote to Guatemala that "the actual interests of Mexico and Guatemala are so identical and indivisible that they cannot erect separate, independent nations without threatening their existences and security. . . . Because of this, a numerous and well disciplined [army] division has left, and soon will cross the border." He wrote other regions that the army possessed 5,000 men. In fact, the army had not departed from Mexico and when troops were finally dispatched they numbered only 600.[3] In Central America at independence there were two companies in Guatemala containing 243 soldiers in all; at the ports and outposts of Omoa, Trujillo, San Carlos, and Petén there was a maximum of 120 mulatto soldiers each, and they were considered unreliable. This weakness and the pressure being exerted by Aycinena and then by a Mexican agent who arrived in late November determined the decision to unite with Mexico. The only alternative to union, according to Gaínza, was "to sustain a war with that nation whose troops were already marching upon us." And this Central America was unwilling to do.[4] The January 3 decision to unite was far from unanimous: 115 towns voted for adhesion, 32 desired independence with Guatemala, 23 chose to leave the decision to a future Congress, and 77 cabildos did not respond. Thus, with less than 50 percent of the municipalities voting in favor of the union, Central America joined Mexico.[5]

Still Central America was far from united. Each cabildo considered itself autonomous, and few recognized the prerogatives of Guatemala as a national capital. When a general persecution of liberals began in Guatemala City, "liberal" regions in the interior (Tegucigalpa, San Salvador) took to arms against "conservative" areas, fearing a restoration of central rule. Regional dissension intensified. The indigo-producing areas of Santa Ana, San Miguel, and Gotera, controlled by families outside the city of San Salvador, pledged union to the central government and separation from the old province. Guatemala sent officials to San Miguel to take command of the civilian militia and some troops were transferred to Santa Ana under Juan Fermín Aycinena. The leadership in Salvador responded, declaring "none of the provinces can be dismembered by the authorities as presently constituted," and threatening retaliation if Guatemala dismembered Salvador. Salvadoran troops were dispatched to Santa Ana under Manuel Arce, forcing a retreat of the Aycinena forces. The neighboring Guatemalan province of Chiquimula revolted and pledged loyalty to Salvador, but was quickly squelched by central authorities.[6] In Nicaragua, León demanded the adhesion of Managua, Granada, and Costa Rica to its authority and sent troops to Managua in a unsuccessful attempt to force that town to join the old provincial capital. The Honduran towns of Comayagua and Tegucigalpa both mobilized, each challenging the other's authority. "What divides the inhabitants . . . that previously formed the provinces of the Kingdom of Guatemala is not the type of government, but a furious hatred that the provinces hold towards the capital for the damages that were caused them under Spanish rule," an observer reported. "The integral nature of the Kingdom that Guatemalans pretend to maintain is a little less than impossible to keep with force." Meanwhile, in Guatemala, Mariano Aycinena complained to Iturbide that "all conspire against Guatemala, impudently not respecting their government."[7]

With the sole exception of the suppression of the Granada rebellion in 1812, for almost three centuries no Spanish or Creole armies had ever faced each other in combat in Central America. This stability was now shattered. In June 1822 a Guatemalan force invaded Salvador, easily outflanked its troops, and took San Salvador. The Guatemalans immediately disbanded and began sacking the city. The Salvadorans reformed quickly, marched on San Salvador, caught the Guatemalans disorganized, and easily defeated them.[8] Soon after the Guatemalan defeat, the Mexican commander Vicente Filísola arrived, took command, organized the regime, freed those liberals who remained in jail, and imposed some stability. He could not, however, deal with the secessionist tendencies of the provinces. After three months of negotiations with the Salvadorans, he reached an accord, granting them separation from Guatemala, but within the Mexican empire. Iturbide rejected the pact, not comprehending the situation. "There does not exist," he wrote, "in Salvador sufficient representation to form an adequate Congress." With the failure of negotiations, Filísola invaded Salvador in January, easily defeating the 2,000 defenders of the city.[9]

Iturbide complicated the delicate balance of Central America. On November 4, 1822, he decreed that Central America should be divided into three provinces of Mexico: "Chiapas," with Ciudad Real as the capital, and including Quezaltenango; "Costa Rica" with León as its capital and including Costa Rica, all of Nicaragua, and all of Honduras except the port of Omoa; and "Sacatepéquez," with Guatemala as the capital, controlling the remainder of Central America. This organization pleased few, alienated many who had previously supported union with Mexico, and sparked military confrontation. The capital of Guatemala lost two-thirds of its possessions; Salvador fell to Guatemala; Honduras to Nicaragua. The smaller towns were not given the autonomy for which they had fought. "The only object of its separation from Guatemala," a representative from Quezaltenango argued, "was to erect itself into a separate province." Comayagua protested that, like Guatemala, León would not protect "the true interests of Honduras." In Nicaragua, Iturbide's decision led to warfare—Granada revolted, defeating a militia sent from León. In Costa Rica, conservatives in Cartago favoring Mexican union overthrew the liberal government. Liberals in San José and Alajuela defeated the Cartago militia, establishing the capital of Costa Rica at San José. Federation with Mexico was a failure. War erupted everywhere; attempts to draw boundaries were a fiasco. Even troops under the able Mexican commander Filísola could not keep the area together.[10]

Political collapse precipitated fiscal collapse. The dissension in the interior provinces cut off their revenues from the capital. When Filísola arrived in 1822 he remarked that the decline was a decade old, and was not solely a consequence of independence. Between the quinquennials of 1811 to 1815 and 1816 to 1820, there had been a noticeable drop in the collection of sales taxes and in receipts from aguardiente, tobacco, and gunpowder. With independence and the "resistance and division between the provinces," each region tried to hold its own tax income, which meant a loss of 385,693 pesos to the capital city. Suspension of the tribute by the Mexican government cut another 176,000 pesos. The critical problem was the separation of the provinces, but the general decline in revenue contributed to the collapse.[11]

During the three hundred years of relative peace there had been little need of a large military establishment, only an army strong enough to defend each town and unite the region. Upon his arrival Filísola informed Iturbide that "the budget to pay the troops and other employees grows to 50,000 pesos [monthly] and to satisfy it, I had to ask for a loan of various subjects of this capital because in the coffers, not a real exists." Additional "loans" were drawn from Guatemalans to support the troops and to finance the march on Salvador. Finally, with the collapse of the Mexican empire, the Guatemalans had to finance the expenses of Mexican troops on their way home.[12]

Civil government faced similar fiscal problems. The city of Guatemala could not pay its deputies to the Mexican Congress and had to borrow money from Oaxaca. The Mexican Congress attempted to resolve the problem by raising the sales tax and creating new municipal levies. Custom taxes originally set at 8 percent were raised to 12 percent in August 1822, but when merchants avoided payment they were lowered to 6 percent in December.[13] But to Guatemalan and other merchants, independence meant freedom to trade openly for those who had been contraband traders. With the collapse of government in September 1821 goods entered and left the country paying no taxes, and the Guatemalan government's ban of all external trade did not dam the "inundation" of foreign goods.[14]

Warfare did interrupt this vital trade, however. The Salvadoran-Guatemalan hostilities cut the major road through Central America, between the indigo fields and the capital, between the Nicaraguan Pacific ports and the north. Roads ran through Honduras, but conflict there prohibited trade as well. "Commerce has vanished; skills and agriculture have been ruined." Salvador was reduced to misery, because it lacked managers for the indigo plantations owned by Guatemalans and Spaniards.[15]

The sad experience with Mexico came to an end in March 1823 with the overthrow of Iturbide in Mexico. A group of liberal Guatemalans petitioned the Mexican general for a Central American Congress, which Filísola convened by recalling the liberal provincial deputation and ordering a new congress with representatives from León, Costa Rica, Comayagua, Chiapas, and Quezaltenango to decide the nation's fate. He withdrew his troops in August.[16]

The end of the Mexican empire isolated Filísola in Guatemala. Although he was respected personally, his Mexican troops were resented, and with the economy's collapse and the eruption of warfare in all parts, the Guatemalan conservatives who had supported the Mexican empire—notably the Aycinena group—were discredited. Filísola had to turn to the only other important political group, the liberals, who had the backing of two thousand troops in Salvador. Most of them representatives from interior Guatemala, Tegucigalpa, and Salvador, these liberals established a constituent congress, which, after prolonged debate, formed a federal government in March 1825 with the Salvadoran Manuel Arce as president.

The motives for the establishment of the national government differed. To some, a form of centralized rule was needed to enforce liberal hegemony, that is, the power of San Salvador, Tegucigalpa, and Granada over or shared with Guatemala, Comayagua, and León; and to others, a liberal, federal government was needed to fight any attempt by the old centralists under the Aycinenas to take hold again. "Now is the time," the liberals proclaimed, "for the monopolies to disappear; for centuries Guatemala has monopolized everything that attracts man. There [in Guatemala] is the university, the government, the superior tribunals, the mint, the army, the archdiocese, the high school, etc., all sustained by the taxes coming from the unfortunate provinces, always disregarded, and always treated horribly."[17]

Most Central American Creoles felt the need for some form of unity to forestall foreign invasion. Mexico had taken control of Guatemala simply by a threat of force in 1821, and, when Filísola withdrew, he left sufficient troops in Ciudad Real to support those Chiapans who favored union with Mexico. After 1823 Guatemala or the federal government maintained troops along the Mexican border. To the south, Bolívar was expanding his Gran Colombia, which, from time to time, claimed parts of Central America, particularly along the Caribbean coast. Furthermore, during this early period, there was no assurance that Spain had accepted Central America's independence. The frailty of the nation, with the loyalties of the church and of some merchants held suspect, underlined the need for unity. Reports were received continuously from 1823 until 1833 that the Spanish were about to invade.

There was among Creole families a tradition of Central American unity. Interfamily marriage, schooling at common monasteries and universities, and commercial connections united many Creoles. Still, this heritage was not a strong one. Antagonisms and, eventually, warfare would destroy most of it. But it was sufficiently strong to lead some Creoles to think of "Central America" rather than Guatemala, Honduras, or Salvador.

The different interests of all the supporters of national government were never and could never be resolved. Suspicions between regions led to periodic battles which furthered distrust. Soon after Filísola left for Mexico, for example, the battalion in Guatemala City revolted, in protest at not being paid. The populace took up arms and persuaded the battalion to withdraw from the capital, but Salvador suspected the attack was an assault against their leaders and immediately sent 900 troops to Guatemala. To counter Salvadoran influence, Quezalten-ango sent 300 troops, Chiquimula, 300, and Guatemala itself raised a civilian militia of 1,000. Before the Salvadorans arrived, local Gua-temalans forced out the liberal provisional government, replacing it with conservatives. From October until March opposing forces faced each other, liberal Salvadorans versus conservative Guatemalans, until a compromise installed a neutral triumvirate to lead the provi-sional government.[18]

Meanwhile, within the constituent assembly, there was debate over the form of political system. The interior demanded a loose system and Guatemalan merchants urged a centralized political structure. The most telling—and, as events later showed, accurate—criticism of the proposed liberal federation came from a cleric, José Francisco Córdoba, who listed the reasons federalism could not function, de-scribing, at the same time, the conditions of Central America after Spanish rule: first, the majority of the nation—the Indians—would not understand the new government and were, indeed, opposed to all types of innovation; second, it was difficult to unite all towns to form a state with conflicting families in nearby areas; third, there were few men capable of holding the many positions a federal form of govern-ment required; and, finally, the "general poverty of the nation" was incompatible with the expenses of the system and would continue the long-standing fiscal problems.[19]

Still, what cannot succeed does not necessarily determine what is attempted. A constitution was completed, providing for a federal government with state governments "being free and independent in its interior government and administration." Both federal and state governments were provided with executive, legislative, and judicial branches. Representation to the federal congress was to be chosen in a proportion of one to thirty thousand and a federal senate, composed of two delegates from each state, had to sanction all bills passed, which provided a veto power over Guatemala's numerical preponderance over the nation.[20]

While the federal government completed its organization, the states attempted to form their own governments. In Tegucigalpa, Sal-vador, and Guatemala, liberals reenforced by Salvadoran military power were in control. Salvador seized the indigo-producing regions of Santa Ana and Sonsonate, under the control of the Aycinena group after the Mexican occupation, in 1824. Tegucigalpa was no longer threatened by Comayagua, as all areas reinforced one another in a liberal "holy alliance." Only Nicaragua remained outside the liberal hegemony—León and Granada rivaled each other regardless of political affinity. There was warfare in 1824; troops from Granada laid seige to León for four months, destroying the "second city of Central America." An observer claimed that during one battle 900 houses were burnt, "some neighborhoods were left in ashes, with a multitude of innocent victims in its midst: one sees the elderly and others begging in the streets without shelter or bread." The region was painfully pacified by Manuel Arce, who merged 500 Salvadoran troops with Granada forces to pacify the province. He organized a tenuous compromise that guaranteed Nicaragua's adhesion to federal rule.[21]

In December 1824 Central America appeared to be unified by liberal regimes under Salvadoran hegemony. But the unification was a mirage, more the reflection of a common position held by diverse families against rival towns and families than a feeling of national community. All feared Guatemala, and few were willing to give up their power to the central government. The true measure and test of the central authority was its ability to muster sufficient fiscal resources for control of the interior by the military and the administration. And fiscal revenues were limited, with few areas willing to allow central, either Guatemalan or Salvadoran, administrators to collect and withdraw revenues from their region.

Early in its tenure the provisional government ordered a fiscal system organized "according to the enlightenment of the century and the progress of the science of economics." Records were missing and disorganized; many had been shipped to Mexico under Iturbide, and interior regions refused to supply Guatemala with the data that would have allowed a rebuilding of the Bourbon fiscal administration. By February 1824 the government conceded that it could not estimate the amount of taxes currently collected or salaries paid. The finance minister confessed that there was such a "disorder of the administration" that the central government could not establish its fiscal base.[22]

The national government was bankrupt. Deputies to the first national congress in 1825, who relied upon outside sources for their support, could not publish their decrees for lack of funds. A general contribution that resembled the tribute tax had been decreed in Guatemala, but collection was limited and was finally absorbed by the authorities of the Guatemalan state government when it was formed in late 1825. Guatemalan merchants periodically made forced loans to maintain the small company of troops in the city, to preserve order, and to ensure that the troops would not rebel again.[23]

To deal with the crisis in revenue, the leaders of the nation sought a loan from a foreign banking house. A British firm, Barclay, Herring and Richardson of London, was awarded in competition the right to serve as agent for a loan of seven million pesos—only five million to be effectively received. The banking house failed, the bond market in London collapsed, and Central America received 328,316 pesos, having contracted a debt of one million.[24]

The loan itself created dispute. Originally intended for defense and public instruction, the first funds were used to repay outstanding debts to merchants. The state governments' response to the federal loan was to try to make loans themselves. Guatemala sent an emissary to Belize to ask for 200,000 to 300,000 pesos, and Honduras and Costa Rica undertook to contract loans with other foreign banks. The National Assembly declared these overtures illegal, thus frightening foreign investors. The federal government's action brought this retort from the executive secretary of Honduras, Francisco Morazán, who was later to be called the "Father" of the Central American Federation:

> The State of Honduras is free, independent, and sovereign, the same as the other states of the Federation. As a consequence, [it] can do whatever it wishes in this manner. To create taxes, administer them, borrow on them, distribute them, are inherent faculties of a free, independent and sovereign state. This [state] isn't a minor, not a pupil. It is sovereign, it is independent, and it does not have to ask permission from anybody to contract an obligation that obliges nobody else except itself.[25]

The national authorities attempted to smooth the rough situation, decreeing that one-half of all the money coming from the English loan would be placed in a fund reserved for the use of the states. To gain access to the fund, however, "the states must remit data on [all] their income."[26]

The superficial unity of Central America dissolved in the search for revenue—the crux of the problem lay in the fact that resources were scarce. There was insufficient revenue for even the state governments to function. As the federal government had no sovereignty in the states, so the states had little sovereignty within their own regions. The jefe of Honduras wrote the national government in November 1824 about the collection of taxes: "I differ with you on the proposition that it should be centralized. . . . Public opinion is against centralization and the administration of the revenue will not be well managed from Guatemala."[27]

This opinion was perhaps best seen in the fight for control of receipts from the tobacco monopoly. The amount of money involved was significant enough to cause conflict among the various adminis-

Table 13.1: Annual Income from Tobacco, 1821–1828 (in pesos)

Time Period	Amount Received	Annually Prorated
Annual income, 1821	438,349	438,349
July-Dec. 1822	7,882	15,764
Aug.-Oct. 1823	42,204	168,816
Jan.-Sept. 1824	14,000	18,667
Annual income, 1826	112,032	112,032
Annual income, 1827	104,551	104,551
Annual income, 1828	83,016	83,016

SOURCES: "Report of the Minister of Finance" P.R.O., F.O., 15/3, Appendix, 13; A.G.G. B5.8, Leg. 70, Exp. 1920, fol. 1; B107.3, Leg. 1833, Exp. 7741; B6.7, Leg. 95, Exp. 2623; Haefkins, *Viaje a Guatemala* p. 307, Smith, "Financing the Central American Federation," p. 492.

trations of the region. The money produced by tobacco under Spain financed most of the colonial government and supported, in particular, authorities in Nicaragua and Honduras. After independence, the amount of money received in Guatemala from the monopoly declined precipitously (see table 13.1). If the average income to the central coffers between the years 1807 and 1819 was some 380,000 pesos, it was obvious that after 1821 this revenue was lacking. National authority controlled only two tobacco factories, one in Quezaltenango and the other in the capital, with the proceeds from the former going to support the troops at the Mexican border. In other interior areas, failure to pay was caused by the wars in Salvador and Nicaragua, combined with the antipathy of Comayagua (which controlled the rich Los Llanos/Gracias tobacco areas). In the end, the interior did not aid the central government, and if the receipts were up in 1826, it was the result of the merger of the leadership of Guatemala and the federation.

There were two reasons for this collapse of tobacco revenue. With independence there was a rise in the planting and selling of unlicensed tobacco. Just as Guatemalan traders had taken advantage of the weak period after September 1821 to trade clandestinely with the British, the farmers fulfilled their old wish of freedom to plant and sell the commodity. Prices were set at artificially high levels by the government; so that it was easy to undercut the monopoly and still make a substantial profit. Both the weakness of the government and the internal civil wars made prosecution impossible. The director of the tobacco administration in Salvador complained in April 1824 that it was impossible to enforce rules against contraband. The next year Guatemalan state authorities complained about the failure of the national government to "enforce the laws against clandestine farming and selling of tobacco." Haefkens reported that the administration of tobacco was virtually extinct in 1827 because of the competition of the contraband product.[28]

Second, the interior refused to pay its share of tobacco revenue to national authorities. Guatemala, which produced only 16 percent of the colony's tobacco under Spain and after independence had had to use some of that income to support troops along the Mexican border, was forced to survive, together with federal authorities, on a small portion of the revenues the colonial national government had received.[29]

The states' refusal to support the federal government indicates more their inability to finance both themselves and a national structure than a revolt against federation. We have seen the steep fiscal decline and the indebtedness of a public bureaucracy under the colonial administration, which supported a mere fraction of the number of the government officials of the national period (see table 13.2). The top-heavy government of national assembly and senate, of a national judiciary, and of new and similar state offices was difficult, if not impossible, to support. Under Spain the colonial administration had been constantly in debt and had struggled to survive. Independent and federal, the government easily employed five or six times the number of individuals.

There were other additional expenses with independence. Under Spain the defense of the colony had been, by and large, ignored. With the exception of the Gálvez administration in the 1780s, Spain and

Table 13.2: Structures of Colonial and Independent Governments in Central America

	Colonial Government	Federal Government
Central authorities	Captain General Audiencia	President National Assembly Senate National Judiciary
State and provincial authorities	Intendant Governor Alcalde Mayor Corregidor	Governor Political Chief
		Legislative Assembly Legislative Council State Judiciary Civil Judges
Local authorities	Cabildo	Municipality

other countries had fought over the richer areas of Mexico, Cartagena, and Havana; Central America was a backwater. With independence, the citizens were forced to defend themselves against the potential threat of Mexico, Spain, and Colombia, and, perhaps most important, against neighboring towns and cities. Aside from the destructive civil war and the cost of taking men away from production, defense was expensive. In the early years of independence, there was a great influx of armaments, so that relatively peaceful Central America became an armed camp. Each town had a militia to supply and, when battles were fought, to support.

With top-heavy administrative costs and the rise in military needs, income at all levels of government fell. The tobacco income fell at both the central and local areas. The tribute had been suspended, replaced by a direct contribution that met with enough resistance at first to render it valueless. The major source remaining was the sales tax, which contraband and the economic and military disruption reduced.

Burdened by higher governmental costs and lower fiscal income, the liberals had set unattainable goals. They wanted to establish schools, but, despite attempts in the early period, were not successful until the 1830s. New roads were needed and the old routes to the hinterlands had to be repaired. Regional rivalries, as much as the lack of revenues, thwarted construction. Their ambition to introduce new industry and agriculture in the hope of national prosperity was frustrated as foreign financing did not materialize substantially.

The failure of localities to support distant and rival cities created the crisis of government revenue. In Guatemala City itself, the merchant class perceived the bureaucracy as a sponge absorbing commercial resources, during the Bourbon reforms and through independence. With independence and the constant request by national and state governments alike for lands and contributions, the merchants had no reason to change their perception of the bureaucracy. The control of the federal apparatus by liberals and non-Guatemalans reenforced this antipathy. The government had not, as yet, aligned itself with business in a common front.

Though the fiscal situation of federal and state governments was precarious, international commerce with Central America—or, more accurately, with Salvador and Guatemala—expanded. The only benefit the government achieved from prosperity was an increase in customs revenue (see table 13.3). By prorating tax figures on an annual basis, one can deduce an approximation of that commerce that paid

Table 13.3: Customs Income in Central America, 1823-1826
(in pesos)

	1823	1824	1825	1826
Imports	n.a.	69,720[a]	117,878[b]	143,008[c]
Exports (2%)	n.a.	2,405	14,838	17,532
Totals	51,740	72,125	132,716	160,540

SOURCES: A.G.G. B107.3, Leg. 1871, Exp. 43284; B6.7, Leg. 96, Exp. 2632, fol. 13; B107.3, Leg. 1884, Exp. 43407, Leg. 1881, Exp. 43381.

[a] Import tax was 6 percent. The figures run from January 1 until November 12, 1824.

[b] Import tax was 6 percent through March and 10 percent between April and December.

[c] Import tax was 10 percent. Figures run from January 1 until October 1.

duties to Central America during these critical years (see table 13.4). Total custom taxes received in ten months in 1826 was three times that in all of 1823, and was probably charged on three times as much commerce.

The increase in custom tax collection was not an indication of a success by the government to "fortify" or "defend" its ports. The revenue coming from imports and exports was collected in Guatemala City. Indigo and cochineal had to pass through the capital in order to get to the Caribbean and Belize, while British goods to Salvador and the interior of Guatemala had to return along the same route. With a majority of the nation in Guatemala, and the wealth in Guatemala and Salvador, the merchants could not resist a minimal levy on their commerce.

There was little success in tax collection in outlying areas. "Smuggling and bribery are carried on to such a serious extent," claimed the

Table 13.4: Estimated Annual Legal Commerce in Central
America, 1823-1826 (in pesos)

	1823[a]	1824	1825	1826
Imports	780,411	1,301,233	1,669,938	1,716,100
Exports	81,922	136,650	741,900	1,051,900
Totals	862,333	1,435,883	1,411,838	2,768,000

SOURCE: Deduced from table 13.3.

[a] The 1823 import and export division is estimated, applying the same import/export ratio as that of 1824 to the total 1823 income. This assumes that exports were either maintaining the same level or constantly rising during the period.

comptroller of customs, "that the authorities have no power to prevent it." The only function of the customs' officers, the official stated, seemed to be to "shield clandestine commerce."[30]

The British were accused of being the prime smugglers in Central America, to which their consul replied that "in nineteen cases out of twenty, the merchants of [Central America] went to Belize with hard dollars, indigo, or other produce and bought or bartered with the merchants for British goods—therefore their own citizens were the smugglers."[31]

Ironically, as central power (in the collection of taxes) declined, and as the national government teetered on the brink of extinction for lack of resources, the economy of Central America was expanding. Government frailty had reached such a point that business could operate and prosper in the seat of national government without substantially contributing to the administration's upkeep.

A rise in the demand for indigo pushed the economic upswing. Trade could flow directly between England and Guatemala with the removal of the Cádiz middlemen at independence. The English economy recovered from the depression following the Napoleonic Wars around 1820, and the textile trade renewed previously established links with Central American indigo. Guatemalan indigo became competitive on the world market. In 1824 prices were consistently on the rise, from 10.5 to 11.5 reales the pound (as compared with 6 reales a decade earlier), with 12 reales offered at the end of the year. In 1825 the constant price was 14 reales for the dye. As prices rose, production followed, so that in 1825 some 1.2 million pounds of indigo were produced, a figure not seen since the eighteenth century. The dye produced was still the inferior corte quality, which did not bring the prices that it had thirty years earlier.[32]

Trade in cochineal dye was just beginning to develop. In 1815 Bustamante had introduced the dye into the region around Antigua Guatemala to replace the depressed cotton and indigo trades; some 4,350 pounds of cochineal were produced in 1820, but five years later some 135,000 pounds were exported at three pesos the pound.[33]

With the influx of textiles after independence, silver was crucial to exchange. The Central American peso was under valued and represented an additional profit for merchants. By November 1823 the government complained "that the extraction of our money is causing our decay." Mexican merchants agreed, in 1827, that their peso was worth 5 percent less than the Central American coin, and in 1832 merchants claimed that they made an immediate 2 to 2.5 percent profit on the export of Central American money.[34]

Table 13.5: *Minerals Minted in Central America, 1817-1825*
(in pesos)

	Silver[a]	Gold[b]	Total
1817	428,661		428,661
1818	554,564		554,564
1819			n.a.
1820	351,127		351,127
1821	389,376		389,376
1822	137,822		137,822
1823	294,347	19,856	314,203
1824	55,037	71,536	126,573
Jan.–July, 1825	103,318	34,408	137,726
Aug.–Dec., 1825	?	?	78,396

SOURCES: Deduced from A.G.G. B9.2, Leg. 2495, Exp. 2506; B6.7, Leg. 93, Exp. 2529; Haefkens, *Viaje*, p. 298; "Guatemalan Report, 1825," P.R.O., F.O., 15/1, fol. 228.
  [a] Silver figured at 8.5 pesos the mark.
  [b] Gold figured at 136 pesos the mark.

With the end of Guatemalan power in 1821, it became impossible to compel Honduran miners to send their minerals to the mint. There were advantages, however, in having the silver assayed and coined. The purity and weight of the silver was guaranteed by the government with the mint consistently upholding its standards through the early 1830s. Still, some Honduran miners found it easier to export their production directly to Belize.

Between 1821 and 1825 (see table 13.5), the amount of silver minted declined consistently; total amounts were half those of the period prior to independence. The master of the mint overstated his point, claiming that "scarcely a tenth part of the mineral produced has been delivered to our mint" between 1821 and 1827, but the decline at the mint, together with the outflow of coinage, caused a scarcity. By 1824 there was a stream of reports of the making of "false money" in interior areas. Tegucigalpa, Comayagua, León, Granada, and even areas within the State of Guatemala coined money that was often weak, disrupting normal commercial patterns. The government accepted Tegucigalpa coin at first, but by 1825 a new minting mixed silver with copper, and the federation ordered all areas to ignore the money.[35]

Foreign entrepreneurs tried to exploit Central American mines, some with noticeable success. Marshall Bennett brought a steam engine from Belize to Honduras and invested 23,000 pesos in a profitable operation. A Mr. Gerard discovered a rich gold lode in Aguacate (Costa Rica) that produced 408,000 pesos in its first five years. Not all enterprises succeeded. An English company invested 15,000 pesos in mining areas in Honduras, Nicaragua, and Costa Rica without success, and a French engineer complained that though there were rich areas in Honduras, he could not find sufficient labor to exploit them.[36]

Imports to Central America were limited chiefly to British dry goods. In 1824 a commission house opened in Belize to supply merchants. A year later Belizans estimated that some 3,200,000 pesos worth of goods were imported annually into Central America.[37]

The economic situation of Guatemalan merchants was thus quite good. In the years 1824 and 1825 merchants received 1.5 million pesos for the indigo annually traded and 370,000 pesos for cochineal. Mariano Aycinena and two other merchants claimed foreign trade "in recent years" had amounted annually to four million pesos. The remaining 1.3 million pesos in trade was paid for with silver bars and coins.[38]

Trade on the Pacific reached levels never known under the Spanish empire. Although the trade was still a fraction of that in the Caribbean, it represented an opening for Salvador and other areas of the interior to gain commercial independence from Guatemala. The port of Acajutla serving Sonsonate is a good example. In 1823 a government official claimed there was insufficient indigo harvested to meet the demand of Pacific port traders. The following year almost 75,000 pesos were imported, with exports probably double that amount—or approximately 5 percent of all Central American transactions—and its function as an entrepôt became clear. Central American and Colombian vessels were used exclusively, it was said, to export "foreign" (almost definitely English) goods to other areas. Thus, Central America was developing a profitable re-export trade in British items.[39]

The merchants in Guatemala had indeed prospered. The house of the "the Marquis of Aycinena is both the most notable and numerous, it might perhaps also be said that it is the richest," an Englishman reported. "There is scarcely a house in the city of Guatemala, however noble or respectable it might be, that has not a warehouse, or mostly, a retail shop attached to it for the . . . European goods which the proprietor has taken in exchange for indigo or cochineal or other produce of his hacienda or country estates." In every merchant house, silver articles were used "for the meanest domestic purposes," and each lady of the house had "at least half a dozen seamstresses and flower and embroidery workers, giving her apartments the appearance for the time of a millionaire's ship."[40]

Few complained of government interference, high taxation, a decline in commerce, or economic stagnation, as they had under Spain twenty years earlier. The government was weak, some might say non-existent, but commercial power was strong. By the beginning of 1826, however, the economic expansion brought on by the flow of British goods to Central America began to retract. A drought ruined the crop of cochineal, and Mariano Aycinena reported that the price of foreign goods had become "very unsteady" with the glut on the market. Prices were "so low that if the assortment be ordinary, it sells at first cost, and if bad, with a loss; so that they are now worth in comparison to last year about 20 to 30 percent less." At the end of the year the British consul reported that "trade is exceedingly full here, British cotton goods on the average do not bring more than the prime cost and charges."[41]

The boom was coming to an end, and its negative effects began to plague the region. The rise in commerce and the subsequent outflow of silver created an inflationary effect. A local newspaper claimed in 1825 that the rise in "the rent of land has resulted in a proportionate rise in [the price of] its products." There is no evidence of a corresponding rise in wages. Rice rose from 2 to 6 reales, and beans, from 2 to 4 pesos the pound. Corn, which had cost 16 reales the fanega at market in 1797 and 1808, cost twice that solely to produce in the fields of Escuintla in 1827. With transportation and profit, the market price rose to 48 reales. Peons were still daily paid 1.5 reales, and masons 4 reales, as they had been for the past fifty years.[42]

In Guatemala, the old problem of food shortages continued. A drought caused famine in Verapaz, Chiquimula, and the areas surrounding the capital in 1822. Two years later the deputy from Chiquimula claimed that for the previous three years there had not been sufficient grains and the "citizenry now has no food." Despite pleas from outlying areas, governmental disorganization and lack of finances prohibited any effective amelioration of the problem.[43]

Commerce between the provinces consisted of some silver trade from Tegucigalpa and indigo from Salvador in exchange for cloth products. Salvador could not overcome Guatemalan domination as long as the road network determined the trade routes. Indigo could not be exported safely through Nicaragua (and the San Juan River) because of the political problems between Granada and León, and Pacific trade was not sufficient to absorb the total indigo production.

The old controversy between cattle producers in the interior and the merchants in Guatemala ended as the merchants took over production in regions nearest to the capital. The complaint by Comayagua in 1820 that cattle were being sent to the capital from the interior for breeding purposes seems to have been borne out: it was estimated that the annual consumption of beef in Guatemala was 1,000 head in 1825, but that the price was too low for the cattlemen of the interior to compete because of the additional cost of transportation. Honduran and Nicaraguan cattle were "solely restricted to internal consumption," while the Guatemalan cattle trade was controlled completely by the "high families" of the capital.[44]

Government interference in the economy was minimal, even at the state level. Its frailty on the local level paralleled that of the national government. There were discussions about how to improve economic conditions, but the lack of finances limited action. José del Valle, a Honduran with mining interests, urged that a mineralogist be brought to Central America to assist in developing mines. He suggested that Indians be employed to exploit the silver. But nothing was done, and, for the most part, it was the British who moved in and took advantage of the few silver resources available.

The government passed laws to rehabilitate ports to stimulate commerce, but little was accomplished until the thirties. It also enacted legislation placing all vacant lands on the market (except Indian ejidos and common lands), but in the inflationary economic conditions, with money leaving the country or involved in commerce, these first agrarian measures had little effect.[45]

Thus, between 1821 and 1826, the regional families of Central America—be they Guatemalan merchants or Honduran miners—established their political positions as the national government struggled to survive. The federation did not control, nor did it profit from, the brief, economic prosperity of these early years. At the same time the conflicts between merchants and producers and government bureaucrats that had existed under Spanish rule continued, with business resisting encroachments on their affairs. The Guatemalans, in particular, viewed with suspicion the federal government located in their city. As long as the interior dominated the government, the merchants would not assist or cooperate. Thus, the federation was slowly developing, mistrusted by all, its motives suspect with each decision it made.

CHAPTER FOURTEEN

States Into Nations

MOST OF CENTRAL America maintained a tenuous peace from 1823 until late 1826. Except for Nicaragua, no area was strong enough to challenge the stability imposed by the alliance of liberals in Salvador, Tegucigalpa, and Guatemala. There was resistance, however, to any attempts by the federal government either to raise a strong army or to collect taxes to finance national institutions.

This stability was shattered in 1826 when the central government tried to regain its prerogatives. The provinces rebelled, and for two years Central America fought, destroying the land, razing farms, and interrupting commerce. Perhaps most important, an armed Central America destroyed the sense of order and peace that had existed throughout the colonial epoch, fostering a militaristic mentality that led to a decade of internecine struggles and a century of disorder—a bitter legacy to Central America. As regional families fought over disputes the crown had mediated, heretofore peaceful castes and classes, who had recognized Creole and Spanish authority, resorted to violence and rebellion to improve their position. The order of the colony dissolved into the disorder of the nation, until the Indian, mestizo, and mulatto "bandits" and rebels coalesced around regional leaders at the end of the 1830s to create a semblance of stability for the mid-nineteenth century. Thus, in many ways, the true revolution occurred, not in 1821, but from 1838 to 1840.

The destruction of Creole power began with their attempt in 1826 to establish a true, national, and federal government, an attempt that the interior states perceived as a threat to their autonomy. The tragic figure of this period was the Salvadoran liberal Manuel Arce. An indigo farmer, a veteran of the unsuccessful 1811 rebellion, and commander of Salvadoran troops in the battles under the Mexican Empire, he was elected president of the federation in March 1825 when Salvador and

Nicaragua threatened secession if his conservative opponent were chosen. Arce compromised with conservatives, tried to build a national army and to deal with the fiscal revolt in the interior. His compromises with the Aycinena-led conservatives, however, earned him the enmity and distrust of Guatemalan liberals. As he worked for national solidarity, his allies, the liberals of the interior, rejected him, forcing him to draw nearer to the conservatives. Finally, when he attempted to enforce the national prerogatives of taxation and the conduct of military affairs, the interior towns openly warred against him and his conservatives allies.[1]

Central America needed an army to defend its borders. Both Mexico and Colombia sought "to occupy an interesting part of our territory." Mexico continued to occupy Chiapas and staged an election in 1824 that ratified the annexation of that area. When the Chiapan town of Soconusco revolted and pledged loyalty to Central America in 1825, both Mexico and Guatemala sent troops to the border where they remained until internal problems in both countries dissipated the tension in 1827. Meanwhile, New Granada established a customs house at the mouth of the San Juan river in Nicaragua in an effort to enforce its sovereignty over the Mosquito Coast. Rumors were also rampant that the "island of Cuba is full of troops . . . to attempt an invasion of some part of the continent." In Costa Rica, a "Spanish agent" attacked Alajuela, and upon capture one of the conspirators confessed that "as a vassal of the King of Spain in whose government I was a Lieutenant Colonel, I had a special commission to provoke revolutions in the Americas."[2]

All recognized the need for a strong military, but no one group could agree on a candidate to command it. Arce proposed an army drawn from the state militia but controlled by the national executive. The national congress modified his proposal by taking the power to appoint officers from the president and giving authority over the armed forces to the states' representatives. Some areas rejected a national force altogether, suggesting a union of regional forces whenever national defense required it.[3]

Arce further aggravated the situation by trying to resinstate the national government's tobacco monopoly, which had financed, to a considerable degree, the growth in centralized power and the military presence to enforce it. Salvador, in particular, refused to allow a national tobacco administration. Guatemala resented the fact that it alone was financing the federal government. Arce was pressured to force his native Salvador to enforce the tobacco monopoly, and when he was unsuccessful there was a plot organized to oust him. When

Salvador threatened invasion to keep him in office, Guatemalan representatives withdrew, depriving the national congress of a quorum. By May 1826 observers wrote "the federation was already in a process of dissolution," the only deterrents to civil war were "the apathy of the people and the civic troops who form the principal force in the city, having deserted to avoid a conflict." With a rump congress, no authorization for a national military, and no national budget, the government of the federation existed in name only.[4]

The final incident leading to civil war concerned the actions of a French emigré, Nicholas Raoul, a liberal army officer befriended by the Guatemalan liberals. Claiming that he obeyed the orders of the liberal Guatemalan state officials, Raoul disobeyed the commands of President Arce. Personal animosity enflamed the controversy, but the issue was the control of the military forces. Guatemala announced its refusal to contribute to the federal budget and began organizing an army. "This state, loyal to the pact of federal union has religiously observed its conditions . . . the other states have ignored [their] obligations." Arce suspended the state officials. State and federal militias fought a series of battles which the national government won. Liberal Guatemalans fled to Chiapas and Salvador as Arce united with the only remaining force in Guatemala, the Aycinena conservatives.[5]

Alliances were drawn throughout the rest of the nation. Comayagua revolted against Tegucigalpa's hegemony, and the Nicaraguan cauldron overflowed again. Arce made no secret of his plans to pacify Honduras and Nicaragua with conservative Guatemalan support as he had two years earlier. When Arce "made common cause with the most fanatical and bigoted of the monastical orders of the clergy," who opposed raising a diocese in Salvador, that province abandoned Arce too.[6]

War lasted until 1829. Arce united in common cause with Aycinena and, when the centralists failed to gain victory, the Salvadoran was deposed and Aycinena became head of the federation and state governments. In Salvador, Aycinena's lands and properties were seized. "Liberals" from the interior finally achieved victory in early 1829, owing mostly to the efforts of a Tegucigalpan Creole, Francisco Morazán, who overcame Guatemalan predominance by uniting troops of his region with those of Nicaragua and Salvador.

Ironically, Central America, which had achieved independence peacefully, suffered the same ravages of war that destroyed so much of Spanish America in the early nineteenth century. Farms owned by Guatemalans in Salvador were sacked, razed, or, at best, seized. Annual production of indigo between 1826 and 1830 was a fifth of that between 1824 and 1826. Conservative and liberal forces alike seized ecclesiastical property.[7]

The magnitude of lawlessness and the destruction of society that the war produced could be seen only much later. Contemporaries reported that "robberies by bands of armed deserters . . . commenced [in 1827], and men who would have fled in dismay from a musket or pistol a few months [earlier], now shoot whole families in cold blood." Incidents of troops running wild, ravaging regions, stealing cattle and horses, occurred on both sides. At war's end, Salvadoran and Honduran occupation troops demanded support from the Guatemalan residents taking funds and foodstuffs by force. The victorious army seized the goods of Luis Aycinena, taking all his cattle and horses, and a hacendado in Villalobos lost all his holdings for working "against the cause of liberty." In various regions of Sacatepéquez, many lost their wealth for being "enemies of the state." Finally, when soldiers left Guatemala and returned home, they engaged in cattle and horse thievery and armed extortion of the citizenry.[8]

Central American liberalism under the Honduran Morazán held complete power; the Aycinenas and their allies were exiled. This liberalism took the forms already established in other areas of Spanish America, but ideological sophistication had developed late, the result of the peaceful evolution to independence.

Anticlericalism was a case in point. Hispanic anticlericalism was inspired by the French Revolution and was strongly expressed in the 1820 Spanish Cortes. In September the Cortes set the tone for nineteenth-century liberalism with a series of acts that resembled enlightened Bourbon measures: nuns, orders, and hospitals were secularized; all capellanías were destroyed; clerics were no longer immune from civil prosecution; the tithe was reduced by half and its elimination was projected. In liberal Spain, as well as independent America, anticlericalism reached its peak over the issue of the patrimony. The Spanish monarch had the right to appoint bishops and determine the administration of church funds. Did not sovereignty now revert to the people and their representatives? Until 1824, in liberal Spain, hostile bishops were replaced; clerics were exiled as enemies of the state. Indeed, the political division in Europe between a conservative Holy Alliance and advancing liberalism was re-enacted here. "The restoration of the Spanish throne," the papal nuncio wrote in 1824, "is entwined with the pontificate." After the Holy Alliance restored Ferdinand VII to his throne and the church to its old rights, the Pope ordered all prelates to "work for the recolonization of [American] colonies using whatever means you have."[9]

Anticlericalism was widespread in the Americas when this order became public. José San Martín, the veteran of the Spanish war of independence, marched from Buenos Aires through the Andean regions, declaring after each victory that the ecclesiastical patrimony fell to him, that he could dispose of church taxes and employees as he wished. Most of the archbishops and bishops of South America were expelled. This was also true of Bolívar's Gran Colombia. In Iturbide's Mexico, the Bishop, offered the choice of recognition and obedience to the new government or exile, chose the latter.[10]

Compared to the rest of the Spanish world, the actions of the Guatemalan archbishop Ramón Casaus y Torres were moderate and conciliatory, despite the rhetoric of nineteenth-century liberal historians. Unlike the Mexican bishop, he pledged loyalty to the independent government and cooperated with most of its policies. There were tensions, chiefly over the church's contribution to the state's upkeep, but these did not become important until the 1827–29 civil war, when Casaus allied with Guatemala and Aycinena's conservatives, issuing declarations of his support and providing funds.

The intensification of anticlericalism in Central America developed around the liberal prelate José Matías Delgado's attempt to establish a Salvadoran diocese. Since the heyday of eighteenth-century indigo cultivation Salvador had wanted its own diocese, independent of Guatemala. The revolts by the prelate Delgado in 1811 and 1822 raised the issue of a diocese in Salvador, and the reconquest of that area by Guatemala was both times supported by Archbishop Casaus. Salvador considered its lack of a bishopric, the symbol of central domination, a sign of discrimination, because dioceses existed in the much poorer areas of Honduras and Nicaragua. In December 1818 the court in Spain had requested the documents pertaining to the dispute, an indication that action might have been taken if independence had not interfered. With independence the Salvadorans assumed the patrimony and erected the diocese by fiat, "believing that the tithe [here produced] is more than sufficient to support an episcopal seat." In 1824 the state's constituent assembly ratified the act, and although Archbishop Casaus declared it illegal, the federal congress (under liberal control) banned the circulation of his declaration. In April 1825 Delgado was installed as bishop and immediately exiled forty-three clerics from Salvador who had opposed the move. The papacy, now closely allied with Ferdinand VII and the Holy Alliance, rejected the

Salvador petition as a "horrible scandal" and exhorted Delgado in 1825 to end the schism. The pope's order arrived six months prior to the outbreak of the civil war and was a contributory factor. With Morazán's victory in 1829, Honduras and Salvador ruled Guatemala. The church's remaining wealth was seized and its lands were sold. The archbishop and all regular clerics, except the Belemites, were exiled, together with the Guatemalan conservatives. In all, three hundred clerics and sixty military and civil servants were expelled.[11]

Although the liberal alliance dominated, once again unity continued to be illusory. Like Arce before him, Morazán became a tragic figure, attempting to impose a unity for which there was no base. His army began to dissolve in mid-1829 as soldiers deserted, returning home to "protect their families and properties" from looters. The Guatemalan liberal state government balked at supporting the federal government, which led, once again, to a revolt and riot by the remaining soldiers in the capital. Officials, whom Morazán had appointed to the federal government, left, disillusioned by the lack of money and power.[12]

Despite the government's weakness, another attempt was made to impose a national structure. At the end of July 1829, the federal authorities decided to send a force of men to Honduras and Nicaragua to pacify those areas still fighting the civil war, the expenses of the expedition to be met by each of the states. Morazán marched on Honduras with five hundred Guatemalan and Honduran soldiers, crushed the rebellion, and then dispatched his uncle Dionisio Herrera to Nicaragua to pacify it by combining mediation and the threat of arms, as Arce had done the previous decade. Herrera remained in Nicaragua as governor and Morazán's brother-in-law was installed as governor in Honduras. Both organized their areas to pay, retroactively, for the military expeditions.[13]

By the end of 1830, Morazán dominated Nicaragua and Honduras, was military head of the federation, and maintained close ties with the Guatemalan liberals. Fearing a national government, once again, in 1831, "conservatives" in Salvador revolted. Concurrently, and in alliance with the Salvadorans, Central American conservative emigrés invaded from Belize, seizing Omoa, while Manuel Arce gathered his supporters in southern Chiapas. But Morazán again destroyed the threat to liberal government. Guatemalan forces invaded Chiapas unexpectedly, routing Arce's followers, and Morazán's army defeated the Salvadorans in one major battle. The occupiers of Omoa were beseiged and forced to surrender, defeated more by the diseases of the hotlands than by military encounters.[14]

Though he defeated all conservative threats, Morazán lacked the power to organize a national government. "The five sovereign states forming the federation," an observer reported, "in many instances do not obey the federal government, neither do they furnish their expenses thereof." The national government "exists but in name; it has no money nor troops." In 1831 Pedro Molina proposed a confederation of five republics on the model of the Swiss canton system, with "one common body to decide international relations, without double powers in the state." Morazán would not consider the proposal, and with no substantial support from other areas, it was never considered.[15]

Indeed, Morazán's sole purpose was to lead Guatemalan troops— or perhaps some Hondurans whom he could pay from time to time— to defeat the enemies of the liberal states, not of the federal government. He maintained order militarily in most of the region as state governments developed, in particular, in Guatemala. Indeed, I suspect the chief reason Morazán is considered a hero in most of Central America today is that he was, in reality, the founder of five independent governments, rather than one centralized government.

The wars sapped his strength, and as Guatemala grew in power, it no longer considered Morazán important. When, in 1833, a revolution in Salvador again overthrew the liberals of that state, Morazán could not oppose it, having "no money or troops." In Nicaragua, a state assembly issued a decree "calling upon the federal congress to make the necessary reforms in the constitution" that would weaken the federal system. In Guatemala, the hundred troops remaining in the federal army were described as dying of hunger, as "the government does not have money to pay them." Morazán thus felt compelled to resign "temporarily" and return to his home in Honduras. "The nation is completely disunited," it was said in June 1833, "for the states have separated from the federal government and seem disposed to act independently and have sent envoys or [as they are here termed] diplomatic agents one to another. . . . The anti-national idea . . . has become too prevalent in the states."[16]

While Morazán protected Central America, state authority developed. This was particularly true in Guatemala and Costa Rica, though by the mid-1830s most people in Honduras and Salvador recognized their state governments as their nation. The creation of smaller, more stable, political entities—they did not call themselves "nations" until 1840—was best seen under the administration of Governor Mariano Gálvez in Guatemala.

Gálvez used his political base in Antigua Guatemala to expand the authority of the state. Although a liberal, he did not partake in the hostilities between 1827 and 1829. After the war he became active in re-forming the state. His particular genius was his ability to create alliances with local elites, guaranteeing their peace and authority in exchange for their cooperation. He developed a network of allies that allowed him to rule autocratically, controlling all elections. A liberal Guatemalan historian testified that "Gálvez presented lists of deputies and representatives, and his agents made sure that the names triumphed in all regions."[17]

Gálvez ruled from 1831 until 1838, his legislation setting the model for nineteenth-century liberalism throughout Central America. He attempted to establish secular schools, and he reformed the curriculum at the University of San Carlos. He made literacy a prerequisite for army officers and ordered that all officials spend their spare time educating soldiers. Gálvez attacked traditional church practices, allowing nuns to leave their orders if they desired, and outlawing interment of bodies within church walls for reasons of health. He curtailed religious holidays, "alleging the habits of dissipation and idleness which such distractions from industry encourage amongst the common people." Finally, he attempted some agrarian reform, allowing squatters to buy land they held for half its value and granting Indians the right of settlement on certain vacant lands.[18]

But the financial base of Guatemala was weak, like that of the national government. Although Gálvez could establish tax collection agencies in Guatemala City and Antigua Guatemala, the centers of his support, taxing outlying areas was more difficult. Contraband commerce in tobacco, aguardiente, and chicha was rampant, and the control of regions by local hacendados made the imposition of a central tax collection as difficult at the state level as it had been at the national.

Gálvez's genius lay in his strategy of uniting the interests of local families with those of the state government and in developing taxes that could be collected with a minimum of compulsion. Although the alcabala sales tax and monopolies of tobacco and liquor existed, they were collected only in Guatemala and Antigua Guatemala where his control was greatest. In the interior of the state he depended upon a head tax called the direct contribution, which resembled closely the colonial tribute tax except that it covered all citizens. It was, in reality, a return to the Hapsburg dependence upon tribute for government support. The tax, suggested in the Larrazábal "Instructions," had been

*Table 14.1: Schedule of the Rate of Taxation for the Direct
Contribution in Guatemala (in pesos, reales)*

Category	Tax	Category	Tax
Laborers, domestic servants, and every other native not a proprieter	0,4	Every person enjoying rents or salaries	×[b]
Artisans	0,6	Purveyors of cattle by wholesale in the capital—large	15
Shopkeepers	1,4	Purveyors . . .—medium	7,4
Manufacturers of cloth (for each working loom)	0,6	Purveyors . . .—small	2
Serge-makers with shops[a]	2,4	Purveyors of cattle in towns—small	2
Salesmen of Guatemala made linen	2,4	Muleteers and carriers for each mule	0,1
Salesmen of foreign-made linen	5	Billiard tables	3
Merchants	20	Innkeepers	3
Proprieters of merchandise	10	*Officials:*	
Cashiers for both	2	Advocates	5
Wax chandlers	4	Scribes, letter writers	3
Sellers of spirits	5	Scribes, public with office	5
Sellers of chicha	3	Scribes, receptors	1
Public houses (inns)	6	Procurators	1
Bakers in the city	3	Writers	1
Bakers in the country	1	Physicians	5
Tanners	2	Surgeons	5
Every mill stone	3	Apothecaries	5
Great proprieters	20	Printers with a press on their property	8
Middle proprieters	5		
Small proprieters	1	Ice shops in the capital	1
Owners of property let out on hire	×[b]	Ice shops in the villages	1

SOURCE: P.R.O., F.O., 15/4, fols. 37-41.
 [a] Serge: A woolen fabric for the poorer classes (i.e., Indians)
 [b] 0.5% of receipts.

established in 1823, but its administration had never been adequate.
All collections were made in the city and here "forced loans" often
were combined and confused with the "direct contribution" to eliminate a regular collection. There is a striking similarity between this
tax and the seventeenth-century Hapsburg alcabala collected as a head
tax. Like the 1603 measure, Gálvez built his resources with this measure. While Indians were charged 2 pesos annually, non-indigenous
populations were divided according to their economic positions in
society (see table 14.1). Workers were given the lightest tax burden
(4 reales), while "merchants" (as distinguished from "proprietors of

merchandise," or, in other words, "middlemen") and "great proprietors" had the heaviest burden of 20 pesos annually. Those who rented land or mules, or who received rents or salaries, had to pay a percentage of their income. Ice shops in the capital paid six times more than in the villages. Surgeons, physicians, and advocates paid the same as vendors of spirits, and "middle farmers" paid less than those that ran "public houses." But the tax weighed heaviest upon the Indians, who were compelled to pay more (2 pesos or 16 reales) than all but the wealthiest non-Indians in the region.[19]

Gálvez turned to the dominant Creole families in the predominantly Indian interior to collect the levy, and to serve, as did the Creole alcaldes mayores in the later days of the Bourbon state, as his political representatives in the region, with one of them acting as the jefe político. No matter that the jefe collected a percentage of the tax for himself, as long as the central government received support (some still called it "tribute") from the interior.[20]

The monopolies of tobacco, aguardiente, and chicha remained, but unlike the federal government of the previous decade, Gálvez did not have to depend upon them for his support. He realized that "the entire department of Verapaz is a factory of aguardiente and between [the towns of] San Geronimo and Salamá there exist perhaps one thousand factories," but prosecution was useless. Although, by law, the government purchased tobacco at one real and sold the same leaf for four, few farmers supplied the government (no one in the interior!), preferring to make a greater profit in the open but illegal trade. In Quezaltenango and Suchitepéquez, the second and third most populated cities of the state, free traffic in tobacco was declared, because the authorities could not purchase any at the low legal price. The most lucrative source of revenues for the Bourbons had now been eliminated.[21]

Because of the direct contribution, Gálvez received greater revenues. In the last seven months of 1830, the state received 5,977 pesos from all sources in the interior of the state, and in the (June–May) fiscal years 1835 and 1836, 183,933 and 181,033 pesos. Still, even though tax revenue and centralized control were increasing, there was not sufficient money to finance the state government. The support of the debt amassed during the 1827–29 civil war and during the later hostilities placed a heavy burden on the treasury. Gálvez listed the priorities on which the money was to be spent: first, for the maintenance of the army; second, for the payment of past debts; and third, to cover back salaries. Like the earlier federal government, the raison d'être of the Guatemalan administration was the maintenance of its military position and the administration of its own salaries.[22]

The increase in revenue was remarkable, however, in that it occurred when international trade was in a great decline. Like the Hapsburgs, Gálvez preferred to depend upon taxation of local basic commodities rather than the vicissitudes of international commerce as the Bourbon fiscal system did. Thus, when there was a disruption in Salvadoran indigo or a drop in demand for indigo, the state's power was not immediately affected.

Commerce in indigo suffered greatly from the effects of the war. The military activities between Guatemala and Salvador that continued intermittently from 1827 onward disrupted cultivation and traffic. Meanwhile, the price of indigo on the world market collapsed as Bengal indigo sold in London at 79 percent the price of Central America's. The price paid in Guatemala "scarcely pays the expense of cultivation," restricting any expansion of the trade. In 1834 indigo was purchased at 6½ reales the pound, or less than half the price paid before the 1826–29 war.[23]

The civil war seriously affected production (see table 14.2), which constantly rose through the early thirties. Nevertheless, the high point of production in 1834 was almost half that of the years 1824 to 1826. Combined with the 50 percent drop in price, producers and merchants received one-fourth their pre-civil war incomes. The eruption of the volcano Cosiguina in 1835 destroyed most of that year's crop. Two years later an observer claimed that "the awkward, dilatory and expensive method of preparing indigo was harming the commerce." The constant civil disorders and government seizures at the end of the decade persuaded Salvadoran planters to ignore the indigo fair of 1839, and trade shifted almost completely to the Pacific. The annual pro-

*Table 14.2: Production of Indigo in Central America,
1826–1834 (in pounds)*

Annual Average, 1826-1830	305,672
1831	600,000
1832	n.a.
1833	450,000-600,000
1834	792,750[a]

SOURCES: These are the rough estimates from French and English consuls. Ministre du Commerce au Ministre des Affaires Etrangères, 5/2/32. A.M.A.E.F. CC-1, 185; Dashwood to Backhouse, 3/3/31, P.R.O., F.O., 15/11, fols. 8-11; Hall to Bidwell, 12/26/33, F.O., 15/13, fol. 36; Chatfield to Palmerston, 9/1/34, F.O., 15/4, fol. 174; Chatfield to Wellington, 5/22/35, F.O., 15/16, fol. 81.
[a] "Worth 638,000 pesos."

duction of indigo was represented in 1844 as being "at most" 450,000 pounds.[24]

As trade in indigo declined, the commerce in cochineal rose. The development of the commodity was as important for the Guatemalan merchant as for the state government. The loss of Salvadoran indigo meant a loss in commerce and taxes for Guatemala City, but production of cochineal centered chiefly on Amatitlán and Antigua, both geographically close to the powers in the capital. The dependence upon Salvadoran indigo for the sustenance of Guatemalan commerce and government finance lessened.[25]

Production of cochineal rose (see table 14.3) to the highest levels since the crop was introduced. Trade in the dye increased more than 150 percent between 1830 and 1834. In the three subsequent years, it was said that production grew substantially, and by 1837 formed "the staple article of export." The annual average export of cochineal between 1840 and 1846 rose to approximately 630,000 pesos. Paradoxically, the product promoted by José de Bustamante, the enemy of Guatemalan merchants, became the staple for their existence. Yet the income from cochineal never reached that from indigo during the boom years of the previous century. The maximum amount given for cochineal between 1840 and 1846 represented a third of that received for indigo in the earlier years, and the tax receipts were substantially lower.[26]

Cochineal did assuage, to some degree, the pain of the losses in the cloth trade. Areas near Antigua that had produced cotton now cultivated the dye. Merchants no longer paid Salvadorans for indigo and the money from cochineal remained within the small Guatemalan economy. With indigo trade directly from Salvador to the Pacific, and cochineal, under Guatemalan control, economic boundaries were being drawn between the two developing nations.

In the southern part of Central America, commercial traffic rose despite the civil disorders in Nicaragua (see table 14.4). Imports from Europe and South America were said to be "British items," and exports, chiefly in Brazil wood, derived from Nicaragua. At the end of the decade, the rise in Costa Rican coffee production added to the commerce, most of which was carried on through the port of Puntarenas.[27]

The absence of a strong export commodity continued the poor balance of trade with foreign countries. It was said in 1832 that the only expensive item in the country was "the rent of capital," which ran between 2 and 3 percent a month, "and this well-guaranteed." It was five to seven times the interest rate the church offered in the

Table 14.3: Production of Cochineal in Guatemala,
1830–1835

Year	Amount (pounds)	Price (pesos)
1830	70,000	140,000
1831	90,000	
1832	n.a.	
1833	120,000–150,000	180,000–225,000
1834	180,000	275,000
1835	600,000–700,000	

SOURCES: See sources, table 14.2, and Chatfield to Wellington, 3/1/36. P.R.O., F.O., 15/18. fol. 65.

colonial epoch. Lacking silver, the mint reduced the weight of the peso in 1832 and again in 1836. The coinage crisis forced the government to cede the mint to a private company, which was given control over the production of silver and coinage in Guatemala.[28]

This crisis furthered decentralization in Central America. Tegucigalpa minted coins at various times in the decade, but a lack of control created inconsistencies in weight—some coins were short one or two grams of silver and others forty grams. Guatemala and the federal authorities ruled in 1836 that Honduran coinage could not circulate as legal tenure. Differences in Guatemalan and Honduran moneys meant "commercial relationships between the states have suffered infinite damage." As the economies of each region separated, coinage further defined the divisions between the states.[29]

Table 14.4: Imports and Exports from the Port of Realejo,
1837–1839 (in pesos)

	Imports			Exports	
	1837	1838	1839	1838	1839
Europe	212,750	427,500	366,000	300,400	305,000
Central America	——	16,500	17,500	17,375	23,000
Peru	20,000	16,000	——	49,875	——
Colombia	20,000	13,500	110,000	8,750	122,500
United States	15,000	——	——	——	——
Totals	267,750	473,500	493,500	384,400	450,500

SOURCES: Based upon the reports of the British vice-consul in Realejo in Chatfield to Palmerston, 1/25/37, 1/15/38, and 1/29/39, P.R.O., F.O., 15/19, fol. 42, F.O., 15/20, fol. 39, and F.O., 15/22, fol. 47.

The politics and economics of free trade merged in the relations of Gálvez and Morazán with foreign merchants and entrepreneurs in a process that typified nineteenth-century Latin American liberalism. Gálvez allied with Carlos Klée of the commercial house of Klée and Skinner, which lent the state money, supplied it with arms and ammunition, and "to answer [Gálvez'] own purposes . . . displayed a steady hostility to Belize," even though Klée and Skinner had its main offices there. The Gálvez government awarded Klée the license to manage the state mint. Together, Klée and Gálvez were involved in an attempt to populate Verapaz with British settlers in the hope that the colony would form an independent state under the federation, a buffer between the expanding Belize settlement and the underpopulated northeast sector of Guatemala.[30]

Marshall Bennett of Belize made a similar attempt at colonization. In exchange for the 168,000 acres of San Geronimo land seized from the Dominicans and a pledge to colonize it within twenty years, Bennett furnished the state with 1,000 muskets. Foreign incursions supplanted church guardianship of local resources.[31]

Bennett did not limit his activities to colonization. In the 1820s he had developed a mining operation in Honduras, becoming friendly with the Herrera-Morazán family. When Morazán became president, Bennett received contracts to cut mahogany on the Mosquito Coast. Morazán used his political authority, gained in the early thirties, to get the right to cut wood from the states of Honduras and Nicaragua, both of which he controlled militarily through his uncle and brother-in-law. He signed the license over to Bennett for a percentage.[32]

These commercial arrangements incited xenophobia. There was a conspiracy, discovered in October 1834, to assassinate foreigners and seize their property. The British consul explained that the causes of the plot were "the late occurrences in Belize, the question of boundary between the two territories, and the grants of land made to the British in different parts of the country." The mahogany arrangement sparked the rebellion that expelled Morazán and his family from Nicaragua.[33]

The dealings were beyond the concerns of most of the nation. The warfare, fiscal policies, and natural disasters combined with disruptions in commerce and the declining economy to cause periodic upheavals. Most important was the continuing problem of food shortages. Reports of the loss of crops or a lack of grain were made from 1830 onward. "Extraordinary measures" narrowly averted an "epidemic of hunger" in both 1831 and 1832. Similar reports continued through 1837, reflecting both the lack of adequate grain production and the collapse in the colony-wide food distribution system of the late eighteenth century.

Gálvez was able to maintain his power despite weakening economic conditions. The English consul considered him "by his talent and influence in the country as the ruler of the republick." Still, Gálvez was bothered by troublesome annual revolts in the state of Salvador. To deal with his problems beyond Guatemala's borders, Gálvez persuaded the Honduran Morazán to return and re-form the federation, financing his force with the tax receipts from the ports of Sonsonate and Omoa. The strength of the federal force, combined with the 320 men Guatemala maintained under arms, was sufficient to quell most rebellions. The British envoy observed that "notwithstanding the diversity of opposite opinions that exist, no appeal to arms seems likely to take place; but if war has been averted it may be attributed more to the extreme state of poverty to which the country is reduced than to any peaceable contented feeling."[34]

Morazán and Gálvez organized a federal government, called a federal congress composed almost exclusively of Guatemalans, and created a federal district of the city of Salvador, without the approval of the ruling Salvadorans. Guatemalan troops invaded the province to accomplish it, easily vanquishing the defenders. Installed in Salvador, Morazán could finance his government from taxes on the indigo trade as he defended Gálvez' liberal hegemony over Central America.[35]

Still, the federal government of Central America, with control over what had been the captaincy-general under Spain, was a mirage, an illusion of centralized rule that served the needs of Guatemala and of Morazán. To be sure, Gálvez did not want centralization as the Aycinenas had and was willing to allow regional autonomy in all areas outside his state, but he would interfere, as he did in the "federation" in Salvador, to support his authority in Guatemala.

At the height of his military and political power, with growing fiscal resources, Gálvez attempted a series of reforms that challenged the political authority of the local political chiefs as well as the clergy. These liberal measures challenged a heritage of three hundred years of Spanish rule. "Everything new, everything Republican," Gálvez declared in 1836, "nothing of the colonial monarchical system. This is my belief. We must be innovators, because if we are not, independence has not done anything more than change the names of things."[36]

His radical innovations enflamed the populace. Civil marriages and divorce were permitted and a labor law was instituted according to which "nobody would be obligated to work" without a contract between laborers and owners. Gálvez' most important step was his attempt to base Guatemala's judicial processes upon the Livingston Codes, which, significantly, gave the power to appoint all judges to the governor of the state. In effect, repeating the 1820 attempt to create civil judges under the control of the provincial deputation, Gálvez sought to remove the power of the landed interests and the jefes políticos. The code provided for trial by jury and the right of habeas corpus, and even established schools in every district of the state, "where everyone [would] learn the rights of man."[37]

The political position of Gálvez seemed strong enough to withstand any attacks from the church or from regional leaders threatened by the reforms, but the weak economic situation at the local level combined with a cholera epidemic that swept across Central America in 1837 to destroy the Gálvez government.

The cholera morbus menaced Central America for many years. In 1832 measures were taken to ensure that it did not enter from Martinique and New York through Central American ports. The epidemic reached Mexico, descended southwards into Chiapas, and miraculously was halted by an effective *cordon sanitaire* near Soconusco in May 1834. The disease returned in May 1836, first appearing in Belize. This time a cordon failed and in late February 1837 the first cases of cholera were reported in Omoa.[38] The disease devastated Central America. Actual figures of incidence and mortality varied. The towns in the district of Mazatenango reported a rate of illness varying from 5 to 37 percent and of mortality from 1 to 9 percent. The overall rate of illness was 17 percent and there were 5 percent fatalities. The British consul in Salvador reported that all his servants had been taken ill. In Guatemala City some 2,812 people were affected, with 918 dead, or about 8 percent of the central population.[39]

The epidemic affected most areas of government and society. Because cholera afflicts adults more than children, with a greater rate of illness and mortality among the mature population, many children were left homeless. Gálvez authorized local jefes to resettle the orphans with families. Emergency measures created another financial crisis, which was further aggravated by the disruption of agriculture and commerce. At the local level, quarantines made exchange between towns impossible, and illness meant cultivation was difficult. The epidemic in Belize a year earlier and that in Guatemala suspended most commerce with the Caribbean for two years.[40]

But the most important effect of the cholera epidemic was the Indian revolt throughout the state and the subsequent anarchy. From March onward reports of Indian unrest arrived in the capital. All agreed that the epidemic was the primary cause, but the rebellion was intricately tied to the reaction to Gálvez' liberal reforms that impinged upon local life. Stirred by the local clergy, the Indian communities connected the promulgation of divorce and civil marriage decrees with the epidemic. Indians resisted the cordons. Rumors spread that the doctors sent from Guatemala poisoned the rivers and streams and that cholera victims were buried alive. A major Indian revolt erupted in Salvador in late May, "several large Indian villages in this vicinity arose upon the white and mulatto population, murdering them, and plundering their houses." The federal troops easily defeated them because they attacked "all parties indiscriminantly, which prevent[ed] their physical power from being applied to potential designs." The troops dealt with the Indians with "great severity."[41]

Similar revolts occurred throughout Guatemala. Gálvez declared martial law, suspending the liberal laws enacted in the previous two years. But it was too late; for the first time the lower classes in Guatemala, some Indians, many mestizos and mulattoes rose and became aware of the power that they held. The rural laborers, the masses, those groups that had been conquered by the Spanish colonial system reacted against the radical changes in law, in order, and in the basic traditions that independence had brought.[42]

The most important revolt took place in the province of Chiquimula, led by the great mestizo Guatemalan leader Rafael Carrera. Gálvez ordered troops to the region to enforce the cordon against cholera and to put down a rebellion. The troops were told to burn the villages, sell the produce of the lands, and execute the leaders of the revolt:

> I do not wish to fatigue your Lordship by relating the barbarities perpetrated by these troops, but merely to state that a man named Carrera, who it seems held a small property at Santa Rosa, after seeing his wife abused, his house and property destroyed, fled into the woods with several others to whom no alternative remained but to resist or die, and there raised a standard of revolt, around which the continued severities of the government officers caused numbers to flock.[43]

Famine, disease, and warfare plagued Guatemala, but Gálvez had been able to maintain control through the jefes; now their support failed because he had tried to eliminate their power by the Livingston Codes. The jefes' interests joined those of the Indians when the new judges attempted to collect taxes in interior regions. "The Indians, who, of course, could comprehend nothing of a jury system and had never seen judges and lawyers visit them, except for the purpose of inflicting punishments, revolted against the intrusion, and their anger lost all bounds when the persons appointed to carry the vexatious and absurd financial law into usurpation, proceeded to take an inventory of their huts and to assess the value to their patches of ground."[44] The central state government was trying to assert authority in the Indian village, an area where government had always tacitly allowed life to continue undisturbed. Under Spain, the Indian pueblos had merely paid an annual tribute through their Indian alcalde, the cleric, the only Spaniard in the town. Now the cleric was no ally of centralized rule, and, under the liberal laws, civil authorities invaded the Indian hut to tax.

The epidemic and revolts threw Guatemala into financial straits again. Gálvez estimated the state deficit to be at least 150,000 pesos by the end of 1837, and with Carrera posing a major military threat, further expenditures were required. Gálvez compromised with the conservative merchant class by appointing Juan José Aycinena and Marcial Zebadura Ministers of State and of Finance in return for financial assistance. When Carrera's army approached the capital in late January, Gálvez forced the conservatives to resign. A month later, Carrera took Guatemala City:

> . . . awhile after came the hordes of barbarians headed by Carrera. Only think what a sight—You would have thought there was a return to the age of Alaric, when he invaded Rome—the sight was awful and horrible—to witness 4,000 barbarians, rude, half-naked, drunk and elated, vociferating with all their might 'long live Religion and death to all foreigners'—some had only staves, others Muskets . . . at the hour of 'oracion' they all knelt down in the [central] square and sang the *Sanctus Deus* and *Ave Maria*.[45]

Like Hannibal, Carrera was persuaded to leave the city and return home. He was given 1,000 pesos for himself, another 10,000 pesos for his followers, and a thousand muskets together with ammunition. The liberal government of Mariano Gálvez was forced to abdicate and conservatives were installed. Still, Carrera was not satisfied, threatening a new sacking of the capital. At this point the powerless Guatemalans turned to Francisco Morazán, asking him to return from Salvador to protect Guatemala.[46]

Without the strong Gálvez government, Central America's disintegration proceeded. As Carrera entered Guatemala City in February, the departments of Sololá, Totonicapán, and Quezaltenango rebelled, forming a new state called "Los Altos" and refusing to make the "exorbitant contributions to maintain numerous [armed] forces." They declared they "had always been oppressed by the naming of functionaries that oppose[d] and degrade[d] them."[47] In the meantime, other states moved to abolish the federal system. Lacking any force in Guatemala to support it, the federation was abolished by the state government in 1839, and finally, in May 1839, the small body that constituted the federal congress in Salvador decreed: "The States are free to constitute themselves in the manner they judge convenient, conserving the republican, representative form of government and division of powers."[48]

Although the federation was expiring, Central America had to endure the death pangs of national government. Through 1838 and into the following year, Morazán fought a series of battles with Carrera and other mestizo and Indian chiefs in Guatemala and Salvador, and with state leaders in Honduras, Nicaragua, and Salvador, who openly and totally rejected Morazán's position. The remnant of the national congress halted operations, leaving three functionaries as the federal government.

Still, Morazán was needed; conservatives and liberals both appealed to him to defend Guatemala with his small army against Carrera. They arranged financing with Pedro Aycinena and other conservatives, providing the state government with 25,000 pesos in return for control of all taxes. Carrera had no such financial problems. He did not have to "recruit or pay men who come to him as volunteers on speculation, to whom clothes are an incumbrance and to whom a maize cake, a few black beans, or a bunch of plaintains afford sufficient sustenance." Although Carrera had trouble acquiring muskets, "the knives, hatchets and pikes of his people are formidable instruments when united in a crowd."[49] Morazán could not stop Carrera and his followers. In August 1839 Morazán's army "lost everything, and after seeing the greater part of their force massacred . . . fled." In September the federal army defeated Carrera, killing a thousand rebels. Carrera's forces withdraw to the hills to regain their strength.[50]

Morazán might have had time to reorganize if Honduras and Nicaragua had not resisted. The two states agreed to oppose Morazán's occupation of Salvador, and in April 1839 their united forces met an outnumbered federal army in battle. Morazán's superior military experience enabled him to carry away a federal victory. His army was winning battles, but, unable to conquer the vast domain of Central America, it was destined to lose power. Between 1838 and 1840 Morazán repeatedly fought Carrera in Guatemala, only to watch his defeated opponent fade into the mountains to recoup. Meanwhile, other provincial mestizo and Indian leaders plagued the federal army, as the states continued to oppose the Honduran. In September 1839 a coup in Salvador overthrew the federal government and Morazán attacked and defeated the city. A few weeks later, he defeated another combined Honduran and Nicaraguan army. According to the British consul, "The war which is carrying on between several of the States of this Republic involves no public principle whatever, and is a mere struggle between the members of two or three families for acquiring direction of public office."[51]

This deplorable state of affairs continued until 1840 when Morazán attempted to create a federal government, although his forces were incapable of completing the task. All the states convoked congresses to rewrite their constitutions as their governments signed treaties as independent nations. As a final step, the title of the leader of the Guatemalan state government was changed to president.[52]

Central America was truly and totally exhausted. "All the villages that one finds between San Miguel, San Vicente until San Salvador, tired of regimentation, without men, horses or silver that are violently demanded of them, revolt against the two sides, preferring to kill either one or the other, rather than take part in a war that isolates their country," the French consul reported.[53] The American John L. Stephens described the effect of the war upon one town near Carrera's home:

> . . . we came to the village of St. Stephanos, where, amid a miserable collection of thatched huts, stood a gigantic church, like that at Chiquimula, roofless, and falling to ruins. We were now in a region which had been scourged by civil war. A year before the village had been laid waste by the troops of Morazán. . . . At six o'clock, we rose upon a beautiful table of land, on which stood another gigantic church. It was the seventh we had seen that day, and, coming upon them in a region of desolation, and by mountain paths which human hands had never attempted to improve, their colossal grandeur was startling. . . . The grass was green, the sod unbroken even by a mule path, not a human being was in sight, and even the gratings of the prison had no one looking through them. It was, in fact, a picture of a deserted village.[54]

Describing a controversy between León and Granada over the financing of the earlier expedition against Morazán in Honduras, Stephens wrote of the military state of Central America:

> Expenses had been incurred in sending troops into Honduras. Granada refused to pay its portion, on the ground that, by the constitution, it was not liable except for expenses incurred in defending the borders of its own state. This was admitted; but the expense had been incurred; León had fought the battle, and had the same materials with which she gained it to enforce the contribution. In order that Granada might be

taken unawares, it was given out that the troops were destined for San Salvador, and they were actually marched out on the San Salvador road; but at midnight made a circuit, and took the route for Granada.[55]

Under orders from the United States government to find and talk to the leaders of the Central American Federation, Stephens had great difficulty in finding them. Finally, in Salvador he encountered Diego Vigil, a relative of Morazán, and nominally vice president of the country:

> If there was any government, I had treed it. Was it the real thing or was it not? In Guatemala they said it was not; here they said it was. It was a knotty question. . . . I referred to the shattered condition of the government; its absolute impotence in other states; the non-existence of Senate and other coordinate branches, or even of a secretary of state, the officer to whom my credentials were addressed; and he answered that he had in his suite an acting secretary of state, confirming what had been told me before, that the "government" would, at a moment's notice, make any office I wanted.[56]

The remnants of the once captain generalcy of Guatemala were reduced to a few men in a small area of Salvador. In Guatemala City, the illiterate Carrera used a rubber stamp to sign legislation annulling all liberal measures of the past seventeen years. Conservatives led by Juan José Aycinena associated with him, creating the policies of the new Guatemalan nation for the next thirty years. The liberals were exiled.

Carrera reconquered "Los Altos" easily, forming once again the nation of Guatemala. Finally, Morazán invaded Guatemala for the last time, taking the center of the capital. Carrera's counterattack surrounded the federal army and destroyed most of it. With his military force routed, Morazán narrowly escaped and fled to Salvador, pursued by Carrera. Without hope, Morazán boarded a ship and left the country. With him went the last vestige of Central America.[57]

CHAPTER FIFTEEN

Caudillos, Castes, and Conclusions

CENTRALIZED RULE VANISHED. Caudillos replaced enlightened liberal governments. Civil strife continued within new national boundaries as regional Creole families vied for control. In some areas government ceased to exist, in others, government and families waged war. In Nicaragua the internecine struggle continued into this century. In Honduras national weakness has persisted to the present. Only in Salvador and Costa Rica did the needs of commerce—the trade in indigo in the former and the developing commerce in coffee in the latter—compel regional leaders to cooperate.

The Carrera Guatemalan revolution differed from the other upheavals in that it was a social revolution, led by a caste and supported by castes.[1] Its objectives were social: the return to the traditional society that had existed before the instability caused by the world economy and the governmental disruptions of the Bourbon and liberal bureaucracies. This social revolution was a "reactionary" movement, restoring the church to its earlier position, returning common and church lands to their original occupants, and even changing the titles of local leaders from "jefes políticos" to "corregidores." Legislation again compelled Indian labor.

To be sure, the Carrera reaction was incomplete, tempered by the rule of conservative ministers and their mercantile interests. Carrera, too, needed to finance his army and pay foreign loans, and his only source of wealth was the Guatemalan merchant community. The Creole elite was allowed to farm and trade in cochineal dye in that central region that was the valley of Guatemala, but it was not allowed to extend its holdings. Commerce was restricted and foreign merchants were actively discouraged. At their highest point under Carrera, Guatemalan exports never reached half of those traded to the metropolis in the last third of the eighteenth century.[2]

Guatemala was a curious blend of Hapsburg and Bourbon institutions. Much like the Bourbons after 1750, Carrera relied upon commerce for taxes, though it was in cochineal rather than indigo. In fiscal 1856, for example, import, export, and sales taxes yielded half of all government income, of which fully two-thirds was spent on the military or for the repayment of military loans. Like the Bourbons, Carrera and his government were linked to the Aycinena family. For most of the caudillo's reign, an Aycinena or a close relative was minister of government. Aycinenas held the most important posts in the church, the merchant guild, and the University of San Carlos. Blending Hapsburg and Bourbon customs, the child of the Bourbon epoch, an Aycinena, was appointed to the archetypical Hapsburg position, the corregidor of the valley of Guatemala, controlling labor for the city and the cochineal plantations.[3]

Central institutions may have borne a resemblance to Bourbon ancestors, but government and society in outlying areas, in regions far removed from cochineal production, descended from the Hapsburgs. Communal property and clerics were restored to their patrimony. Once again the Amerindian defended his birthright, resisting incursions, though they did indeed occur. Withdrawing from the integrated Central American and world economy, Indians took up their inheritance, the semisubsistent economies, producing staples of corn, wheat, and cotton. As in the seventeenth and early eighteenth centuries, corregidores insured a share of foodstuffs and cotton for the city and compelled labor on Creole ranches or on public works. No longer a dependent relation of the city, the Indian again had to be legally compelled to labor.

Still, the Bourbon and liberal attacks on church authority had made an impact. Archbishop Casaus declined an invitation to return— he was too old and had too many responsibilities in Havana, he said. The law established the regular orders again, but there were no friars to resume their works. Despite the ecclesiastical sympathies of the Carrera government, the church as a whole was still in crisis in 1854. Those orders that had been allowed to remain in 1829 were barely surviving. The Belen monastery, for example, was empty and five nunneries were without resources "because their funds were seized by the Spanish government, because of debts and because of the political turmoil." In the twenty-five years after the liberal expulsion from Guatemala, 112 secular clerics died, while only 12 were ordained, and 7 came from Europe.[4]

Both traditional and modern forces struggled in Guatemala. A caste president who supported traditional institutions was forced to compromise with a Creole merchant society. In central Guatemala there was a modern labor system with salaries and debt peonage. Elsewhere in the nation corregidores controlled labor as local economies produced commodities that only marginally affected the national and international market places.

The dominant Creoles in central Guatemala controlled the distribution of pueblos to cochineal farms, the same pueblos that had worked for centuries under the repartimientos of the alcaldes ordinarios of the Creole cabildo. Free labor and a money economy existed as well, as landless ladinos and castes worked, some in debt peonage, on the cochineal plantations.

Thus there were two economic systems, two societies, and two philosophies of government, each countering the other. The pattern for the national period was set as these trends clashed: modern and traditional cultures, outward- and inward-looking, and the world market versus local semi-subsistence. Today, mestizo soldiers rule over European-oriented merchants and Amerindian laborers; the world marketplace continues to erode the traditional sector.

These trends in Guatemala were general throughout Central America in 1840. Labor was more free in the cattle regions of Honduras and Nicaragua than it was in Guatemala, where corregidores controlled the Amerindians. Mulattoes and mestizos fended for themselves or tied their fortunes to dominant families, combatting one another to maintain or extend their power. In these grazing lands land held relatively little value, most laborers rounded up cattle, selling their hides to Granada or sending them to the Caribbean for export.[5]

The Zelaya family of Olancho was typical of this pattern of dominant families who controlled small areas within nations. It was wonderfully described by William Wells, who visited the family in the mid-nineteenth century.[6] He found that the "national" officials in Tegucigalpa recognized the autonomy of the Zelayas. The family paid no taxes, nor were there national officials in the province. The only signs of the national government were titles. José Manual Zelaya was the governor of Olancho, his brothers were alcalde primero, juez de primera instancia, and general of the army for the region. The area's residents respected the family: Francisco Zelaya was thought the best horseman in the province, no small compliment in cattle country. Workers came to the Zelayas for loans and for advice. The Zelayas were, collectively, the caudillo of Olancho.[7]

The regional autonomy of the Zelaya cattle barony was paralleled in Nicaragua, where independence resulted in warfare between cattle families struggling for domination, continuing the blood feuds that had existed since at least 1812. Ranch hands and private armies became one and the same. The work force was devastated as men fled to outlying regions or left the nation for the relative peace of salaried labor on Costa Rican coffee farms or Salvadoran indigo plantations.[8]

There was debt peonage in Nicaragua, but it did not follow the pattern in the rest of America. Peonage was not total subservience. Peones or mozos lived in towns, not on haciendas, and their alternative of flight during civil altercation protected them from abuse. Indeed, the lack of manpower and the threat of runaway workers made labor expensive and, unable to support a labor system, many hacendados abandoned their estates. Land was plentiful and available; about 80 percent of Nicaragua's land was the "property of the state," that is, it was vacant. But the shortage of labor made the land valueless.[9]

Centralized government did not exist in Nicaragua. As if Bourbon rule had never occurred, local authorities dominated their areas, with landed families controlling the political situation. Vestiges of the Bourbons remained: some government titles, some local jurisdictions, and the names of some uncollectable taxes. But in Nicaragua, Bourbon centralization did not survive. Indeed, Nicaragua was threatened with territorial dissolution because of decentralization. The British claimed the Mosquito Coast. The southwestern province of Guanacaste seceded and joined Costa Rica. And then, in 1856, the North American filibuster leader William Walker attempted to conquer the state.

The only areas where liberal central authority was at all effective were Costa Rica and Salvador. In Costa Rica, the coffee plantations of the central tablelands encouraged peace and order. There were coups and family rivalries, but the coffee trade meant Costa Rica prospered, unlike any other area in Central America. Similarly, Salvador united around the annual indigo fair. Although a nativist uprising led by Malespin caused considerable turmoil, by 1850 order was restored and agreement reached among most indigo producers. In Salvador, Bourbon central administration and measures continued, including the taxes on indigo exports and the effective monopolies on tobacco and liquor.

Taken as a whole, the foreign commerce of Central America in 1850 seemed more like that of Hapsburg period 150 years earlier than that of Bourbon epoch. Most trade was in the Pacific, carried on directly between producer and shipper. True, English, French, and North

American ships, rather than Spanish vessels, brought South America and European commodities to the ports and to the fairs to exchange for indigo, cochineal, hides, and coffee. More importantly, there was no central metropolis, no Guatemala to dominate the region as under the Bourbons. If a region dominated, it was a local town or city, as it had been under the Hapsburgs.

The period of centralization begun by the Bourbons had, by and large, ended. Commerce, economy, and government returned to more traditional patterns. Each region developed its own institutions without external forces imposing their will through Guatemala.

Yet, throughout the nineteenth century, weak governments, regional sovereignty, and traditional Hapsburg institutions could not halt the expanding western economy and culture that continued to press inward, into the cities, the towns, and pueblos. The discovery of gold in California spurred encroachments. The liberal Guatemalan revolution and coffee exploitation accelerated the process. it was not until the twentieth century that this process culminated.

Perhaps the best description of Central America in these turbulent years was provided by the American traveler, diplomat, and archeologist, John L. Stephens, who traveled through the region in 1840 and 1841. His words are vivid and precise, like the engravings made by his traveling companion and intimate friend Frederick Catherwood. They recall the narratives written two centuries earlier by the English prelate Thomas Gage and in the early eighteenth century by the English sailor John Cockburn. Without the vituperative English criticisms of the Spanish clergy recorded by his two predecessors, Stephens was struck by the dominant role played by ecclesiastics and religion. Soon after his arrival in Guatemala he met the prelate Castillo, who was being carried "on the back of an Indian in a *silla*, or chair, with a high back and top to protect him from the sun." Stephens viewed the ritual passing of the figure of Santa Lucia, whose tour of the provinces was a symbol of the restoration of religion in the nation, "as a prelude to the restoration of the influence of the church and the revival of ceremonies dear to the heart of the Indian. As such, it was hailed by all the villages through which she (Santa Lucia) passed." It was evident to Stephens that "Carrera and his Indians, with the mystic rites of Catholicism ingrafted upon the superstititions of their fathers, had acquired a strong hold upon the feelings of the people . . ."[10]

Stephens' description of the power of the clergy in rural Guatemala can be applied to any time since 1600. It is an indication of the remarkably slow change in Amerindian society:

In the course of the day I had an opportunity of seeing what I afterward observed throughout all Central America: the life of labour and responsibility passed by the cura in an Indian village, who devotes himself faithfully to the people under his charge. Besides officiating in all the services of the church, visiting the sick, and burying the dead, my worthy host was looked up to by every Indian in the village as a counsellor, friend, and father. The door of the convent was always open, and Indians were constantly resorting to him: a man who had quarrelled with his neighbour; a wife who had been badly treated by her husband; a father whose son had been carried off as a soldier; a young girl deserted by her lover: all who were in trouble or affliction came to him for advice and consolation, and none went away without it. And, besides this, he was the principal director of all public business of the town; the right hand of the alcalde; and had been consulted whether or not I ought to be considered a dangerous person.[11]

Here was traditional Amerindian society, seemingly unaffected by Bourbon or liberal republican government. The cleric guided pueblo social and spiritual life and provided guidance to Indians whenever they had any doubt.

The reform of government and society by the Bourbons, the consequences of the invasion of the western Atlantic economy, and the experimentation by liberal republicans—all the subjects of this book— had not changed that. Traditional society had survived; it had regained its defenses and preserved its customs. Government had returned, by and large, to the control of local powers, and in most areas semi-sufficient economies developed again. Although there were great differences between the two periods, Central America in mid-nineteenth century resembled Central America of 1700 far more than at any other time in between.

This volume has analyzed the Hapsburg, Bourbon, and liberal republican systems of government in an effort to determine their strengths, their weaknesses, and their influences upon society and upon later history. Central to this analysis is the struggle between tradition and change as expressed in Hapsburg and Bourbon institutions. How did implanted institutions survive change and why did modern reforms fail? What were the values behind tradition and the forces for change?

We have seen the resilient quality of those Hapsburg institutions that the Bourbons wished to remove. The loose control that the Hapsburg bureaucracy exerted upon Central America allowed for a greater economic and political independence of the colonial body politic. Tradition and order were considered the highest of all laws; and the

Hapsburg monarchy and its administrators deemed them worthy of the greatest respect. As long as Central America remained loyal—symbolized by the annual remission of funds to the metropolis—the crown respected regional prerogatives and traditions. To be sure, differences existed between the state and the colony, and the crown did attempt to erode local independence. But it understood its limits and, as a result, even at the weakest moment in Hapsburg rule, the colony remained steadfast and loyal, without traces of intellectual or political disaffection. We must credit this to the bureaucratic institution of the empire: the church that maintained a spiritual connection with both Creole and Amerindian and the secular state that respected local needs, rewarded loyal Creoles, and allowed personal profit by individual bureaucrats.

Of course, the very philosophy that legitimized imperial strength in Central America, this weakest of all regions of the empire, ultimately led to the destruction of Hapsburg rule. Foreign enemies whittled away at Hapsburg power as the crown could not husband the fiscal and human resources to build defenses and maintain strong frontiers. The Hapsburg reliance on a steady annual fiscal income led to a failure (or an inability) to expand tax collection among the Creole and Spanish populations. With the rising costs of government and of waging wars, this policy resulted, in turn, in military and bureaucratic weakness.

There are signs that the Hapsburgs appreciated this at the end of their reign. They took some of the income from elites' encomiendas and pensions and attempted reforms in the collection of the sales tax. But this was not sufficient. By 1700 Hapsburg rule—with or without an heir—had come to a definitive end.

The Bourbons appreciated the problems of the Spanish crown through their experiences in France. They understood that national power could not be preserved and enlarged without creating an efficient, centralized bureaucracy, which, in turn, could not be created without challenging local authority. Perhaps most important, national power could be achieved only by attacking those areas of the economy that did not produce fiscal wealth. The traditional economies, the semisufficient towns and pueblos, the nonproductive, church-controlled land, and the noninflationary society, all fell under attack. And the success of the Bourbon reforms could be achieved only by destroying these traditional Hapsburg institutions.

Bourbon institutions *were* implanted and *were* working in 1790. But this success was only momentary, because under the strain of the Napoleonic Wars, the Bourbon structure disintegrated. Without many of those Hapsburg institutions that reinforced loyalty and provided for internal support, with the alienation of those church and secular groups that under the Hapsburgs guarded Spanish rule, Bourbon authority collapsed.

And thus the historical paradox: the strength of the Hapsburgs, the internal reinforcement of loyalty, became the weakness of the Bourbons; just as the Bourbon strengths, their ability to implement modernizing reforms needed to protect their empire were the Hapsburg weaknesses. The Bourbon reforms had been instituted by destroying Hapsburg institutional strength, just as the Hapsburgs had found it impossible to install modernizing reforms.

To a large degree the eighteenth-century Bourbons passed on their intellectual bases to nineteenth-century Spanish and Central American liberals. The heritage of anticlericalism, the desire to retain central fiscal authority, and the belief in the nation as a single unit rather than as a conglomerate of disparate entities and sectors led Central American independence leaders into the debacle of the Federation years. The republic lacked the one strength of the Bourbon (and the Hapsburg) era, the symbol of the crown as a central authority, and thus what had been intense rivalries under the colony became civil wars. And the centralized states disintegrated into regions, into power by municipality, and into local autonomy. The dilemma of the Bourbons in centralizing power by alienating local interests became the dilemma of republican leaders and, as such, without a single major source of military power to maintain control, with the fiscal structure in shambles, Central America disintegrated.

The correlation in political and economic developments is striking: just as Bourbons attacked Hapsburg institutions, the new merchant class tied to the expanding western economy attacked traditional economies. Was the expansion in government caused by economic expansion? Was the economic expansion the result of a deliberate government policy that relaxed trade restrictions as well as implementing other measures? Clearly, the two are complexly interrelated. The growth of trade in mid-eighteenth century provided sufficient resources for expanding government power, while government measures led to economic expansion soon after their implementation.

A correlation between the level of centralization of government authority and the level of trade in indigo is also apparent. Government power was at its greatest height when indigo was enjoying its greatest production and highest prices. When the demand for indigo fell off at the beginning of the nineteenth century, so too did government power. The same process was repeated later, in 1826, when the market for the dye dried up and civil war occurred.

But we should not overdramatize these correlations. Certainly other factors also came into play. The differences in populations, in topographical features, in resources, and in past experiences created different realities for different regions within Central America. If Nicaragua and Costa Rica were economically removed from Guatemala, so too were they by virtue of their historical experiences and racial differences. Guatemala with its highland Indians and traditional economies little resembled Nicaragua with its cattle ranches and marauding Mosquitos Indians. Indeed, it is apparent that the demographic crises suffered by Nicaragua and Honduras as the consequence of the sixteenth-century slaving expeditions created some of the conditions for national dissolution three hundred years later.

Still, by 1840, the central fact was the destruction of centralized authority and the resurgence of a traditionalism that allowed demographic, topographical, and historical differences to emerge. But to end at this date—this artificial, finite point imposed by the author—would be a mistake. For if Bourbon institutions and the strength of the western economy were in decline, the seeds for the future had been planted. The Hapsburg ideal of government and society that remained in traditional societies no longer existed in Creole society. Guatemalan merchants yearned for centralization in government and commerce albeit at a Guatemalan rather than a Central American level. They looked to the North Atlantic for their wealth and for their political ideas. If the dominant authority in 1840 was traditionalist, the minds of the urban classes had been won over to Bourbon ideas.

This intellectual success pervaded urban Central America: unheard of in 1700, only a whisper in 1820, anticlericalism permeated much of Creole society in 1840; the general acceptance of free trade and the sanctity of the market place violated fundamental Hapsburg tenets; and the schizophrenic idealization and hatred of the foreigner, the English, French, or American merchant, or of foreign ideas was a product of the Age of Enlightenment.

Although Bourbon governmental institutions were destroyed by 1840, their social and economic impact remained in the cities. The church was no longer the source of credit, and economies fluctuated depending upon the availability of land, food, and imported commodities. Power was no longer determined by tradition and familial alliances or by positions in the ecclesiastical and urban cabildos, but rather by financial wealth and contacts with foreign merchants. Loans from foreign nations became as important as contributions from local merchants, and trade with the outside world in armaments, cloth, and tools was a necessity. Despite Carrera and caste rule, despite the anarchy in Nicaragua, foreign commerce had to continue, and the influence of the world economy and its agents in the cities, the merchants, remained predominant.

And thus, as the Hapsburgs left their influence long after their demise, so too had the Bourbons. The history of the nineteenth and twentieth centuries in Central America has been, in essence, the struggle between the Hapsburg heritage of economic and political traditional society, regional autonomy, and Christian ideals and the Bourbon legacy of liberal economics, centralized authority, and "enlightened" thought.

Twentieth-century ideologies echo this dichotomy. In Central America, where the world market continues to invade and traditional societies continue to be destroyed, it is impossible to avoid. Still, there is a confusion in contemporary thought that we can place in historical perspective: twentieth-century caudillos attempt to defend some traditional values while permitting the world economy to invade. Socialists decry the destruction of Amerindian society while advocating greater government centralization, continuing the Bourbon process. Clerics are confused. Some advocate social reform, others defend the colonial heritage. Meanwhile, Amerindians continue to employ traditional defenses against twentieth-century technological and social invaders. And as Central American nations lose their economic and cultural autonomy to a larger world system, so Amerindians lose their struggle for existence.

Appendix A

Annual Income from the Church Tithe

THE TITHE SHOULD not be used to measure year-to-year economic production. Rather, the data are valuable for overall trends and as an indicator of church income. Like the alcabala, it was farmed out until the second third of the eighteenth century, when dioceses assumed collection themselves. However, poorer internal regions such as Guëguëtenango continued to be farmed out to prelates and alcaldes mayores into the nineteenth century.

Indians, Indian and Spanish cofradías, and ecclesiastical haciendas did not tithe until the eighteenth century. Thus agricultural production of some Spanish food, such as wheat that Indians or friars produced, or cattle that Honduran cofradías owned, never paid the church tax. Most sugar consumed in Guatemala derived from the Dominican hacienda of San Geronimo and also escaped the tithe. The Bourbons, however, compelled cofradías and ecclesiastical haciendas to tithe by at least 1732.

The tithe, the *diezmo*, was charged at 10 percent on all vegetables, most notably wheat, and on honey, chocolate, bananas, tobacco, cotton and wool, cattle, milk, and lime. But some other "products from the earth" paid less, most notably indigo, which paid 4 percent. Pitch, fish, sugar, bricks, roof thatching, and sugar also paid 4 percent.[1]

A concerted attempt to reform the tithe collection was attempted in the diocese of León in 1748. Clerics and the cabildo eclesiástico accused tax farmers of arranging the licensing for a "minute price"

*Table A.1: Annual Income from the Church Tithe
in the Diocese and the Archdiocese of Guatemala,
Diverse Years 1626–1820 (in pesos)*

Year	Income	Year	Income	Year	Income	Year	Income
1626	19,300	1668	25,500	1701	21,100	1760	22,548
1627	20,000	1669	25,500	1702	23,100	1761	26,082
1628	21,000	1670	25,500	1703	21,000	1762	25,952
1629	21,050	1671	26,000	1704	22,200	1763	25,391
1630	21,000	1672	25,600	1705	23,000	1764	25,764
1635	8,750	1673	26,000[a]	1706	22,000	1772–76	62,523[a]
1636	20,000	1674	25,500	1707	23,500	1777	105,079
1637	21,750	1675	29,000	1708	26,000	1778	80,626
1641	30,000	1676	30,000	1709	27,000	1779	102,312
1644	30,000	1677	30,000	1710	24,510	1780	20,513
1645	30,300	1678	33,000	1711	28,000	1781	172,901
1646	29,500	1679	27,500	1712	23,125	1782	177,383
1647	29,000	1680	29,000	1713	27,000	1783	94,750
1648	26,555	1681	29,000	1714–17	25,404[a]	1786	90,717
1649	27,000	1682	31,000	1724	20,012	1787	90,717
1650	26,300	1683	27,000	1725	22,012	1790–94	165,426[a]
1651	25,500	1684	25,000	1726	20,092	1805	99,694
1652	26,975	1685	25,000	1727	19,220	1806	115,232
1653	30,000	1686	23,000	1728	22,648	1807	102,154
1654	26,000	1687	25,500	1730	19,892	1808	104,226
1655	25,250	1688	26,000	1731–35	23,027[a]	1809	109,255
1656	23,498	1689	24,000	1737	27,215	1810	82,730
1657	26,771	1690	25,000	1739	27,216	1811	61,593
1658	25,500	1691	25,000	1743	20,653	1813	80,854
1659	26,500	1692	25,000	1744–48	28,378[a]	1814	91,181
1660	25,499	1693	29,800	1752	16,372	1815	68,225
1661	24,889	1694	34,650	1753	19,282	1816	58,523
1662	25,100	1695	36,000	1754	24,178	1817	74,193
1663	27,000	1696	35,000	1755	23,513	1818	99,831
1664	22,000	1697	31,000	1756	12,773	1819	8,347
1665	24,000	1698	30,500	1757	20,998	1820	131,116
1666	24,000	1699	29,000	1758	23,423		
1667	25,500	1700	22,619	1759	25,988		

Table A.2: *Annual Average of Tithe Collected in Nicaragua,*
1731-1777 (in pesos)

1731–35	6,750
1736–40	8,310
1741–45	9,084
1750–55	36,672
1759–63	22,825
1764–68	20,439
1769–73	23,990
1774–77	31,026

SOURCES: A.G.I. *1731–50:* Guatemala 950; *1750–55:* Guatemala 362; *1755–75:* Guatemala 909; *1775–77:* Guatemala 921.

and making so much money that they did not have to collect the tithe carefully. The cabildo thus took over control of the tax and began to license it to outside regions while collecting it within León. The success of the reform was obvious over the long term (see table A.2), with receipts rising dramatically in the years that followed. After a period of six years, receipts began to decline once again but still remained at more than double the earlier level.

←──

SOURCES: *1626–30, 1641:* A.G.N. Clero Regular y Secular 184, fols. 303–09, 332; *1635–37, 1666, 1672–73, 1688–96: ibid.,* 38, fols. 1, 44, 50, 144, 149, 153, 163, 164; *1644–65:* A.G.I. Guatemala 166 (Informe . . . cerca de la necessidad que padece la Iglesia Cathedral, 15 de marzo de 1666); *1667–71:* Guatemala 166, Oficiales Reales, 11/ 20/1671; *1674–87:* Guatemala 166, Quenta formada con cargo y data para la nueva fabrica matterial de la Sᵗᵃ Iglesia; *1688–92:* María Concepcíon Amerlinck, *Las catedrales de Santiago de Loś Caballeros de Guatemala,* pp. 95–97; *1708–13:* A.G.I. Indiferente General 81, Año de 1715: Quenta ajusta por un quinquenio lo que an emportado los diezmos; *1714–17:* Indiferente General El Razón de lo que corresponde en un año los diezmos. . .; *1724–28, 1730:* Guatemala 361, El Obispo de Guatemala, 3/11/1735; *1731–35:* Guatemala 724, Testimonio del todo el ingreso en . . . la Real Caja. . .; *1737:* Guatemala 361, Año de 1741: Testimonio de la Religión formada que importó la renta decimal de Obispado de Guatemala; *1739:* A.G.I. Santo Domingo 1238, Thesorero de la Caja, 5/20/1740; *1743:* A.G.I. Guatemala 921, Testimonio de lo que observa . . . de la Gruesa Decimal de Goathemala; *1744–48:* Guatemala 724, Cargo general de la Real Hacienda; *1752–64:* Guatemala 947, Estatutos y reglas formadas por el Arzobispado de Guatemala; *1772–76:* Guatemala 561, Testimonio . . . de la Real Cédula . . ., 7/24/1779; *1777–78:* A.G.G. A3.5, Leg. 1969, Exp. 30267, fol. 109; *1779–83:* A3.5, Leg. 1812, Exp. 28838, fol. 45; *1786:* A3.27, Leg. 1757, Exp. 28229; *1787:* A3.27, Leg. 1757, Exp. 28226, fol. 250; *1790–94:* B1.13, Leg. 18, Exp. 554; *1805–9:* A3.1, Leg. 2533, Exp. 37019; *1810:* A3.1, Leg. 2158, Exp. 32348; *1811, 1813–14:* A3.1, Leg. 2158, Exp. 32345; *1815–16:* A3.1, Leg. 1345, Exp. 22539; *1817–20:* A3.1, Leg. 2158, Exp. 32354.

ᵃ Annual average.

Still, the effects of the reform wore off over the next twenty years. Although income in 1769 was two-and-a-half times that of 1745, both population and commercial activity had also increased greatly. The tithe was farmed out once again in 1772 for a three-year period for 25,882 pesos per annum, and again licensed in 1775 for 32,570 pesos, increasing income some 50 percent. This return to private collection was thus, in effect, a return to the old Hapsburg system of licensing, of dividing jurisdictions among private individuals where the public sector could not function efficiently.

Tithe income represents only partially the wealth of each region. The levy taxed agricultural goods and not trade. In Nicaragua wood, sugar cane, balsam, vanilla, achiote, honey, suet, milk, butter, and salt, as well as other items were exempt from it. Then, regions closer to the metropolitan center were taxed more efficiently than outlying areas. Data from Nicaragua show income from Granada, Masaya, and Nicoya to be worth almost twice that from all other areas combined. Masaya was a center of cacao and indigo production during this period, with both articles in great demand and thus perceived by the tithe. Being close to a political center the cacao production of Masaya was more easily taxed than, say, that of Cartago with its large cacao plantations that supplied Cartagena.

The relative value of the tithe income during the eighteenth century varied from region to region. Chiapas collected more money than Nicaragua between 1737 and 1741, but twelve years later Nicaragua gathered more tithe than all other areas in Central America. In 1752 Nicaragua collected 31,500 pesos versus 16,372 pesos in the Archdiocese of Guatamala. These fluctuations, then, reflect bureaucratic efficiency as much as relative prosperity, although with a declining economy, receipts must, perforce, also drop off.

Table A.3: Annual Income from the Diocese of Nicaragua, by District, 1760–1775 (in pesos)

	1760–64	1765, 1767–70	1771–75
León and Metapa	4,688	4,444	5,130
Realejo	768	964	762
Granada, Masaya, and Nicoya	13,554	12,494	17,011
Nueva Segovia	1,263	1,108	1,581
Cartago	1,821	2,278	2,116
Total	22,094	21,288	26,600

SOURCE: A.G.I. Guatemala 909.

Table A.4: *Average Annual Income from Central America,*
Diverse Years, 1731–1777 (in pesos)

	1731–35	1734–39	1737–41	1743–48	1750–55	1773–77
Guatemala	23,027			27,090		61,458
Nicaragua	6,750		8,592		36,672	29,999
Honduras		4,205				16,075
Chiapas			8,733	9,971		11,542

SOURCES: For Guatemala, see table A.1. For Nicaragua, see tables A.2 and A.3. For Honduras, *1734–39:* Guatemala 361 and A.G.G. A.18, Leg. 211, Exp. 5020, and *1773–77:* A.G.I. Guatemala 432. For Chiapas, *1737–41:* A.G.I. Guatemala 239 and *1769–79:* Guatemala 949.

With more efficient tax collection, an increase in the non-Indian population, and the involvement of more people in a national marketing system, tithe receipts from all areas of Central America increased in the last half of the eighteenth century. With a preponderant Indian and mestizo population that produced food and indigo and cotton products and with the coming of the commercial revolution, Guatemala collected more tithe from 1773 to 1777 than the rest of Central America combined.

Appendix B

Table B.1: Annual Remissions to the Royal Coffers, by
Administration 1781–1819

Year	Guatemala (Administration)	Guatemala (Interior)	Salvador	León (Nicaragua)	Tegucigalpa/ Comayagua (Honduras)	Tuxtla/ Ciudad Real (Chiapas)
1781	121,888	7,320	33,646	24,383	14,116	16,078
1782	n.a.	12,405	44,842	28,294	14,925	19,379
1783	173,416	17,621	62,385	31,665	15,509	17,530
1784	117,267	16,616	72,155	32,253	11,756	16,348
1785	91,713	14,115	81,132	29,276	23,824	26,794
1786	n.a.	11,465	69,738	25,590	14,881	22,776
1787	178,613	n.a.	n.a.	n.a.	n.a.	
1788	146,556	n.a.	n.a.	n.a.	n.a.	
1789	183,228	n.a.	n.a.	n.a.	n.a.	
1790	79,445	19,337	92,741	28,618	10,670	9,078
1791	183,625	17,787	90,478	32,695	10,552	8,609
1792	128,455	17,862	99,381	41,484	9,192	11,173
1793	99,725	n.a.	87,179	28,320	6,061	10,179
1794	67,662	26,183	67,485	31,666	7,175	11,302
1795	78,259	n.a.	64,826	36,510	4,380	11,179
1796	98,312	n.a.	n.a.	n.a.	n.a.	n.a.
1797	119,190	27,715	45,589	34,217	11,103	10,095
1798	175,680	32,669	59,851	33,253	8,973	10,796
1799	175,747	38,530	48,855	31,160	11,413	12,817
1800	116,023	36,480	45,163	20,041	18,967	13,012
1801	n.a.	36,393	43,984	28,725	28,536	16,081
1802	80,118	17,723	42,893	32,640	24,383	14,710
1803	53,899	45,276	50,599	34,979	11,719	8,865
1804	91,255	45,918	30,081	31,179	13,646	15,369
1805	128,033	16,362	40,339	25,584	12,528	8,047
1806	71,527	20,252	31,806	14,750	13,233	6,605

Table B.1: (Continued)

Year	Guatemala (Administration)	Guatemala (Interior)	Salvador	León (Nicaragua)	Tegucigalpa/ Comayagua (Honduras)	Tuxtla/ Ciudad Real (Chiapas)
1807	76,858	17,022	41,629	20,595	10,237	9,627
1808	75,909	10,806	69,572	18,796	12,153	5,776
1809	51,703	15,980	76,577	24,081	11,399	8,127
1810	77,827	28,008	72,960	19,428	10,566	10,798
1811	168,943	18,571	51,878	12,711	7,148	11,942
1812	90,597	14,254	43,296	21,986	n.a.	n.a.
1813	76,502	13,224	27,169	23,716	n.a.	n.a.
1814	45,434	17,917	31,759	20,595	5,620	9,967
1815	61,456	17,139	41,021	12,618	6,711	6,938
1816	66,731	13,483	30,303	19,011	7,139	n.a.
1817	48,985	16,753	26,309	13,018	2,895	7,306
1818	57,970	15,030	28,092	14,810	10,727	6,980
1819	72,067	17,620	20,068	19,346	2,355	7,598

SOURCES: All sources derive from A.G.G. A3.5. Sometimes it was necessary to use two or three different documents in order to gain complete figures. For the year 1781, Leg. 850, Exp. 15802. Hereafter: *1781*: 850–15802; *1782*: 1384–23135; *1783*: 1965–30475; *1784*: 1116–20086; *1785*: 1392–23216; *1786*: 2180–32658; *1787*: 855–15850 & 2183–32683; *1788*: 2187–32704; *1789*: 2187–32706; *1790*: 332–6975 & 6976, & 333–6986; *1791*: 859–15908; *1792*: 536–11167; *1793*: 990–18218, 18219, & 18221; *1794*: 2194–32788; *1795*: 2195–32793 & 343–7156; *1796*: 736–13606; *1797*: 349–7253, 7254, 7255, 7256, & 7258; *1798*: 507–10393 & 463–9578; *1799*: 355–7390 & 617–11943; *1800* 359–7448 & 1418–23488; *1801*: 1430–23700 & 696–13033; *1802*: 364–7508; *1803*: 1158–20519; *1804*: 993–18259 & 875–16017; *1805*: 875–16024 & 1159–20522; *1806*: 997–18326 & 1427–23665; *1807*: 625–12065; *1808*: 743–13761 & 626–12073; *1809*: 2207–32889; *1810*: 2208–32903; *1811*: 381–7952; *1812*: 881–16210 & 492–10117; *1813*: 1442–23907; *1814*: 387–8045; *1815*: 1343–22521; *1816*: 1452–24109; *1817*: 886–16323; *1818*: 1186–20834; *1819*: 1346–22557.
n.a. = Not available.

Appendix C

Table C.1: Sales of and Profits from Tobacco, Diverse Years,
1766–1828 (in pesos)

Year	Net Profit	Year	Gross Sales	Net Profit
1766	56,628	1800	331,640	136,008
1767	88,523	1801	401,037	230,431
1768	88,544	1802	409,142	157,776
1769	85,699	1803	396,342	198,759
1770	87,613	1804	429,043	197,030
1771	110,056	1805	405,546	235,667
		1806	440,257	308,756
1779	95,544	1807	481,368	341,139
1780	94,784	1808	513,893	346,674
1781	86,004	1809	552,902	303,165
1782	94,496	1810	544,188	158,200
1783	93,121	1811	500,811	199,701
1784	121,027	1812	469,634	126,187
1785	91,588	1813	436,976	212,689
		1814	485,786	321,321
1787	93,048	1815	541,742	383,730
1788	119,063	1816	570,776	314,033
1789	214,608	1817	510,079	220,188
1790	161,364			
1791	110,432	1818–19		338,250
1794	70,519			
1795	85,009	1821		438,349
1796	141,643			
1797	155,554	1826		112,032
1798	142,367	1827		104,551
1799	202,235	1828		83,016

←
_____

SOURCES: *1766–71:* A.G.I. Guatemala 680, Demostración. . .y Estado de la Renta Del Tavaco. . .; *1779–91, 1794–97:* Guatemala 772; *1798–1817:* Guatemala 530, Estado Que Manifiesta Los Productos. . . Que ha tenido la renta de tabacos . . . , (and) Guatemala 742, Estado Que Manifesta Los Productos de Tabaco Huidas en los cinco años corridos desde el de 1797 hasta el de 1801 y el de 1807 hasta el de 1811; *1818–19:* deduced from A.G.G. B1.11, Leg. 2356, Exp. 47453, and *El Amigo de la Patria,* febrero 5 de 1821, p. 189; *1821, 1826–28:* A.G.G. B5.8, Leg. 70, Exp. 1920, fol. 1; B 107.3, Leg. 1833, Exp. 7741; Haefkens, *Viaje,* p. 307.

Appendix D

Population Statistics

OUTSIDE OF SANTIAGO de Guatemala, no accurate, statistical based demographic surveys are possible from currently available data. Population fluctuations must be determined from other types of evidence accompanied by statistics used with extreme care.

Indian tribute is a case in point. "Corruption" too often intervened for any accurate assessment of its relation to population. Indian alcaldes underestimated population, either to minimize the pueblo's payment or to pocket the difference between the actual amount and that given to the government. Spanish corregidores underreported tribute payment to the crown and profited from the difference, or, in the event of population decline, continued to collect the same amount of tribute to keep their profits high from the sale of tribute commodities. Clerics and farmers kept Indians on their farms without reporting them. Indian *laborios* in Guatemala City were excused from tribute payment. Forasteros went from one province to another, paying tribute sometimes, and sometimes not. As early as 1562 a census was taken in which officials warned that the responsibility for accuracy and completeness fell to the local chiefs and elders. Spanish officials gathered the data, nothing more. The 1570 census warned that the data were based upon "common knowledge" and that there were actually more persons in the province than had been recorded. By the early seventeenth century, tribute collection was farmed out (*rematado*) in important areas such as Soconusco.[1]

Although we have the most documentation for the eighteenth century, it cannot be used effectively either. Head counts were infre-

Table D.1: Partial Tributary Accounts in Central America, 1685–1818

	1685	1698	1783	1788	1802	1808	1811	1818
Chiapas	17,319			12,091	14,729		18,505	
San Salvador	3,557			10,748	13,375		14,800	
Comayagua	18,430			5,548	6,309			
León					10,285		10,471	
Sonsonate	2,055			4,450	4,458		4,641	
Chimaltenango			7,829	7,380	8,316		8,804	
Amatitlán/Sacatepéquez	3,025		9,201	8,700	10,054		10,804	
Chiquimula de la Sierra	2,338		7,675	8,049	7,578		7,195	
Escuintla	4,397		3,101	2,982	2,051		3,022	
Suchitepéquez	4,085		2,321	3,047	2,558		2,773	
Sololá			5,747	5,671	6,860		6,488	
Totonicapán	6,516		9,939	9,489	11,803		13,128	
Quezaltenango	3,798		4,773	3,941	6,148		7,363	
Verapaz	10,753		11,061	9,783	11,311		11,636	
Central America		93,862				128,144		111,966

SOURCES: 1685: A.G.I. Guatemala 159, Autos que se remítan . . . tocantes . . . los indios del Pueblo de Esquintenango; Contaduría 815, Razón de las Ciudades, Villas y Lugares Vecindarios y Tributarios de Que se componen las provincias del distrito de esta audiencia; 1698: A.G.I. Guatemala 679, Relación de todos los tributos, rentas y demas efectos . . .; 1783 García Paláez, *Memorias*, 3: 272; 1788: A.G.G. A3.16, Leg. 246, Exp. 4912, Plano General en que . . . se demuestra el Numero de Pueblos de cada Partida . . .; 1802: A.G.G. A3.16, Leg. 243, Exp. 4856; 1808: A.G.G. A3.1 Leg. 2153, Exp. 32345; 1811: A.G.G. A3.16, Leg. 953, Exp. 17773; 1818: A.G.G. A3.16, Leg. 1073, Exp. 19435.

Note: Jurisdictions above include: Chiapas (Ciudad Real, Tuxtla, and Soconusco); San Salvador (San Miguel); Comayagua (Tegucigalpa); Totonicapán (Güeguetenango); Chiquimula (Sacapa); Verapaz (Tecpanatitlán); Escuintla (Guazacapán).

quent. In the center of administration, Guatemala, some pueblos went ten or twenty years without new estimates, others fifty-six, and still others sixty-six years. In Chiapas it was said some pueblos went eighty years without recounts. Frequent head counts were not necessarily reliable either, since towns repeated the same data. Government reform further obfuscated population figures. After mid-century, most Indians paid in coinage rather than goods and paid different amounts. When women were eliminated from tribute rolls in 1759, total tribute numbers dropped as much as 50 percent.[2]

Demographic trends were never the same in all pueblos, as regional diseases, weather, and labor conditions affected each town differently. From 1680 until 1730 the population of Santiago de Guatemala and its valley declined as a whole. But this was not true for all pueblos. Between 1768 and 1773 a treasury official reported a rise of 11,195 tributaries throughout the colony, but stipulated, "some towns rose, others declined."[3]

The most frequently cited source for colonial population figures, Pedro Cortés y Larraz, specifically informed the crown that he did not believe some data that were given him by pueblo clerics. Other figures, he said, were purely rough estimates. In his travels, however, he was impressed with the numbers of forasteros in most provinces and "the speed with which the most flourishing provinces decline."[4]

Indians fled not only to other provinces, but also to towns and cities. They became ladinos. And ladinos were frequently confused with mestizos in documents. Mestizos, on the other hand, were sometimes included in Spanish documents. It is clear that no estimate is possible for the caste population of the colony.

All contemporary accounts agree upon a dramatic growth in Central America's total population at the end of the eighteenth century. Rough censuses show: in 1778, 797,214; in 1796, 822,579; in 1803, 1,037,421; and in 1825, 1,287,491.[5]

These figures and those mentioned in this volume are useful for comparative purposes only. They show how contemporaries viewed the demographic structure of their time. For the only careful demographic study of one Central America region, see the work of Christopher Lutz based upon Santiago de Guatemala parish records. He too, though, is forced to estimate patterns from his data.[6]

Abbreviations

A.E.G.	Archivo Eclesiástico de Guatemala
A.G.G.	Archivo General de Guatemala de Centro-America
A.G.I.	Archivo General de Indias
A.G.N.	Archivo General de la Nación (Mexico)
A.M.A.E.F.	Les Archives du Ministre des Affaires Etrangères (Paris)
Anexión	*La Anexión de Centro America a Mexico.* Rafael Heliodoro Valle, comp. 6 vols. (Mexico, 1924–1929)
A.R.S.I.	Archivum Romanum Societatis Iesus
A.S.V.	Archivo Segreto Vaticano
B.A.G.G.	Boletin del Archivo General de Guatemala
H.A.H.R.	*Hispanic American Historical Review*
N.Y.P.L.	New York Public Library
P.R.O., F.O.	British Public Record Office, Foreign Office Series

Notes

Preface

1. If we are to believe the *Annals of the Cakchiquels* and the Quiché *Popoh Vuh*. See the translations by Adrián Recinos.

2. Barbara L. Stark and Barbara Voorhies, eds., *Prehistoric Coastal Adaptations*.

3. Mario Góngora, "The Institutions and Founding Ideas of the Spanish State in the Indies," in his *Studies in the Colonial History of Spanish America*, pp. 67–126. Also see John Leddy Phelan, *The Kingdom of Quito in the Seventeenth Century*.

4. François Chevalier, *La Formation des grands domaines au Mexique* and Charles Gibson, *The Aztecs Under Spanish Rule*.

5. Jaime Vicens Vives, *Approaches to the History of Spain* (Berkeley; University of California Press, 1972), p. 108.

1. The Conquest and the Settlement

1. The estimate is in Murdo J. MacLeod, *Spanish Central Central America: A Socioeconomic History 1520–1720*, p. 41. Four recent works describe the conquest and its aftermath: Murdo MacLeod's work; William L. Sherman, *Forced Native Labor in Sixteenth-Century Central America*; Salvador Rodríguez Becerra, *Encomienda y conquista*; and Christopher H. Lutz, "Santiago de Guatemala, 1541–1773: The Socio-Demographic History of a Spanish American Colonial City." Also see Robert S. Chamberlain, *The Conquest and Colonization of Honduras, 1502–1550*; Domingo Juarros, *Compendio de la historia de la ciudad de Guatemala*, vol. 1. Except where cited, this chapter is based upon these works.

2. Rodríguez Becerra, *Encomienda y conquista*, pp. 19, 42, 113–14.

3. Sherman, *Forced Native Labor*, pp. 113–14.

4. See Chamberlain, *The Conquest and Colonization of Honduras*, for the history of the fight between Montejo and Alvarado. Also see MacLeod, *Spanish Central America*, pp. 56–61, and Clarence H. Haring, "American Gold and Silver Production in the First Half of the Sixteenth Century," p. 467.

5. For an excellent description of the cacao trade, see MacLeod, *Spanish Central America*, pp. 68–79; also see David Browning, *El Salvador, Landscape and Society*, pp. 58–59; Ivar Erneholm, *Cacao Production of South America*, p. 33; Francisco de Paula

García Paláez, *Memorias para la historia del Antiguo Reyno de Guatemala*, 2:43; Eduardo Arcila Farías, *Comercio entre Venezuela y México en los siglos XVI y XVII*, p. 37.

6. Lutz, "Santiago de Guatemala," p. 5; David R. Radell and James J. Parsons, "Realejo—A Forgotten Colonial Port and Shipbuilding Center in Nicaragua," pp. 295–312.

7. For an examination of the Cerrato reforms, see Sherman, *Forced Native Labor*. While Sherman believes the reforms were effective MacLeod does not. He suggests that Cerrato's impact was mixed. "Indian slavery disappeared but it was a secondary and dying system when [Cerrato] arrived. [Sherman disputes this] Minor abuses were corrected and many of the smaller encomiendas reverted to the Crown; but the richer encomenderos were not attacked and in fact consolidated their power." *Spanish Central America*, pp. 109–19.

8. See all of MacLeod for the impact of disease upon Central America.

9. See appendix D.

10. MacLeod, *Spanish Central America*, pp. 68–79.

11. *Ibid.*, pp. 152–75; Pierre and Huguette Chaunu, *Séville et l'Atlantique*, 8a:850–51.

12. Chaunu, pp. 850–51; Robert S. Smith, "Indigo Production and Trade in Colonial Guatemala," pp. 181–82; Manuel Rubio Sánchez, "El añil o xiquilite," pp. 313–49; Browning, *El Salvador, Landscape and Society*, p. 70.

The cabildo of San Salvador complained as early as 1628 that indigo producers could not make a profit because the cost of production equalled the sale price. Manuel Rubio Sánchez, *Historia del añil o xiquilite*, 1:43.

13. For specific examples of how Indians were used in the obrajes and fields, see A.G.I. Guatemala 157, Bishop of Guatemala, 3/15/1671; "Algunos vecinos de Guatemala," 5/8/1644; Manuel Rubio describes the visitas by alcaldes and the fines levied for the use of Indian laborers in the seventeenth century and early part of the eighteenth century in *Historia del añil*, 2:55. Also see his article on "El añil o xiquilite," pp. 313–49; the articles by Robert S. Smith, "Indigo Production," pp. 186–92, 197, and "Forced Labor in the Guatemalan Indigo Works," pp. 318–19, 321–28; Browning, *El Salvador, Landscape*, pp. 45, 76; José Joaquín Pardo, *Efemérides para escribir la historia de la muy noble leal ciudad de Santiago de los Caballeros del Reino de Guatemala*, pp. 179, 184; and MacLeod, *Spanish Central America*, pp. 187–90.

14. MacLeod, *Spanish Central, America*, pp. 187–90; S. Smith, "Indigo Production, p. 185. Between 1693 and 1695 the alcalde mayor of Salvador collected a minimal amount in fines—495 pesos. A.G.G. A1.24, Leg. 15711, Exp. 10215, fol. 124.

15. The seventeenth-century repartimiento of indios was "the key piece of the economic system of the colony"—Severo Martínez Peláez, *La patria del criollo*, p. 95; also see pp. 474–518. Writing in Guatemala in the late seventeenth century, Fuentes y Guzmán testified that "it was rigorously prohibited for hacendados to have centers of Indian workers in their haciendas or cattle ranches." *Recordación Florida*, 1:302.

Also see the considerations of the crown in its deliberations over whether to ban the repartimiento in 1662–63 in A.G.I. Guatemala 132, which is, unfortunately, unpaginated. The deliberations present the views of all sectors of colonial society: secular clerics, regular clerics of the different orders, Creoles, Indians, and officials who represented different interests. See Guatemala 166, German de Betanzos y Quiñones, 5/17/1662, for a description of repartimiento in Guatemala; Guatemala 132, Cabildo Eclesiástico, 11/25/1663. For lists of repartimientos of Indians in the valley of Guatemala see: *1702*: A.G.G. A3.16, Leg. 2321, Exp. 34272; *1712*: A3.12, Leg. 2105, Exp. 31932; *1725*: A3.21, Leg. 2457, Exp. 36060; and *1744*: A3.12, Leg. 2457, Exp. 36063.

16. A.G.I. Guatemala 132, Testimony of Fray Christóbal Servano, 9/11/1663. For complaints concerning the repartimiento of Indians around the city of Guatemala from 1603 until 1739 see A.G.I. Guatemala 354, Expediente de la Ciudad de Santiago . . . sobre que se hagan tres corregimientos, año de 1751, particularly fols. 418–33. The repartidores, "serve no other end," a friar testified, "than to tyrannize the Pueblos."

17. A.G.I. Guatemala 132, Autos Sobre Repartimiento.

18. When *haciendas de campo* are sold, their wealth is more or less determined by the number of Indians they have in repartimiento." Guatemala 132, testimony of Fr. Francisco de Peña, 9/17/1663. Lists of repartimientos to wheat haciendas for 1675–1679 are in A.G.G. A, 3.12, Leg. 2775. See also the sales contract of farms in Sumpango with six *cavallerías* of land and "22 Indios de mandamiento" in 1735, and of a farm called Villalobos "with cattle, mules, horses and Indios de mandamiento," and another called San Antonio with land, horses, and "indios de mandamientos that are assigned to it," in A.G.G. Al. 2, Leg. 487, Exp. 419, fols. 35 and 438–39.

Repartimientos were made continuously until the end of the eighteenth century. They supplied laborers to the indigo fields during the commercial boom of that period, and they built Guatemala City after the major earthquake and transfer of the capital in the 1770s. Reports concerning how they were made, and their effect upon populations rarely differed throughout the epoch. For further evidence of the labor-land value, see Martínez Peláez, *La patria del criollo*.

19. Debt peonage also occurred in seventeenth-century Central America, although not to the great extent it did in Mexico. In order to escape from abusive officials or from the pueblo itself, Indians entered hacienda grounds to labor and live and be protected. In Mexico they became indebted to the hacendado. In Central America, pueblos became attached to haciendas and integrated within their economic influence without being absorbed and taken within hacienda grounds. Indian pueblos that were repartido to the same hacienda for tens of years became attached and indebted to it. Still, there did not exist a need for Indians to flee to haciendas for protection because of a lack of food or destruction of pueblos as had happened in central Mexico in the early seventeenth century. Debt peonage occurred most prominently in the Salvadoran hotlands, where depopulation created a demand for labor and the money crop, indigo, made the area a center for production. When the demand for indigo increased in the mid-eighteenth century, so too did the frequency of debt peonage. MacLeod, *Spanish Central America*, p. 296.

20. Sherman, *Forced Native Labor*, pp. 333–39.

21. Charles Gibson, *The Aztecs Under Spanish Rule*. "The interests of the crown, especially in Mexico, were completely different from those in Guatemala. There, there were mines and there, the repartimiento was abolished in 1633. In 1620 in Mexico, the Mexican hacendados were authorized to hold Indians for debt . . . which was prohibited in Guatemala until the end of the colony." Martínez Peláez, *La patria del criollo*, p. 394. Silvio Zavala concurs: "since 1633 there existed a difference between Mexico and Guatemala in the evolution of agricultural work." *Contribución a la historia de las instituciones coloniales en Guatemala*, p. 85.

2. The Kingdom Under the Hapsburgs

1. John Leddy Phelan, *The Kingdom of Quito in the Seventeenth Century*.

2. When Spanish merchants attempted to market Central American indigo to Flanders in the 1650s, they lost considerable amounts of money in the enterprise. A.G.I.

Mexico 1007, the Consulado of Seville, 10/18/1663. The concern of the crown over the Peruvian traffic is best seen in Indiferente General 2711, which deals with the period 1692–1716 but contains earlier documents that were used as precedent. For a history of the wine trade and other analyses of its importance see MacLeod, *Spanish Central America*, pp. 264–73; and García Peláez, *Memorias*, 2:40–47.

3. Permission to send 200,000 pesos in coinage to Central America from Peru was needed because of legislation in 1600 against the sending of silver from Peru to New Spain as a measure aimed against the traffic of Asian cloth (from the Manila Galleon) to Lima that was competing with the Spanish product. Rubio *Comercio Terrestre*, p. 165; A.G.I. Guatemala 279, Council of the Indies, 1/12/1667 and 6/10/1688; Cabildo of Guatemala, 4/11/1668; Bishop of Guatemala, 11/23/1677; Consulado of Seville, 4/18/1711 and 8/25/1713. For other testimonies of blatant violations of the wine trade see Guatemala 219, President of Guatemala, 4/25/1707, and Guatemala 215, Joseph Descals, 6/13/1697; MacLeod, *Spanish Central America*, p. 269.

4. A.G.I. Guatemala 279, Guatemala Deputation, ?/1670.

5. A.G.I. Guatemala 279, Council of the Indies, 3/30/1685.

6. Permission was granted in the cédula of 5/21/1685 and reiterated in 1688 and 1695. The latter order allowed the trade "for the time of two armadas (from Spain) and lasted—because of the war and lack of trade—technically until 1707, although boats sailed until 1713. A.G.I. Guatemala 279, Real Cédulas of 8/25/1713 and 5/21/1685, Council of the Indies, 10/15/1672.

7. When the wine permission was renewed in 1695, trade in Guayaquil cacao was banned "because it seems that it goes together with wine," A.G.I. Guatemala 279, Fiscal of the Council of the Indies, 1/10/1713; Rubio *Comercio terrestre*, 1:164. Rubio believes that Peruvian merchants were the largest market for Salvadoran indigo around 1690. *Historia del añil*, 1:58.

8. In León, the city's leaders decried the "calamities that afflict the Provinces of Honduras and Nicaragua for the suspension of commerce with Peru through Sonsonate and Realejo and with Havana, Cartagena, and Portobelo." The Guatemalan cabildo appealed to the crown in 1709 to allow direct commerce with Havana because the cost of Spanish goods coming via Mexico was too high.

The new interdict involving Spanish wine reopened the debate between colonial merchants and the commerical sector in Spain. The Seville consulado claimed that it was impossible to trade with Guatemala profitably. It pointed to one Paxcual de Estrado of Mexico, who sent 16,000 pesos worth of clothing to Central American and lost 40 percent of his investment. "Also, it is certain for many years that . . . [illegal] merchandise entered [Guatemala] with the wine and oil." See A.G.I. Guatemala 279 and Rubio *Historia del añil*, 1:239–42.

9. A.G.I. Guatemala 279, the Council of the Indies, 4/7/1713 and 6/1/1717; the President of Guatemala, 6/23/1716.

10. Juarros, *Compendio*, 2:40; MacLeod, *Spanish Central America*, p. 85.

11. See table 7.2.

12. See, for example, the "Libros de Reales Almonedas" for 1701–13, A.G.G. A3.24, Leg. 1635, Exp. 26, fols. 771-26, 774.

13. For correspondence concerning the lack of specie and the inability to convert tributary goods into currency, see letters from the royal officials in A.G.I. Guatemala 639 and Contaduría 981. See MacLeod, *Spanish Central America*, pp. 281–87, for a discussion of how the currency shortage led to problems of clipping and debasement. See the same work for a discussion of demographic trends. Also see Antonio Batres Jáuregui, *La América Central ante la historia*, 1:405–06.

14. The practice was rife throughout most of the colonial period, for some excellent descriptions in the early seventeenth century see Thomas Gage, *Travels*; and, for later on, in the A.G.I. Guatemala 179, Bernardo Gines Ruiz, Maestre Escuela de León, 5/14/1673; Guatemala 387, Real Cédula, 1/12/1667; Guatemala 222, Año de 1708: Testimonio del escrito presenta de Dn Clemente de Ochoa; Guatemala 363, Obispo de Chiapas, 4/4/1717. For later descriptions see chapter 9.

15. A.G.I.Guatemala 221, Año de 1709: Testimonio del primer escriptulo de Capitulos puestos por los Cabildos . . . de la Ciudad de San Miguel y Villa de San Vicente de Austria.

16. A.G.I. Guatemala 132 for the 1660s, Guatemala 222, Año de 1708: Testimonio del escrito presenta de Dn Clemente de Ochoa; and Guatemala 222 for other Correspondences on conditions in 1709.

17. Gage, *Travels*, pp. 321–22.

18. See the complaints of prelates listed in A.G.I. Guatemala 132.

19. *Ibid.*, Auto sobre repartimientos de Indios de Guatemala para servicio ordinario.

20. Ismael Sánchez-Bella, *La organización financiera de las Indias*, p. 52; Rubio, *Comercio terrestre*, pp. 155–56; García Peláez, *Memorias*, 1:203.

21. Many of the details and conclusions reached on the administration of the *alcabala* and *barlovento* taxes derive from the *cuentas* of these taxes. For 1685–1712, see A.G.I. Guatemala 217, 245, and 682, the informes of the contadores; for 1727–28, see Guatemala 724, and for 1728–56, see Guatemala 342. For Mexico, see A.G.I. Mexico 93, Razón . . . de Alcabala.

22. A.G.I. Guatemala 279, Council of the Indies, 1/12/1667, and also see correspondences in Guatemala 387. Between 1664 and 1668 Salvador and San Vicente together paid 800 pesos annually, but the government voluntarily lowered the amount 200 pesos in the last three years because of poor crops.

23. See Mario Góngora, *Studies in the Colonial History of Spanish America*, pp. 82–97.

24. Such a conclusion is also reached by Phelan, *The Kingdom of Quito in the Seventeenth Century*.

25. Encomiendas were usually given for two generations (*vidas*), although they were prolonged whenever a family maintained its influence and "service to the crown." The average encomienda given by the crown in the seventeenth century was worth 755 pesos annually. A.G.I. Guatemala 212, Relación de las mercedes que S.M. ha hecho en encomiendas de Indios . . . desde el año 1600 hasta fin de 1681.

26. José Milla, *Historia de la América Central*, 2:327; Troy Floyd, *The Anglo-Spanish Struggle for Mosquitia*, p. 31; A.G.I. Guatemala 279, Martín de Mencos, 4/14/1669; MacLeod, *Spanish Central America*, pp. 356–57.

27. A.G.I. Guatemala 131, Año de 1651: Expediente sobre haber o no en Guatemala y su Provincia Jueces de Milpas; President of Guatemala, 10/30/1645, 11/7/1646; Guatemala 157, Bishop of Guatemala, 3/14/1671.

28. See the testimonies of the Franciscans in A.G.I. Guatemala 131, Expediente sobre . . . Jueces de Milpas.

29. *Ibid.*; Guatemala 157, Bishop of Guatemala, 3/14/1671.

30. A.G.I. Guatemala 279, Council of the Indies, 1/12/1667; also see correspondance in Guatemala 387.

31. The Mencos family received over 500,000 pesos during the seventy years of the encomienda's existence. It was suspended July 4, 1739, nineteen years after the major Bourbon legislation eliminating the pension. A.G.I. Guatemala 239, Joseph Alexandro Mencos, 8/2/1748. MacLeod, *Spanish Central America*, pp. 356–57.

32. See A.G.I. Guatemala 213 for different *relaciones* of various encomiendas, including that held by the Duke of Medina Celi. For a general summary of most of the encomiendas granted in the seventeenth century see Guatemala 212, Relación de las mercedes que S.M. ha hecho en encomiendas de Indios del distrito de la Audiencia de Guatemala . . . desde el año 1600 hasta fin de 1681 and Guatemala 167, Año de 1671: Testimonio de Los Autos hechos sobre la Vacante de las Encomiendas, and the Real Cédula of 10/29/1671. Also see the Real Cédula of 6/9/1701 in Guatemala 213.

33. A.G.I. Guatemala 419: Los Ramos de Que se Componen la Real Hacienda, 6/20/1698. Guatemala 679, Relación de los Jueces, 5/19/1719; Real Cédula of 12/6/1720 A.G.I. Al.23, Leg. 4636, fols. 9–14. A.G.I. Guatemala 679, Relación de los Jueces Oficiales de la Real Hacienda, 5/19/1719.

34. A.G.I. Mexico 1007, Council of the Indies, 4/29/1667.

35. Pardo, *Efemérides*, pp. 74, 77.

36. MacLeod, *Spanish Central America*, pp. 357–60.

3. Cross and Crown

1. Schedules (*aranceles*) were published listing the charges clerics could levy for each service, although each cleric had leeway in the fees he charged. See A.G.I. Guatemala 162; Arancel de los derechos que han de llevar los Curas . . . ; Guatemala 159, Año de 1687: Testimonio de los Autos Fechos Sobre las raciones que de los bienes de Comunidades, Arancel de los Derechos . . . , fols. 41–43; Guatemala 226, Año de 1720; Testimonio de los Autos Fechas sobre las Raciones y Servicio Personal. For Chiapas see the Visita of Descals in Guatemala 215.

MacLeod suggests that prelates withdrew from highland pueblos in the mid-seventeenth century (*Spanish Central America*, p. 344). The evidence I have seen disputes this. As many as 162 Franciscans lived in 120 pueblos and 24 convents in the mid-seventeenth century. Dominicans continued to administer pueblos in Chiapas, Verapaz, and the Guatemalan highlands. For the Franciscans see the lists in A.G.I. Guatemala 724, Doctrinas de Curas, ?/1665, fols. 17–24, and the reports in letters of 9/24/1661, A.G.I. Guatemala 181, 11/18/1671, A.G.I. Guatemala 157 (that claims 128 pueblos), and 10/24/1673, A.G.I. Guatemala 179 (that claims 120 pueblos). The entire legajo of A.G.I. 132 provides letters from Franciscans between 1661 and 1663, many of whom had spent twenty or thirty years in Totonicapán and Quezaltenango. A detailed list of Dominican prelates is given in A.G.I. Guatemala 181, Jueces Officiales de Guatemala, 9/24/1661. In 1693 the order was said to administer 35,000 tributaries "that equals more than 150,000 Indians in Chiapas and Guatemala." Indiferente Generale 1747, Decree of Consejo, 2/17/1693.

Histories that date from the sixteenth century and listings of the numbers of prelates in convents, on farms, and in Indian pueblos, together with the worth of each order are in: for the Franciscans, (1740) A.G.G. Al.18, Leg. 211, Exp. 5026, for the Dominicans, *ibid.*, Exp. 5028, and A.G.I. Guatemala 214, Año de 1740, Testimonio de la diligencia de Erección del Convento del Señor Sto. Domingo de Esta Ciudad. For another list of Dominican holdings and prelates see the letter from Archbishop Pedro, 7/31/1769, in A.G.I. Guatemala 935. For the Mercedians see A.G.G. Al.18, Leg. 211, Exp. 5025. For the holdings of other orders in 1740 whose members were located chiefly in cities, see *ibid.* Exp. 5029 (Sn Felipe Neri–; Exp. 5024 (Hospital Real de Sta. Catarina); Exp. 5027 (Colegio de Christo Crucificado); Exp. 5031 (four Guatemalan convents).

2. The power and presence of cofradías continued unabated through the mid-eighteenth century, although the fortunes of each fluctuated with those of the pueblos. Compare the auto of 3/20/1637 in A.G.G. A1.2, Leg. 2245, Exp. 16190, fols. 169–70, and the letter from the fiscal of the audiencia, Pedro Frasso, 4/20/1663, A.G.I., 4/20/1663, that decry the abuses of cofradías in Nicaragua and Chiapas with the large expediente written in 1734 that complains about the same problems in A.G.I. Guatemala 511. In 1741 it was said that "the principal reason for bishop's visitas" to pueblos was to charge three pesos each for the inspection of cofradías books. There were 5,000 cofradías in the jurisdiction of the Guatemalan archdiocese. A.G.I. Guatemala 919, Fr. Buena Ventura, 8/16/1741. For reports of abuses by clerics in 1686 see A.G.G. A1.11.2, Leg. 5775, Exp. 48,525, and by ladinos in 1713 A1.24, Exp. 1580, Exp. 10,224, fol. 241.

3. A.G.G. A1.20, Leg. 1485, fols. 48–50, 644. A.G.I. Guatemala 369, Fr. Francisco de Cordova, 8/25/1738, describes large Indian cofradía cattle holdings in Guatemala, and David Browning, *El Salvador*, p. 107, cites the complaints of the pueblo priest in Opico, Salvador, that most of the common lands were being used by cofradía cattle. The debate over whether cofradías should pay the alcabala sales tax is found in A.G.I. Guatemala 919, Informe del Contador, 10/13/1756, and A.G.G. Leg. 1954, Exp. 30,524, and Leg. 1956, Exp. 30,529.

The A.E.G. has whole series of volumes on cofradías from 1720 onward that show both very rich and very poor sodalities. The San Juan Amatitlán accounts are in A.E.G. Cofradías A4.14, Leg. 181, Doc. 2, and the Mita accounts in Docs. 10 and 25. The most complete and widespread examination of cofradía wealth was accomplished in 1769 and will be discussed later.

4. Barbara Bode, *The Dance of the Conquest of Guatemala* (New Orleans, La.: Tulane University Press, 1961), pp. 213–90; Nathan Wachtel, *La Vision des vaincus*, pp. 75–83; Francisco de Solano, *Los Mayas del siglo XVIII*, pp. 381–86.

5. At the end of the seventeenth century, a visitador claimed that in the major Chiapan towns he visited, the Indians paid together more than 12,500 pesos to their clerics annually (A.G.I. Guatemala 982). Reales cédulas issued in 1738 attempted to alleviate the abuses of too many contributions to community funds (Guatemala 215); also see Guatemala 159, Año de 1687: Testimonio de los Autos fechos Sobre las raciones que de los bienes de Comunidades . . . that mentions an auto of 1645 that also attempted to reform community funds.

6. Gage, *Travels*, pp. 294–95.

7. The Paya Indians situated in the partido of Olancho el Viejo (Honduras) provide a good example of those who lived just outside Spanish colonial civilization. Situated between settlers to their west and the hostile Sambos to their east, they were considered (as one official wrote) "as our guard against the enemy Sambos de Mosquito." Attempts by friars to "reduce" the Indians to pueblos repeatedly failed. In the early seventeenth century, friars reduced the Payas, but by 1680 "most had died in the mountains." In that year another reduction was attempted. Five pueblos were established by Franciscan missionaries with 700 to 800 people. After 1691 no friar was available, many Indians died from a measles epidemic, and the rest fled into the mountains. Four pueblos were again established in 1710 with 200 people, but by 1728 the Indians were "returning to the mountains," and by 1748 there were but four families remaining on the site. Sixty-five years later the Indians were said "to live by their own methods in the mountains, returned to the laziness that they are naturally inclined to without having an official that would make them obey the orders of this government to grow what is necessary for their own sustenance as well as for the sustenance of all." See A.G.I. Guatemala 164, El Obispo de Honduras, 2/27/1696; Guatemala 223, El Presidente, 8/20/1712, and Fray Raimundo

Barrutia, ?/1712; Guatemala 371, fr. Francisco Segura, ?/1751; Indiferente General 1525, Visita General de la Provincia de Honduras (1815).

For a similar history of the failure of reductions in the Talamanca mountains of Costa Rica, see A.G.I. Guatemala 240 Report of the Governor of Costa Rica, Diego de la Haya, 3/15/1719, and León Fernández, *Historia de Costa Rica durante la dominación española 1502–1821.*

See Jacques Soustelle, *The Four Suns* (New York; Grossman, 1971), for a description of dying, Indian cultural resistance to external influence among the Lacandon in the 1960s in his chapter, "The Depths of the Past," pp. 63–86.

8. Gage, *Travels*, pp. 250–53.

9. The prelates claimed that whenever two Indians were caught in infidelity they were tied to a tree and attacked with arrows and lances until they died. A.G.I. Guatemala 371, Relación de los Religiosos . . . de San Francisco.

10. "Jicaque" was the general denominator used by colonists for the diverse Indian tribes of the area. See Guatemala 180, Bishop of Guatemala, 12/13/1691.

11. A.G.I. Guatemala 164, Fr. Alonso, Bishop of Comayagua, 2/27/1696.

12. *Ibid.*

13. Fuentes y Guzmán, *Recordación* 1:200–01; Lutz, "Santiago de Guatemala."

14. A.G.I. Guatemala 179, Real Cédula of 8/27/1664; Guatemala 426: Testimonio de . . . lo que importa anualmente los sueldos, salarios, y demas pensiones . . . ; Gage, *Travels*, p. 189.

15. The same year Alonso Cuellar y Cristóbal de Salazar gave a gift of 36,000 pesos to establish the church of Santa Catarina. Scheifler, "Riqueza de los Religiosos en Santiago de los Caballeros de Guatemala" p. 10, For the reports on the Jesuit institutions see A.R.S.I. Mexico 17, "Collegio de Guatimala desde el Año del 1644; Puntos del anua," fols. 240–42, and Fondo Gesuitico 94, fols. 508–14; Schiefler, "Rafael Landivar y su Rusticatio Méxicana," *Estudios Centro Américanos*, p. 34; Pardo, *Efemérides*, p. 59.

16. Fuentes y Guzmán, *Recordación Florida*, 1:203; John Tate Lanning, *The University in the Kingdom of Guatemala*, pp. 32–86.

17. A.G.G. A1.20, leg. 1479, fols. 151–58.

18. Testament of Manuel Cracía Candoso, A.G.G. A1.20, Leg. 1050, fols. 323–27. There are many examples of the founding of capellanías in late seventeenth- and early eighteenth-century Guatemala to be found in the *Libros de Protocolos* in the A.G.G. See, for example, the testament of the Alférez Jacinto de Irrazavábal, who gave most of his landed wealth to the Mercedians in 1662. A.G.G. A1.20, Leg. 1030, fols. 153–54. The Regidor Alonso Albarez put a fifth of the estate of his late, first wife into capellanías for masses to be said in her behalf. *Ibid.*, fol. 315. When Lucia Frense Portes died, childless, after but one year of marriage, she gave her slaves to her husband (for the remainder of his life, after which they were to receive their freedom) and the rest of her 10,400 pesos estate to capellanías. A1.20, Leg. 1478, fols. 56–57. Every testament filed in 1721 by people of even modest wealth provided for capellanías. Al. 20, Leg. 1112. A wealthy woman, Doña Isavel María de Campos from San Vicente de Salvador, held more than 30,000 pesos of loans outstanding and gave the notes to capellanías upon her death in 1731. This seemed a wise course, since she mentions no heirs in the testament. Now the money would be collected by the church for her behalf. A1.20, Leg. 486, fols. 374–75. Poorer people sometimes ignored the church. See the testament of Francisco Joseph de Romero, who in 1731 left nothing but a store to his only heir, a twelve-year-old daughter, to be used for her "good education and state." *Ibid.*, fols. 40–42.

19. The descriptions of the origins and holdings of Guatemalan nunneries written in 1740 show that almost all their wealth came from the dowry of nuns. A.G.G. A1.18,

Leg. 211, Exps. 5,022–29. The *Libros de Protocolos* list many dowries for nuns. In 1733 Pedro de Lara gave dowries, one each for his sister and his sister-in-law, worth 4,500 pesos. The money was placed in "mortgage" (*censo*) upon a large house in Guatemala. The nunnery of [Purísima] Concepción was thus assured of an annual income for their support. A.G.G. Al.20, Leg. 486, fols. 510–18. See also an interesting dowry left in a will in 1735 that gave funds to a nunnery for a female slave, who was to be protected until she was forty and then given her freedom. Al.2, Leg. 487, fol. 369; Scheifler, "Riqueza," p. 5.

20. A.G.G. Al.20, Leg. 1481, fol. 407; Testament of Lic. Dn Pedro de Lara, Al.20, Leg. 486, fols. 510–12.

21. Fuentes y Guzmán, *Recordación Florida*, 1:303.

22. A.G.I. Guatemala 437, Año de 1740: Testimonio de las diligencias de Erección de Convento del Señor Sto. Domingo de Esta Ciudad . . . ; Guatemala 935, Bishop of Guatemala, 7/31/1769; A.G.G. Al.18, Leg. 211, Exp. 5028.

23. *Ibid.*

24. Jesuit property—two haciendas and a convent—was sold some thirty years later for 171,929 pesos. See A.G.I. Guatemala 748, Carta Cuenta of 1781; Scheifler, "Riqueza," p. 11.

25. A.G.G. Al.18, Leg. 211, Exps. 5022, 5027.

26. A.G.G. Al.118.2, Leg. 211, Exp. 5029.

27. A.G.I. Guatemala 363, Bishop of Guatemala, 6/24/1712.

28. The power and wealth of Creole cofradías are described in detail in the visita performed in the Archdiocese of Guatemala in 1769. The complete visita is in A.G.I. Guatemala 948 and will be examined in greater detail later. The *Libros de Protocolos*, discussed above, testify in wills to the membership in cofradías held by most colonists and by all wealthy creoles. Juarros, *Compendio* 1:196–97.

29. See A.G.I. Guatemala 282: Residencia of Dn Francisco Sarassa Y Arce, 6/24/1688; Guatemala 366, Bishop of Guatemala, 6/14/1704; A.G.G. Al.20, Leg. 1481, fols. 302–59; Leg. 1479, fols. 145–202; Sánchez-Bella, *La organización*, pp. 120, 228.

4. Colonial Society

1. Fuentes y Guzmán, *Recordación Florida*, p. 7.

2. The assertion by Bishop Fr. Juan de Zapata that all other Central American settlements had less than 150 vecinos is contradicted by Antonio Vázquez de Espinosa, *Compendium and Description of the West Indies*, pp. 573, 607, 655, 692, 702, 713, 740, 755, and MacLeod, *Spanish Central America*, p. 218. A.G.I. Guatemala 156, Bishop Fr. Juan de Zapata, 6/5/1623. The population figures for the vecinos of Guatemala are from Lutz, "Santiago de Guatemala," pp. 516–20.

3. Lutz's demographic study is revealing. Marriages of Spaniards rose from 1570 until 1670, leveled off for a decade, then generally declined for reasons that will later be suggested. The population of mestizos and mulattos rose continuously through the colonial period. "Santiago de Guatamala," pp. 13–16.

4. García Peláez, *Memorias*, 1:226. The "tribute" of alcabala dated from medieval times. In 1622 the Duke of Osuna gained an exemption based upon the traditional practice of paying a set sum. In 1637, 3,621 settlements in Castille paid tribute in alcabala (Antonio Domínguez Ortiz, *Política y hacienda de Felipe IV*, pp. 198–99).

5. García Peláez, *Memorias*, 1:226–29.

6. *Ibid.*
7. *Ibid.*, pp. 229–34.
8. Juarros, *Compendio*, 2:40–44; MacLeod, *Spanish Central America*, p. 219.
9. Severo Martínez Peláez, *La patria del criollo.*
10. The dowries are contained within notarial (Protocolos) records. This discussion is based upon records in A.G.G. A1.20, Leg. 1030–1112 and Leg. 1479–1485, for the period between 1660 and 1740.
11. Testament of Alonso Alfarez de Vega, A.G.G. A1.20, Leg. 1030, fols. 315–22. For a detailed description of the investment of a dowry in various enterprises, see the testament of Jacinto de Irrazábal, *ibid.*, fols. 153–54.
12. Testament of Josepha Inez de Asperilla A.G.G. A1.20, Leg. 486, fols. 202–07. Gálvez gave Asperilla some 400 pesos to settle the suit, more in charity than for legal restitution.
13. Testament of Juana de Osegueza, *ibid.*, fols. 208–09.
14. A.G.G. A1.20, Leg. 1479, fols. 32–33.
15. "This is how it is done in most provinces, in this [province] of Guatemala, as is well known [and] in Guadalajara where I lived for more than seventeen years." A.G.I. Guatemala 363, Bishop of Chiapas, 4/4/1717; Guatemala 179, Bartolomé Ruiz, 5/14/1673. In Mexico the establishment of the alhondiga failed to halt speculation. See Enrique Florescano, *Precios del maíz y crisis agrícolas en México (1708–1810).*
16. Lutz, "Santiago de Guatemala," pp. 462, 546–47, 569, 597, 588, 591. See also the Cabildo Eclesiástico of Guatemala, 3/15/1709: "many descendants of the first conquerors and settlers of these lands and others no less in number than the known families of Spain live under the need to flee to the pueblos and haciendas to maintain themselves moderately" A.G.I. Guatemala 279.
17. The Bishop of Guatemala asked permission to tithe Indian production in 1712, because the "fruits and grains that Spaniards farmed used to give 11,000 to 13,000 pesos and today gives only 300." A.G.I. Guatemala 363, Bishop of Guatemala, 6/12/1712. This "free market" still existed in 1735. See A.G.I. Guatemala 919, Fr. Pablo, 2/1/1735; Scheifler, "Riqueza," p. 10; Martínez Peláez, *La patria del criollo*, p. 221; and Fuentes y Guzmán, *Recordación Florida*, 1:208, 303.
18. Lutz, "Santiago de Guatemala," pp. 559–65. See the description of different types of labor that supported Guatemala in A.G.I. Guatemala 354, "Expediente de la Ciudad de Santiago sobre la cobranza de los tributos y otras rentas del Valle de dicha ciudad y sobre que se hagan tres corregimientos, año de 1751," that has within it documents that date from 1601 concerning the issue of Indian labor.
19. See Lutz, "Santiago de Guatemala."
20. *Ibid.*, pp. 425–426, citing A.G.I. Guatemala 74, El Sargento Mayor Felipe de Fuentes, 5/27/1680.
21. A.G.G. Guatemala A1.20, Leg. 112, fols. 352–55.
22. In 1735 John Cockburn told of his experiences after he was marooned in Honduras. His narrative is filled with descriptions of wild horses and cows. At night they "heard a great noise of horses running full speed which, we supposed, were as swiftly pursued by the wolves." Near Gracias a Dios "we came to a large Savannah or Plain, where we saw great numbers of wild cattle." Two days later they saw great numbers of wild cattle "which had occasioned so many paths." In Costa Rica he observed the manner in which milk was gotten from wild cows: "here as in other parts of this country; they go into the savannas and catch young calves which they bring home and enclose in a pen, raised high on purpose to preserve them from tigers and other beasts of prey, but leave one place open for the cows to get in, who will not fail to come in the night

to suckle them. In the morning they . . . tie a calf to the foreleg of each cow and whilst she is licking her young one, they milk her." Cockburn says the Indians killed the cattle only for their hides and tallow. *A Journey Over Land from the Gulf of Honduras to the Great South Sea*, pp. 27, 30, 33, 65, 68, 152–53, 157.

23. MacLeod, *Spanish Central America*, pp. 71, 217–19.

24. MacLeod (p. 427) cites documents from 1631, 1642, and 1695–1714 that discuss 200 obrajes. Rubio cites a 1658 document that lists 90 of the largest obraje owners *Historia del añil*, 1:50.

25. One very large hacienda, 67 large holdings, and 237 smaller farms were owned individually. Some 23 other farmers owned 12 of the large holdings and 46 of the smaller. A.G.I. Guatemala 224, Testimonio de los autos fhos sobre la recaudacion del donativo de las haciendas de San Salvador, San Miguel y Villa de Sn Vicente de Austria (1708).

26. Rubio *Historia del añil*, 2:45–107, details the fines from the early seventeenth century until the use of Indian labor was allowed in 1737. In 1671 the Bishop of Guatemala complained that the visitas of alcaldes mayores caused more damage to the Indians because the inspecting officials extorted funds from them.

27. A.G.I. Guatemala 159, Año de 1687: Testimonio de los Autos fechos sobre las raciones que de los bienes de comunidades. . . .

28. A.G.I. Guatemala 362, Bishop of Nicaragua, 4/13/1717; Guatemala 240, Dn Diego de la Haya, 3/15/1719.

29. A.G.G. Guatemala 362, Bishop of Nicaragua, 6/18/1704. The colonists' fear of the Mosquitos and Sambos was quite justified. Cockburn claimed to have observed a raid by Mosquitos in Chiriqui, Costa Rica: "They scalped the priest, tore off his skin, leaving the skull bare, then they fixed the skin on a spear and danced round it a considerable time; after which they reared up a long pole, one end of which they fastened to the ground, and on the other they stuck his body while he was yet alive, and then made their barbarous mirth of his exquisite tortures, scoffing at it" *A Journey Over Land*, pp. 236–41.

30. See, for example, A.G.I. Guatemala 162, Bishop of Nicaragua Juan de Rosas, 1/34/1684.

31. A.G.I. Guatemala 279, Cabildo Eclesiástico, 4/16/1688, The Cabildo of Guatemala (undated, ca. 1669) and Martin de Mencos, 4/14/1669. See the series of correspondances from various sectors of the Guatemalan and Central American community from 1665 until 1715 in Guatemala 279.

32. The amount of trade is impossible to measure. The goods of two merchants from Granada in April 1661 that were confiscated in Portobelo were worth some 13,000 pesos, not a great amount. The numbers of people involved in the trade in Guatemala as well as the other colonies is also unknown. A.G.I. Guatemala 133, Pedro Frasco, visitador, 11/25/1663.

33. A.G.I. Guatemala 164, Procedimientos de Dn Lorenzo Ramírez de Guzmán que fue Governador de Honduras de Interim, 1/20/1684.

34. A.G.I. Guatemala 162, Bishop of Nicaragua, 7/20/1647 and 4/18/1679; Guatemala 279, Cabildo Eclesiástico, 5/29/1709.

35. The Guatemalan merchants controlled taxation until 1667, with levies on indigo never collected "because the most interested (in the trade) are the richest and most powerful citizens (of Guatemala)." After the government assumed responsibility for tax collection in that year Salvadoran producers and Guatemalan merchants sold the dye to church officials, who, enjoying tax-free status, could export it to Mexico or even Spain without fear of levies and consequently could offer higher prices for the commodity at the point of origin. Other subterfuges were also used, the bribery of officials being

the most prevalent. A.G.I. Guatemala 387, Real Cédula, 1/12/1667; A.G.G. A1.20, Leg. 1481, fols. 149, 288, 302–59.

36. A.G.I. Guatemala 279, President of Guatemala, 4/24/1688; Guatemala 47, Oficiales Reales, 7/3/1665; Guatemala 387, Reales Cédulas of 1659 and 1663, fols. 4–5, 213.

37. At Campeche the Council of the Indies recognized the right of the Spanish colonists to cut and trade the dye with the English "considering that God has not bestowed the Province of Campeche with gold, silver nor other goods, he left that province free from sustenance so that hardwood brings the only sustenance . . . by trading with the (Caribbean) islands." A.G.I. Mexico 1007, Council of the Indies, 4/29/1667.

38. *Ibid.* See also Troy Floyd, *The Anglo-Spanish Struggle for Mosquitia*, pp. 55–61.

39. For the growth and importance of the logwood and indigo trade in Europe, see Arthur M. Wilson, "The Logwood Trade in the Seventeenth and Eighteenth Centuries," pp. 1–15; Susan Fairlie, "Dyestuffs in the Eighteenth Century," pp. 488–510, Jean O. McLachlan, *Trade and Peace with Old Spain, 1667–1750*, pp. 93, 178; Ralph Davis, "English Foreign Trade 1660–1700," pp. 160–64; A. H. John, "Aspects of English Economic Growth in the First Half of the Eighteenth Century," in W. E. Minchinton, ed., *The Growth of English Overseas Trade in the Seventeenth and Eighteenth Centuries*, p. 169. For the aspect of this trade in Central America, see Léon Fernández, *Historia de Costa Rica durante la dominación española 1502–1821*, p. 286; García Peláez, *Memorias* 2:298–99; Vera Lee Brown, "Contraband Trade: A Factor in the Decline of Spain's Empire in America," p. 183; Floyd, "The Guatemalan Merchants, the Government, and the Provincianos, 1750–1800," p. 91. The history of this region is best covered by Floyd in *The Anglo-Spanish Struggle for Mosquitia*.

5. Crisis and Continuity, 1680–1730

1. It was said that the city had "a growing number of Indians." A.G.I. Guatemala 354, Petition from Sargento Antonio Pineda (1683); Lutz, "Santiago de Guatemala," p. 16; Pardo, *Efemérides*, p. 99; Fuentes y Guzmán, *Recordación Florida*, 1:215.

2. See MacLeod's excellent lists of pandemics and localized epidemics that afflicted Central America from the conquest until 1750. *Spanish Central America*, pp. 98–100. See also Pardo, *Efemérides*, pp. 103–86; Fuentes y Guzmán, *Recordación Florida*, 1:209; Lutz, "Santiago de Guatemala," pp. 263, 519, 561, 747–51; Solano, *Los Mayas*, p. 262; A.G.I. Guatemala 279, President of Guatemala, 4/24/1688; Guatemala 214, Relación de los Méritos y Servicios de Dn Manuel de Farinas; Guatemala 219 Oidor Pedro de Ozaeta, 10/12/1706; Guatemala 221, President of Guatemala, 3/8/1709; Contaduría 981, President of Guatemala, 1/13/1731 and 2/15/1731; Guatemala 230, Año de 1735: Testimonio de los Autos de Reglamentos de las Reales Cajas del Provincia de Nicaragua.

3. A.G.I. Guatemala 354, Expediente . . . sobre la cobranza de los tributos, fols. 223–46; Lutz, "Santiago de Guatemala," pp. 13–21.

4. See, in particular, A.G.I. Guatemala 159, "Año de 1687: Testimonio de los Autos fhos sobre la perdición general de los indios;" and "Testimonio de los Autos Fechos sobre las raciones que de los bienes de comunidades . . . ;" fol. 74; Guatemala 164, Bishop Alonsso de Várgas of Honduras, 2/27/1696. A.G.I. Guatemala 217 has a number of petitions from Indian towns asking for remission of tribute between 1700 and 1710.

5. Fuentes y Guzmán, *Recordación Florida*, 1:352, and Solano, *Los Mayas*, ch. 3 and p. 122.

6. A.G.I. Audiencia of Guatemala, 7/18/1736; Guatemala 230, Año de 1735, Testimonio de los Autos de Reglamentos de las Reales Cajas del Provincia de Nicaragua, fol. 2;

7. Fuentes y Guzmán, *Recordación Florida*, 1:139–40.

8. A.G.I. Guatemala 354, Expediente . . . sobre la cobranza de los tributos, fols. 152–74.

9. For a history of the administration of Santiago de Guatemala and the "Valley of Guatemala," see A.G.I. Guatemala 354, Expediente de la Ciudad de Santiago sobre la cobranza de los tributos y otras rentas del Valle de dicha Ciudad y sobre que se hagan tres corregimientos, año de 1751, that provides a resumé of many of the documents of the previous 175 years.

10. The distinction is interesting from a legal viewpoint: the alcaldía mayor had Spanish secular and ecclesiastical haciendas, whereas Escuintla was mostly—but not exclusively—Indian. The alcaldías mayores were Petapa and Amatitlán and the corregidor, Escuintla.

11. Garcia Peláez, *Memorias*, 2:24–27.

12. The Bishop of Honduras related the early history of the mine and named its discoverer in a letter to the crown, 4/17/1696, A.G.I. Guatemala 363. The oidor, Joseph Descals sent many complaints to the crown concerning the La Corpus mine dispute, of which his letter of 5/16/1696 in A.G.I. Guatemala 215 is most representative. For later reports on the mine, see Guatemala 216, the Royal Cédula of 1/24/1698; Guatemala 246, Año de 1707: Autos de Taladero; Guatemala 220, Dn Joseph Osorio Espinosa, 1/30/1707, who, as oidor of the audiencia of Mexico traveled to Guatemala to report on the mine situation; and A.G.I. Guatemala 218, Joseph Eustachio de León, 1/27/1743, who reported the history of the mine. La Corpus is discussed frequently in much of the correspondence between royal officials and the Council from 1695 until 1720.

13. A.G.I. Guatemala 215, letters from Joseph Descals, 5/19/1696, 6/13/1697, and 5/16/1696.

14. The Guatemalans used a force of 80 Spaniards and 200 Indians, These invasions were required to reach their goal; two Dominicans were killed in the attack. See A.G.I. Patronato 237, especially Ramos 1 and 15; Guatemala 180, Bishop of Guatemala, 12/13/1691; Contaduría 981, President of Guatemala, 3/27/1727. An earlier entry (entrada) in 1670 yielded 3,000 souls, A.G.I. Guatemala 179, Fr. Joseph Ramirez, 11/29/1680. See also A.G.I. Patronato 237, Ramo 14; Guatemala 237, Año de 1755: Testimonio . . . sobre la reducción de los Indios que han desamparado los pueblos del Petén.

15. The visita is in A.G.I. Guatemala 215; García Peláez, *Memorias*, 2:271–72.

16. García Peláez, *Memorias* 2:271–72.

17. Fray Francisco Ximénez, *Historia de la provincia de San Vicente de Chiapa y Guatemala de la orden de predicadores*, 3:398–400; Cayetano Alcázar Molina, *Los virreinatos en el siglo XVIII*, pp. 199–200.

18. García Peláez, *Memorias*, 2:278; Hubert H. Bancroft, *Works*, 7:659–62; J. Antonio Villacorta C., *Historia de la Capitanía General de Guatemala*, p. 84; A.G.G. A1.11.40, Leg. 5885, Exp. 49,856, Leg. 5887 Exp. 49,904; Pardo, *Efemérides*, pp. 124–33.

19. Lascals reported that Sebastian de Alva was the silversmith to whom the president brought his silver and gold. A.G.I. Guatemala 215, 7/9/1696. After the bishop of Guatemala died in 1702 some 271 marks of untaxed worked silver (*plata labrada*) was found among his effects. A.G.I. Guatemala 216, President of Audiencia, 6/30/1702. In 1733 it was noted that no mines in Tegucigalpa or La Corpus had ever sent fiscal revenue to the Guatemalan audiencias, "even when their production was opulent." A.G.I. Contaduría 981, note accompanying remissions, 7/7/33. In 1749 the President of Guatemala

said that the silversmiths of Guatemala were the best in the Indies and had much silver to work. A.G.I. Guatemala 236, 12/22/1749. Also see Guatemala 243, Joseph Eustacio de León, administrator of the mint, 1/27/1743; Guatemala 795, President of Guatemala, 10/10/1748; García Peláez, *Memorias*, 2:298–99; *Breve appunti del Guatemala*, MS. Gesuiti 1255/4 (3384), in the Biblioteca Nazionale (Rome); Informe de Don Geronymo de la Vega y Lacayo, 1/19/1759, in the Bibliothèque Nationale (Paris).

20. A.G.I. Guatemala 164, Fr. Alonso of Honduras, 7/20/1690. For the decline of cabildos see A.G.I. Guatemala 286, the Cabildo of Guatemala, 1/29/1698; Juarros, *Compendio*, 2:36, 44, 108; García Peláez, *Memorias*, 2:8–19.

21. A.G.I. Guatemala 724, Año de 1748, Razón de los sueldos . . .

22. A.G.I. Guatemala 48, Reales Cédulas of 1671 and 1687; Guatemala 167, Testimonio de los Autos fhos sobre la vacante de las encomiendas . . . A.G.I. Guatemala 239 has the cédulas that suspended encomiendas in 1720, others in 1739, and the remainder (or so it was said) in 1748. After 1720 some encomiendas continued to be charged because of old debts from towns to encomenderos that had yet to be paid (because of population loss?) A.G.G. A1.23, Leg. 4636, fols. 9–14. In 1778 the Duke of Medina Celi was still owed 14,787 pesos from the 585 pesos annually that had not been paid between 1692 and 1721, plus some interest. A.G.I. Indiferente General, Council of the Indies, 1/21/1778.

23. The pattern of mestization will be discussed later. A.G.I. Guatemala 368, Año de 1724, Testimonio de los autos hechos sobre el descubrimiento de los Indios que se hallabase extraidos . . . ; A.G.I. Guatemala 240, Real Orden (1718).

24. The Chiapas revolt caused a loss of 70,000 pesos between 1712 and 1721. See A.G.I. Contaduría 981, note accompanying remission of 1712–21; A.G.I. Guatemala 216, Informe del Contador, 5/31/1702. A.G.I. Contaduría 981, the report of the *Contador*, 1722; Guatemala 228, Año de 1723: Autos fechos en razón de la paga que pretende cargo de Bocanegra. For defense expenditures see, in particular, Guatemala 639, "Lo Que Necesita los Castillos" (1709).

25. A.G.I. Contaduría 981, Contador del Real Hacienda, 1/15/1711.

26. A.G.I. Contaduría 977, "Extracto de las noticias . . . sobre la mala administración de su Real Hacienda . . . ; Guatemala 228, Dn Andres del Corobaeutia, 6/30/1772.

27. A.G.I. Guatemala 243, Fiscal, 5/17/1754, and answer of the Council of the Indies, 8/30/1754; A.G.G. A1.2, Exp. 16,190, Leg. 2245, fol. 182; "Auto acordado de la Audiencia de Guatemala sobre la cuota de tributos, mayo de 1585;" Martínez Paláez, *La patria del criollo*, p. 233; Fuentes y Guzmán, *Recordación Florida*, 2:79, says that both sexes pay tribute in his encomiendas.

28. A.G.I. Guatemala 342, Real Cédula, 6/16/1728; Guatemala 682, Contador de Alcabala, 3/16/1725; A.G.G. A3.5, Leg. 2407, Exp. 35432.

29. A.G.I. Guatemala 286, the Cabildo of Guatemala, 1/29/1698; Guatemala 279, Bishop Fr. Mauro of Guatemala, 6/1/1709; García Peláez, *Memorias*, 2:19–20.

30. The pattern of migration is clear. Lutz sees it from 1690 until 1730. I would agree. Neither Fuentes y Guzmán, the corregidor of Totonicapán, nor Francisco Vázquez perceived large numbers of Spanish or castes in Totonicapán at the end of the seventeenth century. In 1707, however, the Bishop reported "many Spanish vecinos living in this valley." By 1769 Archbishop Pedro Cortés y Larraz calculated that from a third to a half of the population of Guatemala lived outside of Spanish towns and cities. See Lutz, "Santiago de Guatemala," p. 523; Pedro Cortés y Larraz, *Descripción geográfico-moral de la diócesis de Goathemala*, 2:200. For further discussion see Jorge Luján Muñoz "Reducción y fundación de Salcaja y San Carlos Sijo (Guatemala) in 1776," *Anales de la Sociedad de Geografía e Historia de Guatemala* (1976), no. 44.

31. Petitions in 1813 and 1815 asked the crown for permission to reduce the Lacandones and "all the Indians that live dispersed in the mountains." The Council denied the request, perhaps because of the revolutionary situation across the border in southern New Spain A.G.I. Guatemala 423, Mariano Robles, 7/26/1813, and Fernando Antonio Dávila, 11/29/1815. For the revolt, see A.G.I. Guatemala 293–96, and Herbert S. Klein, "Peasant Communities in Revolt: The Tzeltal Republic of 1712," pp. 247–63; A.G.I. Contaduría 981, President of Guatemala, 3/27/1727.

32. Juarros, *Compendio*, 1:269, 314; Pardo, *Efemérides*, p. 145; Bancroft, *Works*, 2:656–57; Scheifler, "Riqueza."

33. Pardo, *Efemérides*, pp. 145–49; Lanning, *The Eighteenth-Century Enlightenment in the University of San Carlos*, p. 271.

34. A.G.I. Guatemala 240, Don Juan Chiafino, Alcalde Mayor of Verapaz, 2/22/1728; Juarros, *Compendio*, 1:269.

6. The Transformation of the Colony

1. The new 10 percent quinto tax yielded 16,000 pesos in 1726, suggesting an annual production of 160,000 pesos. See A.G.I. Contaduría 976, Cuenta of 1725; Pardo, *Efemérides*, p. 158.

2. The low price of *azogue* (mercury) was renewed in 1740 and continued until at least 1750. Indians who discovered new veins were given exemption from labor in the mines and tribute payment for themselves and their heirs. A.G.I. Guatemala 232, President of Guatemala, 1/6/1742.

3. A.G.I. Guatemala 246, Año de 1749, Testimonio . . . de el Director de la Casa de Moneda; Guatemala 234, Año de 1745, Testimonio de varios instrumentos que comprueban las barras de plata . . . .

4. A.G.I. Guatemala 795, President of Guatemala, 10/10/1748; Guatemala 236, President of Guatemala, 12/22/1749; Royal Cédula of 12/21/1748.

5. A.G.I. Guatemala 242, Merits and Services of Joseph Gonzalez Rancaño.

6. See A.G.I. Guatemala 370, Año de 1749: Testimonio de los Autos hechos por Dn Manuel Antonio de Guzmán, Justicia Mayor de la Provincia de Chiquimula, fols. 5–17; Guatemala 371, Consejo de Indias, 7/13/1751.

7. A.G.I. Guatemala 371, Consejo de Indias, 7/13/1751

8. Ronald Dennis Hussey, *The Caracas Company 1724–1784* (Cambridge, Mass: Harvard University Press, 1934).

9. In 1749 Ramón de Lupategui went to Realejo to build two boats for the company. He found the port depopulated, with only a Franciscan monk and a few Indians living there. He gathered laborers for the construction and found that he needed to import food from León, twelve leagues away. He was able to build only one vessel before exhausting his financial resources. See A.G.I. Guatemala 240, Salvador Dávila, 5/21/1758; A.G.I. Guatemala 232, Año de 1744: Testimonio de los Autos Sobre la erección de la Compañía que se quiere establecer en esta Ciudad para el Beneficio de Minas y Saca de frutos del Reino; *Breve Muestra de la Muchas Utilidades que puede producir . . . una compañía que se podrá establecer . . . .* Pardo, *Efemérides*, p. 166, observes that the Guatemalan cabildo "was constantly preoccupied with free commerce with Peru." However, the desire for trade was not now linked to the need to export indigo, although a need still existed. Rather, the preoccupation was concerned with a regular supply of Huancavelica mercury.

10. A.G.I. Guatemala 342, Pedro Herrarte, 5/10/1746; Guatemala 525, President, 3/30/1752. Mosquito raids intermittently interrupted the trade between Granada and the Caribbean after 1724 (informe de Don Geronymo de la Vega y Lacayo, 1/19/1759, in the Bibliothèque Nationale). In 1722 a 708-head mule train from Costa Rica to Panama carried 22,698 pounds of indigo. Four years later 1,115 mules carried over 6,000 pounds of indigo and 10,875 pounds of sarsaparilla. Other good years for the trade were 1750 (28,631 pounds of indigo), 1753 (7,000 pounds of sarsaparilla), and 1757 (10,894 pounds of indigo. See Robert Dilg, "The Collapse of the Porto Belo Fair," Ph.D. dissertation, Indiana University, 1970; and Juan Carlos Solórzano, "El comercio exterior de Costa Rica en la época colonial," Ph.D. dissertation, Universidad de Costa Rica, 1977.

11. From the sales contracts of slaves in the *Libros de Protocolos* in A.G.G. A1.20, I have deduced that most male and female slaves between the ages of sixteen and fifty cost from 300 to 500 pesos between 1663 and 1681 and from 150 to 300 pesos from 1722 until 1756. There were a few exceptions and some slaves were bartered for other commodities, but these prices tended to be the general rule. A.G.I. Guatemala 221, Año de 1709, mentions thirty-two slaves sold from a French boat in the Gulf of Honduras. The new influx lasted until the second half of the eighteenth century, when a rise of native and caste populations made slavery uneconomical. Manumitted slaves performed the work they or their forebears once did in slavery for wages, falling in many cases into debt peonage. The use of slaves became limited to wealthy merchants for domestic purposes or to the government, which used slaves to man and populate frontier regions along the Mosquito Coast that Spaniards and other freemen would not. In 1785, there were 389 slaves at the Omoa fortress. A.G.G. A3.5, Leg. 692, Exp. 12992.

12. The growth of Tegucigalpa as a center for contraband activities in the first third of the eighteenth century—previously it was farther south in Gracias a Dios and Segovia—reflects the expansion of mineral production during this period. A.G.I. Guatemala 872B, Año de 1745: Testimonio del informe hecho . . . por Dn Luis Díez Navarro, 4/14/1745; and "Descripción de toda la costa del mar del Norte y parte de la del Sur, de la Capitanía General de este reyno de Guatemala que hizo el Ingeniero Ordinario, Dn Luis Díez Navarro . . . en este Año de 1743. A.G.I. Guatemala 254, Año de 1744, Testimonio de las Diligencias . . . ; Vera Lee Brown, "Contraband Trade: A Factor in the Decline of Spain's Empire in America," *H.A.H.R.*, 8:185; Floyd, *The Anglo-Spanish Struggle for Mosquitia*, pp. 113–14; MacLeod, *Spanish Central America*, p. 373.

13. See A.G.I. Guatemala 214, Joseph Estacio de León, ?/1746. The Council of the Indies claimed that Central America did one million pesos annually in trade (*ibid.*, 4/4/1750).

14. In 1723, Indian indigo was preferred by Parisian druggists to that of Guatemala but after that date the Indian commodity appeared rarely on European markets until 1800. Louisiana and Caracas joined in indigo production in 1785, at the height of its demand. See Savary des Bruslons, *Dictionnaire universel* (Paris, 1723), 2:411; Jean Cavignac, *Jean Pellet, Commerçant de Gros 1694–1772*; Dauril Alden, "The Growth and Decline of Indigo Production in Colonial Brazil," pp. 35–60; Lewis Cecil Gray, *History of Agriculture in the Southern United States to 1860*, 1:73–74, 81, 83, 290–95, 610–11, 740, 1024.

15. "Indigo is sold for a much lower price to Peru than to Europe because neither *flor* indigo nor *sobresaliente* is sent there [to Peru]." A.G.I. Guatemala 235, Testimonio de los autos formados sobre que en el puerto de San Fernando de Omoa . . . se cobre el Impuesto de 4 pesos por cada Zurron de Añil . . . .

16. See A.G.I. Guatemala 540 for petitions to build and run a vessel between Guatemala and Cádiz in 12/5/1758 and 1763.

17. A.G.I. Guatemala 923, Extracto autorisado en competente forma de las justi-ficaciones de calidad y descendencia de los Vidaurres, Minas y Carriones . . . .

18. For the presence of Simon Larrazábal see A.G.I. Guatemala 342, Cabildo of Guatemala, 9/30/1739, and Contaduría 976, Cuenta of 1725; For Gaspar Juarros, Con-tratación 2605; Joseph or José Piñol, Contratación 1595; also see Floyd, "The Guatemalan Merchants, the Government, and the Provincianos, 1750–1800," pp. 90–110, and "The Indigo Merchant," p. 468.

19. On the eve of his death, José Piñol had close commercial dealings with Ayci-nena. See A.G.I. Guatemala 745, in which Piñol pays 15,760 pesos for 217 slaves to the account of his wife's future husband.

20. An incomplete list of Central American exports from 1778 to 1785 shows that Aycinena controlled 27 percent of the commerce. The *marquesado* title cost 6,000 *du-cados* annually and was supported by the rent from two houses in Guatemala and the produce of an indigo hacienda in Salvador.

The descendants of the first marquis had immense power and wealth. His son José Alejandro Manuel Ignacio de Aycinena was regidor, sindico and alcalde ordinario of the *ayuntamiento* in Guatemala City, as well as being Director of the Economic Society, Intendant of Salvador, a member of the Consejo de Indias in Spain, and an *alguacil mayor* of Mexico City. When Guatemala sent money to its representatives in the Spanish Cortes in 1814 it was sent via the House of Aycinena. From 1805 until independence the commercial house had some 180,000 pesos deposited in the Lima colonial treasury.

When freedom from Spain was declared and the independent federal government formed, the Aycinenas pleaded poverty. Nevertheless, we have the testimony of a con-temporary American visitor in 1825 to counter these claims: "I was invited into the house of the Marquis of Aycinena . . . [seeing some pearls], I thought of course [they] could not be so from their extraordinary size. I found, however, that I was mistaken. I had hardly supposed it possible that such enormous pearls existed and wishing to ascertain their value, I guessed them at 10,000 pounds. The Marquis, I understood, had given more for them: the necklace consisted of twenty-one pearls, the centre one being in the shape of, and as large as, a pigeon's egg, and the others large in proportion, but round and decreasing in size, gradually, towards each end." Thompson, *Narrative of an Official Visit to Guatemala*, p. 191.

The existing literature on the Aycinena family is biased and thus unreliable. The late-nineteenth-century liberal historian, Ramón Salazar, wrote an anti-Aycinena dia-tribe, *Mariano de Aycinena*, to which Edwin Enrique del Cid Fernández responded in an equally defective, pro-Aycinena work, *Origen histórico de la Casa y Marquesado de Aycinena*. Also see Floyd, "The Guatemalan Merchants," pp. 97–98, and "The Indigo Merchant," pp. 90–110; Rafael Heliodoro Valle, comp. *La anexión de Centro América a México* (hereafter cited as *La Anexión*), letters from Mariano Aycinena, 3:235, 4:131–33.

21. The presence of the *Cinco Gremios* in the indigo trade is seen in the registries in A.G.I. Contratación 1595, 2498, 2598, 2599, 2605, 2607, 2612, and Guatemala 880; Rubio, *Historia del añil*, I, 249–252, 267; Richard Herr, *The Eighteenth-Century Enlightenment in Spain* pp. 121, 148, 150.

22. The number of vecinos in Salvador in 1740 was 58, in San Vicente, 46, and San Miguel, 60. Rubio *Comercio terrestre*, p. 344.

23. For the different sides to the disputes and an account of the major actors in the incident see A.G.I. Guatemala 238, Año de 1757: Testimonio Relativo de los Autos Formados por Dn Luis Díez Navarro, en la Ciudad de San Salvador . . . sobre varios disturbios acaecidos en ella, por oposicion de los Criollos contra algunos Europeos

24. See A.G.I. Guatemala 242, Año de 1758: Testimonio de las Diligencias practicadas sobre el nombramiento echo de Thenientes de la Provincia de Sn Salvador, San Miguel y Villa de Sn Vicente de Austria; Guatemala 246, Joseph de Pinedo, 7/22/1752.

25. The denounced official was persecuted for ten years and was unable to obtain work or salary until 1768. A.G.I. Guatemala 595, Bernabe de la Torre, Alcalde Mayor de San Salvador, 4/21/1768.

26. Valentin Solórzano, F., *Evolución económica de Guatemala*; Floyd, "The Guatemalan Merchants," p. 106; A.G.G. A3.1, Leg. 139, Exp. 1545, fol. 27; Leg. 2724, Exp. 39040; A3.3, Leg. 2368, Exp. 34985; A3.5, Leg. 997, Exp. 18342; Leg. 875, Exp. 16038.

27. For the effect of the 1769–1773 plague, see A.G.I. Guatemala 423, Manuel Fedruque de Goyena, Alcalde Mayor de San Salvador, 6/28/79.

28. Aycinena took from Juan de Taranco the haciendas Cerro de Avila, La Concepción, and San Juan de Vista in San Vicente, and from Manuel Bolanos, the haciendas Archichiquitos and Los Naranjos, also in San Vicente. See A.G.I. Guatemala 573, Año de 1785: Testimonio de los Autos, sobre si devera pagar Alcavala de las Haciendas nombradas la Concepción y Sn Juan de Vista que Dn Juan de Taranco ha cedido al Sr. Marquesa de Aycinena, fols. 1–6, 53–57.

7. The Bourbon Reforms in Central America

1. Campillo y Cosío, *Nuevo sistema de govierno económico para la América*. See also Josefina Cintrón Tiryakian, "Campillo's Pragmatic New System," pp. 233–57; for the evolution of Campillo's reforms in Mexico, see David A. Brading, *Miners and Merchants in Bourbon Mexico 1763–1810*.

2. In the eighteen disparate years for which records exist between 1603 and 1635, the annual remissions to Spain averaged 88,826 pesos. A.G.I. Contaduría 981, Domingo de Zurrain Irigoyen, Contador and Oidor, 5/2/1678; see also supplemental figures in Contaduría 983B.

3. Herr, *Eighteenth Century Enlightenment in Spain*, p. 13; Scheifler, "Riqueza," p. 6.

4. Herr, *Eighteenth-Century Enlightenment in Spain*, pp. 18–31; Pedro Rodríguez de Campomanes, *Tratado de la regalía de amortización* (Madrid, 1765).

5. See the Real Cédula of ? 1717 and accompanying correspondence with the Governor of Nicaragua, 3/25/1718, in A.G.I. Guatemala 240.

6. See the Real Cédula of ? 1738, A.G.I. Contaduría 981; letter from Fr. Buena Ventura, 8/16/1741, Guatemala 919; and Guatemala 511 for discussions about abuses of sodalities. The fight against church power continued until the end of the century. Guatemala 920, Año de 1770, Testimonio al exhorto echo por el Governador de la Provincia . . . sobre cofradías y sus visitas.

7. A.G.I. Guatemala 941, Expediente de Fr. Lorenzo del Río, 3/30/1772.

8. A.G.I. Guatemala 972, Pantaleon Ibañez Cuevas, 10/8/1753.

9. Pardo, *Efemérides*, p. 173; Scheifler, "Riqueza," pp. 6–7.

10. A.G.I. Guatemala 531, Informe No. 5 (by Fernando Antonio Dávila, 1814).

11. Real Cédula of 2/1/1753, A.G.I. Indiferente General 2952.

12. A.G.I. Guatemala 935, Declaración del Fiscal, 4/29/1776; Guatemala 495, Año de 1813: Testimonio . . . sobre se exceptua de secularization los quatro curatos del Partido del Kiché. . . . See the review of clerics in Central America about 1760 in *Brevi notizie sull' ambiente . . . della provincia di Chiapa* and *Brevi appunti del Guatemala*

MS. Gesuitico 1255/3 & 4 (3384) Biblioteca Nazionale (Rome). Herr, in *Eighteenth Century Enlightenment in Spain*, reports that between 1762 and 1792 "over a dozen regulations" affected the orders in Spain p. 33.

13. A.G.I. Guatemala 926, Testimonio Instruido a Consulta del Señor Francisco Robleado, Oidor . . . (1805). The oidor reported that friars were recruited from Mexico since 1781.

14. R. Herr, *Eighteenth Century Enlightenment in Spain*, pp. 13–21.

15. Nine of the twenty Jesuits in Guatemala were from New Spain. Of the two Guatemalans expelled, one was the first noted Guatemalan poet, Rafael Landívar. Rafael de Zelis, *Catálogo de los sugetos de La Compañía de Jesus Que Formaban La Provincia de México El Día de Arresto, 25 de Junio de 1767* pp. 121, 129; Lanning, *The University in the Kingdom of Guatemala*, pp. 95–96. The state gained 171,929 pesos from the sale of the Jesuits' property in Central America. The order held two haciendas, one each in Guatemala and Salvador, as well as a convent in Chiapas. A.G.I. Guatemala 748, Carta Cuenta of 1781; Guatemala 542, Bishop of Ciudad Real, 7/2/1764.

16. The crown ordered informes on cofradías in virtually every decade after 1740: *1740*: A.G.G. A1.24.41, Leg. 4651, Exps. 39,728, 39,729, 39,731, 39,736; *1768*: A1.11, Leg. 99, Exp. 2122, 2123, and Cortés y Larraz, *Descripción geográfico-moral*; (1776) A1.1, Leg. 101, Exp. 2159, Leg. 104, Exps. 4752–58; *1787* A1.23, Leg. 1532, fol. 263 and *Prontuario de las Leyes Patrias*, 57; *1788*: A1.11.2, Leg. 5777, Exp. 48554; *1802 and 1803* A1.11, Legs. 6101–09. For general trends see A.G.G. A3.5, Leg. 2407, Exps. 35432 and 35440; Solórzano F., *Evolución económica*, p. 160. Also see chapters 9 and 10.

17. See A.G.I. Guatemala 928: Año de 1806, Testimonio de las Diligencias . . . de los conventos Dominicanos. . . . Most of the church holdings in 1740 were still held in 1829 when the liberal government seized them. Mary Holleran, *Church and State in Guatemala*, p. 54.

18. Requests for more friars came from every Guatemalan archbishop after 1790; see their letters in A.G.I. Guatemala 926, 962, and 963.

19. The institutions were alike in both southern Mexico and Central America. See Brian Hamnett, *Politics and Trade in Southern Mexico 1790–1821* pp. 2–7; and MacLeod, *Spanish Central America*, pp. 313–18. Creoles in Central America were unable, however, to gain direct control over the audiencia. In marked contrast with every major audiencia in Spanish America, no native Central American was ever an oidor in Guatemala from 1687 until 1806. During this same period only three Guatemalan Creoles served as oidores elsewhere in the empire. Of all oidores who served in Guatemala, almost one third (32 percent) were Creoles from other American colonies. During the "liberal" colonial epoch after 1807, three Guatemalans were oidores in Guatemala. Mark A. Burkholder and D. S. Chandler, *From Impotence to Authority: The Spanish Crown and the American Audiencias 1687–1808*.

20. A.G.I. Guatemala 354, Expediente . . . sobre la cobranza de los tributos, fols. 223–46.

21. *Ibid.*, fols. 366–76.

22. Pardo, *Efemérides*, pp. 209–12.

23. Prior to 1763 the Mexican Contador de Cuentas had authority over Central America, but had never performed any inspections over the Guatemalan territory.

24. See the extraction of notes made by the Contador of Cuentas Dn Manuel Herrarte (1763), A.G.I. Guatemala 679; Guatemala 541, Agustín de Guiraola, Escribanía de Camara, 8/15/1763.

25. A.G.I. Guatemala 679, Manuel Herrarte (1763).

26. *Ibid.* In April 1763 an inspection revealed an outstanding debt of 152,855 pesos

to the treasury which could not be collected. Guatemala 679, Informe of Agustín de Guiraola.

27. A.G.I. Guatemala 541, Agustín de Guiraola, 1/28/1764; Guatemala 595, Testimonio . . . sobre que el Administración General de Alcabalas cobre el tres por ciento . . . .

28. The measures instituted by Guiraola and Valdés were governed by ordenanzas based upon the Instrucción de Alcabalas de México that the visitador Gálvez attempted to institute in New Spain. See A.G.I. Guatemala 542, Año de 1763: Testimonio de la Real Instrucción . . . cerca de la Nueva Administración de Alcavalas y Barlovento, fols. 97–141; A.G.G. Leg. 2407, Exps. 35435 and 35440; Solórzano F., *Evolución económica*, pp. 216–17. A.G.I. Guatemala 595, Dn. Francisco Valdés, 3/31/1766.

29. The constant plea that a practice held since "time immemorial" could not be changed dates back to Hapsburg legal philosophy. But now the Bourbons ignored that reason as a legal defense. See A.G.I. Guatemala 542, Año de 1764: Testimonio del recurso hecho por la Ciudad y Diputación del Comercio de Goathemala . . . ; Guatemala 595, Testimonio de la Instancia seguida por el Procurador Sindico Gral del Noble Ayuntamiento de la Ciudad de Goathemala . . . sobre que el Administración Gral de Alcavalas cobre el tres por ciento. . . .

30. A.G.I. Guatemala 595, the Council of the Indies, 4/6/1765; Guatemala 541, Agustín de Guiraola, 1/28/1764. The entrada and salida taxes were also returned to prior levels.

31. A.G.I. Guatemala 679, Informe de Agustín de Guiraola, 5/21/1768; Guatemala 541, Agustín de Guiraola, 5/10/1765.

32. A.G.G. A3.5, Leg. 2407, Exp. 35440, Leg. 2203, Exp. 32863; Héctor Humberto Samayoa Guevara, *La Intendencia en el Reyno de Guatemala*, pp. 53–54.

33. The reform of the gunpowder and playing-card monopoly, previously under Mexican control, was not opposed, since the establishment of local authority meant retaining receipts in Central America. See Pardo, *Efemérides*, p. 231; Thomas Karnes, "The Origins of Costa Rican Federalism," p. 253.

34. Pardo, *Efemérides*, pp. 229, 231; A.G.G. A3.1, Leg. 1073, Exp. 19434, "Razón de los Ramos Particulares que se administran en las Tesorerías de Real Hacienda del Reino de Guatemala"; A3.3, Leg. 1860, Exp. 29490; B6.7, Leg. 96, Exp. 2630.

35. A.G.I. Guatemala 525, the Cabildo of Guatemala, 10/23–24/1766; Guatemala 680, Julian Arriaga, 7/31/1766.

36. Samayoa Guevara, *La Intendencia*, pp. 55–57; Pardo, *Efemérides*, pp. 232–34.

37. "Estado General que Manifiesta El Producto de Alcavalas . . . en Cinco Años Corridos Desde . . . 1770 hasta . . . 1774," A.G.G. A3.5, Leg. 1720, Exp. 27708, fols. 174–75.

38. A.G.G. A3.5, Leg. 71, Exp. 1359.

39. A.G.I. Guatemala 682, Vicente Equival, 8/4/1784.

40. Salvador was given complete control over all indigo produced in its region after 1780. Although the port of Omoa was given to the general tax administration, it was stressed that it remained under both the diocese and intendency of Comayagua. "Real Orden de Febrero 1787," See A.G.G. A3.1, Leg. 693, Exp. 13002, fols. 74–79; "Estado General," A3.5, Leg. 1720, Exp. 27708, fols. 289–90; "Providencia de 17 de marzo de 1787," A3.5, Leg. 2203, Exp. 32863; A3.5, Leg. 112, Exp. 5466.

41. In 1776, a decree was promulgated by the president that exempted the payment of entry taxes on edibles and articles of primary need coming into Guatemala, but two years later the tax was reintroduced by the officials, and the next year the king was forced to voice his support for the general administration and to criticize the "insubor-

dination against the collection of the entry tax." A.G.G. A1.23, Leg. 1529, Fol. 34; A1.2, Leg. 1540, fol. 163; A3.4, Leg. 70, Exp, 1339, fol. 3; A3.1, Leg. 686, Exp. 12958, fol. 242; "Decreto de 15 de agosto 1779," A3.5, Leg. 2203, Exp. 32863.

42. "Real Cédula de 6 de septiembre 1786," A.G.G. A1.10, Leg. 2275, Exp. 16507, fol. 7; "Decreto de 5 de julio 1786," A3.5, Leg. 2203, Exp. 32863; A3.1, Leg. 1322, fols. 260–98. During the appeals it was claimed that fraud was practiced constantly and with notoriety in the Customs House in Guatemala, A3.1, Leg. 1322, fol. 252.

43. A.G.G. A3.5, Leg. 73, Exp. 1413.

44. Royal order of 4/27/1784, A.G.G. A3.1, Leg. 586, Exp. 11676; Royal order of 10/27/1784, A3.1, Leg. 1322, Exp. 22324, fol. 157.

45. In 1787 permission to grow tobacco was given to Costa Rica. It was later withdrawn, then granted, and then withdrawn again in 1813. A.G.I. Guatemala 733.

46. A.G.I. Guatemala 744, Cuentas of Aguardiente.

47. "Tobacco," it was said by the Intendant of Comayagua in 1815, "although excluded from commerce, grows in all areas without cultivation and for this reason is difficult to monopolize in a province this large." A.G.I. Indiferente General Visita General de la Provincia de Honduras.

48. A.G.I. Guatemala 877, Real Aprovación, 6/16/1783. Settlements were also attempted in Yucatan.

49. The 1783 salaries did not include the money paid interior representatives of the alcabala and tobacco administrations who earned their salaries through commissions on the amount they collected. A.G.I. Guatemala, 11/28/1798. For the cost of the colonization plan, see Guatemala 832, Tomas Wading, 11/28/1798.

8. At the Mercy of the World Market

1. A.G.I. Guatemala 423, President of Guatemala, 7/21/1771; Guatemala 448, President of Guatemala, 3/24/1751; Guatemala 252, Bishop of Guatemala, ?; Villacorta, *Historia de la capitanía general de Guatemala*, pp. 419–27.

2. See *Historia de la capitanía general de Guatemala*, pp. 419–27; Pardo, *Efemérides*, pp. 262–63, and Antonio Batres Jáuregui, *La América Central ante la historia*, 3:76.

3. The royal cédula that approved the move specified that loans and mortages could not be transferred to the new site. The implications of the controversy are revealed in a letter to the king from an eighty-five-year-old prelate, Pedro Martínez de Molina, 9/17/1773, A.G.I. Guatemala 661.

4. A.G.I. Indiferente General 1747 Proyecto . . . para la traslación de la Capital . . . The price of additional land was estimated at 100 pesos the cavallería.

5. A.G.I. Guatemala 561, Año de 1778, Sobre . . . Averiguar el producto de los dos Reales Novenos; Real Cédula, 7/18/1778; President of Guatemala, 8/25/1778; El Fiscal del Consejo de Indias, 11/21/1778.

6. Villacorta, *Historia de la capitanía general*, pp. 86, 418–19, 427–37; Pardo, *Efemérides*, pp. 257, 262–63; Batres Jáuregui, *La América Central*, 3:76; *El Editor Constitucional*, 4/23/1821. Also see the entire legajo in A.G.I. Guatemala 561.

7. New Guatemala had a total of 3,250 people in 1782, one fourth of whom were Spanish, a third each mulatto and mestizo, and the remainder Indian. See Villacorta, *Historia de la capitanía general*, p. 439; A.G.I. Guatemala 450, Dn Antonio Miguel de Lagarte, 9/8/1775; Guatemala 949, Bishop of Chiapas, 11/28/1778.

8. A.G.I. Guatemala 450, Governor of Comayagua, 10/16/1774; Guatemala 919,

Intendant of Comayagua, 4/20/1795; Guatemala 450, President of Guatemala, 7/8/1776; Guatemala 450, Año de 1776: Testimonio . . . de las noticias . . . de San Salvador de los temblores . . .

9. Aycinena served as the general administrator of supplies to the new city during its construction. For the plans of the Aycinena house see A.G.I. Mapas y Planos (Guatemala 243); Ralph Lee Woodward Jr., "Economic and Social Origins of the Guatemalan Political Parties (1773–1823)," pp. 544–66.

10. A.G.I. Guatemala 669, Matías de Gálvez, 10/16/1783; Pedro Molina, *Escritos*, 2.211–12.

11. Floyd, "Bourbon Palliatives and the Central American Mining Industry, 1765–1800," pp. 103–25.

12. Although Floyd ("The Guatemalan Merchants," p. 108) believes that the decree of 1800 which granted complete free trade between cattlemen and merchants "represented a victory for the cattlemen over the merchants," because the producers "could now at least cope with the monopoly under more flexible marketing conditions," my research has found that after 1800 the monopoly controlled the market, much to the intense displeasure of the producers who suffered. In 1811 a cattleman, Manuel Antonio Alcantana, writing for "the remaining hacendados and merchants of cattle" from Comayagua, complained "the diezmos, the alcabala, the levy of two reales for each beast that is eaten in the capital of this province, and two for each that is exported, combined with the taxes to transport the cattle through the most remote areas up until the capital, with growing costs of grazing and losses from death, injury or the loss of a third or half of the cattle's worth (through loss of weight), and when one arrives at the end, what is the price for which it is sold? [With] the trade in cattle being controlled by certain people . . . the cattle trade does not give one the money that is needed to repay very large debts." He complained that he was paid 6,500 pesos for 1,000 head that had to be in "good condition." In 1799, at the government-controlled fair, the price established ranged between 7 and 9 pesos the cow "with mostly at 8 pesos," as compared with 6.5 pesos in 1811 or a decline in price of almost 20 percent. A.G.G. A1.5, Leg. 2266, Exp. 16448; A3.3, Leg. 2368, Exps. 34956 and 34957.

13. Report of Robert Hodgson (1765), A.G.I. Santa Fe 1261, fols. 366–67. The population of Rivas grew five times from 1717 to 1777. Sofonías Salvatierra, "La fundación de la villa de Rivas," pp. 312–23. Cacao was produced in other areas of Central America, particularly in Soconusco (Chiapas). In the Guatemalan province of Suchitepéquez there existed over a million cacao trees in production in 1818. Henry Dunn, *Guatimala*, p. 220; Fernández, *Historia de Costa Rica*, p. 436.

14. A.G.I. Guatemala 832. Expediente Sobre Si ha de subsistir el Montepio . . . For the best description of the attempt to break merchant power in the indigo trade see R. S. Smith's works on "Indigo Production and Trade," and "Documents, Statutes of the Guatemalan Indigo Growers' Society," and Floyd, "The Guatemalan Merchants."

15. A.G.I. Guatemala 445, José María Peinado, 8/17/1812; Guatemala 668, Fiscal of New Spain (1821).

The relationship between the condition of the market and the control of merchants over prices was best seen during the nineteenth century. In 1804, in the midst of a locust plague, when output was down (and demand consequently up) a royal official claimed that "the merchants of the capital and those of Cádiz prefer to put their interests into silver" because of the "high price of indigo established at the fair." After the end of the plague and the end to warfare in Europe—when warehouses were filled with unsold indigo—in 1806, and again in 1810, when a bumper crop of indigo reduced demand, the mediation between farmers and businessmen was suspended, although it was restored in subsequent years. In the decade prior to independence there were sporadic reports of the fixing of prices. A.G.G. A1.5.5, Leg. 51, Exp. 1258, fol. 37; *La Gazeta de Guatemala,* 17 de noviembre de 1810, p. 346; *Apuntamientos sobre la agricultura,* p. 79; Smith, "Statutes," p. 336, and "Indigo Production," pp. 200–3; Juarros, *Compendio,* 2:115; Rubio, "El añil," p. 317; Ralph Lee Woodward, Jr., *Class Privilege and Economic Development: The Consulado de Comercio of Guatemala 1793–1871,* p. 39.

16. Floyd, "Bourbon Palliatives," pp. 117–23; A.G.I. Guatemala 668.

17. See A.G.I. Guatemala 588 for informes on the attempt to regulate the trade in cattle; Guatemala 41, President of Guatemala, 7/20/1780; Guatemala 423, President of Guatemala, 9/19/1800.

18. The original chief officer (Prior) of the merchant guild was the Marquis de Aycinena. The statutes of the guild were taken from the Ordenanzas de Intendentes de Buenos Aires (1782) and those of New Spain of 1786. See the royal orders of 4/27/1784 and 10/27/1784 in A.G.G. A3.1, Leg. 586, Exp. 11676, and Leg. 1322, Exp. 22324, fol. 157. For a detailed study of the institution of Intendencies, see Samayoa Guevara, *La Intendencia en el Reyno de Guatemala.*

19. A.G.G. A1.5, Leg. 2266, Exp. 16437.

20. A.G.G. A3.6, Leg. 2440, Exp. 35779. Also see Smith, "Origins of the Consulado of Guatemala," and Woodward, *Class Privilege and Economic Development.*

21. Woodward, "Economic and Social Origins of the Guatemalan Political Parties," pp. 549–50; and Woodward, *Class Privilege and Economic Development.*

22. B. Barreme (French consul to Coruna;, "Description des colonies espagnoles," ch. 7: Capitanerie générale de Guatemala," 2/28/1818, and "Aperçu statistique de la Capitanerie générale de Guatemala," A.M.A.E.F.-Mémoires, vol. 37, unfolioed.

23. In A.G.I. Santa Fe 1261. For supporting information see Floyd, *The Anglo-Spanish Struggle for Mosquitia.*

24. He repeats the same contraband charge in 1768. A.G.I. Santa Fe 1261, fols. 156–57, 194, 354. England had received a steady supply of dyes from Spain since before the War of Jenkin's Ear, so much so that an anonymous English pamphleteer, who was generally opposed to Spanish trade, advocated the continuation of commerce in dyes even during the war. McLachlan, *Trade and Peace With Old Spain,* p. 10.

25. A.G.I. Santa Fe 1261, 179, 369; Guatemala 459, Año de 1769: Testimonios . . . de que el Capn. Joseph Antonio Bargas tenía ilícito trato con los enemigos . . .

26. A.G.I. Santa Fe 1261, 232, 252, 453

27. Clarence H. Haring, *The Spanish Empire in America,* p. 343, believed that the 1778 general legislation on trade made foreign contraband sales to Spanish colonies less lucrative. Looking from Jamaica, Allen Christelow saw a decline in illegal trade in 1764 caused either by: increased Spanish military presence on their coasts; the actions of a Jamaica naval officer who was demanding excessive fees; a glut on the Spanish market of English goods since the British occupied Havana in 1763; a change in contraband channels to Havana and Pensacola; or bad English legislation that required all dyes to be shipped directly to Great Britain rather than to North America and enforced restrictions on English contraband activities with the French. In Christelow, "Contraband Trade between Jamaica and the Spanish Main, and the Free Port Act of 1766," pp. 312–40.

28. For the original English proposal to attack the Mosquito Coast see Christelow, "Contraband Trade," p. 316; A.G.I. Santa Fe 1261, fols. 502–12, 571–79; Guatemala 450, Joseph de Esteven Sierra, 1/1/1777.

29. Hodgson's son, William Pitt Hodgson, remained in the region after his father's death and became a source of slaves purchased by the Spanish colonial government.

A.G.I. Estado 48 Año de 1795 Testimonio . . . sobre . . . que se sigue el establecimiento de una Sociedad Económica; Estado 49 Letters from Josef Gabriel Hora.

30. A.G.I. Santa Fe 1261, 502.

9. The Indian Under the Later Bourbons

1. See the summary of the process in the report of the President of Guatemala, 8/13/1786, A.G.G. A3.16, Leg. 246, Exp. 4912, fols. 1–61.

2. *Ibid.* The Indians of Matagalpa (Nicaragua) paid less because they lived near Mosquitos Indians in dispersed regions and gave the tribute voluntarily. In Costa Rica, one town paid the exorbitant annual tribute of 4 pesos, 2 reales.

3. *Ibid.*, fol. 61.

4. *Ibid.* A.G.N. Cofradías y Archicofradías 18, Exp. 1, fol. 215, Viceroy Bucareli, 6/17/1775. Abuses resulted from the change. Alcaldes who earned money from repartimientos and sales of goods claimed that the pueblos owed them substantial funds and seized community funds. A.G.I. Guatemala 945, Bishop of Chiapas, 11/28/1778. The complaint was repeated—using the same words—by Francisco Antonio Dávila before the Cortes thirty-four years later. Informe 7/8/1814 in Guatemala 531.

5. A.G.I. Guatemala 917, Intendant of León, 4/11/1815.

6. The administrator of alcabalas in 1771 expressed his confusion over whether to tax the goods that entered Guatemala City from cofradías, because, he felt, they were using ecclesiastical privilege to escape paying the alcabala. It was ruled that Indians did not have to pay taxes, but ladinos who traded indigo did. A.G.I. Guatemala 660, 1/21/1771. Guatemala 459, Año de 1768. Testimonio . . . sobre que se les cobra Dȓo de Barlovento de hilo de sus cofradías; A.G.G. A3.5, Leg. 1954, Exp. 30524.

A series of legajos in the A.E.G. on cofradías provides an intricate description of their internal organization and relationship with Creole society. One cofradía in Mitla, for example, had outstanding loans worth around 16,219 pesos in 1744, one-third of which were held by Christoval de Gálvez, a member of one of the oldest Spanish families in the colony. Interest from the loans supplied the sodality with only 16 percent of its annual income, the rest coming from contributions and from sodality lands. A.E.G. Cofradías A4.14, Leg. 181, Documento 2.

7. The visita and report were delayed because of the Guatemalan earthquake of 1773. The final report of the archbishop has been published in Cortés y Larraz, *Descripción geográfico-moral de la diócesis de Goathemala*, but the critical information here being used comes mostly from the written replies to his queries from local priests, some of which appears in Santiago Montes, *Cofradías hermandades y guachivales* (2 vols.; Salvador, 1977), but much has not been published. It is available in A.G.I. Guatemala 948. The archbishop's visita is the chief source for Francisco de Solano, *Los Mayas del siglo XVIII.* Aside from the cleric's salary, the church hierarchy profited from sodalities by inspecting and taxing them for the visita. See A.G.I. Guatemala 920, Año de 1771: Testimonio al exhorto echo por el Governador de la Provincia . . . sobre cofradías. . . .

8. A.G.I. Guatemala 948: Relación de las Cofradías . . . Quadrante 1, fols. 67–68, 82–83; The spread of indigo lands in Salvador caused conflict with cattle sodalities. The cattle ate the indigo plants, much to the Creoles' displeasure. The solution, they saw, was to transfer the cattle elsewhere and convert the cattle land into indigo farms. See A.E.G., Leg. 4.14, Doc. 8-1757.

9. Deduced from A.G.I. Guatemala 948: Relación de las Cofradías. . . .

10. When, in 1778, the government requested data on annual income from mayordomos of cofradías and from clerics, they refused to furnish any information. A.G.I. Guatemala 561, Relación . . . sobre los dos Reales Novenos.

11. A.G.I. Indiferente General 1747, Santos Sánchez, 12/27/1814; Guatemala 915, Cura of Jocotenango, 3/21/1777; Guatemala 450, Governor of Comayagua, 10/16/1774; Don Antonio Miguel de Lagarte, 9/8/1775; A.G.G. Al. 45, Leg. 163, Exp. 3264, for the construction of the city of Guatemala, and Exp. 3285, for the construction of the Omoa road.

12. García Paláez, *Memorias*, 3:183; Solórzano F., *Evolución económica*, p. 138.

13. For excellent descriptions of the nature of the indigo works see Smith, "Indigo Production and Trade," Rubio, "El Añil," and Floyd, "Bourbon Palliatives," pp. 119–20.

14. A.G.I. Guatemala 948, Año de 1771: Testimonio de las respuestas dadas por los Curas seculares del Arzobispado de Goathemala, 2:126. François Chevalier, *La Formation des grands domaines au Mexique*.

15. A.G.I. Guatemala 669, Año de 1784: Testimonio de los autos sobre arreglo de peones para los trabajos de las haciendas . . . Fr. Matías de Córdova, *Utilidades de que todos los indios y ladinos se vistan y calcen a la Española y medios de conseguirlo sin violencia, Coacción, ni Mandata*, p. 5; Fr. José Antonio Goicoechea, *Memoria sobre los medios de destruir la mendicidad y de socorrer los verdaderos pobres de esta capital*; Smith, "Forced Labor in the Guatemalan Indigo Works," p. 319.

16. Wages were ten reales a week during the planting and growing seasons and twelve reales during the harvest season of March through September. Punishment was not to exceed twenty-five lashes. The reglamento is published in Smith, "Forced Labor in the Guatemalan Indigo Works," pp. 321–28, and the draft labor list appears in Rubio, *Historia del añil*, 2:139.

17. See the Residencia of the Governor of Nicaragua between 1783 and 1789, A.G.I. Guatemala 413; A.G.G. Al.23, Leg. 4636, fols. 195–96, Cavildo of Granada, 4/24/1785; see A.G.I. Guatemala 577 and 582 for reports of abuses of repartimiento and Silvio Zavala, *Contribución a la historia de las instituciones coloniales en Guatemala*, p. 86.

18. See Zavala, *Contribución a la historia*, p. 84. Lesley Byrd Simpson has compiled a partial list of requests and grants of repartimientos in regions in and around Guatemala and the highlands from 1734 until 1798, concluding that the system declined in the later years of the century, *Studies in the Administration of the Indians in New Spain*, pp. 99–116.

19. A.G.I. Indiferente General 1525 Mariano Gálvez, et al., *Instrucciones de Quezaltenango*, 9/22/1810; "Visita General de la Provincia de Honduras," pp. 302–09. Francis Gall, "Revisions for the Diccionario Geográfico de Guatemala," MS.

20. A Visita General of Honduras in 1804 claimed that all mines were supplied by repartimientos of Indians, A.G.I. Guatemala 501, Ramón de Anguiano (1804); Guatemala 797, Año de 1796: Testimonio . . . sobre el desarreglo con que se conduce el Minero Dn Domingo Espino Querros de los Indios que se le han asignado para el Laboreo de su Mineral . . . Rómulo Durón, *La provincia de Tegucigalpa bajo el gobierno de Mallol, 1817–1821*, pp. 27–29. Forced labor continued in the indigo regions but met local resistance. In 1803 the government renewed the 1783 legislation on draft labor because of the "disorder" in the provinces. Rubio, *Historia del añil*, 2:143.

21. See Cortés y Larraz, *Descripción*, 1:239, 244, 275–77, 280; 2:76–78, 116, 281; and A.G.I. Guatemala 948, Cartas Respuestas de los Curas, 77, 81, 120. Also see note 7 of this chapter.

Evidence of the increase in crossbreeding and the decline of the pueblo pervades the works of Cortés y Larraz and others. The alcaldía mayor of Tegucigalpa was 72 percent ladino in 1780. In Nicaragua in 1802, "many Indians live in different classes of haciendas. Many go begging." A.G.G. A3.16, Leg. 243, Exp. 4856, fols. 57, 60, 61 (the Governor of Nicaragua); Floyd, "Bourbon Palliatives," p. 105. García Peláez, *Memorias*, 3:198, lists the growth of ladinos in Itzapa in the valley of Guatemala. Through 1692 the pueblo was purely Indian. In 1700 2 percent of the births were of ladinos, in 1750 5 percent, 1763 8 percent, and 20 percent in 1764. In 1805 Archbishop Luis Peñalver estimated the population of Guatemala and Salvador at 636,822, of which 65 percent were Indian. S.C.A.E.S. Guatemala Pos. 20, Fas. 515.

22. A.G.I. Guatemala 948, Cartas Respuestas de los Curas, 2–18, 43, 94.

23. A.G.I. Guatemala 948, Año de 1771: Testimonio de las respuestas dadas por los Curas seculares, 1:22, 119–20, 172; Guatemala 262, Bishop of Guatemala (undated); Guatemala 681, President of Guatemala, 4/5/1798; Guatemala 561, Audiencia of Guatemala, 7/6/1778; Guatemala 949, Bishop of Chiapas, 11/28/1778. A.G.G. A3.2, Leg. 2535, Exp. 37083, and A2.3, Leg. 1531, fols. 517–18; A.G.I. Guatemala 451, President Matías Gálvez, 10/6/80; Guatemala 423, 8/7/88; La Gazeta de Guatemala, 7/23/1798, and Solano, *Los Mayas*, p. 127.

24. A.G.I. Guatemala 917, Archbishop of Guatemala (1790). Lanning, *The Eighteenth-Century Enlightenment*, p. 211.

25. For tributary figures see (1788) A.G.G. A3.16, Leg. 246, Exp. 4912; (1802) A3.16, Leg. 243, Exp. 4856; and (1811) A3.16, Leg. 953, Exp. 17773.

26. For a list of fifteen revolts between 1801 and independence see Severo Martínez Peláez, "Los motínes de indios en el período colonial guatemalteco," I Congreso Centroaméricano de Historia Demográfica, Económica y Social (San José, Costa Rica, 1973); Also see A.G.I. Guatemala 539, Audiencia de Guatemala, 10/30/1761; and G. Mayes H., *Honduras en la Independencia*, p. 28.

27. Reports came from Mazatenango, Quezaltenango, Totonicapán, and Güeguëtenango. They are found in A.E.G. Cofradias A4.14, Doc. 13.

10. The Economy Collapses

1. Between 1787 and 1790, Mexico annually exported, on the average, 199,562 *piastres fortes* of indigo. Between 1798 and 1801, commerce was suspended because of the war, but in 1802 Mexico exported 3,229,796 piastres fortes of indigo (or an annual average of 807,449) piastres fortes for the four years. This large amount seems to indicate that much of Guatemalan indigo was sent to Mexico because of the more regular and better defended shipping between Cádiz and Vera Cruz. Direct shipping from Mexico to Spain was resumed in 1803, and from Guatemala the following year. Alexandre de Humboldt, *Essai politique*, 2:701, 706, 733. Smith, "Indigo Production," p. 197; Elisa Luque Alcaide, *La sociedad económica de amigos del país de Guatemala*, pp. 32, 34; *La Gazeta de Guatemala*, 11/25 and 11/29/1799, 1:145–47; 11/19/1804, 8:505.

2. The alcalde mayor of Suchitepéquez wrote, in 1802, that "all of the western region of . . . Suchitepéquez is covered by locusts to such a degree that within the sixty hours since they have arrived, they have inundated 200 square leagues. Now, the workers recall with dread the terrible hunger, incalculable mortality and fearful occurrences that the locusts caused thirty years ago in Chiapas. . . . In Soconusco . . . the locusts are now so numerous that they cover the sun and suffocate the most active fire." A.G.I. Estado 49, 5/7/1802. The government was forced to distribute grain collected as tribute, forcing down the prices of agricultural commodities, and the king removed all taxes on grain imported from Mexico and Guayaquil. In 1809 the *Síndico* of the Merchant Guild

claimed that locusts and the war "destroyed the most opulent haciendas, reducing their harvest to a fifth [of usual harvests]." A.G.G. A1.5, Leg. 2266, Exp. 16448; A1.5.5, Leg. 51, Exp. 1258, fol. 34; A3.3, Leg. 2372, Exp. 35014; A1.4, Leg. 4027, Exp. 31010; *La Gazeta de Guatemala* 6/14, 6/28, 7/12, 8/2, 9/27/1802, 6:145, 147, 157, 174, 179, 233; 3/26, 7/9, 9/17, 10/1/1804 and 2/18/1805, 8:17, 359, 402, 456, 576.

3. There were complaints that government assistance was given "partially," with the small indigo grower being excluded. A.G.G. B6.7, Leg. 96, Exp. 2653; A1.5, Leg. 2266, Exp. 16445; *La Gazeta de Guatemala*, 7/26, 8/30, 9/27/1802, 6:187–89, 211, 241–42.

4. In 1795 flor quality was "not present" at the annual indigo fair. A.G.G. Guatemala 668, Minister of Real Hacienda, 4/23/1795; *La Gazeta de Guatemala*, 11/17/1810, 14:346; A.G.G. A1.38, Leg. 1745, Exp. 11716, fol. 685; Fr. José Antonio Goicoechea, *Tratado del xiquilite y añil de Guatemala*, p. 6.

5. A.G.G. A1.5, Leg. 2266, Exp. 16445; Pedro Molina, *Escritos*, 2:212; Rubio, "El añil," p. 329; *La Gazeta de Guatemala*, 9/4/1797, 1:284.

6. A.G.G. A.5.5, Leg. 51, Exp. 1258, fol. 36; Smith, "Indigo Production," p. 208; Arcila Farías, *Comercio*, pp. 84–86.

7. Declining world prices also affected cacao production. At the end of the eighteenth century cacao was purchased from farmers for from 30 to 50 pesos for a *fardo* of five arrobas, prices that fell to 10 pesos in 1815. With inflationary prices and high taxes, producers argued that they could not afford to continue production. Salvatierra "Rivas," pp. 321–22; "Report on the Decline of Indigo from the Real Consulado," April 1817, A.G.G. A1.5.5, Leg. 51, Exp. 1273, fols. 3–20.

8. A.G.G. A1.5.5, Leg. 51, Exp. 1273; Smith, "Indigo Production," p. 186; Rubio, "El añil," p. 337.

9. A.G.N. Consolidación, vol. 1: Real Despacho General de 12/26/1804. Sobre la venta de los vienes de Obras Pias en los Reynos de Indias; vol. 3, fols. 382–403; A.G.I. Guatemala 744, Fiscal of Guatemala, 8/14/1816. Geoffrey A. Cabat, "The Consolidation of 1804 in Guatemala," *The Americas*, 28:20–34. For the "contributions" of the crown during wartime see A1.1, Leg. 6093, Exp. 55337, fol. 19; B1.7, Leg. 10, Exp. 376; and Salazar, *Historia de veintiún años*, pp. 13–14.

10. See the complaints from the Comayagua Cabildo in A.G.I. Guatemala 930 and the Visita General in Indiferente General 1530.

11. A.G.N. Consolidación, vol. 9, Letters from Alejandro Ramírez and Antonio González M., 8/20/1808. Cabat, "The Consolidation of 1804," p. 36.

12. The price of corn in Tuxtla (Chiapas) doubled between 1768 and 1813. A.G.I. Guatemala 934, "Informe Sobre El Estado de Chiapas," 7/15/1813. A.G.G. B1.11, Leg. 79, Exp. 2331, fol. 132; A1.2, Leg. 2189, Exp. 15737; B1.13, Leg. 495, Exp. 8373: Salazar, *Historia de veintiún años*, p. 91; Louis Bumgartner, *José del Valle of Central America*, p. 187.

13. In 1814 a ceremonial procession and mass devoted to the Virgin Mary that had been financed by a small tax on agricultural production had to be abandoned for lack of funds. The rite was annually celebrated to pray for "the fertility of our bodies, and [for] the healthful waters that are so necessary for the harvest and to guard against the rise of hunger." As a result, the cabildo of Guatemala decided to finance the ceremony. A.G.G. B1.6, Leg. 9, Exp. 355; A1.1, Leg. 6093, Exp. 55269, fol. 51, Exp. 55344, fols. 3, 5, 9, 13, 60; A1.2, Leg. 2189, Exp. 15736, fols. 7–8; Leg. 2190, Exp. 15739; A3.3, Leg. 2369, Exp. 23993, Leg. 2372, Exp. 35014.

14. See A.G.G. A1.1, Leg. 6093, Exp. 55344.

15. See David Browning's study of the development of ecological imbalance in Salvador, *El Salvador, Landscape and Society*, pp. 83–87, 114–15, 134.

16. See A.G.I. Guatemala 679 for the royal orders of 9/14/1811 and 11/24/1816 banning the importation of cotton goods.

17. A.G.I. Indiferente General 1525, Instrucción de Quezaltenango, 9/22/1810.

18. G. Desdevises du Dézert, Vice-Rois et Capitaines Généraux des Indes Espagnoles à la fin du XVIII siècle, pp. 38–40.

19. The president of Guatemala reported in 1813 that the Honduran mining industry was in "total decay." A.G.I. Guatemala 679, Informe de la Provincia de Honduras, 2/20/1816; Apuntamientos sobre la Agricultura, pp. 25–26; Bumgartner, José de Valle, pp. 78–79.

20. Miguel González Saravia, Bosquejo político estadístico de Nicaragua (Guatemala, 1824), unpaged; also available in the P.R.O., F.O. 15, vol. 3, fol. 235.

11. José de Bustamante and the Crisis in Colonial Government

1. Herr, The Eighteenth Century, pp. 37–85; "Representation to Carlos IV on the Nature of the Holy Office by G. M. de Jovellanos," in W. N. Hargreaves-Mawdsley, Spain under the Bourbons, 1700–1833, p. 187; Góngora, Studies in the Colonial History of Spanish America, pp. 178–81.

2. See Lanning's The Eighteenth-Century Enlightenment in the University of San Carlos for an excellent description of this important institution. Lanning reveals that the university was one of the most advanced institutions in Spanish America. Rafael Heliodoro Valle, Historia de las ideas contemporaneas en Centro América; Salazar, Historia de veintiún años, p. 59; José del Valle, Obras, p. xlvi; Guillermo Mayes H., Honduras en la independencia de Centro América y anexión a México, p. 14.

Goiecochea never succeeded in implementing curriculum reform. He proposed to offer "precisely the great works of natural philosophy in vogue in Spain, France, Italy, Germany, and England in the eighteenth century." Lanning estimates that despite the failure of reform, San Carlos was, "intellectually speaking" ahead of the University in Mexico City. Eighteenth-Century Enlightenment, pp. 51–75; see also José del Valle, El Amigo de la Patria, 2/19/1821, pp. 363–78.

3. Herr, The Eighteenth Century, p. 444.

4. "Representation . . . by G. M. de Jovellanos," p. 186.

5. As oidor, Villa Urrutia was able to provide powerful protection for radical thought. In 1795 he used his position to aid a Frenchman being persecuted because he "freely and scandalously" discussed the French Revolution, refusing to recognize "the love of God," and proclaiming that "if the French Revolution triumphed, the world would be a paradise, with no place for retrograde institutions like the Spanish monarchy." Villa Urrutia managed to delay prosecution of the case and to have the Frenchman exiled, thus protecting him from jail or death. Lanning, Eighteenth-Century Enlightenment, p. 319; John S. Fox, "Antonio de San José Muro," pp. 410–12. Later, the reactionary President Bustamante accused Villa Urrutia of having "planted in Guatemala the opinions that have produced so many troubles." A.G.I. Guatemala 495, 3/2/1814.

6. Later, others testified to the beginnings of large-scale contraband traffic. A report to the British crown in 1808 claimed that there were fifteen English ships sailing to the Bay of Honduras (in addition to forty-eight vessels "to foreign colonies in the Caribbean"). It was said that three or four American schooners appeared every year, beginning at the turn of the century. In 1811 the cabildo of Granada suggested that the best way to get rid of contraband was to allow free commerce with all nations. José T. Medina

alleges that the regime of González Mollindo was directly chiefly by the liberal Ramírez, *La Imprenta en Guatemala 1660–1821*, p. 423. See also Arcila Farías, *Comercio entre Venezuela y México en los siglos XVI y XVII*, pp. 28–29; Ramón Salazar, *Historia del desenvolvimiento intelectual de Guatemala*, 2:316–17; Lucy F. Horsfall, "The West Indian Trade," p. 182; Orlando Roberts, *Narrative of Voyages and Excursions on the East Coast and in the Interior of Central America*, p. 90; A.G.G. A.1, Leg. 2189, Exp. 5737; B5.7, Leg. 67, Exp. 1847, fol. 5. The first recorded contacts with the North Americans occurred in 1799, when two boats from Philadelphia, owned by Andrew Burke, traded 60,000 pesos worth of goods legally, after getting permission from the colonial government. Two years later the Diana, a boat out of Boston, made contact with Juan Bautista Irisarri, an indigo producer with contacts with the Aycinena family, and as a result Irissari sent a vessel to Boston. Ten years later this shipment became part of the general controversy between the militaristic president of the audiencia, Bustamante, and the merchant class. See below. A.G.I. Estado 49, Ambrosio Cerdán y Pontero, 6/22/1799; Guatemala 833, President of Guatemala, 2/4/1804; *Apuntamientos sobre la agricultura* (Guatemala, 1811), p. 5.

7. Tax revenue declined, according to some government officials, due "particularly to the contraband traffic that is being carried on with foreign goods." A.G.G. A1.1, Leg. 28, Exp. 818, fols. 8–9; Humboldt, *Essai politique sur le Royaume de la Nouvelle Espagne*, 2:467–73; Dunn, *Guatimala*, p. 170.

8. Mario Rodríguez, *The Cádiz Experiment in Central America, 1808 to 1826*, pp. 44–45.

9. *Ibid.*, pp. 47–51.

10. Ricardo Gallardo, *Las Constituciones de la República Federal de Centro-América*, 2:960–61; A.G.G. B1.8, Leg. 11, Exp. 410; B1.12, Leg. 3477, Exp. 79405, fol. 104.

11. Marure, *Bosquejo*, 1:12.

12. Gallardo, *Las Constituciones*, 1:89; A.G.G. A1.2, Leg. 37, Exp. 4345, fols. 59–65, Leg. 2188, Exp. 15735, fol. 6; Salazar, *Historia de veintiún años*, p. 117.

13. But the only evidence I have been able to discover of any activity on the part of the tribunal was a letter sent in October 1810 from that body to the cabildo of Ciudad Real concerning "a certain individual named Andres, of medium build, white, with measle scars, young, between fifteen and seventeen years, dressed poorly like a citizen [citoyen], with a straw hat, a ring on one finger, and he says he's from Andalusia. We wish to request that in the case that this individual comes into your jurisdiction, you interrogate him as to the object of his trip and examine the passport which he carries." A.G.G. A1.1, Leg. 6093, Exp. 55344, fols. 53–58; A1.2, Leg. 2189, Exp. 15736, fols. 14–35, 68; B1.3, Leg. 3, Exp. 44, fols. 1–4; A3.2, Leg. 27, Exp. 506; Salazar, *Historia de veintiún años*, p. 138.

14. The father of José Matías Delgado was one of the founders of the Society of Indigo Producers in 1782. Rodolfo Barón Castro, *José Matías Delgago*, p. 8; A.G.G. A1.30, Leg. 2651, Exp. 22247; A.1, Leg. 6924, Exp. 57003; A3.1, Leg. 2724, Exp. 39028; B2.1, Leg. 22, Exp. 684; B2.7, Leg. 82, Exp. 2376; B2.9, Leg. 38, Exps. 838, 839, 859, 860, 873; Marure, *Bosquejo*, 1:13–14; Salazar, *Historia de veintiún años*, p. 157; *La Gazeta de Guatemala*, 1/13/1812, p. 117; Haefkens, *Viaje*, p. 213; A.G.I. Guatemala 454, Cabildo of Guatemala, 1/23/1811.

15. A.G.G. B2.9, Leg. 38, Exps. 869, 886, 888, 891.

16. Later, San Miguel and San Vicente were "elevated" from "villa" to "ciudad" status for their support. These rewards illustrate the Spanish government's practice of pitting one town against another and rewarding areas for their obedience, thus perpet-

uating regionalism in an almost feudalistic manner. See A.G.G. B2.1, Leg. 22, Exp. 684; B2.9, Leg. 38, Exps. 859, 860, 873; B2.1, Leg. 22, Exp. 715. The rebels in Chiquimula were fined for their attempt at revolt. B1.1, Leg. 6114, Exp. 56281.

17. A.G.G. B2.2, Leg. 24, Exps. 688, 689, 693, and 697, B2.9, Leg. 38, Exp. 837; Marure, Bosquejo, 1:15–16.

18. A.G.G. A.1.1, Leg. 6922, Exp. 56950. Fernández, Historia de Costa Rica, pp. 476–78; Mayes, H., Honduras en la Independencia, p. 33.

19. Ever since 1811 the cabildo of Guatemala had attempted to get as much news as possible of the Mexican revolution. In December 1812 some Guatemalans attempting to travel to Veracruz en route to Spain were denied passports. "The public," the regidores claimed, "is frightened and wishes to discover the true events." Bustamante claimed that he had heard little himself, except that Morelos had invaded Oaxaca and that the Indians in Tehuantepeque had revolted. A month later the Guatemalan cabildo asked its counterpart in Ciudad Real for news, and it responded that Oaxaca had fallen to the rebels. A.G.G. A1.2, Leg. 2190, Exp. 15739, fols. 12, 18, 46.

20. A.G.G. A1.2, Leg. 2190, Exp. 15739, fols. 117–18.

21. Ibid., fols. 130, 185, 193.

22. Bustamante had seen the 1811 Salvadoran rebellion as "supposed to fulfill a general plan of revolt in Colombia, Mexico and Central America." A.G.I. Guatemala 453, José de Bustamante, 12/23/1811; Guatemala 943, José de Bustamante, 5/22/1813.

23. Details of this little-known participation by Central America in the Mexican rebellion are in a letter from Fernando Antonio Dávila, 7/8/1814, A.G.I. Guatemala 531.

24. Marure, Bosquejo, 1:19; Salazar, Historia de veintiún años, pp. 176–77.

25. The conspiracy was discovered four days before the planned uprising. Bustamante issued a decree in which he revealed that his agent had been keeping him informed of the plot throughout the year. A.G.G. A1.1, Leg. 6924, Exp. 57003, fols. 78–88; Marure, Bosquejo, 1:19; Salazar, Historia de veintiún años, pp. 176–77.

26. A.G.G. A1.5.5, Leg. 51, Exp. 1273, fol. 18; A1.1, Leg. 6926, Exp. 57044, fols. 1–6. The royal government also ordered that all salaries and expenses past due to Cortes deputies must be paid, an exaction that again punished improverished municipalities. The collection of past salaries proved to be more difficult than the collection of past debts owed the government. Although other deputies were owed considerable sums by their local governments, the best example of unpaid salaries was that of the representative from Guatemala, Antonio Larrazábal. This deputy not only represented the richest area of the country, but was also closely associated with the Aycinena family (who lent him money during his stay in Spain). After the fall of the Cortes he was persecuted both in Spain (where he was briefly imprisoned) and in Guatemala. After the return of liberal government he was honored as the greatest of all the Central American representatives to the Cortes. In 1820, one of the first acts of the newly restored, liberal cabildo in Guatemala was to approve the inscribing of Antonio Larrazábal's name in the meeting hall for his "resolve in sustaining our rights and that persecution which he suffered."

Despite his fame, Larrazábel had great problems in collecting the salary and expenses due him. The story of his efforts to collect the money is, in reality, a history of the fiscal situation in Central America for the next twenty-five years.

While Larrazábel was still in Spain in 1815, his brother, José Ignacio, wrote the Guatamalan cabildo asking for the funds owed. The request apparently had no success, as nothing more was said about it. In 1822, after independence, Larrazábel personally requested the funds. He stated that he hadn't charged 2,000 pesos that the cabildo had promised him for "travelling in a foreign boat to insure my arrival," nor the 571 pesos that it cost him to print the famous Instructions from the ayuntamiento. Nevertheless, "the terrible circumstances in which I find myself because of the large amount that I still owe for my expenses in Cádiz, obliges me to request that you provide me with this amount." Larrazábel detailed more than 7,500 pesos that the cabildo owed him for daily expenses.

His appeal had some success, as on September 26, 1822, the Mexican general then occupying Guatemala, Filisola, ordered payment of the debt. However, when the funds arrived, they were not "complete." "The pay that you have given me is only partial: the first is a bond against the Customs House that I cannot redeem without considerable loss; and the rest is in (weak) money from Tegucigalpa." Between 1822 and 1830 Larrazábel received eight payments, amounting to 5,580, leaving a debt of 2,000 pesos.

In 1830 a renewed appeal for the remaining funds to the Guatemalan municipality successfully yielded 400 pesos; in 1833, 220 pesos; in 1834, 600 pesos; and in 1836, 100 pesos, thus leaving a debt of 680 pesos. In 1837, a request to the municipality was turned down. Finally, in 1840, almost thirty years after Larrazábel had assumed his position as deputy, the local authorities ruled that "no debt is older, nor more possesses the right to be paid," and ordered that the remaining funds be paid.

Thus, a man who was allied with the most powerful interests in Central America had to wait thirty years to receive his salary, and then, because of the reduced value of the money, was not actually successful. A.G.G. A1.2, Leg. 2193, Exp. 15746, Leg. 2239, Exp. 16105, fols. 2–5; Leg. 795, Exp. 19356; B85.1, Leg. 1146, Exp. 26162, fols. 2–14; B1.8, Leg. 11, Exp. 395; B1.78, Leg. 529, Exp. 10101, fols. 79, 162; B78.48, Leg. 858, Exp. 20664, fols. 3–4.

27. A.G.I. Guatemala 423, Intendant of Honduras, 1/17/1815.

28. The crown issued two orders on 9/14/1811 and 11/24/1816 prohibiting the introduction of European cotton goods into America. A.G.I. Guatemala 679, José Tejada, 9/11/1817.

29. For the judicial proceedings see A.G.I. Guatemala 673, Año de 1814: Testimonio . . . a representacion del Sr. Marques de Aycinena sobre no pagar mas derechos . . . ; Salazar, *Mariano de Aycinena*, pp. 57–62; A.G.G. A1.5.5, Leg. 51, Exp. 1273, fol. 18.

30. For vessels seized, see Guatemala 679, José de Tejada, 2/25/1818; Guatemala 743, Bustamante, 6/11/1815; also see Guatemala 743, Bustamante, 9/6/1814.

31. A.G.I. Guatemala 530, Año de 1819: Testimonio . . . sobre los medios que convendrá para evitar la introducción de Contravandos (Tomas O'Horan).

32. "The decay or decline in income in the coffers comes from the general misery caused by the obstruction of commerce and particularly by contraband that introduces foreign goods that do not contribute anything to the treasury and cause considerable loss of [coined silver] to those countries from where [the goods] derive." A.G.G. A1.1, Leg. 218, Exp. 818, fols. 1–9. A.G.I. Guatemala 679, Informe del Contador General de Indias (José Tejada), 8/6/1818.

33. But by December 1813, when Bustamante suggested that cabildos use Indian community funds to pay the salaries for Cortes representatives, most municipalities responded that there was no longer money in the account, "because it has all been loaned to the public treasury." A.G.G. B1.4, Leg. 4, Exp. 95; B1.2, Leg. 2, Exp. 50, fols. 2–3.

34. The April 1812 "donation" was based upon the precedent, established during the "War of the American Revolution," that had "requested an extraordinary donation of two pesos from each Spaniard and one from the other classes, and moreover, there didn't exist an individual who refused the state this small aid." A.G.G. B1.8, Leg. 76, Exp. 2249, fols. 1–2; A1.1, Leg. 6114, Exps. 56299, 56322, 56328, 56327.

35. A.G.G. A1.1, Leg. 6114, Exp. 56272; Leg. 6115, Exps. 56357, 56369, 56405.

36. A.G.I. Guatemala 454: Estado que manifiesta las salidas de caudales (by José de Bustamante).

37. A.G.G. Bl.4, Leg. 4, Exp. 66.

38. A.G.G. Bl.6, Leg. 9, Exp. 355; Leg. 493, Exps. 8276, 8239–41.

39. Until the end Bustamante defended his role as being that of protector of the crown's authority. "This is how they insult he who has been a victim of so many sufferings only because he does not hold the dangerous opinions of this damned epoch," he said in 1815. Two years later he described his measures as necessary "to contain the progress of the rebellion that exists in this capital." A.G.I. Guatemala 679, Informe del contador general de Indias, 8/6/1818; Guatemala 502, Bustamante, 3/18/1815; Guatemala 744, Bustamante, 8/14/1817.

12. The Widening Gyre

1. See the petitions of Juan Fermín de Aycinena, 1/12/1819, and Gregorio Castriones and the "Sociedad Urruela y Barreda," 1/16/1818, A.G.I. Guatemala 679. By this time the term "neutral nations," which came from the years of the Napoleonic Wars, had become a euphemism for Great Britain and the United States.

2. A.G.G. Al.2, Leg. 2193, Exp. 15744, fols. 35–36, and Exp. 15746, fol. 143; Miguel García Granados, *Memorias*, 1:11–14.

3. *El Editor Constitucional*, 9/25/1820, 1:162, 164.

4. *El Amigo de la Patria*, 12/9/1820, 1:133.

5. *El Editor Constitucional*, 9/18/1820, 1:110.

6. *Ibid.*, p. 132.

7. A.G.I. Guatemala 679. Diputación Provincial de Nicaragua, 5/20/1821.

8. The Provincial Deputation began meeting on August 3rd. Bl.13, Leg. 16, Exp. 479, fols. 1–3; Al.1, Leg. 6930, Exp. 57150.

9. Urrutia "has been very sick with apoplectic attacks from one moment to another that could deprive him of his life; this illness had debilitated his body and has damaged his intellectual powers," a member of the deputation attested. That body petitioned the Cortes to remove him from office for his repeated absence.

But far more was involved than illness. During the same period every move made by the deputation to assume control over government administration was countered. The audiencia did not, it asserted, "recognize the authority of the provincial deputation to ask for those documents that have been requested." In appeals sent to the Cortes the deputation listed the requests made to the audiencia that had not been answered: on September 3, the papers relating to the "urgent need" to erect a diocese in Salvador; October 1, a report on the state of the treasury; October 9, measures to deal with the revolt of Indians at Totonicapán (see below); October 18, the establishment of a health committee (*Junta de Sanidad*); and on October 30, the need to name civil judges. The deputation did receive a report on the state of the treasury, but it was not sufficiently detailed. "What is needed to be known," the deputation wrote, "is the product of each tax, their expenses, their employees, and respective salaries . . . the state of the administration of sales tax, of the tithe, of the consulado, of tobacco, gunpowder, and playing cards, and also [that of] the hospital Hermandad!" In a challenge to the judicial authority, the deputation demanded documents concerning all of the imprisoned, the condition of the jail in Guatemala City, and "specifics of the infractions that have been charged against some alcaldes mayores and corregidores in the Province."

A.G.G. Al.1, Leg. 6930, Exps. 57113, 57114, 57119, 57135, 57154, 57157; Bl.13,

Leg. 16, Exp. 480, fols. 3, 31; Exps. 500, 502, Leg. 17, Exp. 509, Leg. 18, Exp. 551, Leg. 494, Exp. 8337, fols. 1–4.

10. A.G.G. B1.13, Leg. 494, Exp. 8326, fols. 1–8.

11. The *Plan* was announced in Mexico February 24, 1821. Lucas Alamán, *Historia de Méjico*, 5:98, 107–08.

12. It is not exactly clear what had compelled Urrutia to resign. The deputation wrote the Cortes that the official stepped down because of "his advanced age, the epileptic attacks that left him without the use of an arm, and the defiance of the constitutional regime." But Urrutia was strong enough to travel north to Mexico six months later, so illness seems an insufficient reason. Probably it was the combination of pressure from the deputation, the need to have a stronger man to lead the colony should Iturbide's rebellion turn southward, and the state of his health. A.G.G. B1.13, Leg. 16, Exp. 480, fols. 3–21, Leg. 17, Exp. 519; A1.1, Leg. 6928, Exp. 57190.

13. The basic evidence for this interpretation comes from the coincidence in dates. Iturbide had been openly maneuvering in Mexico in late 1820 and issued his Plan on February 21, 1821. News generally took two weeks to arrive in Guatemala—and special events, two days. Thus, it is apparent that the Guatemalans and the Spanish were aware of what was occurring in the north. "Report of the Consulate of the State of Trade, February 1821, P.R.O., F.O., 15/3, 115; Bancroft, *Works*, 8:45.

14. A.G.G. B1.11, Leg. 79, Exp. 2337, fols. 10–11, Leg. 16, Exp. 484, Leg. 79, Exps. 2332, 2335, 2344; A1.1, Leg. 6930, Exps. 57113, 57114.

15. Reports came in from Santa Barbara, Sicapeca, San Raymond, Jacaltenango, Tepanguatemala, Gualán, and Sololá of continued collections and resistance. A.G.G. A1.1, Leg. 6932, Exp. 57307; B1.11, Leg. 79, Exp. 2331; B1.13, Leg. 17, Exps. 510, 511, 513, Leg. 495, Exp. 8432. For the Totonicapán revolt see J. Daniel Contreras R., *Una rebelión indigena en el partido de Totonicapán*, p. 5, and A.G.G. A1.1, Leg. 6930, Exp. 57113. For the Costa Rican/Nicaraguan tribute problem, A.G.G. B1.13, Leg. 494, Exp. 8369.

16. A.G.G. A1.1, Leg. 6930, Exps. 57170, 57114; B1.10, Leg. 77, Exp. 2281; B1.13, Leg. 495, Exps. 8379, 8422; B1.14, Leg. 20, Exp. 641.

17. On June 22, 1821, the deputation in Guatemala decided to wait until another session to decide the question; on July 3 there were reports of disturbances in Paricia "over the exaction of tribute." But, in a separate plea, the ayuntamiento of Sololá claimed that without the tribute tax, it could not function. On August 3 the deputation wrote Consalapa not to make any changes in the collection of tribute. This is the last report that could be discovered on the issue before independence was declared. A.G.G. B1.13, Leg. 17, Exps. 515–17.

18. A.G.G. A1.1, Leg. 6632, Exp. 57372; B1.13, Leg. 17, Exps. 510–12, 516.

19. See A.G.G. B1.11, Leg. 79, Exp. 2331, fols. 19, 20, 53, 61–63, 139–40.

20. A.G.G. B1.13, Leg. 17, Exp. 520, fol. 61.

21. For example, the need to pay deputies to the Cortes produced controversy. At first it was suggested that the representatives be paid with tribute money, but the central government rejected this. It was finally decided that a new tax be placed on the slaughter of cattle. In addition to the two reales per head already being collected by the cabildos, another two would be levied for the sale of the cattle prior to butchering. Additional taxes were to be charged on stores and warehouses. The measures provided cabildo members, who held the butchering monopolies, with the force to finance the representative, whom the cabildo elected from its own group, thus shifting the burden of representative government upon those who wanted representation. A.G.G. B1.13, Leg. 17, Exps. 511 and 529.

22. A.G.G. B1.10, Leg. 79, Exp. 2301, fols. 12–13, 49; A1.1, Leg. 6930, Exp. 57114.

23. A.G.G. Bl.13, Leg. 17, Exps. 510 and 512; Bl.10, Leg. 78, Exp. 2301.

24. An Indian town of Catamers with 2,000 inhabitants had been merged with the ladino settlement of Del Real with 2,500 people, and inhabitants of the former town complained, "What justification is there for the merging of Indians and ladinos, each of whom despise each other?" A.G.G. Bl.14, Leg. 475, Exp. 8407.

25. Comayagua notified the Guatemalan deputation in late July 1821 that it was going to send a representative to that body, but this was a temporary "surrender," a response to the surge of liberal power occasioned by the growing force of rebels in Mexico. The Comayaguan delegate never arrived, and, when independence was declared in September, the Comayagua deputation was quickly reconstituted. Much of this critical dispute is documented in three legajos: A.G.G. Al.1, Leg. 6930, Exps. 57106, 57114, 57220, fol. 46; Bl.1, Leg. 78, Exp. 2301, fols. 1–108; Bl.13, Leg. 17, Exps. 510–14. Also see Mayes H. *Honduras en la independencia*, pp. 39–51; and Durón, *La provincia de Tegucigalpa*, p. 154.

26. A.G.G. Bl.13, Leg. 494, Exp. 8346.

27. Fernández, *Historia de Costa Rica*, pp. 492–93; *El Amigo de la Patria*, 9/7/1821, pp. 162–65.

28. The guild attempted to resist the reform by appealing to the Cortes, but the deputation rejected the move as a delaying action and ordered the immediate institution of the measure. A.G.G. Bl.13, Leg. 17, Exp. 517, Leg. 18, Exp. 525.

29. Liberal historians have described the conservatives in a number of ways that have distorted the events of this period. Alejandro Marure wrote, in 1836, the first definitive liberal history of the 1820 to 1836 period, financed by a liberal Guatemalan government. The conservatives won the 1820 cabildo election, he wrote by "spreading gold among the [most] ignorant and miserable" class. *Bosquejo*, 1:20–21. At the end of the nineteenth century, another liberal historian, Ramón Salazar, wrote that "the Ayuntamiento did not represent the interests of the people of Guatemala. It has been invaded by the Spanish party [that were] anti-constitutionalist and an enemy of independence," although he admits that Valle's opposition to free trade made him the most popular man in the colony. *Historia de veintiún años*, p. 217. The early conservative responses to these historians were as polemical as the liberal treatises, but lacked the documentation that Marure employed. Thus, until today, the effect of these major distortions remains. For the results of the 1820 election, see A.G.G. Bl.10, Leg. 78, Exp. 2300; Al.2, Leg. 2194, Exp. 15747, fol. 2.

30. Reaction to Molina's article was immediate. The conservative Guatemalan cabildo discussed this "dangerous article" and pressed charges against him. A member of the Comayaguan deputation wrote Gainza of his love for the king: "I cannot explain to you the pain and tears that come from my heart" because of the article. All attempts at prosecuting Molina failed, however, because the control of censorship was exercised by the liberal Guatemalan deputation. *El Editor Constitucional*, 6/4/1821, pp. 613–16; A.G.G. Al.2, Leg. 2194, Exp. 15747; Bl.14, Leg. 20, Exp. 663.

31. *El Editor Constitucional*, 8/20/1821, p. 743.

32. Alamán, *Méjico*, 5:344–45; Samayoa Guevara, "Fray Matías de Córdova, Educador y Centro-Americano" *Antropología e Historia de Guatemala*, 16:32; Gallardo, *Las Constituciones*, 1:181; Salazar, *Historia de veintiún años*, pp. 227–50; Marure, *Bosquejo*, 1:25–31; *El Genio de la Libertad*, 10/15/1821, p. 774, and 10/22/1821, p. 834. Among the signers of the Declaration of Independence were nine former students of the University of San Carlos, who had, between them, twenty-six diplomas from the school. Lanning, *Eighteenth-Century Enlightenment*, p. 339; José del Valle, *Obras*, 1:3–4; Villacorta C. "Bibliografía e iconografía de la Independencia," *Anales de la So-*

ciedad de Geografía e Historia (1937), 14:6. A.G.G. B5.4, Leg. 59, Exp. 1380, Leg. 62, Exp. 1655; Mayes H., *Honduras*, pp. 57, 59. Fernández, *Costa Rica*, pp. 498–502, 507–13.
    33. José M. Mendez, *Memoria del estado político y eclesiástico de la capitanía general de Guatemala presentada a las Cortes el día 17 de mayo de 1821*, pp. 17–20.

13. The Republican Experiment: In Search of Order

1. *El Genio de la Libertad*, 10/15/1821, p. 826.
2. In December 1821 the Mexican General Vicente Filísola wrote to Iturbide from his position in southern Mexico describing the confused situation of Central America: León and Comayagua proclaimed freedom from Spain, but declared themselves united to Mexico. Granada and Costa Rica separated themselves from the former area, protesting that they wished to follow the fate of the capital (Guatemala); Tegucigalpa, Omoa, Trujillo, Olancho, and Gracias refused obediance to Comayagua, embracing the opinion of Granada; Quezaltenango first endorsed the Guatemalan act of September 15, and then retracted, uniting itself to Mexico, following the other provinces; Güeguetanango, Sololá, and part of the partido of Mazatenango proceeded in the same manner; San Salvador is not in agreement with Guatemala. Filísola, *La cooperación de México en la independencia de Centro America*, 2:31.
3. Iturbide to Gaínza, 10/19/21, *Anexión*, 1:49–53; Alamán, *Méjico*, 5:345–46.
4. Marcial Zebadua, *Memoria al Congreso Federal* (Guatemala, 1825); "Sketch of the Present State of the Republic of Guatemala," P.R.O., F.O., 15/1, 30–31; Filísola, *La Cooperación de México*, 2:108–09; Marure, *Bosquejo*, 1:35–36.
5. Aycinena to Iturbide, 1/3/22, *Anexión*, 3:112.
6. A.G.G. B5.4, Leg. 61, Exps. 1605, 1609, 1610, 1615, 1618, 1624, 1633, fol. 8, Leg. 62, Exp. 1667, Leg. 63, Exps. 1668, 1694, 1688, fol. 13, 1699, 1708, fol. 20; Leg. 62, Exp. 1667, Leg. 58, Exp. 1294; Acts of the Ayuntamiento and Provincial Deputation of San Salvador, 1 and 20/11/22, *Anexión*, 3:125–26, 144–45. Delgado to Aycinena, 2/5/22, *Anexión*, 2:45–47; Marure, *Bosquejo*, 1:39–41.
7. A.G.G. B5.4, Leg. 62, Exp. 1655, fol. 12, Exp. 1657, Leg. 63, Exp. 1742; the Mexican Secretary of War to Gaínza, 2/18/22; Gaínza to the Junta Gubernativa of Costa Rica, 4/7/22; Memorial of the representatives of Honduras, 5/8/22; Representation by the Señores Lindo, 6/20/22; Filísola to Iturbide, 1/31 and 2/25/22; Aycinena to Filísola, 2/16/22; Aycinena to Iturbide, 1/3/22, *Anexión*, 2:111, 142–44, 212, 3:112, 166–67, 197, 198, 215.
8. Marure, *Bosquejo*, 1:41.
9. Proclamation of Filísola, 10/26/22, Delgado to Filísola, 11/14/22, and Filísola to Delgado, 11/17/22, in *Anexión*, 2:348, 375, 379; Marure, *Bosquejo*, 1:48.
10. Declaration of the Ayuntamiento of Quezaltenango, 12/17/22; a petition from the Ayuntamiento of Comayagua to the Emperor, 12/28/22, *Anexión*, 2:419, 437–42. Filísola to the Secretary of State, 9/8/22, Filísola to the Secretary of War, 8/3/22, *Anexión*, 3:379–81, 5:163; Marure, *Bosquejo*, 1:55, 57.
11. As one of its first acts of independence Salvador suspended the tribute on January 12, 1822. A.G.G. B5.4, Leg. 63, Exp. 1688, fol. 8; B5.8, Leg. 71, Exp. 1967, Leg. 72, Exp. 2037, fol. 8; B10.5, Leg. 176, Exp. 3763; Filísola to the Secretary of the Treasury, 8/3/22, *Anexión*, 3:375–76.
12. A.G.G. B5.79, Leg. 67, Exp. 1827, fols. 43, 49, 146; B5.6, Leg. 65, Exp. 1764; B1.78, Leg. 529, Exp. 10101, fols. 157, 159–60. Filísola to the Secretary of War, 7/5/22, *Anexión*, 3:363.

13. A.G.G. B5.7, Leg. 66, Exp. 1813, fols. 1, 6; B5.8, Leg. 4123, Exp. 92798, fol. 179; Solórzano F., *Evolución económica*, p. 269.

14. A.G.G. B6.7, Leg. 95, Exp. 2623; B1.78, Leg. 529, Exp. 10101, fol. 83.

15. A.G.G. B5.7, Leg. 67, Exp. 1848; Filísola, *La cooperación de Mexico*, 2:39.

16. A.G.G. B6.14, Leg. 86, Exp. 2406.

17. "La Junta del Gobierno de San Salvador a La de Costa Rica, 10/2/1823," *Documentos históricos posteriores a la independencia* (San José, 1923), pp. 161–63.

18. Archbishop Casaus served as mediator in the dispute. A.G.G. B6.28, Leg. 3486, Exp. 79662; Marure, *Bosquejo*, 1:69–79; M. Montúfar, *Memorias*, pp. 223–24; "Sketch of the Present State of the Republic of Guatemala," 7/9/1824, P.R.O., F.O., 15/1, fols. 37–38.

19. "El Voto," in J. D. Gámez, *Archivo histórico de Nicaragua*, cited by Pedro J. Chamorro, *La historia de la federación de la América Central*, pp. 85–86.

20. There were some obvious structural faults. Although the states had veto power, Guatemala maintained a preponderance of power. With popular elections for the executive, congress, and the supreme court, the largest state would be able to control all areas of the government except the senate. On the other hand the central power was very weak. The president had no veto power over the congress and had to obey legislative dictums that he might oppose. Civil militias were to be created by the states in the face of the federal army. The states, therefore, through congressional power and local military force, guarded against the creation of any powerful central authority. Chamorro, *La Historia*, p. 88.

21. Marure, *Bosquejo*, 1:106; Manuel José Arce, *Memorias*, pp. 19, 29–30; M. Montúfar, *Memorias*, pp. 30–31; "Mensaje de C. Manuel José Arce, Presidente de la Republica al Congreso Federal," 5/1/26, P.R.O., F.O., 254/5, fols. 9–10.

22. The constituent assembly ordered the different jurisdictions to report periodically on the state of their finances, but received few responses. By November 1824, at the eve of the formation of the regular government, reports had not been received from Cartago, Granada, Tegucigalpa, Comayagua, Omoa, and Sonsonate. Neither were reports received from the administrations of sales taxes, aguardiente, and tobacco despite their proximity to the assembly. In early 1825 it was said that figures were still not forthcoming from Salvador, Sonsonate, Comayagua, Tegucigalpa, Cartago, Granada, and the national ports of Omoa and Trujillo. At the end of the year, still another attempt was made, but failed because of lack of "data and cooperation." A.G.G. B6.7, Leg. 91, Exp. 2453, fol. 11; B108.6, Leg. 1941, Exp. 44726; B6.7, Leg. 96, Exp. 2628; B107.5, Leg. 1916; Solórzano F., *Evolución económica*, p. 284.

23. A.G.G. B5.7, Leg. 3478, Exp. 79421; B10.5, Leg. 173, Exps. 3635, 3637, Leg. 174, Exp. 3657. The list of voluntary contributions in 1823 and 1824 is confused by the conflicting jurisdictions of the federal and state governments. In March 1824 a voluntary subscription was opened by the federation to purchase armaments, in November it requested a "patriotic subscription," and a month later a loan of 6,000 pesos was asked to establish fortifications along the coasts. For its part, the state requested an 80,000 peso loan as soon as its constituent assembly was formed in September 1824. It promised the federation 23,000 pesos out of the loan, though only 10,000 were sent. The state also attempted to "hechar mano" into the Indian community funds, but found that the funds had been exhausted by federal authorities. It was said that between February 1822 and June 1824 money had been taken from the fund for "diverse reasons," including the support of deputies to the Mexican congress, and by early 1825 only active debts were remaining as assets. A.G.G. B11.6, Leg. 195, Exp. 4241; B10.5, Leg. 176, Exp. 3763; B6.7, Leg. 101, Exp. 2864; B6.7, Leg. 93, Exp. 2527, Leg. 96, Exps. 2628, 2632,

Leg. 101, Exp. 2864; B1.11.6, Leg. 195, Exps. 4291 and 4295; Smith "Financing the Central American Federation, 1821–1838," pp. 494–95, 500–1.

24. A.G.G. B10.5, Leg. 174, Exp. 3668; B6.8, Leg. 94, Exp. 2557; B6.7, Leg. 95, Exp. 2606.

25. A.G.G. B1.08, Leg. 3484, Exp. 7941, fol. 70; B10.5, Leg. 174, Exp. 3685, fol. 6, Exp. 3686; B5.7, Leg. 4127, Exp. 92807; B11.6, Leg. 201, Exp. 46281; B6.7, Leg. 95, Exp. 4628; Chamorro, *La historia*, pp. 124–25.

26. A.G.G. B1.08, Leg. 3484, Exp. 79641.

27. A.G.G. B1.08, Leg. 3484, Exp. 7945.

28. A.G.G. B6.7, Leg. 95, Exp. 2597; B11.7, Leg. 197, Exp. 4398; Haefkens, *Viaje*, p. 300.

29. The two factors—contraband and interior state resistance to paying of receipts—sometimes combined. Honduras would send its tobacco into Guatemala, undercutting the official national price of the product and trading illegally outside its own borders.

In 1824 the National Assembly discussed whether to abolish the tobacco monopoly. José del Valle argued in favor of its continuance because the tax fell chiefly upon Spanish and ladinos since Indians did not smoke. If the monopoly were removed, he claimed, another tax would have to be put in its place that would be imposed on all classes of society. Thus, Valle's argument was based on the protection of Indians. Another factor must have been the huge amount of revenue involved, a sum that would be difficult to receive from any other levy. Thus, the National Assembly voted to keep the monopoly, deciding that the shares the states were to provide the federal government should come from the tobacco revenue. José del Valle, *Discurso . . . sobre la renta de tabacos* (Guatemala, 1824).

30. "Report of the Minister of Finance on the Revenue of the Republic," P.R.O., F.O., 15/7, fols. 35–36; George A. Thompson, *Narrative of an Official Visit to Guatemala*, pp. 71–72.

31. Guatemalans also continued a clandestine commerce with the Mosquito Shore, where Belize and Jamaican merchants came to trade. Nevertheless, the basic trade was with Belize, in what was termed by the British consul in 1826 as holding a "smuggling monopoly." Schenley to Planta, 5/31/26, P.R.O., F.O., 15/5, fol. 345; O'Reilly to Canning, 2/22/26, P.R.O., F.O., 15/5, fol. 67.

32. Mariano de Aycinena, Luis de Aguirre, and Pedro de Sarrando, "Official Commercial Report by the Commission on the State of Commerce," P.R.O., F.O., 15/3, fols. 81–82; *La Gazeta del Gobierno*, 3/1824, p. 8; Aycinena to O'Reilly, 1/10/26, P.R.O., F.O., 15/7, fol. 100. Chamorro, *La Historia*, p. 141.

33. "Official Commercial Report," p. 80; Aycinena to O'Reilly, 1/10/26, P.R.O., F.O., 15/5, fol. 100.

34. 2,000 Mexican pesos were worth 1,920 Central American pesos in 1827; the two coins were at par in 1821. Dashwood to Backhouse, 3/3/31, P.R.O., F.O., 15/11. A.G.G. B6.7, Leg. 93, Exp. 2529; B10.8, Leg. 3484, Exp. 79642.

35. "Mint in Guatemala," 5/8/27, P.R.O., F.O., 15/5, fols. 101–2; *El Indicator*, 11/1/1824, p. 16; A.G.G. B10.5, Leg. 174, Exp. 3673; B108.6, Leg. 1935, Exp. 44434.

36. O'Reilly to Bidwell, 5/30/27, P.R.O., F.O., 15/7, fols. 142–47.

37. It was said that some 2.5 million pesos were annually traded in British dry goods by the local commercial houses. In Jamaica the houses of Benito Pérez and Antonio Imaterio sold an additional 535,000 pesos to the mainland. There were also 153,000 pesos in goods smuggled into Omoa and Nicaragua by diverse sources. "Attempted Explanatory Statement of the Values of His Majesty's Colony at Belize as Connected with its Com-

mercial Transactions with the New Republic of Guatemala 1825," P.R.O., F.O., 15/3, fols. 108–12.

38. Mariano Aycinena et al., "Official Commercial Report," P.R.O., F.O., 15/3, fols. 79–82.

39. "A Statement of Entries of Vessels into the Harbour of Acajutla," P.R.O., F.O., 15/5, Appendix No. 10, fols. 111–12; A.G.G. B9.2, Leg. 3421, Exp. 2495; O'Reilly to Canning, 2/22/26, P.R.O., F.O., 15/5, fol. 64.

40. "Official Commercial Report," fols. 174–76; "Trading Capital or List of the Chief Families in the City of Guatemala," P.R.O., F.O., 15/3, fols. 105–06.

41. Aycinena to O'Reilly, 1/10/26, P.R.O., F.O., 15/5, fols. 101–2; O'Reilly to Bidwell, 8/5/26, P.R.O., F.O., 15/5, fol. 193.

42. *El Indicador*, 1/17/1825, p. 76: *La Gazeta del Gobierno*, 3/1/1824, p. 8; *La Gazeta de Guatemala*, 2/13/1797, p. 16; A.G.G. B78.5, Leg. 625, Exp. 12516; A3.3, Leg. 2368, Exp. 34985.

43. A.G.G. B5.7, Leg. 66, Exp. 1816, fols. 1, 7, Exp. 1819, Fol. 29; B6.7, Leg. 95, Exp. 2589, fol. 10, Exp. 2591.

44. Haefkens, *Viaje*, p. 260; George Thompson, *Narrative*, p. 455; Aycinena et al., "Official Commercial Report," P.R.O., F.O., 15/3, fol. 89.

45. Decrees of the "Supremo Poder Ejecutivo," 1/22, 2/10, 7/13, 11/21/1824 and 1/7, 9/16/1825, all to be found in the N.Y.P.L.; A.G.G. B11.5, Leg. 191, Exp. 4120.

14. States Into Nations

1. Bumgartner, *José del Valle*, pp. 236–37; Philip F. Flemion, "States Rights and Partisan Politics," pp. 600–18, Arce, *Memorias*, pp. 19–20; Marure, *Bosquejo*, 1:138–40; M. Montúfar, *Memorias*, p. 28; A.G.G. B5.7, Leg. 4126, Exp. 92807.

2. Colombia claimed the Mosquito Coast from Cape Gracias a Dios south, because of a cédula of November 30, 1803, that granted that territory to New Granada. Central America argued that the cédula was meant to provide the coast with military defense and was not a transfer in sovereignty. The British consul reported in February 1826 that "the state of affairs between this country and Mexico daily assumes a more serious aspect." A newspaper in Mexico reported a resolution in that nation's *Camara de Diputados* authorizing the government to annex Guatemalan regions, to which the federation's Congress reacted by declaring that, if such a plan was carried out, Central America would take "equal action" toward Mexican towns.

A Guatemalan state commission concluded that the northern regions that threatened secession could not be controlled due to a lack of arms and ammunition. As late as June 1826 the rumors of Mexican hostilities continued. A Guatemalan commander reported the movement of Mexican troops that month. It was later learned that there were just nineteen soldiers involved. On the Guatemalan side, the Minister of War reported that it was almost impossible to maintain troops on the border because so many soldiers deserted. A.G.G. B10.8, Leg. 3483, Exp. 79641, fols. 7–9, 18, 253, 497–98, 549; Exps. 79667, 79679; B11.6, Leg. 195, Exp. 4333, Leg. 197, Exps. 4388, 4396, 4397, 4403, 4406; B61.5, Leg. 106, Exp. 2885; B6.21, Leg. 84, Exp. 2387; B7.8, Leg. 133, Exp. 3127. O'Reilly to Canning 2/17, and O'Reilly to Bidwell, 10/30/1826, P.R.O., F.O., 15/5, fols. 8–9, 216; Thompson to the Minister of Foreign Affairs, 12/31/1824, P.R.O., F.O., 15/1, fol. 99. Gordon Ireland, *Boundaries, Possessions, and Conflicts in Central and North America and the Caribbean*, pp. 24–26, 164–65.

3. Flemion, "States Rights and Partisan Politics," p. 614; A.G.G. B10.8, Leg. 3483, Exp. 79641, fols. 194, 195, 198, 205, 226, 276, 314, 315, 363; "Mensaje del C. Manuel José Arce," P.R.O., F.O., 214/5, fol. 111; Marure, *Bosquejo*, 1:151–53; Arce, *Memorias*, p. 38; M. Montúfar, *Memorias*, pp. 49–50.

4. A.G.G. B7.8, Leg. 135, Exp. 3150, fols. 1–2; B10.8, Leg. 3883, Exp. 79641, fols. 160–61, 460, 487–88; Joseph Lockey, "Diplomatic Futility," pp. 270–71; O'Reilly to Canning, 2/17/1826 and 3/31/1828, P.R.O., F.O., 15/5, fols. 8, 180.

5. *Primera Esposición de los Documentos y Motivos para el Decreto de Arresto del Jefe del Estado* (Guatemala, 1826), unpaginated; Marure, *Bosquejo*, 1:161, 171, 179–91; M. Montúfar, *Memorias*, pp. 52–84; Batres Jáurequi, *La América Central ante la historia*,, 3:112–13; O'Reilly to Bidwell, 10/10, 11/5, 11/18/1826, P.R.O., F.O., 15/5, fols. 210–13, 233, 312; A.G.G. B10.8, Leg. 3483, Exp. 79641, fols. 655, 657, 682, 704, 743–44; B7.26, Leg. 3480, Exp. 79487.

6. The arrival of liberal Guatemalan refugees in Salvador combined with the open plans of Arce to assert central authority throughout all of Central America and his opposition to a Salvador diocese led to a break between the Salvadoran government and the Federation. The diocese issue will be examined shortly.

7. Some battles were influenced by the presence of indigo plantations and the harvest season. The Aycinenas were charged by political opponents in Guatemala with using the national armies to protect their haciendas. Soldiers on the liberal side of the conflict left the army to return to farms to harvest indigo. The dye that was seized by Salvadoran forces from Aycinena haciendas was used to purchase arms from a passing French vessel, the Boyer. In the midst of the civil war a Spanish privateer entered the Bay of Honduras and seized arms and indigo owned by the federal government. For various descriptions of the conflict, see Francisco Morazán, *Memorias*, the *Memorias* of Manuel Arce, Manuel Montúfar, and Miguel García Granados, previously cited, as well as the dispatches of the English consuls O'Reilly and Moyle in P.R.O., F.O., 15/7 and 15/8. Also see the description made by the Dutch consul Jacobo Haefkens, *Viaje a Guatemala y Centroamérica.*

8. A.G.G. B118.9, Leg. 2431, Exps. 50906–51015; B7.2, Leg. 146, Exp. 3194; B10.5, Leg. 174, Exps. 3694, 3695, 3699, 3705; "Decreto de 16 de octubre 1829," in N.Y.P.L.

9. See A.S.V., Arch Nunz., Madrid 270, for the documents concerning Spanish liberalism.

10. *Ibid.*, see in particular in this file "Esposición De Los Documentos Y Motivos Para El Decreto De Estrañamiento Del Territorio de La República Del Obispo . . . D. José Santiago Rodríguez (Santiago de Chile, 1826).

11. The existence of an illegal Salvadoran diocese in the face of opposition by central church authorities forced President Arce into a dilemma in 1826. As a supporter of central power, and now aligned with conservative Guatemalan families, he had to maintain some relationship with the archdiocese. Any alliance between him and the central church would be viewed with antipathy from Salvador. In early December the inevitable split occurred. Archbishop Casaus had proclaimed the following year as a jubilee year, but excluded the State of Salvador from its celebration because of the ecclesiastical revolt. The publication of the document, without any resistance from Arce, led to the realization in Salvador that the president could no longer be trusted. Although the Salvadorans did not know it, the man who advised Rome on the diocese issue was José Aycinena through the papel nuncio in Madrid, where Aycinena still lived. A.S.V., Arch. Nunz. Madrid, Vol. 270, various dispatches in 1824 and 1825; also valuable on this issue are the A.S.V., Segreteria de Stato Esteri 279, and the Sacra Congregazione Degli Affari Ecclesiastici Straordinari: Guatemala Pos 1–3, 4, 5, 9/Fascs. 507, 511, and

512; Holleran, *Church and State in Guatemala*, pp. 65, 108–112; "Informe del Cabildo Eclesiástico de Guatemala, P.R.O., F.O., 15/2, fol. 87; *Anexión*, 2:101; A.G.G. B83.1, Leg. 1111, Exp. 24752, fols. 1–4; Marure, *Bosquejo*, 1:xxv–xxxx; Chamorro, *Historia*, p. 197; A.G.G. B83.1, Leg. 1111, Exp. 24784; Arce, *Memorias*, pp. 85, 113, 156; L. Montúfar, *Reseña históra*, 5:154–57; M. Montúfar, *Memorias*, pp. 33, 170; Haefkens, *Viaje*, p. 231; "Suite des événements de Guatemala" (by Cochelet) A.M.A.E.F., C.C.-1, fol. 21; Quémónt au Ministre des Affaires Etrangères, 11/18/1830, A.M.A.E.F. Dépêches-I, 134.

12. A.G.G. B7.2, Leg. 146, Exp. 3194; B10.5, Leg. 174, Exps. 3694, 3695, 3699, 3705; B5.7, Leg. 4123, Exp. 92809, fols. 51–66; "Decreto de 16 de octubre 1829," in N.Y.P.L.; B118.9, Leg. 2434, Exps. 51511, 51545, 51547; B83.1, Leg. 3520, Exps. 82235, 82236, fols. 3, 93: Haefkens, *Viaje*, pp. 237–38.

13. Haefkens, *Viaje*, pp. 234–35; L. Montúfar, *Reseña Historia*, 1:189–202.

14. See the dispatches of Hall to Bidwell in 1831 and 1832, P.R.O., F.O., 15/11 and 12, and the letter of Pedro Molina to Hall, 5/14/1832, P.R.O., F.O., 253/3, unpaginated.

15. Hall to Bidwell, 5/18 and 10/10/1832, P.R.O., F.O., 15/12, fols. 46, 88–89; L. Montúfar, *Reseña historia*, 1:151–68, 194.

16. See L. Montúfar, *Reseña Historia*, 2:133, as well as the dispatches of Hall to Bidwell in P.R.O., 15/12 and 15/13, and those of DeClairambault to Ministre in A.M.A.E.F., Dépêches-2.

17. Gálvez was originally allied with the Barrundia family, but slowly became more independent. Gálvez served as an official under the Mexican empire, and later became president of the federal congress in 1825. During the civil war he was forced into retirement in Antigua and in January 1829 led a revolt against the weakening forces of Mariano Aycinena. With the reestablishment of liberal government. Gálvez reorganized the finances of the state before becoming governor. His power was so great that Morazán attempted to send him as envoy to France in 1831, in order to rid the president of a potential rival. Salazar, *Historia de veintiún años*, pp. 232–33; Marure, *Bosquejo*, 1:25; L. Montúfar, *Reseña historia*, 1:180, 284; Chatfield to Palmerston, 1/30/1836, P.R.O., F.O., 15/18, fol. 49.

18. Anti-church legislation earned the wrath of the clergy. Gálvez sent inspectors into convents, asking each nun whether she wished to leave. The decree curtailing religious holidays brought declarations from the church that "God ordered that on certain days men should not work, and before one obeys men, he must obey God. "Mensaje del Gefe del Estado de Guatemala Dr. Mariano Gálvez al abrirse las sesiones ordinarias de la Asamblea Legislativa en 1836" and "Mensaje del Gefe del Estado de Guatemala Dr. Mariano Gálvez al abrir sus sesiones ordinarias la Asamblea Legislativa en 1837," in P.R.O., F.O., 254/5, fols. 112–13, 118; Chatfield to Palmerston, 12/12/1824, F.O., 15/14, fol. 331. L. Montúfar, *Reseña historia*, 1:309–23, 2:76–78; Lanning, *Eighteenth-Century Enlightenment*, pp. 258–59; Holleran, *Church and State*, p. 112; "Decreto de la Asamblea Legislativa de 5 de diciembre de 1835" and "Decreto de la Asamblea Legislativa de 29 de marzo de 1836" in Jorge Skinner-Klée, *Legislación in-digenísta de Guatemala*. For the important role Gálvez played in encouraging foreign colonization, see William J. Griffith's *Empires in the Wilderness*.

19. In 1825 a year's revenue from the tax was but 3,457 pesos in the interior, a great reduction from the 100,000 pesos received annually under the Spanish tributary system in Guatemala. A.G.G. B6.7, Leg. 96, Exp. 2625; B10.5, Leg. 173, Exp. 3643, fol. 27, Exp. 3645, fols. 1, 4, B11.6, Leg. 195, Exp. 4275, Leg. 200, Exp. 4275.

20. A.G.G. B108.6, Leg. 1944, Exp. 44743, Leg. 1948, Exp. 44750; B108.5, Leg. 1922, Exp. 44060.

21. A.G.G. B5.7, Leg. 4126, Exp. 92829, fol. 4; B10.5, Leg. 177, Exp. 3778, fol. 2; B108.6, Leg. 1943, Exp. 44741, Leg. 1944, Exp. 44743, Leg. 1947, Exp. 4479.

22. A.G.G. B107.3, Leg. 3656, Exp. 86474; B1.10, Leg. 2353, Exps. 47301, 47302; B110.1, Leg. 2353, Exps. 47303–47321, 47330, B108.5, Leg. 1931, Exp. 44257.

23. Ministre du Commerce au Ministre des Affairs Etrangères, 5/2/1832, A.M.A.E.F. CC-1, fol. 85; Dashwood to Backhouse, 3/3/1831, P.R.O., F.O., 15/11, fols. 8–9.

24. In 1864, 1870, 1875, 1881, and 1891, indigo furnished producers 1,129,105, 2,619,749, 1,160,700, 1,470,300, and 892,092 pesos. Browning, *El Salvador, Landscape and Society*, pp. 160–62, 309–11; Chatfield to Palmerston, 3/1/1836, 6/26/1837, and 12/20/1839, P.R.O., F.O., 15/18, fol. 64, F.O., 15/19, fol. 98, F.O., 15/22, fol. 315; Robert Dunlop, *Travels in Central America*, p. 19.

25. DeClairambault to Ministre, 2/8/1835, A.M.A.E.F. CC-1, 310.

26. Chatfield to Palmerston, 6/26/1837, P.R.O., F.O., 15/19, fol. 98; Rubio, "La grana o cochinella," in *Antropología e Historia de Guatemala*, 13:29; García Granados, *Memorias*, 4:444.

27. Chatfield to Palmerston, 4/4 and 3/5/1838, P.R.O., F.O., 15/20, fols. 112–15, 135.

28. A.G.G. B87.1, Leg. 1191, Exp. 28986; B108.5, Leg. 1921, Exp. 43990, Leg. 1922, Exps. 44049, 44053, 44056; García Granados, *Memorias*, 3:340; Dashwood to Backhouse, 3/3/1831, P.R.O., F.O., 15/11, fol. 13.

29. A.G.G. B10.5, Leg. 179, Exp. 3831, fol. 9; B108.5, Leg. 1921, Exp. 53998; B119.2, Leg. 2521, Exp. 56993, fols. 38, 41; B5.7, Leg. 4126, Exp. 92815, fol. 14.

30. The rifles were worth 5,000 pesos. In March 1835 the British envoy reported that "the grant of territory . . . to a company in London is received with dissatisfaction by the Mexican agents possibly (because) of the impediment it offers to the prospect of extending their frontier into Vera Paz." Seven months later the same consul claimed "that the government of (Mexico) would with a view (sic) to reach the Caribbean sea, seize any opportunity to extend its eastern frontier at the expense of this Republic. . . . the Mexican Government contemplated offering to Central America the province of Soconusco in exchange for the district of Petén in the Department of Vera Paz and adjoining the British settlement in Honduras." Chatfield to Wellington and to Palmerston, 3/16 and 10/8/1835, P.R.O., F.O., 15/16, fols. 39, 259; A.G.G. B108.5, Leg. 1922, Exp. 44053; Chatfield to Palmerston, 8/25/1834, 12/22/1837, P.R.O., F.O., 15/14, fols. 155–60, F.O., 15/19, fol. 208; Chatfield to Wellington, 6/1/1835, P.R.O., F.O., 15/16, fol. 99.

31. "Some cutters who are operating under a grant from the King of the Mosquito Shore were forced off by the Governor of Trujillo and M. Bennett." (Superintendent of Belize) MacDonald to Lord Glenly, 2/12/1837, P.R.O., F.O., 15/19, fol. 230; Chatfield to Palmerston, 8/25/1834, P.R.O., F.O., 15/14, fols. 163–64; L. Montúfar, *Reseña historia*, 1:244.

32. "Mr. Bennett found himself in the comical position of using his best influence to get grants to territory made around Belize, which in Belize as a Magistrate, he votes to be an unwarrantable encroachment on the part of the very persons he a few weeks before urged to make the cession." P.R.O., F.O., 252/15, cited by Mario Rodríguez, *A Palmerstonian Diplomat in Central America*, p. 73.

33. Each ton of mahogany was said to produce a "clear profit" of 100 pesos. Bennett gave the state of Honduras a mint "whose value is estimated at 30,000 pesos."

The logging business seemed to the British envoys very lucrative, but "the whole of their enormous profit passes into the pockets of four or five individuals." Nevertheless,

Morazán later wrote a friend that he had not received much money from the enterprise, claiming that out of 29,000 pesos worth of trees sold, he had received only 2,000 pesos.

The Nicaraguan coup and the assassination of Morazán's ally, Governor Zepeda, occurred when the official attempted to get the approval of a wood-cutting contract from the state assembly. The state leader was to receive a share of the profit. He had, the British consul said, "an insatiable capacity in monopolizing the principal sources of wealth in the state." Chatfield to Palmerston 9/16/1835, 5/27/1836, and 8/19/1837, B.P.R.O., F.O., 15/16, fols. 170, 176; F.O., 15/18, fol. 92; and F.O., 15/19, fol. 181; A.G.G. B85.1, Leg. 1151, Exp. 26611, Leg. 1152, Exp. 26670; B96.1, Leg. 3619, Exp. 8470; B108.5, Leg. 1922, Exp. 44053.

The fear of English expansion led to a number of misunderstandings. In 1830 twenty-five French families attempted to establish a colony along the Mosquito Coast, but were chased by the Indians. When they arrived at Trujillo, the local commander gave them permission to settle on the island of Roatan in the Bay of Honduras. Some days later a British boat from Belize landed them on the island, where they were met by some Central Americans who considered the settlement an invasion. Word was sent to Guatemala and the government responded by sending 100 soldiers to Roatan, with an angry letter to Belize demanding an explanation.

Some forty years later the Guatemalan historian Lorenzo Montúfar wrote: "one of the measures that most honors (President) Barrundia is having saved the island of Roatan which was occupied by the British" *Reseña historia,* 1:271. For a contemporary narrative of the events see Cochelet to Ministry, A.M.A.E.F. CC-1, 92, 8/16/1830; Dashwood to Backhouse, 11/3/30 (and the attached Ibarra to Dashwood, 7/3/1830, that protests the "occupation"), and the correspondence from the commissioner of Belize, Cockburn to Dashwood, 9/9/1830, that explains the error in landing and assisting the French settlers. P.R.O., F.O., 15/10, fol. 209.

34. Hall to Bidwell, 12/20/1833, P.R.O., F.O., 15/13, fol. 34; García Granados, *Memorias,* 3:314; L. Montúfar, *Reseña historia,* 2:133.

35. Hall to Bidwell, 6/7, and Chatfield to Palmerston, 8/11/1834, P.R.O., F.O., 15/14, fols. 145 and 15/15/, fol. 17. A new state of Salvador was established with its capital located in San Miguel.

36. "Mensaje del Gefe del Estado de Guatemala, Dr. Mariano Gálvez al avrirse las sesiones ordinarias de la Asamblea Legislativa," in P.R.O., F.O., 254/5, fol. 113.

37. L. Montúfar, *Reseña historia,* 2:333–43; Skinner-Klée, *Legislación indigenista,* p. 22; A.G.G. B108.5, Leg. 1922, Exp. 44065; Chatfield to Palmerston, 9/20/1837, P.R.O., F.O., 15/19, fol. 143.

38. A.G.G. B82.4, Leg. 1102, Exps. 24407–24429; B82.4, Leg. 3588, Exps. 81913, 82034–82048; B119.2, Leg. 2521, Exp. 56991, fols. 1, 13.

39. The cholera epidemic was not, of course, limited to the state of Guatemala, but spread throughout all of Central America. The epidemic, traveling via Honduras, reached the city of Salvador eleven days prior to Guatemala City's infection. But the best reports of the effect of the epidemic come from Guatemala. The Mazatenango figures represent minimal illness and mortality rates, as many Indians fled to the mountains to escape the epidemic and some probably died. A.G.G. B82.4, Leg. 1102, Exps. 24432–24444; B82.4, Leg. 3588, Exps. 42049–42061; B5.7, Leg. 4126, Exp. 92816, fol. 5; Chatfield to Palmerston, 6/26/37, P.R.O., F.O., 15/19, fols. 95, 96.

40. Of 640 people attacked by May, only twelve (or 2 percent) were children, of whom five died. A.G.G. B108.7, Leg. 1938, Exp. 44606; B82.4, Legs. 1102–1106. "El Gefe del Estado a Los Habitantes del Mismo," P.R.O., F.O., 254/5, fol. 130; "Razon de

las Cantidades que adeuda la Hacienda Publica . . ." A.G.G. B1.12, Leg. 2365, Exp. 48477.

41. L. Montúfar, *Reseña historia*, 2:348–60; A.G.G. B82.4, Leg. 1104, Exp. 24545, fols. 10, 12; Chatfield to Palmerston, 6/26/37, P.R.O., F.O., 15/19, fol. 101.

42. L. Montúfar, *Reseña historia*, 2:363–96; García Granados, *Memorias*, 4:436–40.

43. Chatfield to Palmerston, 2/5/1838, P.R.O., F.O., 15/20, fols. 64–65. For the best description of the rise of Carrera, see Ralph Lee Woodward, Jr., "Social Revolution in Guatemala: The Carrera Revolt," *Applied Enlightenment*, pp. 45–70. For the important role played by the English consul in this turbulent era see Rodríguez, *A Palmerstonian Diplomat in Central America: Frederick Chatfield, Esq.*

44. Chatfield to Palmerston, 2/5/1838, P.R.O., F.O., 15/20, fols. 65–66.

45. Chatfield to Palmerston, 2/16/1838, P.R.O., F.O., 15/20, fol. 80; L. Montúfar, *Reseña historia*, 2:490.

46. Chatfield to Palmerston, 2/16 and 3/7/1838, P.R.O., F.O., 15/20, fols. 82, 116; L. Montúfar, *Reseña historia*, 3:76–79.

47. A.G.G. B1.12, Leg. 2356, Exp. 48536; Chatfield to Palmerston, 5/6/1838, P.R.O., F.O., 15/20, fol. 231; L. Montúfar, *Reseña historia*, 2:275–77, 286, 3:9–13.

48. Chatfield to Palmerston, 6/5 and 8/4/1838, P.R.O., F.O., 15/20, fols. 231, 277. A.G.G. B1.12, Leg. 2356, Exp. 4856; B1.19, Leg. 2543, Exp. 58789.

49. Chatfield to Palmerston, 8/18, 8/22, 10/2/1838, P.R.O., F.O., 15/20, fol. 301–2, 305, 347–48. By January 1839 it could be said that "the merchants and property owners are nearly ruined by the heavy loans." Chatfield to Macdonald, 9/20/1838 and 1/21/1839; P.R.O., F.O., 15/20, fol. 349, F.O., 15/22, fol. 28; A.G.G. B1.12, Leg. 2356, Exps. 48555, 48567, 48576; B119.9, Leg. 2543, Exp. 58773; B1.12, Leg. 2365, Exps. 48453, 48476, 48500, 48526, 48545.

50. The history of the Honduran-Nicaraguan alliance illustrates this conflict between "two or three families." While Morazán controlled Honduras, his brother-in-law's brother claimed an abandoned mine, which, under the law, was his right. Together with Marshall Bennett, he invested money and machinery in the project which proved profitable. The original owner sued to obtain possession of the mine and, when that suit failed, arranged a coup that deposed the pro-Morazán government. The new government sent an agent to Nicaragua and the alliance was formed. Chatfield to Palmerston, 11/15/1838; 3/6/, 4/20, and 6/5/1839, P.R.O., F.O., 15/20, fol. 389, F.O., 15/22, fols. 141–43, 149, 167; L. Montúfar, *Reseña historia*, 3:354–56; A.G.G. B.102.2, Leg. 166, Exp. 3481, fols. 2, 4, 12; Mahelin to Ministry, 9/28, 10/26/1839, A.M.A.E.F. Dépêches-3, 28, 30.

51. The "offensive and defensive" treaties between the nations symbolized more than anything else the destruction of any pretense of a Central American government: 1/18/39, Honduras and Nicaragua; 5/7, Honduras and Guatemala; 6/5, Guatemala and Salvador; 7/24, Nicaragua and Guatemala; 8/1, Costa Rica and Guatemala; 7/1, Honduras and Costa Rica. L. Montúfar, *Reseña historia*, 3:297–302, 310; A.G.G. B99.3;, Leg. 1413, Exps. 33005, 33008; B87.2, Leg. 1195, B11.8, Leg. 2437, Exp. 51825; Chatfield to Palmerston, 2/13, 5/3, and 11/7/1839, P.R.O., F.O., 15/22, fols. 61–63, 154, 267.

52. Chatfield to Palmerston, 7/5/1839, P.R.O., F.O., 15/22, fol. 208.

53. Mahelin to Ministry, 9/28/1839, A.M.A.E.F. Dépêches-3, 28.

54. John L. Stephens, *Incidents of Travel in Central America, Chiapas, and Yucatan*, 1:76–79.

55. *Ibid.*, 2:27.

56. *Ibid.*, 1:323–24.

57. Mahelin au Ministre, 3/24 and 4/18/1840, A.M.A.E.F.-Dépêches-3, 77–78, 84;

336 14. States Into Nations

L. Montúfar, Reseña historia, 3:325, 377, 484; Stephens, Incidents of Travel, 1:211; A.G.G. B87.1, Leg. 1192, Exp. 29042.

15. Caudillos, Castes, and Conclusions

1. Woodward, "Social Revolution in Guatemala," in Applied Enlightenment, pp. 45–70.

2. Ephraim George Squier, Notes on Central America, p. 520; Guía de forasteros de Guatemala para el año 1853, p. 93.

3. Guía de forasteros de Guatemala, pp. 21, 80. For other observations on Guatemala, see Le Père Cornette, Relation d'un voyage de México à Guatémala dans le cours de l'année 1855; G. F. Von Tempsky, Mitla; Karl Scherzer, Travels in the Free States of Central America, Nicaragua, and San Salvador; Squier, Notes on Central America.

4. See A.S.V., S. Congr. Concil. Rel. 383, "Relación del estado de la Iglesia Metropolitana de Guatemala."

5. An excellent description of the economy of cattle lands and other farms is given by Pablo Lévy, Notas geográficas y económicas sobre la república de Nicaragua. Also see Auguste Myionnet Dupuy, Deux Ans de séjour dans l'état de Nicaragua 1850, 1851, 1852.

6. William V. Wells, Explorations and Adventures in Honduras.

7. Ibid., pp. 271–389.

8. Lévy, Notas geográficas y económicas, pp. 441–447, Myionnet Dupuy, Deux Ans de séjour, pp. 28–31.

9. Myionnet Dupuy, Deux Ans de séjour. Also see Lévy, Notas geográficas y económica.

10. Stephens, Incidents of Travel in Central America, Chiapas, and Yucatan, 1:5, 61–62.

11. Ibid., 1:170–71.

Appendix A

1. See A.G.I. Guatemala 947 and 949 for a description of the tithe in Guatemala in the late eighteenth century. See Guatemala 908 for Honduras and Guatemala 909 for Nicaragua. Also, "Memoria de todos los Generos y Especies de que deve pagar el Diezmo en este Obispado de Goathemala" (1732) in the British Museum.

Appendix D

1. Robert M. Carmack, Quichean Civilization, pp. 140, 141, citing A.G.I. Guatemala 45 and 394.; A.G.I. Contratación 4730 A Carta Cuenta, 1618; Guatemala 679, El Informe del gobernador de Guatemala, 8/23/1764; García Peláez, Memorias, 1:180.

2. A.G.I. Guatemala 679, El Informe del gobernador de Guatemala, 8/23/1764.

3. A.G.I. Guatemala 354, Año de 1739, Cuenta de tributos; Guatemala 743, Contador General, 10/22/1778.

4. Cortés y Larraz, *Descripción*, 2:275–77.

5. Rosenblat, 1:188, *La Gazeta de Guatemala*, 11/22/1802; Juarros, 1:16, 46, 91; Marure, *Bosquejo*, 1:148.

6. Lutz, "Santiago de Guatemala."

Glossary

aguardiente   brandy, rum, spirits
alcabala   sales tax
alcalde ordinario   chief official of
   the cabildo
alcalde mayor   provincial official
Alférez Real   royal lieutenant
alhondigas   government grain
   warehouses
almoneda   city stock house,
   auction house
añil   indigo
aranceles   schedules
asiento   monopoly
audiencia   ruling tribunal
barlovento   a sales tax
cabildo   municipal council
capellanía   money for a mass
cavallería   105 acres
cédula   decree
Cinco Gremios   Five Guilds
cofradía   sodality
consulado   merchant guild
contador   official auditor
corregidor   provincial official
corte   ordinary cut (of indigo)
ejido   public or common land
embarciónes   export tax
encomienda   grant of tribute-
   paying Indians; pension
estanco   monopoly
flor   finest quality (of indigo)

forasteros   wanderers
gobierno   government jurisdiction
hacendado   owner of large
   agricultural holding
hato   small plot
jefe político   political chief
juez de milpas   judge of plantings
juros   bonds
media anata   tax on salary and
   encomienda
mesada eclesiástica   tax on clerical
   salaries
milpas   corn, corn fields
mozo   servant
nao   ship, vessel
obraje   work shop
oidor   judge
papel sellado   official paper
quinto   the "fifth" tax on mineral
   production
rancheras   settlements
real   one-eighth of a peso
reducciones   expeditions to gather
   and "reduce" Indians into pueblos
regidores   members of the cabildo
reino   kingdom
repartidores   Spanish officials who
   distribute labor
repartimiento   distribution, division
   of labor
salida   export tax

situados   tribute income
sobre saliente   medium quality (of indigo)
tamemes   slave bearers

trapiches   sugar mill
vara   a measure of length
vecino   citizen
visitador   inspector

Bibliography

Most of the data for this study come from primary, archival research. For the colonial period, work in the Archivo General de Indias (A.G.I.) in Seville, Spain, produced excellent information, particularly on the seventeenth and early eighteenth centuries, about which information is missing elsewhere. The Audiencia de Guatemala section in that archive is the most important source for Central America. However, an examination of the fiscal data and, more important, the comments accompanying them in the *contaduría* section were also extremely helpful. Other sections examined, which are also useful, were *Indiferente General, Mapas y Planos*, and *Estado*. Some loose documents are also spread among the papers of the Audiencias of Mexico and of Santa Fe.

The Archivo General de Guatemala de Centro-America (A.G.G.) has ample information, particularly on the epochs of the Bourbon reforms, independence, and the federal government. Here too much missing information can be recovered in those legajos concerned with fiscal matters. The *Protocolos* records also disclosed the fabric of life in colonial Central America.

Both archives complement each other. No scholar can derive an accurate picture of colonial Spanish American history by examining only one of these two sources. Seville received government reports and judicial appeals; Guatemala contains local documents such as wills, licenses, and account books. Documents lost in one archive can frequently be found in the other.

Most of the research done in the Archivo General de Guatemala was accomplished at a time when scholars could review entire legajos. Since then, however, there has been a change in procedure and investigators can now request only expedientes (usually single pages) one at a time. A study such as this work will never again be accomplished without a return to the old method and, as a result, Central American historiography will suffer.

Aside from these archives, I also consulted the Archivo Eclesiástico de Guatemala (A.E.G.), examining, in particular, the section on *cofradías y archicofradías*, and in the Archivo General de la Nación (A.G.N.) in Mexico, particularly the section entitled *consolidación*. For the national period, the British Public Record Office, Foreign Office Series (P.R.O., F.O.) and in the

Archives du Ministre des Affaires Etrangères (Français) (A.M.A.E.F.) the series on Central America and Guatemala were particularly helpful. So too were the documents on church-state relations in the eighteenth and nineteenth centuries in the Archivo Segreto Vaticano and the Archivum Romanum Societatis Iesus in Rome. There exist diverse manuscripts on both colonial and national periods in the French Bibliothèque Nationale, the British Museum, and the New York Public Library.

The libraries where rare documents listed below can be found are given the initials B.N. (Bibliothèque Nationale, Paris), B.M. (British Museum) and N.Y.P.L (New York Public Library).

Adams, Eleanor B. "A Bio-Bibliography of Franciscan Authors in Colonial Central America," *The Americas* (1952), 8:431–71; (1952), 9:37–86.

Alamán, Lucas. *Historia de Méjico desde los primeros movimientos que prepararon su independencia en el año de 1808 hasta la época presente.* 5 vols. Mexico: J. M. Lara, 1849–52.

Alcázar Molina, Cayetano. *Los virreinatos en el siglo XVIII*, vol. 10. Madrid: Salvat Editores, 1945.

Alden, Dauril. "The Growth and Decline of Indigo Production in Colonial Brazil: A Study in Comparative Economic History." *Journal of Economic History* (1965), 25:35–60.

Alvarez, Juan. *Las guerras civiles argentinas y el problema de Buenos Aires en La República.* Buenos Aires: Biblioteca de la Sociedad de Historia Argentina, 1936.

Amerlinck, María Concepción. *Las catedrales de Santiago de Los Caballeros de Guatemala.* Tesis, Universidad Iberoamericana, Mexico, 1971.

Anderson, Perry. *Lineages of the Absolutist State.* London: Humanities Press, 1974.

Andrien, Kenneth James. "The Royal Treasury and Society in Seventeenth Century Lima." Dissertation. Duke University, Durham, No. Carolina, 1977.

Annals of the Cakchiquels, The. Adrián Recinos and Delia Goetz, trans. Norman: University of Oklahoma Press, 1953.

Antiguo Diplomático, Un. "La Union de Centro-América." *Revista Mexicana de Derecho Internacional* (1920), 2:517–33.

Antuñez y Acevedo. *Memorias históricas sobre la legislación y gobierno del comercio de los españoles con sus colonias.* Madrid, 1797 (B.N.).

Apuntamientos sobre la agricultura y comercio del reino de Guatemala que el Señor Don Antonio Larrazábal diputado en los cortes extraordinarias de la nación por la misma ciudad pidió al real consulado en junta de gobierno de 20 de octubre de 1810. Nueva Guatemala: Manuel de Arevalo, 1811 (B.M.).

Araña, Tomás de. "Relación de los estragos y ruinas que ha padecido la ciudad de Santiago de Guatemala, por los terremotos y fuego de sus volcánes, en este año de 1717." *Anales de la Sociedad de Geografía e Historia* (Guatemala) (1941), 17:148–60, 232–43.

Arce, Manuel José. *Memorias*. San Salvador: Editorial Ahora, 1947.

Arcila Farías, Eduardo. *Comercio entre Venezuela y México en los siglos XVI y XVII*. Mexico: El Colegio de Mexico, 1950.

Ardant, Gabriel. *Histoire de l'impôt*. 2 vols. Paris: S.E.V.P.E.N., 1971.

Aycinena, Juan José. *Discurso pronunciado en la casa del supremo gobierno del Estado de Guatemala*. Guatemala: Imprenta del Gobierno, 1840. (B.M. and N.Y.P.L).

—— *Observaciones críticas con motivo de la impresión de una correspondencia entre el jefe del estado y el Sr. J. Barrundia*. Guatemala: Academia de Estudios, 1837 (B.M. and N.Y.P.L.).

—— *Otras reflexiónes sobre reforma política en Centro-América*. New Amsterdam: José Caieja, 1832 (B.M. and N.Y.P.L.).

—— Otras reflexiónes. New York: José Caieja, 1834 (B.M. and N.Y.P.L.).

—— *Reflexiónes sobre la necesidad de una reforma política en Centro-América*. New Amsterdam: José Caieja, 1832 (B.M. and N.Y.P.L.).

Ayón, Tomás. *Historia de Nicaragua*. 2d ed. Madrid: Escuela Profesional de Artes Gráficas, 1956.

Bagú, Sergio. *Estructura social de la colonia. Ensayo de historia comparada de América Latina*. Buenos Aires: Libreria "El Ateneo" Editorial, 1952.

Bailyn, Bernard, "Communications and Trade: The Atlantic in the Seventeenth Century." *Journal of Economic History* (1953), 13:378–87.

Bancroft, Hubert H. *Works*. Vols. 6–8. San Francisco: A. L. Bancroft, 1883–87.

Barbier, Jacques A. "Tradition and Reform in Bourbon Chile: Ambrosio O'Higgins and Public Finances." *The Americas* (1976), 34:381–99.

Barón Castro, Rodolfo. *José Matías Delgado*. San Salvador: Ministerio de Educación, 1961.

—— *La población de El Salvador*. Madrid: Consejo Superior de Investigaciones Científicas, Instituto Gonzalez Fernández de Oviedo, 1942.

Batres, Luis. *Centro-América, su presente, su pasado, y porvenir*. San José: Imprenta Nacional, 1879.

Batres Jáuregui, Antonio. *La América Central ante la historia*. 3 vols. Guatemala: Tip. Sánchez y De Guise, 1920.

Berenger, Jean. *Finances et absolutisme autrichien dans le second moitié du XVII siècle*. Paris: H. Champion, 1975.

Böcker, Carlos Guzman and Jean-Loup Herbert. *Guatemala: una interpretación histórico-social*. Mexico: Siglo Ventiúno, 1971.

Borah, Woodrow. *Early Colonial Trade and Navigation between Mexico and Peru*. Ibero-Americana, vol. 38. Berkeley and Los Angeles: University of California Press, 1954.

—— *New Spain's Century of Depression*. Ibero-Americana, vol. 35. Berkeley and Los Angeles: University of California Press, 1951.

Brading, David A. *Haciendas and Ranchos in the Mexican Bajío, León 1700–1860*. Cambridge: Cambridge University Press, 1978.

—— *Miners and Merchants in Bourbon Mexico 1763–1810*. Cambridge: Cambridge University Press, 1971.

Brasseur de Bourboug, Charles Etienne. *Histoire des nations civilisées du Mexique et de l'Amérique-Centrale*. 4 vols. Paris: A. Bertrand, 1857–59.

Breve muestra de las muchas utilidades que puede producir a este reyno el comercio de los frutos de el, arreglandose su manejo por dirección de una compañía que se podrá establecer. Guatemala?, 1741 (B.M.).

Brown, Vera Lee. "Contraband Trade: A Factor in the Decline of Spain's Empire in America." *Hispanic American Historical Review* (1928), 8:178–189.

—— "The South Sea Company and Contraband Trade." *American Historical Review* (1926), 31:662–78.

Browning, David. *El Salvador, Landscape and Society.* Oxford: Clarendon Press, 1971.

Bumgartner, Louis, *José del Valle of Central America.* Durham: Duke University Press, 1963.

Burkholder, Mark A. and D. S. Chandler. *From Impotence to Authority: The Spanish Crown and the American Audiencias, 1687–1808.* Columbia: University of Missouri Press, 1977.

Cabat, Geoffrey A. "The Consolidation of 1804 in Guatemala." *The Americas* (1971), 28:20–38.

Calderón Quijano, José Antonio, director. *Los Virreyes de Nueva España en el reino de Carlos III.* 2 vols. Seville: Escuela de Estudios Hispano-Américanos, 1967.

Campillo y Cosío, Jóse del. *Nuevo sistema de gobierno económico para la América.* Madrid: Impr. de B. Cano, 1789.

Cañas, Antonio et al. *Interpelación al pueblo soberano de Centro-América.* Guatemala: Imprenta de la Union, 1833 (B.M.).

Carmack, Robert M. *Quichean Civilization.* Berkeley: University of California Press, 1973.

Carmagnani, Marcelo. *Les Mécanismes de la vie économique dans une société coloniale: Le Chile (1680–1830).* Paris: S.E.V.P.E.N., 1973.

Cavignac, Jean. *Jean Pellet, commerçant de gros, 1694–1772.* Paris: S.E.V.P.E.N., 1967.

Chamberlain, Robert S. *The Conquest and Colonization of Honduras, 1502–1550.* Washington, D.C.: Pan American Union, 1953.

Chamorro, Pedro J. *La historia de la federación de la América Central.* Madrid: Ediciones Cultura Hispanica, 1951.

Chapman, Anne M. "Port of Trade Enclaves in Aztec and Maya Civilization." In Karl Polanyi et al., eds., *Trade and Market in the Early Empires.* Glencoe, Ill: The Free Press, 1957.

Chaunu, Pierre. *Les Philippines et la Pacifique des Iberiques XVIe, XVIIe, XVIIIe siècles.* Paris: S.E.V.P.E.N., 1960.

Chaunu, Pierre and Huguette Chaunu. "Le Climat des rapports franco-espagnols à Cadiz dans la seconde moitié du XVIIe siècle." *Mélanges offerts à Marcel Bataillon.* Bordeaux: Féret et Fils, 1962.

—— *Séville et l'Atlantique.* 8 vols. in 13. Paris: Colin, 1955–59.

Chevalier, François. *La Formation des grands domaines au Mexique. Terre et société aux XVIe–XVIIe siècles.* Paris: Université de Paris, 1952.

Chinchilla Aguilar, Ernesto. *El ayuntamiento colonial de la ciudad de Guatemala.* Guatemala: Editorial Universitaria, 1961.

—— "El ramo de aguas de la ciudad de Guatemala en la epoca colonial." *Antropología e historia de Guatemala* (1953), 5:19–31.

—— *Historia del arte en Guatemala, 1524–1962. Arquitectura, pintura, y escultura.* Guatemala: Ministerio de Educación Pública, Centro Editorial "José de Pineda Ibarra," 1963.

—— *La inquisición en Guatemala.* Guatemala: Ministerio de Educación Pública, 1953.

Christelow, Allan. "Contraband Trade between Jamaica and the Spanish Main, and the Free Port Act of 1766." *Hispanic American Historical Review* (1942), 22:309–43.

—— "Great Britain and the Trade from Cádiz and Lisbon to Spanish America and Brazil 1759–1783." *Hispanic American Historical Review* (1947), 27:2–29.

Cid Fernández, Enrique del. *Don Gabino de Gainza y otros estudios.* Guatemala: Editorial Universitaria, 1959.

—— *Origen histórico de la Casa y Marquesado de Aycinena* 4 vols. Guatemala: privately published, 1969.

Cockburn, John. *A Journey over Land from the Gulf of Honduras to the Great South Sea.* London: C. Rivington, 1735 (B.M.).

Cole, W. A. "Trends in Eighteenth-Century Smuggling." *Economic History Review*, 2d ser. (1958), 10:395–410.

Colección de los Decretos de observancia general expedidos por la Asamblea Constituyente del Estado de Guatemala. Guatemala: Imprenta del Gobierno, 1840? (B.N.).

Colección de documentos para la historia de Costa Rica. León Fernández, ed. 10 vols. San José, Paris, and Barcelona: Imprenta Nacional, Imprenta Pablo Dupont, Imprenta viuda de Luis Tassa, 1881–1907.

Colección Somoza: Documentos para la historia de Nicaragua. Andres Vega Bolanos ed. 17 vols. Madrid, 1954–57.

Comisión sobre convocatoria a una asamblea nacional. Guatemala, 1833 (B.M.).

Contreras R., J. Daniel. *Una rebelión indigena en el partido de Totonicapán en 1820.* Guatemala: Imprenta Universitaria, 1951.

Cordova, Fr. Matías de, *Utilidades de que todos los indios y ladinos se vistan y calcen a la Española y medios de conseguirlo sin violencia, coacción, ni mandata.* Guatemala: Ignacio Beteta, 1798 (B.M.).

Cornette, Le Père. *Relation d'un voyage de México à Guatémala dans le cours de l'Année 1855.* Paris: Julien, Lanier, Cosnard, 1858.

Cortés y Larraz, Pedro. *Descripción geográfico-moral de la diócesis de Goathemala.* Biblioteca "Goathemala," *vol.* 20 in 2 vols. Guatemala: Sociedad de Geografía e Historia, 1958.

Crowe, Frederick. *The Gospel in Central America.* London: Charles Gilpin, 1850.

Davis, Ralph. "English Foreign Trade, 1660–1700." *Economic History Review*, 2d ser. (1954), 7:150–66.

—— "English Foreign Trade, 1700–1774." *Economic History Review*, 2d Ser. (1962), 15:285–303.

DeLarenaudière, Philippe F. *Mexique et Guatemala*. Paris: Firmin Didot Frères, 1843.

Desdevises du Dézert, G. *L'Eglise espagnole des Indes à la fin du XVIII siècle*. Paris: Phillipe Renovard, 1917.

—— "Vice-Rois et Capitaines Généraux des Indes Espagnoles à la fin du XVIII siècle." *Révue Historique* (1917), 125–126.

Discurso del Gobierno Supremo sobre la renta de tabacos. Guatemala: 1824 (B.M.).

Discurso del Presidente del poder executivo a la apertura del Congreso Federal de Guatemala. Guatemala, 1825 (B.M.).

Documentos para la historia. San Salvador: Imprenta del Gobierno, 1862 (B.M.).

Domínguez Ortiz, Antonio. *Política y hacienda de Felipe IV*. Madrid: Editorial de Derecho Financiero, 1960.

Dunlop, Robert. *Travels in Central America*. London: Longmans, 1847.

Dunn, Henry. *Guatimala*. New York: G. & C. Carvill, 1828.

Durón, Rómulo E. *Historia de Honduras desde la independencia hasta nuestros dias.*. Tegucigalpa: Tipografía Nacional, 1903.

—— *La Provincia de Tegucigalpa bajo el gobierno de Mallol, 1817–1821*. Tegucigalpa: Tipografía Nacional, 1904.

Eisenman, Charles. *Centralisation et décentralisation: Esquise d'une thêorie générale*. Paris: Librairie générale de droit et de jurisprudence, 1948.

Elliott, J. H. *Imperial Spain, 1469–1716*. New York: St. Martin's Press 1964.

Erneholm, Ivar. *Cacao Production of South America*: Historical Development and Present Geographical Distribution. Gothenberg, Sweden, 1948.

Facio, Rodrigo. *Trayectoria y crisis de la Federación Centroaméricana*. San José, Imprenta Nacional, 1949.

Fairlie, Susan. "Dyestuffs in the Eighteenth Century." *Economic History Review*, 2d ser. (1965), 17:488–510.

Farnie, A. A. "The Commercial Empire of the Atlantic, 1607–1783." *Economic History Review*, 2d ser. (1962), 15:205–18.

Ferguson, E. James. *The Power of the Purse*. Chapel Hill: University of North Carolina Press, 1961.

Fernández, León. *Historia de Costa Rica durante la dominación española 1502–1821*. Madrid: Tipografía de Manuel Ginés Hernández 1889.

Filísola, Vicente. *La cooperación de México en la independencia de Centro América*. 2 vols. Mexico: Libreria de la Vda. de Ch. Bouret, 1911.

Flemion, Philip F. "States' Rights and Partisan Politics." *Hispanic American Historical Review* (1973), 53:600–18.

Florescano, Enrique. *Precios del maíz y crisis agrícolas en México (1708–1810)*. Mexico: El Colegio de México, 1969.

Floyd, Troy S. *The Anglo-Spanish Struggle for Mosquitia.* Albuquerque: University of New Mexico Press, 1967.

—— "Bourbon Palliatives and the Central American Mining Industry, 1765–1800." *The Americas* (1961), 18:103–25.

—— "The Guatemalan Merchants, the Government, and the Provincianos, 1750–1800." *Hispanic American Historical Review* (1965), 41:90–110.

—— "The Indigo Merchant: Promoter of Central American Economic Development, 1750–1808." *Business History Review* (1965), pp. 466–88.

Fuentes y Guzmán, Francisco Antonio de. *Recordación Florida; discurso historial y demostración natural, material, militar y política del Reyno de Guatemala.* 2d ed. 3 vols. Biblioteca "Goathemala," vols. 6–8. Guatemala: Sociedad de Geografía e Historia 1932–33.

Gage, Thomas. *Travels in the New World.* J. Eric Thompson, ed. Norman: University of Oklahoma Press, 1958.

Gallardo, Ricardo. *Las Constituciones de la República Federal de Centro-América.* 2 vols. Madrid: Instituto de Estudios Publicos, 1958.

Gámez, José D. *Historia de la Costa de Mosquitos.* Managua: Talleres Nacionales, 1939.

—— *Historia de Nicaragua.* 3 vols. Managua: Talleres Nacionales, 1955.

García, Miguel Angel. *Diccionario histórico enciclopedico de la República de El Salvador.* 3 vols. San Salvador: Imprenta Nacional, 1952.

García Granados, Miguel. *Memorias.* 4 vols. Ministerio de Educación Pública, 1952.

García LaGuardia, Jorge María. *La Genesis del constitucionalismo Guatemalteco.* San José, Costa Rica: E.D.U.C.A., 1971.

García Paláez, Francisco de Paula. *Memorias para la historia del Antiguo Reyno de Guatemala.* 3 vols. Guatemala, 1851–52.

Gazeta de Guatemala, La. Vols. 1–14, Guatemala, 1799–1810.

Gerhard, Peter. *Pirates on the West Coast of New Spain, 1565–1742.* Glendale, Calif.: A.H. Clark, 1960.

Gibson, Charles. *The Aztecs Under Spanish Rule: A History of the Indians of the Valley of Mexico, 1519–1810.* Stanford, Calif.: Stanford University Press, 1964.

Goicoechea, Fr. José Antonio. *Tratado del xiquilite y añil de Guatemala.* Guatemala: Ignacio Beteta, 1797 (B.M.).

—— *Memoria sobre los medios de destruir la mendicidad y de socorrer los verdaderos pobres de esta capital.* Guatemala: Ignacio Betata, 1797 (B.M.).

Gómez Carrillo, Agustín. *Historia de la America Central.* 2 vols. Guatemala: Tipografía Nacional, 1895–97.

Góngora, Mario. *Studies in the Colonial History of Spanish America.* Richard Southern, trans. Cambridge: Cambridge University Press, 1975.

Gray, Lewis Cecil. *History of Agriculture in the Southern United States to 1860.* 2 vols. Washington, D.C.: Carnegie Institution, 1933.

Griffith, William J. *Empires in the Wilderness: Foreign Colonization and Development in Guatemala 1834–1844.* Chapel Hill: University of North Carolina Press, 1965.

Guía de forasteros de Guatemala para el año 1853. Guatemala, 1853.

Haefkens, Jacobo. *Viaje a Guatemala y Centroamérica.* Theodora J. M. Van Lottum, trans. Guatemala: Editorial Guatemala, 1969.

Hamilton, Earl J. *American Treasure and the Price Revolution in Spain, 1501–1650.* New York: Octagon Books, 1965.

—— *War and Prices in Spain, 1651–1800.* Cambridge, Mass.: Harvard University Press, 1947.

Hamnett, Brian. *Politics and Trade in Southern Mexico 1790–1821.* Cambridge: Cambridge University Press, 1971.

Hargreaves-Mawdsley, W. N., ed. *Spain Under the Bourbons, 1700–1833. A collection of documents.* London: Macmillan, 1973.

Haring, Clarence H. "American Gold and Silver Production in the First Half of the Sixteenth Century." *Quarterly Journal of Economics* (1915), 29:433–79.

—— *The Buccaneers in the West Indies in the XVII Century.* London: Methuen, 1910.

—— *The Spanish Empire in America.* New York: Oxford University Press, 1947.

—— *Trade and Navigation Between Spain and the Indies in the Time of the Hapsburgs.* Cambridge, Mass.: Harvard University Press, 1918.

Henderson, George. *An Account of the British Settlement of Honduras.* London: R. Baldwin, 1811.

Herr, Richard. *The Eighteenth Century Enlightenment in Spain.* Princeton: Princeton University Press, 1958.

Herrarte, Alberto. *La Union de Centroamérica.* Guatemala: Ministerio de Educación Pública, 1955.

Holleran, Mary. *Church and State in Guatemala.* New York: Columbia University Press, 1949.

Horsfall, Lucy F. "The West Indian Trade." In C. Northcote Parkinson, ed., *The Trade Winds.* London: George Allen and Unwin, 1948.

Houdaille, Jacques. "Les français et les Afrancesados en Amérique Centrale 1700–1810." *Revista de Historia de América* (1957), 44:305–30.

Humboldt, F. H. Alexandre de. *Essai politique sur le Royaume de la Nouvelle Espagne.* 2 vols. Paris: F. Schoell, 1811.

—— *Evaluation numérique de la population du Nouveau Continent.* Paris: Dondey-Iupre père et fils, 1825.

Humphreys, Robin A. *British Consular Reports on the Trade and Politics of Latin America 1824–1826.* London: The Royal Historical Society, 1940.

—— *The Diplomatic History of British Honduras.* London: Oxford University Press, 1961.

Hussey, Roland D. "Analysis of a Document concerning a 'Voluntary Donation' in Guatemala in 1644." *Hispanic American Historical Review* (1944), 24:699–708.

El Indicador (Guatemala). 1824–25.

Informe del gobierno supremo de Guatemala sobre los emprestitos que se le han ofrecido. Guatemala, 1824 (B.M.).

Instrucciones para la constitución fundamental de la monarquía española y su gobierno. Guatemala, 1953.

Ireland, Gordon. *Boundaries, Possessions and Conflicts in Central and North America and the Caribbean.* New York: Octagon Books 1971.

Israel, Jonathan I. *Race, Class and Politics in Colonial Mexico.* Oxford: Oxford University Press, 1975.

―― "Mexico and the General Crisis of the Seventeenth Century." *Past and Present* (1974), 63:33–57.

Jensen, Merrill. *The New Nation.* New York: Knopf, 1950.

Jones, Chester L. *Guatemala, past and present.* Minneapolis: University of Minnesota Press, 1940.

Juan y Santacilia, Jorge and Antonio de Ulloa. *Relación histórica del viaje a la América Meridional.* 4 vols. Madrid: A. Marin, 1748.

Juarros, Domingo. *Compendio de la historia de la ciudad de Guatemala.* 2 vols. Guatemala: Tipografía Nacional, 1857.

Karnes, Thomas. "The Origins of Costa Rican Federalism." *The Americas* (1959), 15:249–69.

Kaufmann, William W. *British Policy and the Independence of Latin America.* New Haven, Conn.: Yale University Press, 1951.

Kenyon, Gordon. "Mexican Influence in Central America, 1821–1823." *Hispanic American Historical Review* (1961), 41:175–205.

Klein, Herbert S. "Peasant Communities in Revolt: The Tzeltal Republic of 1712." *Pacific Historical Review* (1966), 35:247–63.

Konetzke, Richard, ed. *Colección de documentos para la historia de la formación social de Hispano-América.* 3 vols. Madrid: Consejo Superior de Investigaciones Científicas, 1962.

Lanning, John Tate. "The Church and the Enlightenment in the Universities." *The Americas* (1959), 15:33–49.

―― *The Eighteenth-Century Enlightenment in the University of San Carlos de Guatemala.* Ithaca, N.Y.: Cornell University Press, 1956.

―― *The University in the Kingdom of Guatemala.* Ithaca, N.Y.: Cornell University Press, 1955.

Lapolombara, Joseph. *Bureaucracy and Political Development.* Princeton: Princeton University Press, 1963.

Lardé y Larín, Jorge. *Origines de San Salvador Cuzcatlán hoy capital de El Salvador.* San Salvador: Imprenta Nacional, 1925.

Larreinaga, Miguel. *Prontuario de todos las Reales Cédulas, cartas acordadas y órdenes comunicadas a la audiencia del Antiquo Reino de Guatemala desde el año de 1600 hasta 1818.* Guatemala: Imprenta de Luna, 1857.

Lascaris Comneno, Constantino. *Historia de las ideas en Centroamérica.* San Jose, Costa Rica: E.D.U.C.A., 1970.

Leonard, Irving A. *Baroque Times in Old Mexico.* Ann Arbor: University of Michigan Press, 1959.

Leon Borja, Dora and Adam Szaszdi Nagy. "El comercio del cacao de Guayaquil." *Revista de Historia de América* (1964), 57–58:1–50.

Lévy, Pablo. *Notas geográficas y económicas sobre la república de Nicaragua.* Paris: Libreria Española, 1873.

Liss, Peggy. "Jesuit Contributions to the Ideology of Spanish Empire in Mexico" *The Americas* (1973), 29:314–33, 449–70.

Livingston, William S. *Federalism and Constitutional Change.* Oxford: Clarendon Press, 1956.

Lockey, Joseph. "Diplomatic Futility." *Hispanic American Historical Review* (1930), 3:269–94.

Loosley, A. C. "The Puerto Bello Fair." *Hispanic American Historical Review* (1940), 13:314–335.

Luján Muñoz, Jorge. "El desarrollo demográfico de la ciudad de Santiago de Guatemala 1543–1773." *Universidad de San Carlos: Publicacion Anual* (1970), 1:239–51.

—— *La independencia y la anexión de Centroamérica a Mexico.* Guatemala: Editorial Universitaria, 1975.

—— *Permanencia De Antigua.* Guatemala: Editorial Universitaria, 1966.

Luque Alcaide, Elisa. *La sociedad económica de amigos del país de Guatemala.* Seville: Escuela de Estudios Hispano-Americanos, 1962.

Lutz, Christopher H. "Santiago de Guatemala 1541–1773: The Socio-Demographic History of a Spanish American Colonial City." Ph.D. dissertation, University of Wisconsin, 1976.

Lynch, John. *Spain Under the Hapsburgs.* 2 vols. New York: Oxford University Press 1964, 1969.

—— *The Spanish American Revolutions, 1808–1826.* New York: Norton, 1973.

McAlister, Lyle N. "Social Structure and Social Change in New Spain." *Hispanic American Historical Review* (1963), 43:349–70.

McLachlan, Jean O. *Trade and Peace with Old Spain 1667–1750.* Cambridge: Cambridge University Press, 1940.

MacLeod, Murdo J. *Spanish Central America: A Socioeconomic History 1520–1720.* Berkeley: University of California Press, 1973.

Manning, William R., ed. *Diplomatic Correspondance of the United States concerning the Independence of Latin American Nations.* 3 vols. New York: Oxford University Press, 1925.

Martínez Peláez, Severo. *La patria del criollo: Ensayo de interpretación de la realidad colonial guatemalteca.* Guatemala: Editorial Universitaria, 1971.

Marure, Alejandro. *Bosquejo histórico de la revoluciones de Centro-América.* 2 vols. Guatemala: Tipografía de "El Progreso," 1877–78.

—— *Efemérides de los hechos notables acaecidos en la República de Centro América.* Guatemala: Tipografía Nacional, 1844.

Mata Gavidia, José. *La influencia de España en la formación de la nacionalidad Centroaméricana.* Guatemala: Union Tipografica, 1943.

Maxwell, Kenneth R. *Conflicts and Conspiracies: Brazil and Portugal 1750–1808.* Cambridge: Cambridge University Press, 1973.

Mayes H., Guillermo. *Honduras en la independencia de Centro América y anexión a México.* Guatemala: Tipografíca Nacional, 1955.

Mecham, John Lloyd. *Church and State in Latin America.* Chapel Hill: University of North Carolina Press, 1934.

Medina, José T. *La imprenta en Guatemala 1660–1821.* Santiago de Chile: José T. Medina, 1910.

Mejía Nieto, Arturo. *Morazán, presidente de la desaparecida República Centro Américana.* Buenos Aires: Editorial Nova, 1947.

Melendez, Carlos. *Proceres de la Independencia Centroaméricana.* San José, Costa Rica: E.D.U.C.A., 1971.

Memoria presentada por el secretario de estado y del despacho de relaciones interiores y exteriores. Guatemala: Imprenta Nueva, 1832 (B.M.).

Memoria que el secretario general interino del estado del Salvador presentó a la legislatura del año de 1828. San Salvador: Imprenta del Gobierno, 1828 (B.N.).

Méndez, José M. *Memoria del estado político y eclesiástico de la capitanía general de Guatemala presentada a las Cortes el día 17 de mayo de 1821.* Madrid: Tipografía de Manuel Hernández, 1889 (B.N.).

Milla, José. *Historia de la América Central.* 2 vols. Guatemala: Tipografía Nacional, 1879–82.

Minchington, Walter E., ed. *The Growth of English Overseas Trade in the Seventeenth and Eighteenth Centuries.* London: Methuen, 1969.

Molina, Felipe. *Bosquejo de la República de Costa Rica.* New York: S. W. Benedict, 1851.

Molina, Pedro. *Escritos* 3 vols. Guatemala: Ministerio de Educación Publica, 1954.

Monroy, Agustín Estrada. *Datos para la historia de la iglesia en Guatemala.* Biblioteca "Goathemala," vol. 27. 2 vols. Guatemala: Sociedad de Geográfia e Historia, 1972.

Montes Mozo, Santiago. *Etnohistoria de El Salvador: El Guachival Centroaméricano.* 2 vols. San Salvador: Ministerio de Educación, 1977.

Montgomery, George W. *Narrative of a Journey to Guatemala in Central America in 1838.* New York: Wiley and Putnam, 1839.

Montúfar, Lorenzo. *Reseña historia de Centro-América.* 5 vols. Guatemala: Tip. de "El Progreso," 1878–79.

Montúfar, Manuel. *Memorias para la Historia de la Revolución de Centro América.* Jalapa: Aburto y Blanco, 1832.

Moore, Barrington. *Political Power and Social Theory.* Cambridge, Mass.: Harvard University Press, 1958.

Morazán, Francisco. *Memorias.* San Vicente: Edicion del Rol, 1827.

Muro, Fr. Antonio de San José. *Utilidades y Medio de que los indios y ladinos vistan y calzen a la Española.* Guatemala: Ignacio Beteta, 1978.

Myionnet Dupuy, Auguste, *Deux Ans de Sejour dans l'état de Nicaragua 1850, 1851, 1852.* Paris: Imprimerie Poussielgue Masson, 1853.

Navarro García, Luis. *Virreyes de Nueva España (1759–1779) (1779–1787).* 2 vols. Seville: Escuela de Estudios Hispano-Américanos, 1967 and 1968.

Naylor, Robert A. "The British Role in Central America prior to the Clayton-

Bulwer Treaty of 1850." *Hispanic American Historical Review* (1960), 40:361–82.

Nelson, George H. "Contraband Trade under the Asiento, 1730–1739." *American Historical Review* (1945), 51:55–67.

Ots Capdequi, José María. *Historia del derecho español en América y del derecho indiano.* 2d ed. Madrid: Aguilar, 1969.

—— *Instituciones sociales de la América española en el período colonial.* La Plata: Imprenta López 1934.

Palmer, R. R. *The Age of the Democratic Revolution.* 2 vols. Princeton, N.J.: Princeton University Press, 1959, 1964.

Pardo, José Joaquin. *Efemérides para escribir la historia de la muy noble y muy leal ciudad de Santiago de los Caballeros del Reino de Guatemala.* Guatemala: Tipografía Nacional, 1944.

Pares, Richard. *War and Trade in the West Indies 1739–1763.* Oxford: Clarendon Press, 1936.

Parker, Franklin D. *The Central American Republics.* London: Oxford University Press, 1964.

—— *José Cecilio del Valle and the Establishment of the Central American Confederation.* Tegucigalpa: Universidad de Honduras, 1955.

—— "José Cecilio del Valle: Scholar and Patriot." *Hispanic American Historical Review* (1952), 32:516–27.

Parker, Franklin D., ed. *Travels in Central America 1821–1840.* Gainesville: University of Florida Press, 1970.

Parry, J. H. *The Sale of Public Office in the Spanish Indies under the Hapsburgs.* Ibero-Americana, vol. 37. Berkeley and Los Angeles: University of California Press, 1953.

—— *The Spanish Seaborne Empire.* New York: Knopf, 1966.

Phelan, John Leddy. *The Kingdom of Quito in the Seventeenth Century: Bureaucratic Politics in the Spanish Empire.* Madison: University of Wisconsin Press, 1967.

Portig, W. H. "Central American Rainfall." *Geographical Review* (1965), 55:68–90.

Posthumus, N. W. *Inquiry into the History of Prices in Holland.* 2 vols. Leiden: Brill, 1946, 1964.

Radell, David R. and James J. Parsons. "Realejo—A Forgotten Colonial Port and Shipbuilding Center in Nicaragua." *Hispanic American Historical Review* (1971), 51:295–312.

Ragatz, Lowell J. *Statistics for the study of British Caribbean Economic History 1763–1833.* London: Bryan Edwards Press, 1927.

Real cédula de erección del consulado de Guatemala. Madrid: Don Benito Cano, 1793 (B.M.).

Recopilación de leyes de los reynos de las Indias. Madrid: Por Iulien de Paredes, 1681; rpt; Madrid: Consejo de la Hispanidad, 1943.

Redfield, Robert. *The Primitive World and its Transformations.* Ithaca, N.Y.: Cornell University Press, 1953.

Relaciónes históricas y geográficas de América Central. Madrid: Victoriano Suárez, 1908.

Remesal, Antonio. *Historia general de la Indias Occidentales y particular de la gobernación de Chiapa y Guatemala,* 2 vols. Biblioteca "Goathemala." Guatemala, Sociedad de Geografía e Historia, 1932.

Ricard, Robert. *La "conquête spirituelle" du Mexique.* Paris: Université de Paris, 1933.

Rippy, J. Fred. *Rivalry of the United States and Great Britain over Latin America 1808–1830.* Baltimore, Md.: Johns Hopkins University Press, 1929.

Roberts, Orlando. *Narrative of Voyages and Excursions on the East Coast and in the Interior of Central America.* Edinburgh: Constable, 1827.

Rodríguez, Mario. *The Cádiz Experiment in Central America, 1808–1826.* Berkeley: University of California Press, 1978.

—— "The Livingston Codes in the Guatemalan Crisis of 1837–1838." *Applied Enlightenment: Nineteenth Century Liberalism.* Middle American Research Institute, No. 23. New Orleans: Tulane University, 1972.

—— A *Palmerstonian Diplomat in Central America: Frederick Chatfield, Esq.* Tucson: University of Arizona Press, 1964.

Rodríguez Becerra, Salvador. *Encomienda y conquista: Los inicios de la colonización en Guatemala.* Seville: Universidad de Sevilla, 1977.

Rosenblat, Angel. *La población indígena y el mestizaje en America.* 2 vols. Buenos Aires: Editorial Nova, 1954.

Rubio Sánchez, Manuel. "El añil o xiquilite." *Anales de la Sociedad de Geografía e Historia* (Guatemala) (1952), 26:313–49.

—— "El cacao." *Anales de la Sociedad de Geografía e Historia* (Guatemala) (1958), 31:81–129.

—— *Comercio terrestre de y entre las provincias de Centroamérica.* Guatemala: Editorial del Ejército, 1973.

—— "La grana o cochinella." *Antropología e Historia de Guatemala* (1961), 13:15–46.

—— *Historia del añil o xiquilite en Centro América.* 2 vols. San Salvador: Ministerio de Educación, 1976.

—— *Historia del puerto de la Santísima Trinidad de Sonsonate o Acajutla.* San Salvador: Editorial Universitaria, 1977.

—— *Historial de El Realejo.* Managua: Colección Cultural Banco de América, 1975.

—— *Status de la mujer en Centroamérica.* Guatemala: Editorial "José de Pineda Ibarra," 1976.

Saint-Lu, André. *Condition coloniale et conscience créole au Guatemala (1524–1821).* Paris: Presses Universitaires de France, 1970.

—— *La Vera Paz: Esprit évangélique et colonisation.* Paris: Institut d'Etudes Hispaniques, 1968.

Salazar, Ramón. *Historia del desenvolvimiento intelectual de Guatemala.* 3 vols. Guatemala: Tipografía Nacional, 1897.

—— *Historia de veintiún años.* Guatemala: Tipografía Nacional, 1928.

—— *Manuel José Arce.* Guatemala: Biblioteca de Cultural Popular, 1952.

—— *Mariano de Aycinena.* Guatemala: Biblioteca de Cultura Popular, 1952.

Salvatierra, Sofonías. *Contribución a la historia de Centroamérica: monografías documentales.* 2 vols. Managua: Tip. Progreso, 1939.

—— "La fundación de la villa de Rivas." *Revista de la Academia de Geografía e Historia de Nicaragua* (1938), 2:312–23.

Samayoa Guevara, Hector Humberto. *Ensayos sobre la independencia de Centroamérica.* Guatemala: Editorial "Jose de Pineda Ibarra," 1972.

—— "Fray Matías de Córdova; Educador y Centro-Américano." *Antropología e Historia de Guatemala* (1964), 16:21–35.

—— "El gremio de salitreros de Antigua Guatemala." *Antropología e Historia de Guatemala* (1955), 7:25–45.

—— *Los gremios de Guatemala.* Guatemala: Editorial Universitaria, 1963.

—— *Implantación del Régimen de intendencias en el Reyno de Guatemala.* Guatemala: Editorial "José de Pineda Ibarra," 1969.

Sánchez-Bella, Ismael. *La organización financiera de las Indias (siglo XVI).* Seville: Escuela de Estudios Hispano-américanos, 1968.

Santiago Cruz, Francisco. *Breve Historia del Colegio de la Compañía de Jesus de Ciudad Real de Chiapas 1681–1767.* Mexico: Editorial Tradición, 1977.

Savary des Bruslons. *Dictionnaire universel de commerce.* Paris: Jacques Estienne, 1723.

Scheifler, José Ramón, S. J. "Rafael Landivar y su Rusticatia Méxicana." *Estudios CentroAméricanos* (1950), 41:4–10, 42:32–37.

—— "Riqueza de los Religiosos en Santiago de los Caballeros de Guatemala." *Estudios CentroAméricanos* (1950), 45:5–13 and 46:8–18.

Scherzer, Karl. *Travels in the Free States of Central America, Nicaragua and San Salvador.* London: Longman, Brown, 1857.

Scholes, France, V. "Franciscan Missionary Scholars in Colonial Central America." *The Americas* (1952), 8:391–416.

Scholes, France V. and Ralph L. Roys. *The Maya Chontal Indians of Acalan-Tixchel.* 2d ed. Norman: University of Oklahoma Press, 1968.

Schumpeter, Joseph A. "The Crisis of the Tax State." W. F. Stolper and R. A. Musgrave, trans. *International Economic Papers* (1954), 4:5–38.

Schurz, William L. "Mexico, Peru, and the Manila Galleon." *Hispanic American Historical Review* (1918), 1:389–402.

Sherman, William L. *Forced Native Labor in Sixteenth Century Central America.* Lincoln: University of Nebraska Press, 1979.

—— "Indian Slavery and the Cerrato Reforms." *Hispanic American Historical Review* (1971), 51:25–50.

Shumpeter, Elizabeth. B. *English Overseas Trade Statistics, 1697–1808.* Oxford: Clarendon Press, 1960.

Simpson, Lesley Byrd. "A Seventeenth-Century Encomienda: Chimaltenango, Guatemala." *The Americas* (1959), 15:393–402.

—— *Studies in the Administration of the Indians in New Spain: The Repar-*

timiento System of Native Labor in New Spain and Guatemala III. Ibero-Americana, vol. 13, Berkeley: University of California Press, 1938.

Skinner-Klée, Jorge. *Legislación indigenísta de Guatemala.* Mexico: Instituto Indigenísta Interamericano, 1965.

Smith, Robert S. "Documents, Statutes of the Guatemalan Indigo Growers' Society." *Hispanic American Historical Review* (1950), 30:336–45.

—— "Financing the Central American Federation 1821–1838." *Hispanic American Historical Review* (1963), 43:438–510.

—— "Forced Labor in the Guatemalan Indigo Works." *Hispanic American Historical Review* (1956), 36:318–328.

—— "Indigo Production and Trade in Colonial Guatemala." *Hispanic American Historical Review* (1959), 39:181–211.

—— "Origins of the Consulado of Guatemala." *Hispanic American Historical Review* (1946), 26:150–61.

Solano, Francisco de. *Los Mayas del siglo XVIII.* Madrid: Ediciones Cultura Hispánica, 1976.

Solórzano F., Valentin. *Evolución económica de Guatemala.* Guatemala: Centro Editorial "José de Pineda Ibarra," 1963.

Soriano Lleras, Andres. "Episodios de la independencia de Guatemala." *Universidad de San Carlos Publicación Anual* (1970), 1:113–47.

Spalding, Karen, "Social Climbers: Changing Patterns of Mobility Among the Indians of Colonial Peru." *Hispanic American Historical Review* (1970), 50:645–64.

Squier, Ephraim George. *Nicaragua: Its People.* London: Longman, Brown, 1852.

—— *Notes on Central America.* New York: Harper, 1855.

—— *The States of Central America.* New York: Harper, 1858.

Stark, Barbara L. and Barbara Voorhies, eds. *Prehistoric Coastal Adaptations: The Economy and Ecology of Maritime Middle America,* New York: Academic Press, 1978.

Starr, S. Frederick. *Decentralization and Self-Government in Russia, 1830–1870.* Princeton, N.J.: Princeton University Press, 1972.

Stephens, John L. *Incidents of Travel in Central America, Chiapas, and Yucatan.* 2 vols. New York: Dover Publications, 1969.

Stein, Stanley J. and Barbara H. Stein. *The Colonial Heritage of Latin America: Essays on Economic Dependence in Perspective.* New York: Oxford University Press, 1970.

Taylor, William "Landed Society in New Spain: A View from the South" *Hispanic American Historical Review* (1974), 54:387–413.

—— *Landlord and Peasant in Colonial Oaxaca.* Stanford: Stanford University Press, 1972.

TePaske, John J. "Recent Trends in Quantitative History: Colonial Latin America." *Latin American Research Review* (1975), 10:51–62.

Thompson, Donald E. *Maya Paganism and Christianity. A History of the Fusion of Two Religions.* Middle American Research Institute Publication No. 19. New Orleans: Tulane University, 1954.

Thompson, George A. *Narrative of an Official Visit to Guatemala.* London: John Murray, 1829.

Thompson, J. Eric S. "Sixteenth and Seventeenth Century Reports on the Chol Mayas." *American Anthropologist* (1938), 40:584–604.

Tibesar, Antonine. "The Alternativa: A Study in Spanish-Creole Relations in Seventeenth Century Peru." *The Americas* (1955), 11:229–83.

Tilly, Charles, ed. *The Formation of National States in Western Europe..* Princeton, N.J.: Princeton University Press, 1975.

Tiryakian, Josefina Cintrón. "Campillo's Pragmatic New System: A Mercantile and Utilitarian Approach to Indian Reform in Spanish Colonies of the Eighteenth Century." *History of Political Economy* (1978), 10:233–57.

Tobar Cruz, Pedro. "La esclavitud del negro en Guatemala." *Antropología e Historia de Guatemala* (1965), 17:3–14.

Torres Lanza, Pedro. *Relación descriptiva de los mapas, planos, etc. de la audiencia y capitanía general de Guatemala . . .* existentes en el archivo de Indias. Madrid: Tip. de la Revista de Archivos, 1903.

Townsend Ezcurra, Andres. *Las Provincias Unidas de Centroamérica: Fundación de la Republica.* 2d ed. San José, Costa Rica: E.D.U.C.A., 1973.

Trevor-Roper, H. R. "The General Crisis of the Seventeenth Century." In Trevor Aston, ed., *Crisis in Europe, 1560–1660.* New York: Basic Books, 1965.

Ulloa, Bernardo de. *Restablecimiento de las fábricas y comercio Español.* Madrid: A. Marin, 1740.

Valle, José Cecilio del. *Escritos.* Guatemala, 1825 (B.M.).

—— *Manifiesto de. . . .* Guatemala: Imprenta de la Union, 1825 (B.M.).

—— *Obras.* Tegucigalpa: Tipografía Nacional, 1914.

Valle, Rafael Heliodoro. "Dionisio De Herrera 1783–1850: A Centennial Tribute." *Hispanic American Historical Review* (1950), 30:554–58.

—— *Historia de las ideas contemporaneas en Centro América.* Mexico: Fondo de Cultura Económica, 1960.

Valle, Rafael Heliodoro, comp. *La anexión de Centro América a México.* 6 vols. Mexico: Secretaría de Relaciones Exteriores, 1924–49.

Vallejo, Antonio. *Compendio de la historia social y política de Honduras.* Tegucigalpa: Tipografía Nacional, 1926.

Vázquez de Espinosa, Antonio. *Compendium and Description of the West Indies.* Charles Upson Clark, trans. Washington, D.C.: Smithsonian Institution, 1942.

Vicens Vives, Jaime, ed. *Historia social y económica de España y America.* 5 vols. Barcelona: Editorial Teide 1957–59.

Villacorta C., J. Antonio. *Historia de la capitanía general de Guatemala.* Guatemala: Tipografía Nacional, 1942.

Villalobos R. Sergio. "Contrabando frances en el Pacifico, 1700–1724." *Revista de Historia de América* (1961), 51:49–80.

Von Tempsky, G. F. *Mitla: A Narrative of Incidents and Personal Adventures on a Journey in Mexico, Guatemala and Salvador.* London: Longman, Brown, 1858.

Wachtel, Nathan. *La vision des vaincus. Les Indiens du Pérou devant la conquête espagnole 1530–1570.* Paris: Éditions Gallimard, 1970.
Wallerstein, Immanuel. *The Modern World System.* New York: Academic Press, 1974.
Wells, William V. *Explorations and Adventures in Honduras.* London: Sampson, Low, 1857.
West, Robert C. "The Mining Economy of Honduras during the Colonial Period." *Actas del XXXIII Congreso Internacional de Americanistas* (1959), 2:767–77.
West, Robert C. and John P. Augelli. *Middle America: Its Lands and Peoples.* Englewood Cliffs, N.J.: Prentice-Hall, 1966.
Whitaker, Arthur, ed. *Latin America and the Enlightenment.* New York: D. Appleton-Century, 1942.
Williams, Mary. *Anglo-American Isthmian Diplomacy.* Washington, D.C.: American Historical Association, 1916.
—— "The Ecclesiastical Policy of Francisco Morazán and the Other Central American Liberals." *Hispanic American Historical Review* (1920), 3:119–43.
Wilson, Arthur M. "The Logwood Trade in the Seventeenth and Eighteenth Centuries." In Donald C. McKay, ed., *Essays in the History of Modern Europe.* Freeport, N.Y.: Books for Libraries Press, 1968.
Woodward, Ralph Lee, Jr. *Class Privilege and Economic Development: The Consulado de Comercio of Guatemala 1793–1871.* Chapel Hill: University of North Carolina Press, 1966.
—— "Social Revolution in Guatemala: The Carrera Revolt." *Applied Enlightenment: Nineteenth Century Liberalism.* Middle American Research Institute Publication No. 23, New Orleans: Tulane University, 1972, pp. 45–70.
Wortman, Miles L. "Bourbon Reforms in Central America, 1750–1786." *The Americas* (1975), 32:222–38.
—— "Government Revenue and Economic Trends in Central America, 1787–1819." *Hispanic American Historical Review* (1975), 55:251–86.
—— "Legitimidad política y regionalismo—El Imperio Mexicano y Centroamérica." *Historia Mexicana* (1976), 26:238–62.
Ximénez, Francisco. *Historia de la provincia de San Vicente de Chiapa y Guatemala de la orden de predicadores.* Biblioteca "Goathemala," vols. 1–3. Guatemala: Sociedad de Geografía e Historia, 1929–31.
Zavala, Silvio. *Contribución a la historia de las instituciones coloniales en Guatemala.* Guatemala: Ministerio de Educación Pública, 1953.
—— *De Encomiendas y Propiedad Territorial en algunas regiones de la América Española.* Mexico: Antigua Librería Robredo, de José Porrua e Hijos, 1940.
—— "Los esclavos indios en Guatemala." *Historia Mexicana* (1970), 19:459–65.
—— *New Viewpoints on the Spanish Colonialization of America.* Philadelphia: University of Pennsylvania Press, 1943.
Zebadua, Marcial. *Proyecto de reforma de las instituciones políticas de Centro-América.* Sonsonate: Imprenta Libre, 1834 (B.N.).

Zelaya, Chester. *Nicaragua en la independencia.* San José: Editorial Universitaria Centroamericana, 1971.

Zelis, Rafael De. *Catálogo de los sugetos de la Compañia de Jesus Que formaban la Provincia de México el día de arresto, 25 de junio de 1767.* México: Imprenta de I. Escalente, 1871.

Index

Absolutism, xiii–xiv, 107, 112, 116, 129,
132–33, 136, 137, 146, 154, 158, 166,
168, 171, 196, 203, 215–16, 227, 229,
272; *see also* Bourbon reforms
Acajutla, 244
Acapulco, 117
Acasaguastlan, 60
Achiote, 29
Agrarian reform, 254
Agriculture, 130; *see also individual*
agricultural products, e.g., Cotton,
Indigo; Wheat, Rural life
Aguacate, 244
Aguardiente, 169, 205, 232, 254;
licensing, 66; monopoly (*estanco*), 140,
144, 153, 190, 256, 271
Aguía, Miguel, 15
Aguirre, Joachim de, 143
Alajuela, 232, 248
Alcabala (sales tax), 31–33, 36, 37, 59,
62, 67–68, 96, 100, 104–5, 107, 138,
139, 141–43, 144–45, 146–52, 153, 160,
180, 190, 274, 279, 301*n*; after
independence, 232–33, 240–41, 254,
269; *see also* Fiscal administration
Alcaldes, Indian, 10, 13, 66–67, 264, 289
Alcaldes mayores and *corregidores*, 10,
11–12, 13, 19, 25–31, 33, 34–35, 36,
38, 63, 68, 69, 94, 100, 102, 105,
115–16, 126, 127, 128, 133–34, 138,
140, 146–47, 149, 166–67, 172, 173–74,
177, 178, 180, 224, 239, 256, 268, 269,
279, 289, 305*n*. *see also Repartimiento*
of goods; *Repartimiento* of labor

Alcaldes ordinarios, 13, 28, 65, 66, 95–96,
122, 123, 124–26, 270; *see also*
Repartimiento of labor
Alcoholism, 44, 173
Alférez Real, price of, 106
Alhondigas (graineries), 72, 192
Almojarifazgo (customs tax), 138, 148–49
Almonedas (auction houses), 26, 73
Alotenango, 180, 181
Alotepeque, mines of, 99, 115–16
Alternativa system, 65
Alvarado, Jorge, 5
Alvarado, Pedro, xii, xiv, 4, 5, 6, 7, 42,
49, 65
Amatitique, 25
Amatitlán, 51–52, 55, 56, 67, 83, 93, 181,
191, 258, 289; *see also* San Juan
Amatitlán
"American" Treaty (1670), 89
Amerindian rebellions, 6, 103, 318*n*;
Cakchiquel, 4; Chiapas (1712), 101,
106; highland Guatemala (1773),
182–83; Totonicapán (1820), 222;
Guatemala and Salvador (1837),
262–67; Salvador (Malespin's) (1840),
271
Amerindians, 25–31, 77–82, 133–34, 135,
172–83, 200, 209–10, 215, 270, 272–73,
277, 279; and internal trade, 73–74;
effect of commercial revolution upon,
115, 162, 191–93; effect of Bourbon
reforms upon, 116, 130, 172–80;
forasteros, 175, 178, 180–81, 289, 290;
and independence, 183, 235, 246, 247,

Amerindians (*continued*)
254, 256; mortality (*see* Disease;
Population), *see also* Common lands;
Labor; Tribute; "Two republic" policy
Amsterdam, indigo market in, 162
Antigua (or Antigua Guatemala),
160–62, 164, 193, 218, 219, 223; after
independence, 242, 254, 258; *see also*
Santiago de Guatemala
Aquajapa, 13–14
Arce, Joseph, 126
Arce, Manuel, 125, 231, 233–34, 236,
247–49, 252
Arce, Thomas de, 124–25
Arequipa, 88
Arroyave family, 106
Arroyave y Beteta, Ventura de, 115
Artisans, 72, 74, 145, 160, 193, 201, 202,
207, 217–19, 226–27, 255
Asian goods, 98, 117
Asiento (slave trade monopoly), 118
Audiencia (royal tribunal): at Gracias a
Dios, 6; of Guatemala, dissolved and
restored, 8, 25, 31, 33, 34, 68, 71, 95,
107, 148, 159, 200–01, 211, 215–16,
239
Augustinian order, 95
Avería, 167
Aycinena, commercial house of, 123–24,
127–28, 162, 167–68, 189–90, 200, 201,
216, 217, 269, 309n; 310n; contraband
trade by, 193, 321n; harassment by
Bustamante, 201–11; and
independence, 220, 224, 226, 234, 235,
244, 250
Aycinena, José, 203, 204, 211, 220
Aycinena, Juan Fermín, 231
Aycinena, Juan Fermín de, first marquis
of, 123, 159, 161–62, 314n, 315n
Aycinena, Juan José, 264, 267
Aycinena, Mariano de, 125, 229, 230,
231, 244, 245, 248, 249, 251
Aycinena, Pedro, 265
Ayuntamientos, *see* Cabildos

Bacon, Francis, 196.
Bagaces, 76
Balance of authority, under the
Hapsburgs, 17, 20–21, 38, 99–100
Balsam, 29

Barcelona Company, 123, 124
Barclay, Herring and Richardson,
English commercial firm, 236–37
Barlovento tax, 31, 36–37, 39, 68, 104,
138, 141–43, 146
Barrios Leal, Jacinto de, 97–99
Barrundia, José Francisco, 123, 206–07
Barrundia, Martín, 123
Barter, 88, 113; *see also* Semi-subsistent
economies
Batres, Manuel de, 145, 159
Bay of Honduras, 11, 22, 34, 86, 92, 113,
118, 119, 121, 154, 169–71, 178, 199,
208, 219
Beans, 26, 28, 174, 245
Beef, 73, 127, 128; sale of, 191, 246; trade
in, 157; *see also* Cattle
Belen monastery, 206–07
Belize (Walis), 119, 120, 171, 241, 243,
252, 333n; settlement of, 38, 89–90;
dispute of, 154; trade with, 199, 208,
217, 218, 219, 241, 260, 262
Bennett, Marshall, 243, 260, 333n
Betlemites, 49, 139
Bluefields, 171
Bolívar, Simón, 221–22, 234, 251
Bonds, fiscal, (*juros*), 56–59, 61, 68
Bordeaux and the indigo trade, 120, 162
Bourbon reforms: strategy of in Central
America, 62–63, 107, 113–14, 116,
129–56, 171; and the church, 63, 130,
132–37, 145, 152–53, 160, 172–73; and
merchants, 104–05, 114–15, 124,
139–43, 157–58, 161, 162–68; and
producers, 113–14, 145, 162–66; and
fiscal administration, 130–32; and
fiscal policy, 138–56, 190–91; and
Guatemalan rebellion against, 140–43;
and the Guatemalan cabildo, 141–45,
150; and Indian tribute, 143, 145–46;
and the tobacco monopoly, 143–45,
152–53; fiscal results of, 146, 150–51,
152–53, 279; jurisdictions implanted,
146–50; intendancies, 148–49; and
increased state power, 151–52, 154;
and increased state expenses, 154–56;
aimed against merchant credit,
162–66; and Amerindia, 172–180
Bourbon rule, 23, 91–92, 100–1, 104,
107, 111–13, 195–97, 199, 268, 269,

271; and the Hapsburgs, xv, xvi, 17–18, 31, 40, 50–54, 59, 63, 69, 91, 94, 105, 111–13, 116, 129, 131, 145–46, 151–52, 156, 158, 171, 173, 180, 195–96, 200, 203, 229, 257, 271–77, 312n; crisis in, 190, 193–94, 215–16, 222–24, 227, 229

Brazil, indigo production in, 120

Britain, 12, 123, 130; intrusions into Central America, 89–90, 91, 154, 168–72, 243–44, 271, 334n; and the Mosquito Coast, 92, 117–20, 130, 168–171; contraband trade, 99, 106, 164, 180, 184, 208; textile revolution in, 111, 120, 162; duties on indigo imports, 162, 187–88; trade with, 215, 216–219; and independent Central America, 241–46, 271–72, 276

Buccaneers, 38, 39, 100; *see also* Piracy

Buenos Aires, 88, 167, 184, 201, 202, 203, 251

Bulls of the Sacred Crusade, 61–62, 88

Bureaucracy, 19, 65, 91, 107, 198–99, 273–77; corruption in, 10, 32, 33, 102, 105, 120, 138, 147, 160, 169, 289, 311n; venality in, 17; weakness of, 33, 99–100, 111, 222; alliances with creoles, 68, 138, 167; expansion of, 139–56, 168, 171, 195–96, 282; after independence, 239; *see also Alcaldes mayores and corregidores; Alcaldes ordinarios; Audiencia;* Bourbon reforms; Cabildos; Federation of Central American States; Hapsburg monarchy; *Juez de milpas*

Bustamante, José de, 168, 201–11, 216–17, 222, 226, 242, 258, 324n

Cabildo of Guatemala, 190, 220; and José de Bustamante, 202–211; and independence, 216–17

Cabildo of Santiago de Guatemala, xiv, 65–72, 73, 74, 106–107, 128, 138, 159–61, 200–201, 205–207, 270; fiscal authority of, 141–45, 150

Cabildos, Indian, 17

Cabildos, Spanish, xii, 17, 64, 65, 68–72, 100, 149, 180, 239; after independence, 69, 200–1, 202, 215–16, 220, 226–28, 229, 230, 239; fights to control, 124–26

Cabildos eclesiásticos, 42, 50, 53

cacao, trade of and production in, 5, 7, 9–10, 11, 13, 15, 23, 26, 27, 29, 34, 39, 55, 62, 65, 68, 75, 76, 81, 87, 89, 194, 199, 215, 279, 282, 319n; Guayaquil, 9, 23, 89, 98, 112, 194; Caracas, 9–10, 117, 194; and the Matina Valley, 119, 164 *see also Juez de milpas*

Cacos, political faction, 220

Caja de comunidad, see Community funds

Cakchiquels, xii, 4

Calvo de la Puerta, Sebastian, and the Bourbon offensive, 144

Campeche, 98, 99; trade with, 87, 117; lagoon, 89, 120

Campillo y Cosío, José de, 112, 130

Campomanes, Pedro Rodríguez de, 130, 133

Cañas family, 162

Capellanías, 52, 55, 59, 71–72, 84, 105, 137, 250, 300n

Capital, 258–59; flow of into Central America, 124, 131–32, 157; flow of out of Central America, 184, 190–91, 219, 323n; *see also* Specie

Capuchines order, 57, 134

Caracas, 167, 201; cacao production in, 9–10, 117, 194 the Real Compañía of, 117, 169; indigo competition from, 186–187

Caravello, Juan González, 96

Caribbean, 86, 154, 157, 270; hotlands bordering the, 2, 3, 4; English in, 34, 38, 118–20; French in 34; fortifications near, 34; Dutch in, 38; Spanish naval weakness in, 117, 208

Carmelite order, 57, 59

Carolina, indigo production in, 120, 162

Carrera, Rafael: revolt of, 8, 263–67; rule of, 268–70, 272, 277

Cartagena, 167, 208, 240; trade with, 12, 87, 105, 117, 151, 164, 282

Cartago, 77, 80, 86, 119, 164, 169, 205, 232

Casas, Bartolomé de las, 7, 29, 42

Casaus y Torres, Ramón, 221, 251–52, 269, 331n

Castile, 8

Catholicism, 41–63; of the Counter-

Catholicism (*continued*)
  Reformation, xii, xiii; and the wine trade, 20; in Central America, 272–73; *see also* Church
Cattle, 7, 44, 52, 53, 54, 55, 75, 77, 82, 84–85, 126, 127, 136–37, 147, 176, 190–91, 194, 225, 245–46, 270, 276, 279, 302–303n; rustling, 73; ranches, 76, 215, 271; ranchmen, 163, 194, 215; effect of consolidation of debts upon, 177; *see also* Beef, sale of
Caudillismo, 268–272, 277; *see also* Carrera, Rafael
Central America: as land bridge, 3, 4; cultures of, 4
Central American Federation, *see* Federation of Central American States
Cerrato, Lic. Alonso López de, reforms of, 8–9, 31, 42, 49, 177, 294n
Chalcasapa, 176
Charles I of Spain (Charles V of the Hapsburg Empire), xii, 18
Charles II of Spain, 91
Charles III of Spain, 149, 170, 196–97, 198, 200
Charles IV of Spain, 167, 198
Chaunu, Pierre and Huguette, 10
Chavarria, Nicolas Justiniano, 51
Chevalier, François, xiii
Chiapas, iii, xiii, xv, 9, 13, 28, 32, 42, 45, 46, 49, 50–51, 55, 56–57, 59, 65, 75, 79, 97, 98, 102, 106, 116, 128, 134, 135, 137, 144, 148, 150, 151, 161, 165, 166, 173, 175, 176, 179, 181, 203–206, 215, 227, 232, 233, 248, 249, 252, 262, 282–83, 284–85, 289; town of, 44, 73, 147
Chicha, 223, 254, 256
Chile, 28
Chimaltenango, 60, 164, 223, 289
Chipilapa, 78, 181
Chiquimula, province of, 33, 60, 77, 82, 84, 94, 101, 115–16, 148, 178, 204, 231, 245, 263
Chiquimula de la Sierra, 76, 80, 83, 94, 289
Cholera, 262–64, 334n
Church, the, xii, xiv, 41–63, 64, 69, 71–72, 273–77, 279–81, 298n; and Amerindian labor, 12, 133, 137, 174; and the Hapsburg state, 18, 91, 100,

132, 196; regular vs. secular clergy, 19; as guardian against abuses, 29–30, 45, 133; income, 32, 56–62, 103–4, 137, 154–55, 175; rituals, 43, 45, 49; as bank and credit institution, 53–54, 68, 105, 106, 111, 132, 133, 136–37, 190–91, 259; anti-clericalism, 59, 63, 221, 250–52, 276, 332n; and the Bourbon offensive, 112, 130, 132–37, 145, 152–53, 159–61, 172, 175–77, 190–91; church-state relations, 133–37; and the Enlightenment, 135, 200; ultramontanism, 136, 198; and liberalism, 137, 201, 221, 254, 259, 260; the Salvador Diocese issue, 221, 249, 331n; and independence, 234, 249; under Carrera, 268, 269, 272–73; *see also* Bulls of the Sacred Crusade; *Cabildos eclesiásticos*; Capellanías; Cofradías; Consolidation of church debts; *individual religious orders*
Cimarrones, 12; *see also* Mosquito people; Sambo nation
Cinco Gremios Mayores de Madrid, 124, 170
Ciudad Real, 25, 28, 42, 56, 69, 77, 79, 82, 85, 148, 166, 206, 227, 232, 284–85; intendency of, 209
Clerics, 43, 45–46, 133–34, 174, 210, 219, 224, 250, 262, 264, 272–73, 289, 298n; as contraband traders, 32, 99, 120, 134; dearth of, 135, 269, 311n. *see also* Church; *individual religious orders*
Cloth, *see* Textiles
Cobán, 47, 55, 56, 60, 98
Cochineal, 10, 28, 219, 241, 242, 244, 245, 258–59, 268, 269, 270, 272
Cockburn, John, 272
Coffee, 219, 258, 268, 271, 272
Cofradías (confraternities or sodalities), xiv, 43–45, 61–62, 84, 98, 105, 106, 107, 133, 134, 137, 160, 172, 175–77, 178, 190–91, 279, 299n, 311n, 316n, 317n
Coinage, *see* Specie
Colbert, Jean Baptiste, 112, 117
Colegio de Jesús, 51–52
Colegio Universitario of San Lucas, 51–52
Colombia (Gran Colombia), 234, 240, 244, 248, 251, 259, 330n

Colonization, 153, 154, 155, 210, 260
Columbus, Christopher, xii, 3–4, 5
Comalapa, 56–57, 181
Comayagua: province of, xv, 25, 32, 42, 48, 56–57, 58, 77, 80, 85, 116, 209, 224–25 (*see also* Honduras); town of, 39, 69, 71, 80, 87, 114, 122, 128, 147, 148, 149, 155, 161, 166, 179, 190, 193, 205, 208, 224–26; after independence, 230–35, 238, 243, 245–46, 249, 284–85, 289
Comitlán, 55, 56
Commerce, *see* Trade
Commercial revolution, western, *see* World economy
Common lands, xiv, 43, 173, 175, 215, 246, 268, 269; invasions of, 173, 191, 192, 323*n*
Community funds, 45, 133, 134, 135, 136, 137–38, 223, 269; state absorption of, 173, 191, 192, 323*n*
Concordat of 1753, 136
Conquest, the, xii–xiii; of Central America, 3–16, 132, 133, 176
Conservative political thought and movement, 207–8, 218–19, 221, 226–27, 326*n*; after independence, 229–35, 250, 251, 252, 265, 267, 268–69
Consolidation of church debts, 59, 137, 166, 177, 191, 199
Constituent Assembly, 235
Consulado of Guatemala, 122, 167–68, 207–8, 226
Consulado (merchant guild), of Seville, 20, 21, 23, 101–2, 189, 315*n*
Contraband trade, 39, 92, 97, 98, 100, 105, 131, 153, 154, 193, 194, 207–8, 216, 226, 308*n*, 315*n*, 320*n*, 323*n*; in wine, 21–22; in silver, 32; with the Dutch, 34, 39; with the English, 39, 180, 184, 185, 186, 193, 199–200, 202, 329*n*; along the Mosquito Coast, 117–20, 168–71; in cacao, 164; in tobacco, 179; North American, 184; after independence, 238–40, 254; *see also* Trade
Contreras family, 4, 5
Convents, *see individual religious orders*
Copernicus, Nicholas, 196
Córdoba, José Francisco, 235

Corn, 73, 75, 93, 105, 126, 151, 174, 175, 192; production of, 1, 26, 28; prices of, 191, 245
Corregidores, see Alcaldes mayores and *corregidores*
Cortés, Hernán, 3–4, 47
Cortes, liberal, 200–1, 202–3, 207, 209, 210, 220, 221, 222, 223, 224–25, 226, 228, 250
Cortes y Larraz, Pedro, *visita* of, 176–77, 180–81, 290
Costa Rica: province of, 3, 23, 25, 38, 46, 75, 76, 77, 80, 84, 99, 100, 101, 106, 117, 126, 128, 144, 152, 164, 165, 205, 224, 226, 227, 230, 232, 233; state of, 239, 244, 248, 253, 258, 302–3*n*; nation of, 268, 271, 276
Cotton, trade in and production of, 7, 13, 26, 28, 29, 67, 148, 164, 173, 193, 194, 202, 216–18, 219, 242, 245, 269, 279, 282; *see also* Textiles
Council of the Indies, 19–24, 25, 33, 35–36, 39, 41, 42, 94, 97–99, 118
Credit: the church as source of, 53–54, 68, 105, 106, 111, 132, 133, 136–37, 190–91, 259; merchant control of commerce through, 123, 125, 127–28, 157–58, 159, 162–66, 170, 184, 189–90, 194; *see also* Debt; Capital
Creoles, xiii, 19, 34, 42, 64–72, 95–96, 106, 215, 224, 227, 234; rivalry with peninsulares, 28–29, 36, 46, 64–65, 69, 72–73, 117, 124–26, 158, 201; society of and the church, 48–51
Crespo Suarez, Pedro, 51–52
Cuba, 4, 143
Curaçao, 39, 164, 169, 199

Danli, 190–91
Debt, 44, 204; peonage, xiii, 75, 77, 112–13, 125–26, 172–73, 174–75, 177, 178–79, 192, 270–71, 295*n*; loss of farms because of, 62, 125, 127–28, 166, 217; foreign, 236–37, 268, 276; *see also* Credit
Declaration of the Rights of Man, 200
Defense, 58–59, 90
Defense, Central American: colonial, 24, 38–40, 85, 100–1, 103, 118–19, 130, 131–32, 153, 170–71, 195, 196, 197,

Defense, Central American (*continued*)
205–6, 221, 225; post-independence,
230, 232–33, 234, 237, 238–40, 241; *see
also* Military
Delgado, José Matías, 204, 220, 250–52
Demography, *see* Population
Dependency: economic, xv, 113, 270;
internal, 126, 129, 151, 163–66, 174,
179, 192–93, 194, 258; external, 157,
170; *see also* Semi-subsistent
economies; World economy
Descals, Joseph, 97–99
Descartes, René, 196, 197
Díaz del Castillo, Bernal, 74
Díez Navarro, Luis, 118–20, 154–56,
168–71, 197
Diputación del comercio (committee of
the city's commerce), 22, 32, 104,
142–43
Direct contribution tax, 236, 240, 254–56
Disease, 5, 11, 71, 92, 93–94, 101, 141,
180, 181–82, 262–64; epidemics and
pandemics, 3, 7, 9, 26, 46, 51, 77,
93–94, 139, 158, 181–82; malaria, 48;
smallpox, 181; vaccine, 183; cholera,
262–64, 334*n*
Dominican order, 20, 42, 43, 46, 47,
51–52, 54–58, 66, 74–75, 81, 83, 86,
95, 98, 106, 124–25, 132, 134, 135, 136,
137, 178, 279
"Donations," for state expenditures, 290
Dowries: for nuns and priests, 50, 52–53;
for marriage, 70–71
Draft labor, *see Repartimiento* of labor
Drought, 92, 93, 174, 191, 245
Dunn, Henry, 189
Dyes, 39, 105, 162; *see also* Cochineal;
Dyewoods; Indigo
Dyewoods, 7, 119, 120, 168–71

Earthquakes, 34, 59, 61, 71, 92, 94, 204;
of 1688, 93; of 1717, 93, 101, 105,
106–7; of 1751, 158; of 1773, 158–59,
164, 179, 182–83, 190; of 1773–74
(Comayagua), 161, 179, 193; of 1773
(Salvador), 161, 179
Economy, 13–16, 72–90, 111–28, 129,
139, 151, 157–58, 171, 172, 179,
184–94, 199–200, 216–19, 275–77; and
the silver belt, 6, 15; economic

depression, 26, 189–94, 202, 208;
internal, 39, 45, 54, 174–75; and the
church, 50, 53–54, 62–63, 133; after
independence, 240–46, 257–59, 270;
see also Barter; Dependency; Semi-
subsistence economies; trade;
individual commodities
Elites, colonial, 41, 49–50, 54, 61–62,
64–72, 92, 136; change in, 106, 107,
116, 122–23, 130, 137, 158, 197–99;
under Carrera, 268–71
Encomienda; as labor system, xii, 5, 8,
13, 65; *encomenderos*, xiv, 7, 9, 15, 25,
30, 42, 66, 94; *see also* Pensions
Enlightened despotism, 196–97, 198, 200
Enlightenment, xv–xvi, 135, 154; in
Central America, 51, 136, 197–99, 201,
268, 276–77; influence on Spain and
Central America, 112–13, 173, 196–97
Enriquez, Pedro, 96
Entradas and *reducciones*, seventeenth
and eighteenth century, 46–48, 85, 98,
114, 116, 134, 135, 307*n*; *see also*
Conquest
Epidemics, *see under* Disease
Escribanía de Camara, 140
Escuintla, 13, 51, 60, 67, 78, 93, 101,
181, 245, 289
Esparza, 76, 77, 78

Factories, Bourbon, 117, 120, 124
Familial alliances, 65, 66, 124, 128, 130,
134, 158, 166, 167, 190, 191, 224, 229,
230–31, 235, 236, 246, 247, 254, 256,
270, 271, 276, 335*n*
Famine, 35, 51, 73, 93, 116, 141, 163–64,
182, 185, 191–93, 245, 260, 263
Federation of Central American states,
123–24; trade of, 217, 240–46; as
framework for regionalism, 229;
formation of, 230–35, 328*n*; fiscal crisis
of, 236–40; economy of, 244–46; and
the end of order, 247–50; dissolution
of, 252–53, 261–67
Ferdinand and Isabela, 18
Ferdinand VII of Spain, 200, 202, 207,
210, 211, 250, 251–52
Feyjóo, Benito Gerónimo, 196–97
Filísola, Vicente, and union with
Mexico, 231–35

Fiscal (King's lawyer in the audiencia), 30, 147

Fiscal administration, 7, 20, 24–27, 31–32, 44, 90, 116, 117, 153, 197, 198, 200, 273–77; weakness in, 17, 38, 100–5, 113, 311–12n; and wine, 22; remissions of revenue to Spain, 26, 31, 107, 131; reform of, 36–37, 94, 96, 114–15, 130–31, 137–56, 164, 171, 173–76, 180, 195, 196, 312–13n; and the church, 41, 50, 58, 59, 60, 62, 133, 136; and the Guatemalan cabildo, 67–69, 138–43; rates of taxation, 127, 141, 148–49, 168, 186; receipts, 146, 150–53, 175, 284–85, 321n; jurisdictional changes in, 146–50; and intendencies, 148–49, 166–68; reporting methods of, 149; crisis in, 154–56, 184, 190, 193–94; collapse of, 196, 208–11, 222–24, 232–33; in republican government, 236–40, 247, 248, 255, 328n; foreign loan dispute, 236–37; tobacco revenue crisis, 248–49; in the States, 254–57, 264; the direct contribution, 255; collapse of the Federation, 260; *see also* Bourbon reforms; Tax-farming; *individual categories*

Flores, Jose de, 82

Food, 128, 139, 157; availability of, 15, 72–74, 172; dearth of, 160, 163–64, 191, 245, 260

Forasteros, *see* Amerindians

Forced contributions and loans, 100, 101–2, 184, 209, 210, 232–33, 236, 323n

France, 91, 111, 155, 198; of the Bourbons, 111, 130, 132, 135, 175, 197

Franciscan order, 30, 35, 43, 46, 47, 48, 49, 53, 57, 66, 135, 137, 182, 193

French Revolution, 127, 167, 198, 250; influence on Central America, 200, 201

Fuentes y Guzmán, Felipe, 74

Fuentes y Guzmán, Francisco Antonio de, 54, 65, 74, 92–93, 94

Gage, Thomas, 29–30, 45, 47, 272

Gaínza, Gabino, 221, 226, 230

Gálvez, Bartholomé, 71

Gálvez, José de, 130, 140, 143

Gálvez, Mariano, 254–57, 260–64, 332n

Gálvez, Matías de, 154, 164–68, 170–71, 197

Gazeta de Guatemala, La, 191, 199

Gazistas (political faction), 220, 226–27

Gobiernos (bureaucratic division), 25, 166, 197

Godoy, Manuel de, 198

Goicoechea, Fr. José Antonio, 179, 197–99, 218, 320n

Gold production, 5, 6, 13, 96, 114, 120; *see also Quinto*

González, Melchor, 51–52

González Mollindo, President of Guatemala, 199, 202, 203

Gotera, mines of, 180, 230

Government, as social force, 8

Gracias A Dios, 6, 65, 69, 80, 85, 87, 119, 152, 193, 238

Gracias A Dios, Cape of, 3, 119

Granada, xv, 28, 68, 73, 80, 81, 84, 85, 86, 88, 117, 122, 141, 164, 166, 194, 204, 205, 215, 219, 226, 227; after independence, 234–36, 243, 245, 266–67, 270, 282

Grande domaine, 5

Great Britain, *see* Britain

Guachivales, see Cofradías

Guadalajara, 167

Guanacaste, 271

Guatemala: state, 216, 236, 237, 238–39, 243, 244, 247, 248, 252, 253–57, 259, 265; nation, 268–70, 272, 276

Guatemala, highland, xiv, 28, 75, 77, 82, 103, 115, 116, 126, 128, 135, 157, 164, 181, 182–83, 184–85, 192, 193, 215, 218, 219

Guatemala, province of, 32, 42, 45, 49, 60, 97, 98, 116, 123, 124, 125, 126, 127, 128, 134, 144, 148, 150, 151, 152, 160, 163, 164, 176–77, 179, 209, 220, 224, 225, 228, 234, 235, 280, 282–83, 284–85, 289

Guatemala, valley of, xiii, 9, 13, 44, 60, 77, 79, 82, 83, 93, 103, 135; control of labor in, 95–96, 107, 115, 138–39

Guatemala City, 113, 122, 159–61, 164, 176, 182, 185, 191, 192, 194, 199, 200, 205–07, 210, 215, 219, 220, 222, 227;

Guatemala City (*continued*)
  after independence, 229–36, 238, 240,
  241, 246, 250, 254, 262, 264, 267; *see
  also* Santiago de Guatemala
Guatemala Company, 117, 123, 307*n*
Guayabal Valley, 178
Guayaquil, *see* Cacao
Guazacapán, 60, 78, 181
Guëguëtenango, 60, 79, 82–83, 84, 179,
  180, 181, 182, 279
Guiraola, Agustín de, and the Bourbon
  offensive, 140–43
Gulf of Honduras, *see* Bay of Honduras
Gunpowder, 114, 143, 162, 232, 312*n*

Hacienda, xii, xiii, 140–41, 164, 172, 175,
  177, 178–81, 254, 271, 272, 279, 295*n*
Haefkens, Jacob, 239
Haiti, 155
Hapsburg monarchy: philosophy of xii,
  xiv, xv–xvi, 17, 24, 31, 33–40, 50;
  system, 17–40, 41–43, 54, 62–63, 74,
  90, 91, 99–100, 105, 107, 111–13, 176,
  195–96, 199, 215, 257, 268, 272–77,
  282; law, 64–65, 66; reforms of, 94–96,
  145; *see also* Bourbon rule, and the
  Hapsburgs
Hardwoods, *see* dyewoods
Hatos (small agricultural plots), 4, 7
Havana, 74, 86, 87, 117, 121, 167, 185,
  208, 216, 221, 224, 240, 269
Headcounts, 140, 289–90; *see also*
  Tribute
Headtax, 200; *see also* Tribute
Henrietta, island of, 86
Herrarte, Manuel de, 140–43
Herrera, Dionisio, 252, 260
Hides, 39, 184, 272
Hispanidad, 17, 18, 42, 196
Hispaniola, *see* Santo Domingo
Hodgson, Robert, 168–71
Holland, 91, 111; illegal commerce with,
  12, 34, 36
Honduras, xiii, 4, 23, 32, 38, 44, 46, 48,
  49, 56–57, 58, 59, 61, 69, 83, 84–85,
  87, 89, 93, 97, 98, 99, 100, 101, 103,
  106, 114–15, 117, 118–19, 124, 126,
  128, 134, 143, 144, 148, 150, 151, 152,
  158, 162, 163, 164, 165, 166, 176, 178,
  184, 185, 190, 192, 193, 199, 210,
    215–16, 220, 224–25, 279, 283,
    302–03*n*; after independence, 231–35;
    state of, 237, 238, 243, 244, 246, 249,
    250, 251, 252, 253, 259, 265–66;
    nation, 268, 270; *see also* Comayagua
Honey, 28, 84
Horses, 82, 83, 176, 190
Hospitals, 49, 50, 55, 56–57, 107

Idolatry, *see* Paganism
Immigrants to Central America, 122–23;
  see also *Nouveaux-arrivés*
Independence in Central America, 113,
  123, 129–30, 145, 153, 166, 183, 191,
  192, 194, 195, 200, 208, 211, 215–16,
  219–20, 221, 225, 226, 227–28, 233,
  240; *see also* Rebellions, 1811–12
Independence movement in Mexico,
  151, 184, 201, 202, 204, 208–9; Hidalgo
  and Morelos rebellion, 203, 205, 322*n*;
  Iturbide rebellion, 221, 227
Independence movement in South
  America, 151, 201, 203, 251; Bolívar
  and, 221–22
India, indigo production in, 120, 187
Indians, *see* Amerindians
Indigo (*indigofera tinctoria*), 10–12, 15,
  25, 39, 61, 62, 68, 71, 75, 81, 83, 86,
  87, 88, 89, 92, 96, 105, 123, 138, 139,
  143, 147, 153, 222, 271, 279, 282, 283,
  294*n*, 295*n*, 308*n*; production of, 6–7,
  92, 120, 137, 162–63, 175–76, 275;
  labor in, 11–12, 28–29, 43, 112–13,
  115, 172, 177–79; eighteenth-century
  expansion of, 113, 120–22, 124–26,
  151, 157, 162–66, 177, 184, 251;
  commerce in, 120, 168–71, 187,
  188–89, 207, 216, 217, 219, 318*n*;
  decline in production of, 184–91, 192,
  194, 199, 202, 204; Guatemala's
  superior flor product, 185–87, 319*n*
Industrial revolution, eighteenth
  century, 12
Inquisition, Court of the, 98, 122, 132,
  196, 197, 198, 200
Insularity, 9
Intendants and intendancies, 105, 130,
  148, 149, 155, 166–67, 190, 195, 204,
  224, 239

Interior Central America, 6, 103, 162–66, 219, 220, 224, 226; receipts from, 146–47; subadministrations in, 147–51; after independence, 230, 235, 236, 239, 241, 246, 248
Irisarri, trading house, 123, 199
Irisarri-Arrillaga commercial alliance, 123
Itenco, 80
Iturbide, Agustín de: and the independence of Central America, 221, 227 and union with Mexico, 229–34; the empire of, 251
Itzá, 4, 46, 47, 98, 101
Izalcos, 10, 15, 65, 78, 94

Jacaltenango, 182
Jalapa, 192
Jamaica, 38, 84–85, 86, 88, 89, 120, 123, 164, 168–72, 199
Jerez de la Choluteca, 80
Jesuits, 49, 51–52, 56–58, 61, 75, 95, 136, 196; expulsion of, 136, 311n
Jicaque Indians, 48, 118, 119
Jocotenango, Indian barrio, 67, 160
Jovellanos, Gaspar Melchor de, 149, 197
Juarros, Antonio, 203
Juarros, Domingo, 123
Juarros, Gaspar, 123
Judges, civil, 220–21, 222, 223–24, 261–64
Juez de milpas (agricultural judge): and cacao production, 7, 10; and agricultural production, 34–36
Juros, see Bonds
Jutiapa, 44, 225

Klée and Skinner, commercial house, 260

Labor: availability of, 6, 9, 13–16, 18–19, 75, 105, 114, 160, 173, 270, 271; change in pattern of, 124–26, 129, 159, 177–81, 193, 269; *see also* Labor, Amerindian
Labor, Amerindian, xii, xiv, 5, 13–16, 24, 34–36, 43, 46, 94, 111, 112, 135, 138–39, 146, 172, 177–81, 268; abuse of 8, 41, 161; in indigo works, 11–12, 28–29, 43, 112–13, 115, 172, 177–81; in public works, 15–16, 66, 69, 160–61,

178; *see also* Amerindia; Encomienda; *Repartimiento* of labor; Slaves; *Tamemes*
Lacandon Indians, 46, 101, 181, 307n
La Corpus Mine, 59, 96–99
Ladinos, 143, 178, 179
Lake Atitlán, 73
La Madriz, Francisco Gómez de, Tequelí, 98–99
La Madriz, Lorenzo de, 97
Landivar family, the, 106
Land tenure, 61–62, 72–86, 192, 194, 246; in America, 5; in Mexico 5; land value and *repartimiento*, 14, 76; land value, 53, 245, 295n; women land owners (*see* Women)
Larrazábal, Antonio, 123, 322–23n; "Instructions" to, 254–55
Larrazábal, Simon, 122–23, 159
Larrazábal family, 106
Latifundia, *see* Land tenure
Law: and custom, 19–20; and enforcement, 19–20
Lenca Indians, 178
León: province of, xv, 13, 25, 32, 42, 88, 105, 279, 284–85, 289; town of, 69, 73, 76, 80, 85, 122, 144, 147, 164, 169, 194, 205, 215, 219, 226, 227, 228; intendancy of, 175, 209; in independence and post-independence struggles, 230–36, 243–45, 266–67; *see also* Nicaragua
Liberalism, Central American, 123, 169, 201–11, 218–19, 220–28, 268, 269, 272–77, 326n, 331n; and anti-clericalism, 137, 221, 269; and independence, 199, 217–18; after independence, 229–36; and the Federation, 247–53, 268; and the Salvador diocese issue, 250–52; and Mariano Gálvez, 254–57, 260–64; *see also* Cortes; Larrazábal, Antonio
Liberal thought, xv, 198
Lima, xiii, xv, 32, 87, 88, 92, 105, 123; viceroyalty of 18, 21
Limpieza de sangre (pure blood doctrine), 64, 66
Linnaeus, Carolus, 197
Livingston Codes, 261–63
Locust infestation, 34, 71, 88, 93, 127,

Locust infestation (*continued*)
  158, 166, 185, 191–92, 194, 199, 204,
  318–19*n*
Logging, 38, 260, 333*n*; loggers on the
  Caribbean coast, 89–90, 154
Logwood, 38, 89–90
Los Altos, state of, 264, 267
Los Llanos, 240
Lutz, Christopher, 74, 290

MacLeod, Murdo, 10, 76
Malespin, Francisco, 271
Managua, 80, 230
Manila Galleon, 117
Manumission, 75
Marriage, xiv, 66, 70–72, 74–75, 93, 106,
  123, 158, 301*n*
Marroquín, Francisco, 7, 42
Martínez, Peláez, Severo, 69
Masaya, 80, 227, 282
Matagalpa, 80, 166
Matina Valley, 75, 119, 130, 164, 169
Mayan Civilization, 87
Mayorga, Martín de, 159–62, 182–83
Mazatenango, 182, 223, 262
Measles, 158, 181
Media anata, tax, 27, 32, 68, 100, 103
Medina, José de, 122
Medina Celi, Duke of, 20
Mencos, General Martín Carlos de,
  34–36, 39, 96, 100, 104, 297*n*
Mendicancy, 133, 173, 179, 197
Mercantilism, 130
Mercedian order, 46, 49, 53, 55, 56–57,
  61, 66, 74, 139, 193
Merchant power, 18–19, 65, 67, 112,
  123–24, 126–27, 129, 157, 159–68, 184,
  192, 194, 224, 275–77, 303–4*n*,
  314–15*n*; and food, 72–74; and miners,
  114–15, 128, 162–63, 165, 193–94; and
  Bourbon absolutism, 116, 130, 136–37,
  137–43, 147, 166–68, 190–91, 197, 200,
  202, 207; and indigo producers,
  127–28, 162, 164–65, 186, 189–90; and
  cattlemen, 128, 163, 165–66, 245–46,
  314*n*; and independence, 216–20, 225,
  226; after independence, 230, 233, 236,
  240, 241–46, 255, 257–59; and Carrera,
  268–69, 270; *see also Cabildo* of
  Santiago de Guatemala
Merchants, xiv, 22, 25–26, 32, 64, 91,

122–23, 199, 215, 219; of Cadíz and
  Seville, 10, 121, 122–23, 161–62, 216,
  242; Mexican, 27, 121, 242; Central
  American, 34, 86, 167–68; British, 46;
  see also Consulado
Mercury, or quicksilver, 23, 98, 113–15,
  117, 128, 162, 307*n*
Mesada eclesiástica, tax, 32, 103
Mestizos, xiii, 19, 30, 64–65, 67, 74,
  75–86, 92, 93, 126, 143, 162, 179, 215,
  247, 263–67, 270, 281, 290, 301*n*;
  mestization, 83, 85–86, 101, 103, 126,
  180–81, 282, 317–18*n*
Mexico, 7, 8, 10, 12, 15–16, 17, 18, 20,
  23, 25, 26, 30, 32, 46, 62, 68, 71, 72,
  73, 76, 86, 88, 92, 97, 98, 105, 115,
  117, 120, 123, 130, 135, 136, 148, 155,
  157, 175, 184, 190, 191, 200, 201, 204,
  206, 208, 209, 221, 227, 240; Aztec,
  xiii, 4; Central American union with,
  223, 229–34, 247, 251; the nation of,
  248, 262, 330*n*
Mexico City, 31, 88, 123
Military: expenses, as a budgetary drain,
  100, 103, 154–55, 196, 210, 232, 236,
  256, 274–75; needs, 241, 248, 253, 264,
  265, 268, 269
Milpas, 1, 7
Miners, 184, 215, 224, 225; and merchant
  power, 162
Mining, 32, 34, 62, 84, 92, 94, 96–97, 99,
  105, 112–13, 116, 126, 128, 148, 151,
  178, 180, 181, 193–94, 217, 243–44,
  246, 305–6*n*, 320*n*; *see also* Gold
  production; *Quinto*; Silver, production
Mint: in Guatemala, 59, 92, 107, 114–15,
  116, 164, 221, 234, 243, 259, 260; in
  Mexico, 99, 114; *see also* Specie
Missionary attempts, *see Entradas*;
  individual religious orders
Mita, 44, 80
Mixco, 79, 164, 191
Molina, Pedro, 218, 227, 229–30, 253
Molina, Vicente, 126
Moñino, José, 130
Montejo, Francisco de, and the
  settlement of Honduras, 4, 5
Montepío de añil, 164–65, 189
Montesquieu, Charles-Louis de
  Secondat, 197, 200
Montevideo, 203

Montúfar, José Maria, 206–7
Morazán, Francisco: opposing federal
power, 237; as leader of federal forces,
249; as leader of the Federation,
250–53, 260–67, 333–34n
Mortgages, 52, 53, 54, 59, 61, 106, 137,
159, 160, 190; *see also Capellanías*
Mosquito Coast, 106, 118–20, 132, 154,
168–71, 199, 224, 248, 260, 271
Mosquito people, 32, 38, 47, 48, 84–85,
90, 92, 100, 101, 106, 118–20, 168–71,
199, 276, 303n
Motín de Esquilache, 136
Mulattos, xiii, 30, 65, 74, 75–86, 93, 126,
143, 162, 179, 215, 224, 247, 263–67,
270; as soldiers, 101, 145, 206, 222, 230
Mules, 76, 77, 82, 83, 86, 117, 123, 256

Napoleonic Wars, 162, 242, 274
National Assembly, 237, 239, 249
Navas y Quevado, Andrés de las, 96–99
"New Laws" of 1542, 8, 42
New Granada, xv, 87, 216, 248
New Spain, Viceroyalty of, *see* Mexico
Newton, Sir Isaac, 196
Nicaragua: province of, 10, 23, 28, 32,
38, 44, 48, 49, 56–57, 58, 75, 84–85,
93, 97, 99, 100, 101, 126, 144,
147, 149, 150, 151, 152, 155, 157, 163,
164, 165, 166, 170, 174, 175, 179, 184,
194, 199, 205, 215–16, 219, 222, 224,
226, 227, 281–83, 284–85; after
independence, 232, 233, 235, 238, 244,
245, 246, 247–49, 251, 252, 258, 260,
265–66; as nation, 268, 270, 271, 276,
277; *see also* León, province of
Nicoya, 25, 29, 78, 166, 282
Nobility, in Central America, 123,
161–62
Nouveaux-arrivés, 7; in eighteenth-
century Central America, 106, 112,
117, 122, 129, 161–62, 197
Nueva Guatemala, *see* Guatemala City
Nueva Segovia (Nicaragua), 6, 28, 48,
54, 75, 80, 85, 88, 205
Nuns and nunneries, 49, 50–51, 55,
56–57, 300–301n; *see also individual*
orders

Oaxaca, 205, 206, 233; trade with, 75, 83,
88–89, 105, 126

Obrajes, indigo, illness in, 11–12, 77
Officials, Spanish, 25, 154; economic
needs of, 27–28; merchant alliances
with, 27–28, 68, 138
Oil, 58, 59; trade with Peru, 20
Olancho (el viejo), 6, 80, 85, 119; (el
nuevo), 80, 85, 190, 225, 270–71
Olives, 20
Omoa, 118, 148, 167–71, 206, 209, 210,
215, 216, 219, 222, 225, 226, 230, 262;
construction of fortress, 121, 154, 178;
colonization efforts at, 153, 154, 155,
210; illegal commerce from, 199; after
independence, 252–53, 261
Osuna, Duke of, 20

Pachuca, mines of, 117
Pacific, hotlands bordering the, 2, 3
Pacific commerce, 20–26, 87–89, 117,
129, 157, 199, 244, 245, 271–72
Pacific Company, *see* Guatemala
Company
Paganism, 45, 46, 48, 173, 176, 183
Panama, 4, 8, 75, 76, 87, 117
Papel sellado (official paper), 32, 68
Patrimonial society, xii, xiv
Patronato Real, 41, 49, 60, 134, 250–51
Patucas Indians, 119
Pavón, Cayetano, 115
Pavón, Manuel José, 203
Pavón family, 106
Paya Indians, 299n; *entradas* against, 116
Pedraza, Cristóbal de, 42
Peinado, José Maria, 204
Pensions, or *encomiendas*, xiv, xv, 13,
26, 32, 34–38, 51, 55, 68, 72, 73, 74,
85, 91, 92, 100, 112, 141, 297n, 298n;
suspension of, 34, 100–01, 105, 107,
130, 274, 306n; vacated, 39
Peru, 4, 7, 8, 10, 12, 15, 17, 20–21, 25,
30, 34, 75, 86, 88, 92, 98, 105, 117,
120, 151, 184
Petapa, 44
Petén, 4, 47, 98, 101, 141, 230
Philip V of Spain, 17–18, 91
Piche (Pitt), William, 99, 119–20, 134
Piñol, José, 123
Piracy, 17, 20, 23, 84–85, 86–87, 88, 89,
120, 208, 216, 222; *see also* Buccaneers
Pitch, 279; production of 7, 10, 28, 75,
84, 85, 88; trade in, 21

Playing cards monopoly, 143, 312n
Political parties: *see* Cacos; Conservative political thought; Gazistas; Liberalism
Population, xii, 3–16, 67, 77, 92, 93–94, 111, 126, 137, 178, 191, 276, 288–90, 306n; Amerindian, 26, 48, 93–94, 103, 139, 173, 181–82
Portobelo, 86, 117, 118
Post office, 221
Potosí (Peru), xiii, 15
President of the Audiencia, 25, 26, 27, 30, 31, 45, 95, 159
Prices, 113, 127, 139, 166, 191, 218–19, 245, 319n; tobacco, 144, 152; merchant control of, 184, 194, in cattle, 163, 165–66, meat, 246, indigo, 120–21, 162, 164–65, 186, 242, 257, 294n, silver, 114–15, 162, 165
Producers, *see* Merchant power
Propaganda Fide order, 46, 56–57
Property, *see* Land tenure
Providencia, island of, 86, 164
Provincial Deputations, 200–1, 205–7, 211, 220–28, 233, 324n
Public works, 15–16, 66, 69, 160–61, 178, 269
Puebla de los Angeles, 80
Puerto Caballos, 87
Puerto Cartago, 119
Puerto Escondido, 118
Puerto Sal, 118
Puntarenas, 258
Purísima Concepción, order of, 50, 53, 57, 59

Quezaltenango, xiii, xv, 27, 28, 56, 60, 79, 126, 135, 148, 164, 179, 180, 182, 192, 193, 289; and independence 232, 233, 238, 256, 264; *see also* Los Altos
Quiché nation, xii, 4, 45, 183
Quicksilver, *see* Mercury
Quinto (royal fifth tax on mining), 6, 32, 113, 139, 146
Quito, xiii, 21

Rabinal, 60
Race mixture, 74–75; *see also* Mestizos, mestization
Ramírez, Alejandro, 199, 202
Raoul, Nicholas, 249

Real Compañía Guizpuzcoana, 117
Realejo, 7, 10, 23, 28, 88, 117, 120, 166, 215, 226, 259
Rebellions: Carrera, xv, 262–67; creole, over wine import interdicts, 23–24; of cabildo, over tax, 67–68; of 1717, over transfer of city, 107; against peninsular encroachments, 124–26; against Bourbon reforms, 140–43, 152; of 1773, over transfer of city, 159–62; of 1811–12 (Central American), 202, 204–06, 211, 231, 247, 251; Belén conspiracy, 206–7, 322n; 1820–21, Comayagua, 224–26; 1823 (Guatemala City), 234–35; *see also* Amerindian rebellions; *specific* Independence movement; Warfare, civil
Reducciones, see Entradas and *reducciones*
Regidores, see Cabildos, Spanish
Regionalism, 205, 215–16, 224–28, 275, 321–22n; in Hapsburg rule, 63, 133; as reinforced by producer-merchant rivalry, 125, 145, 158, 164–66, 184, 190; post-independence, 125, 153, 194, 230–32, 240, 258–59, 327n; *see also* Federation of Central American states
Regular clerics, *see individual orders*
Religious orders, 133; secularization of, 134–135; decline of, 137, 172–173
Repartimiento of goods (*derrama*), 27–31, 35–36, 76–77, 84, 105, 128
Repartimiento of labor, xiii–xiv, 8, 12, 13–15, 25–27, 30, 38, 43, 59–60, 66, 67, 75–76, 77, 84, 87, 89, 92, 94, 95–96, 97–98, 105, 112–13, 125–26, 127, 128, 160–61, 164, 172, 173–74, 177–81, 294n, 295n, 317n; ban of, 35–36, 173, 174, 179–80, 193, 200; inclusion of non-Indians, 114, 126, 161, 179; under Carrera, 268
Rice, 245
Río Chamalecon, 118
Río de Aguan, 119
Río de Carpintero, 119
Río de Leones, 118
Río de Mais, 119
Río de Mainao, 119
Río de Motagua, 118
Río de Suerte, 119

Río de Ulua, 118
Río Limosmas, 119
Río Payas, 119
Río Platano, 119
Río Reventezon or Ximenes, 119
Río San Juan, 100, 117, 119, 130, 171,
    199, 245, 248
Río Tinto, 119, 154
Rivas, 164, 189, 205, 227, 314*n*
Roads: construction, 14, 66, 178;
    network, 126, 130, 167, 240, 245
Roatán, island of, 119, 154, 199
Rodríguez de Rivas, Francisco, 102,
    106–7
Roque, Antonio, 85
Rosica de Caldas, Sebastián Alvarez
    Alfonso, 39
Rousseau, Jean-Jacques, 197
Rural life, 65, 70–72, 75–86

Sacapa, 60, 76, 82, 83–84, 94, 115–16,
    118, 178, 181
Sacatepéquez, 79, 181
Salaries, *see* Wages
Salaries and expenses, government, 27,
    58, 59, 154–56, 175, 210, 313*n*; after
    independence, 236
Sales tax: *see* Alcabala; Barlovento
Salpaltagua, 14
Salt, 67, 87
Salvador: province of, xiii, 11, 28, 33, 44,
    55, 57, 68, 75, 76, 77, 83, 84, 86, 87,
    93, 100, 105, 113, 121, 123, 124, 125,
    126, 127, 144, 150, 152, 160, 174, 176,
    178, 192, 194, 215, 220, 228; slaving in,
    4; Diocese issue, 221, 249, 250–52,
    332*n*; after independence 230–36, 238,
    240, 241, 244, 245, 247–52, 253,
    257–58, 261, 263, 265, 284–285; nation
    of, 268, 271; *see also* Indigo; San
    Salvador
Sambo nation, 32, 38, 47, 48, 84–85, 90,
    92, 100, 101, 106, 116, 118–20, 154,
    168–71, 199, 224, 225, 303*n*
Samsaquez, 35
San Andrés de Zaragoza, 25
San Antonio Suchitepéquez, 25, 27, 33,
    60, 78, 89, 97, 101, 148, 181–82, 191
San Carlos, 230
Sánchez de Berrospe, Gabriel, 98–99

San Christoval Amatitlán, 79
San Felipe Neri, congregation of, 106
San Francisco el Alto, 182
San Geronimo, sugar hacienda, 55, 83,
    137, 250, 279
San Ignes Petapa, 79
San Jorge Olanchito, 119
San José (Costa Rica), 1, 232
San Juan Amatitlán, 44, 79, 94, 95; *see
    also* Amatitlán
San Juan Ostuncalco, 79
San Luis Potosí, mines of, 117
San Martin, José, 251
San Mathío, Juan de, 94–95
San Miguel (Salvador) xiv, 11, 56–57, 60,
    69, 76, 126, 190, 204, 230, 266
San Miguel Petapa, 79
San Miguel Totonicapán, 81
San Pedro Petapa, 176
San Pedro Sacatepéquez, 79, 181
San Pedro Sula (Honduras), 7, 80, 85,
    118
San Salvador, xi, xiv, 11, 25, 56–57, 60,
    69, 78, 97, 102, 116, 124, 126, 147,
    148, 149, 161, 164, 175, 179, 190, 204,
    205, 207, 229, 294; after independence,
    233–34, 261, 262, 266, 267, 289
Santa Ana (Salvador), 11, 60, 204, 230,
    235
Santa Catharina order, 53, 57, 59
Santa Cattharina, 79
Santa Clara order, 57, 59
Santa Cruz Chiantla, 79
Santa Cruz de Quiché, 56, 181
Santa Cruz de Yoro, 80
Santa María de Jesús, 67
Santiago Atitlán, 79, 181
Santiago Cosumago, 78
Santiago de Chile, 167
Santiago de Guatemala, iii, xiii, xiv, 33,
    36, 49–53, 54, 55, 56–57, 61, 65–68,
    71–75, 79, 85, 86, 87, 92–93, 101, 106,
    123, 126, 129, 134, 138–39, 147, 149,
    152, 157, 290; transfer of capital away
    from, 158–61, 313, 314*n*; *see also
    Cabildo* of Guatemala; Guatemala
    City; Antigua
Santo Domingo (Hispaniola), 4, 120
Santo Domingo de los Hortelanos
    (Indian barrio), 67

San Vicente de Austria (Salvador), 60, 69, 76, 122, 126, 204, 266
Sapottitlán, 78
Sarsaparilla, 10, 39, 75, 84, 87, 120, 169
Schools, 240, 254, 262
Segovia, *see* Nueva Segovia
Semi-subsistent economies, xv, xvi, 39, 45, 53, 193; decline of, 126, 129, 157–58, 179, 181; under Carrera, 269, 270, 273–74
Sevaco, *see* Matagalpa
Seven Years War, 127
Seville, as wine producer, 20
Sheep, 82–83
Sherman, William, 15
Shipbuilding, 7, 10, 88
Silver: production of, xv, 5, 40, 113–17, 162, 164, 191; dearth of, 6, 15, 26, 184, 193, 207, 242, 258–259, 323n; *see also* Mint; *Quinto*
Silver trade, 105, 120, 126, 137, 138, 217, 225, 244, 245, 296n; from Peru, 21, 98
Silver-working industry, 99, 305–306n
Situados, 100, 103, 141
Slaves: escaped, 2; African, 19, 30–31, 38, 55, 64, 67, 72, 74–75, 77, 85–86, 89, trade in, 6, 12, 118, 169, 308n, 315–316n, breeding of, 86; and slaving Amerindian, 4, 5, 8, 49, 66, 85
Smallpox vaccine, 173, 183, 226
Smuggling, *see* Contraband
Sociedad Económica de Amigos del País de Guatemala, 197
Soconusco, 7, 9, 10, 25, 33, 35, 65, 75, 76, 78, 89, 99, 148, 166, 248, 262, 289
Sodalities, *see* Cofradías
Sololá, 6–7, 79, 148, 264, 289
Sonsonate, 11, 22, 23, 24, 25, 58, 60, 65, 69, 78, 97, 116, 120, 181, 235, 244, 261
Spain, 155–56, 184, 190, 196, 202–3, 206, 209, 289; institutions of, 3, 26, 92, 198; trade with, 34, 92, 113, 117, 124, 130, 157; *see also* Wine
Spanish, in Central America, 4, 7
Spanish America, 4, 184
Specie, 114, 172, 329n; dearth in, 21–22, 26–27; outflow of, 120, 184, 193, 207, 217, 219, 242, 244, 246, 258–59, 323n; counterfeit, 259

Stephens, John L. and Frederick Catherwood, 266–67, 272
Subsistence, *see* Semi-subsistent economies
Suchitepéquez, 250, 256, 289; *see also* San Antonio Suchitepéquez
Suet, 77, 87
Sugar, 153, 170, 219, 279, 282; production of, 43, 74; plantations, 54, 62, 77, 81, 83, 86, 137, 215

Tabasco, 6
Talamanca Indians, 46
Tamemes (Indian bearers), 5, 14
Taxation, *see* Fiscal administration
Tax-farming, 32–33, 61, 66, 138–39, 145, 150, 279, 289, 303n
Tecpanatitlán, 60
Tecpatitlán, 28, 55, 56
Tegucigalpa, 25, 71, 80, 99, 114, 119–20, 128, 134, 147, 148, 165, 166, 180, 205, 219, 224, 225, 284–85, 308n; after independence, 230–235, 243, 245, 247, 249, 270
Tequelí affair, 96–99, 101, 106
Textiles: from Spain, 10, 39; workhouse, in Guatemala, 74; trade, 87; British, 89, 162, 180, 184, 193, 194, 207–8, 216–19, 242, 244, 323n; in Central America, 126, 128, 147, 157, 164, 170, 193, 194, 216–19, 245; production, 143; decline, 207, 258; *see also* Cotton
Textutla, 181
Thread (of pita), 26, 29, 67
Tinoco, José, 224
Tithe, 32, 50, 51, 59–61, 73, 137, 160, 161, 170, 250, 251, 279, 283, 302n
Tobacco, 87, 179, 204, 219
Tobacco monopoly, 190, 210, 221, 271, 313n; implanting of, 59, 143–45; revolts against, 140–43, 152, 205; revenues from, 152–53, 167, 180, 232, 286–87; end of, 237–39, 248–49, 254, 256, 329n
Totonicapán, 28, 56–57, 148, 181, 192, 222, 264, 289
Trade, 15, 86–90, 92, 105–6, 111–13, 196, 207–8, 275–77, 296n, 308n; to other American colonies, xv, 20–24;

government role in, 6, 111–12, 130,
162–63, 199; internal, 7, 25–29, 32–33,
139; with Spain, 20, 89–90; with
Europe, 121, 271–72; change in
patterns of, 121, 124–25, 129, 148–49,
151, 154, 157–58, 170, 172, 175–76,
179, 184–90, 192–93, 194, 195, 197,
198, 199, 215; fairs, 162, 163, 165, 257,
272; "free trade," 211, 215, 216–19,
221, 226–27; post-independence,
240–46, 257–59, 262, 268–69, 271–72,
329n; with the United States, 259, 272;
see also Contraband trade
Traditionalism, 9, 122, 128, 133, 158,
172, 196, 263, 268, 269, 272–77
Treaty of Paris (1783), 154, 171
Tribunal de cuentas (treasury inspection
board), 31
Tribunal of loyalty, 203–4, 321n
Tribute, Indian, xiv, xvi, 8, 9, 25–27,
43–44, 45, 48, 58, 78–81, 83, 93, 94,
100, 101, 102–3, 104–5, 106, 107, 114,
116, 131, 133, 135, 136, 139, 140–41,
143, 145–46, 153, 263, 289–90, 316n;
conversion of goods into, 21, 26, 113;
as stimulus for trade, 26, 73; and
repartimiento of goods, 27, 31; and
encomienda pensions, 38; payment in
coin required; 173–75, 177;
suspension, 200, 209–10; direct
contribution as restoration of, 236,
240, 254–56
Tribute, of free mulattoes and blacks, 32
Trinidad, trade with, 87
Trujillo (Honduras) 6, 39, 80, 84, 85, 86,
100, 118, 130, 154, 209, 219, 226, 230
Tuxtla, 148, 284
"Two republic" policy, 64–65, 66–67,
69–70, 173
Tzutuhil nation, 4

Ulloa, Bernardo de, 112
Union of Arms, 31
United States, 259, 272, 276
University of San Carlos, 51–52, 92, 136,
190, 197, 234, 254, 320n
Urban life, 72–75, 92, 191
Urruela, Gregorio, 123
Urruela family, 106

Urrutia Montoya y Matos, Carlos de,
216–17, 219–20, 226, 324n, 325n
Utrecht, Treaty of, 118
Uztáriz, Geronimo de, 112

Valdés, Francisco de, and the Bourbon
offensive, 142, 144, 197
Valdeviera, Fray Antonio de, 42
Valle, José Cecilio del, 191, 218, 246
Vanilla, 28, 29
Venality, 66
Veracruz, 20, 21, 121, 167, 185
Verapaz, xiii, xv, 4, 25, 27, 46, 55, 79,
82, 83, 84, 86, 88, 98, 118, 152, 181,
218, 245, 256, 289
Vicens Vives, Jaime, xv
Vidaurre family, 122
Villa Urrutia, Jacobo de, 199, 320n
Vitoria school of Salamanca, xii
Volcanic cordillera, 1, 4
Volcanoes, 1; eruptions of, 257
Voltaire, François Marie Arouet, 197

Wages, 29, 114, 245, 317n
Walker, William, 271
War, 127, 154–56, 190, 194, 199, 204,
215; and the Hapsburg State, 91, 100,
195; *see also* Military
Warfare, civil, 92, 96–99, 101, 205, 216,
275; and disruption of trade, 166; after
independence, 229–36, 240, 247–50,
252–53, 256, 257, 261, 264–67; and rise
of lawlessness, 249–50, 252, 260, 263,
268, 331n; *see also* Rebellions;
Amerindian rebellions
War of the American Revolution, 127,
154, 161, 162, 170
War of the French Revolution, 184, 185
War of Jenkin's Ear, 112, 117, 120, 134,
139, 154, 170, 184
War of Spanish Independence, 175, 190,
191
War of the Spanish Succession, 23, 63,
91, 92, 101, 111, 112, 117–18, 132
Wars, Napoleonic, 162, 242, 274
Wells, William, 270–71
Western economy, *see* World economy
Wheat, 13–14, 26, 30, 43, 55, 59, 60, 61,

Wheat (*continued*)
66, 67, 73, 74, 75, 76, 77, 83, 93, 105, 126, 127, 139, 141, 151, 192, 279
Wine, 15, 39, 58, 59, 68, 87, 88, 175, 218; Spanish, 10; Peruvian, 10, 111–12; the seventeenth century debate over, 20–26, 105, 295*n*
Women: Spanish, 70–72, 82–84; Indian, payment of tribute by, 103, 140–41, 290
Wool production, 13, 26
World economy, xvi, 9–10, 113, 122, 157–58, 171, 174, 177, 180–81, 184, 190, 191, 268, 272, 273, 277, 283

Xenophobia, 260, 274
Xiquilite, see Indigo

Yoro, Valley of, 48, 85
Yucatan, 4, 6, 47, 86, 98, 120, 182

Zebadura, Marcial, 264
Zelaya family of Olancho, 270–71